JOHN CONNELLY is Associate Professor
of History at the University of California,
Berkeley.

From Enemy to Brother

From Enemy
to Brother

THE REVOLUTION IN CATHOLIC TEACHING
ON THE JEWS, 1933–1965

John Connelly

HARVARD UNIVERSITY PRESS

Cambridge, Massachusetts, and London, England

2012

Library of Congress Cataloging-in-Publication Data

Connelly, John.
  From enemy to brother : the revolution in Catholic teaching on the Jews,
1933–1965 / John Connelly.
      p. cm.
  Includes bibliographical references (p.) and index.
  ISBN 978-0-674-05782-1 (alk. paper)
    1. Catholic Church—Relations—Judaism.   2. Judaism—Relations—Catholic
Church.   3. Christianity and antisemitism—History.   4. Racism—Religious
aspects—Christianity.   5. Vatican Council (2nd : 1962–1965)   I. Title.
  BM535.C627 2012
  261.2′6—dc23   2011035338

To Fiona

Contents

Introduction

The Christian who rejects individual merit and guilt denies the work of Jesus.

Czesław Miłosz

The Jesuit Stanisław Musiał was among the most courageous opponents of antisemitism in our time. He denounced officials in the Polish Catholic hierarchy who tolerated hostility to Jews, castigated the chauvinism of Catholics staking crosses at Auschwitz, and at times even obliquely criticized John Paul II, who is regarded by many Poles as a saint. From passionate involvement stretching back to his days as a young priest at the Second Vatican Council (1962–1965), Musiał knew Catholic-Jewish relations in all their complexity. Shortly before his death in 2004, he surprised an interviewer by claiming that the Declaration made about Jews at Vatican II—in which the church renounced all antisemitism—seems to contain nothing special or new.[1]

A quick glance at chapter 4 of this Declaration—approved in October 1965 by 2,221 against 88 bishops and known by its Latin name *Nostra Aetate* ("In Our Time")—confirms Musiał's impression. Every word seems unexceptional. Christ, his mother, and the apostles were Jews. The church began in the Old Testament. The Jews—whether from that time or ours—may not be held responsible for Christ's death. The church decries all forms of hatred, including antisemitism. And finally, the church looks forward to a day when all humans will be united. To dispute these assertions seems absurd. Does not the New Testament say clearly that Christ and his mother were Jews? Could one possibly hold a people numbering in the millions culpable for acts done by a few almost two thousand years ago? Is not Christianity a religion of love set against all hatred?

Yet first impressions deceive. In fact, Father Musiał tells us, the church had never in its history looked upon the Jews in the ways specified in *Nostra Aetate*. A second pioneer in the Christian-Jewish dialogue, the American Paulist Father Thomas Stransky of Milwaukee, who helped draft *Nostra Aetate* as an advisor at Vatican II, makes the point more radically. The Declaration signaled a "180 degree turnabout," he said in a speech of 2006, reversing all that the church had thought about Jews since its early days, a time when teachings about Christ's divinity or the Trinity had yet to be formulated. From the third century at the latest, church authorities taught that the Jews' destiny was to wander the earth suffering retribution from God for rejecting Christ, serving in their destitution as the most direct evidence that the church's claims to God's favor were correct. By acts of discrimination passed by councils through the centuries, the church then created conditions calculated to keep the Jews destitute.[2] This situation was supposed to endure until the end of time when the Jews finally turned to Christ.

The teaching of Vatican II could not have been more different. Beyond saying that the promises—thus the Covenant—made by God with the Jews were still in force, the document asserted—quoting St. Paul's letter to the Romans—that the Jews remained "most dear" to God. That is, they continued to enjoy God's favor. This radical shift in teaching worried many, including Father Stransky, who wondered whether Catholics could suddenly assimilate ideas that contradicted everything they had been taught to believe. Furthermore, if the teaching on the Jews, established with the foundations of the church, could be dug out and recast, what was safe from change? In our own day, because of the patent absurdity of the old anti-Judaic teachings, we have the opposite point of view noted by Father Musiał: that everything in *Nostra Aetate* makes perfect sense and needs no elaboration. It is between these opposing views that this book traces the history of this Vatican II revolution.

Like all history, this book is not about a dead past. The past does not die. Because Catholics fail to appreciate the change that took place in the 1960s, they continue to return to pre-revolutionary patterns of thought without knowing it. The church of our day claims to understand the Jews in the terms provided by *Nostra Aetate*, but its leaders keep reverting back to the pre-Vatican II period in their pronouncements. In *Nostra Aetate*, the church was content to think of reconciliation of humankind by God in an indistinct future, with no compulsion for Jews to turn to Christ, yet the pope recently enjoined Catholics to pray for the Jews, "that God our Lord should illuminate their hearts, so that they will recognize Jesus Christ, the Savior of all men." Even more recently, American bishops asserted that Catholics must look forward to the inclusion of the "whole people of Israel" in the church: something the bishops of Vatican II were careful not to proclaim.[3]

The failure to comprehend *Nostra Aetate* in its historic development makes such misunderstanding all but unavoidable. People ignorant of the past lack orientation for the future; in our day that means that Catholics lack guidance on how to relate the teaching of Vatican II to other sources for thinking about the Jews, especially scripture. What about the section in Matthew 28 where Christ enjoins his followers to bring the Gospel to "all nations," baptizing them in the name of the Father, Son, and Holy Spirit? That call does not seem to exclude the Jews, and indeed supports the idea that Catholics should—at the very least—pray that Jews accept Jesus Christ as Messiah. Yet in 1965, despite insistent urging from the personal theologian of Pope Paul VI, the drafters of *Nostra Aetate* refused to say that the church must conduct a mission to the Jews, or that the Jews must turn to Christ. In the statement that the bishops overwhelmingly accepted and Paul VI promulgated as authoritative church teaching—teaching that cannot be rescinded by later popes—the drafters likewise ignored other sections of scripture suggesting that Jews were responsible for Christ's death (Acts 3:15) and lived under a curse (Matt. 27:25), and that the covenant God had made with the Jews was obsolete (Heb. 8:13). Instead, they shifted the church's understanding of its relation to the Jews to three chapters of Paul's letter to the Romans, which contain the Apostle's most mature reflections on the Jewish people.

This shift was possible because the church's teaching authority—the magisterium—reserves to itself the right to interpret scripture according to the needs of a particular time, though in conversation with the church's tradition. But the question is why the shift happened. Before anything else, historians of *Nostra Aetate* must ask why the church ignored other references from scripture, as well as many centuries of tradition, and centered its understanding of the Jews on three chapters of one of Paul's epistles. To figure out how the church reached this end point, the pages that follow trace the Declaration's origin from the intellectual milieu out of which this shift to Paul occurred, namely, groups of Catholic anti-Nazis operating in Central Europe in the 1930s. Among them was one of *Nostra Aetate*'s authors, the priest Johannes M. Oesterreicher, originally a Jew from Moravia, who served as theological consultant at the Vatican Council, but began his struggle against antisemitism in Vienna in 1933. Oesterreicher worked within tiny groups of Catholics who published and spoke out against Nazi ideology from cities just beyond Hitler's reach, first in Austria and Switzerland, and then France until the German attack in 1940. At that point, Oesterreicher joined a number of his comrades-in-arms—the philosophers Jacques Maritain and Dietrich von Hildebrand, the political scientist Waldemar Gurian—in exile in the United States. Other collaborators stayed behind in Europe. Oesterreicher's intellectual sparring partner for three decades, the German theologian Karl Thieme, took refuge near Basel, Switzerland, in 1934, and remained there through the dark war years, continuing to think and write about Christian-Jewish relations. The theologian Annie Kraus, a Jew who became Catholic in 1942 and inspired Oesterreicher and Hildebrand with pathbreaking thought on antisemitism written in 1933, hid from the Gestapo first in Berlin, then Southern Germany. Others were not so lucky. The priest who baptized Kraus and Oesterreicher, peace activist Max Metzger, was tried and executed for treason in Berlin in 1944. A year earlier the Gestapo arrested Ferdinand Frodl, a Jesuit who wrote about racism for Dietrich von Hildebrand. In 1944, the Nazi People's Court sentenced Frodl to three years prison for failing to report on resistance activities he knew about.

These activists found themselves drawn to St. Paul because chapters 9 through 11 of his letter to the Romans directly refuted claims made by the racist antisemites. According to Paul, if the question was "race," then Jews actually stood above "Aryans" (Gentiles) in their predisposition to lead faithful lives. And far from being permanently lost and contaminated—as the racists claimed—the Jews remained "most dear to God"—the very phrase that went into the Vatican II statement. In fact, St. Paul proclaimed, at the end of time, all Israel would be saved. He had no such certainty about the Gentiles (Aryans).

Why the activists surrounding Johannes Oesterreicher got involved in fighting Nazi racial antisemitism is a question of personal biography that we ultimately cannot answer. Yet one fact stands out in their histories: they were converts. This trend did not begin in 1933. From the 1840s until 1965, virtually every activist and thinker who worked for Catholic-Jewish reconciliation was not originally Catholic. Most were born Jewish. *Without converts the Catholic Church would not have found a new language to speak to the Jews after the Holocaust.* As such, the story of *Nostra Aetate* is an object lesson on the sources but also the limits of solidarity. Christians are called upon to love all humans regardless of national or ethnic background, but when it came to the Jews, it was the Christians whose family members were Jews who keenly felt the contempt contained in traditional Catholic teaching. A group called Amici Israel, which emerged in the 1920s at the initiative of the Dutch convert Franziska van Leer, demanded an end to liturgical references to Jews as perfidious and a halt to efforts to "convert" the Jews.

But critical mass in this struggle accumulated only in the decade that followed, when Catholics farther to the East, in the lands where German was spoken, observed an intensification of anti-Jewish contempt among fellow believers in ways that should have been impossible. The racism of Nazism—which these converts called neo-paganism—was beginning to enter the teaching of some of the most eminent Catholic teachers of the day. It was well known that Catholics could be racist; what was new was the use of arguments based in theology to undergird racism, indeed to make racism seem a necessary consequence of Catholic faith. By 1936, one of the most influential and popular preachers of this era, Georg Bichlmair, later the Jesuit Provincial of Austria, was proclaiming from the pulpits of Vienna that Jews carried special defects in their genes for the historic sin of rejecting Christ—defects so severe that baptism was powerless to remove them. For that reason, he argued, Jewish converts had to work hard to undo the effects of apostasy within themselves—a task they might not conclude within their lifetimes. Bichlmair was only forcefully stating what other Catholic intellectuals, like theologians Karl Adam or the scientists Hermann Muckermann and Wilhelm Schmidt, were teaching in books and learned articles.

At this level, the prehistory of *Nostra Aetate* forces us to question a basic assumption we hold about Catholicism in the modern age: that it resisted racism. Even critics of the church are willing to grant a clean distinction between modern antisemitism, which preaches hatred of Jews as an unredeemable and dangerous race, and Christian anti-Judaism, which foments contempt by considering the Jewish people cursed by God and carrying a special burden of suffering through history. The Catholic Church is generally considered the rare institution that resisted racism.[4] Yet in a time when Christianity ceased treating Jewish converts as Christians with equal rights, the older anti-Judaism had clearly become enmeshed with modern racist antisemitism.[5] What the convert friends of Johannes Oesterreicher discovered in their polemics with Catholic racists was that this connection, clearly visible in the intergrown branches of racist antisemitism and religious anti-Judaism, extended much deeper than they imagined, into the soil of common assumptions about Jewish character and fate. Antisemitism and anti-Judaism were thus distinct as ideal types in the Weberian sense, but in practice they were inseparable in ways that Christians of the 1930s failed to comprehend.[6]

The history of the document embraced by the church in 1965 is therefore also a story of how Christians learned to oppose antisemitism with the tools given by their faith in their time. This learning occurred within the language of chapters of Paul's letter to the Romans that had been neglected for centuries, and it took place in roughly two phases: first, before the war, against the superficial if popular assumptions of Catholic racism; second, after the war, against the deeply rooted beliefs of Christian anti-Judaism. In the former period, the converts argued that, yes, Jews can be baptized and become Christians of no worse standing than Christians of Gentile background. However, they continued to insist that Jews must be baptized to escape the curse resting upon the Jewish people for rejecting Christ. In the second period, these thinkers began to wonder about the nature of the curse. If the history of the Jews was a series of trials sent to punish them for failing to accept Christ, then what meaning did Auschwitz have? Were the Nazis instruments of God's will, meant to make the Jews finally turn to Christ? To answer yes to this question was obscene, but it was the only answer Catholic theology provided as of 1945. In the years that followed, the converts had to stage a revolution in a church that claimed to be unchanging.

After the war, a new generation of converts joined Oesterreicher (now known as John) and Karl Thieme in their efforts to undo the anti-Judaism on which antisemitism thrived. In Freiburg, Germany, the concentration camp survivor Gertrud Luckner published the *Freiburger Rundbrief* and enlisted Thieme as her theological advisor. There Thieme developed ideas later taken into the documents of Vatican II. In Paris, Father Paul Démann, a converted Hungarian Jew, began publishing the review *Cahiers Sioniens*, and, with the help of fellow converts Geza Vermes and Renée Bloch, refuted the anti-Judaism in Catholic school catechisms, especially the idea that Jews lived under a curse. Three years later Miriam Rookmaaker van Leer, likewise a convert (from Protestantism), founded the Dutch Catholic Council for Israel (Katholieke Raad voor Israel), and engaged the priest Anton Ramselaar as her theological advisor. Ramselaar had known the founders of the Amici Israel initiative of the 1920s.[7]

In 1958, Ramselaar, at the suggestion of Ottilie Schwarz (a convert from Vienna) convened an international symposium in Apeldoorn, Holland which brought together the leading Catholic thinkers from France (Paul Démann), Germany (Karl Thieme, Gertrud Luckner), Israel (Abbot Leo Rudloff, Father Jean-Roger Hené), the United Kingdom (Irene Marinoff), and the United States (John Oesterreicher). Besides Ramselaar, all were converts. At its third meeting, in 1960, this group produced theses that were passed onto the new Pope John XXIII—along with recommendations of John Oesterreicher's Institute for Judeo-Christian Studies at Seton Hall University in South Orange, New Jersey. Oesterreicher founded this institute in 1953 with help from the eminent Chinese legal scholar John C. H. Wu, professor at Seton Hall and a convert to Catholicism.[8] In 1961, Oesterreicher went on to the Second Vatican Council. At one critical moment in October 1964, the priests Gregory Baum and Bruno Hussar joined Oesterreicher to draft the statement that would become the Vatican Council's decree on the Jews. Like Oesterreicher, Baum and Hussar were converts of Jewish background.

What we see by looking at the Catholic converts who argued against antisemitism was the necessity but insufficiency of secular arguments. As Karl Thieme wrote in the 1950s, hatred of Jews always had some relation to their religious character. Even the Nazis, who made race science into a religion, never specified a Jewish identity that was divorced from Jewish religion. The Catholic story is therefore part of the more general story of the intellectual and moral struggle against antisemitism in the modern era. Scholars once thought that secularization had pushed religion to the margins of social relevance by the late nineteenth century, making religious forms of Jew hatred irrelevant.[9] Modern racist antisemitism had allegedly displaced religious anti-Judaism. Yet in recent decades historians have shown that religion by no means declined into insignificance during the secular age and that, similarly, religious forms of Jew hatred did not disappear.[10] Though weakened, churches in Central Europe in the 1930s were still vital institutions, populated by people who were devout but confused about the relationship of racism, antisemitism, and Christianity. In Germany, the bishops added to the muddle by condemning Nazism and issuing prohibitions against it in 1930 and 1931, but then lifting warnings and prohibitions after the Nazis seized power.[11]

Catholics who opposed antisemitism could not ignore the worldly aspects of the problem. In the 1930s, they began using the arsenal of social and natural science to upend ideas about Jewish domination of the economy, or Jewish coherence as a "race," or alleged Jewish conspiracies aiming at world domination. They did not have to start from scratch, but rather could draw upon a growing corpus of literature by authors such as Abraham Sachar, Bernard Lazare, Anatole Leroy-Beaulieu, or Solomon Fineberg, who patiently overturned the antisemites' claims with impressive arrays of evidence and arguments.[12] Ultimately, their opponents could not sustain antisemitic stereotypes because they lacked grounding in fact.

But religion is not about grounding in fact. Christians believe in "things not seen." A devastating argument based in reason—for example, that Jewish blood is empirically no different from non-Jewish blood—may not deflate racism, but it begins letting out the air. Racism has a tenuous relation to reality, but it is not about things not seen. Yet Christian anti-Judaism was not only about things not seen, it proclaimed things not meant to be understood, things that were subjects of mystery, not chosen by individual

Christians of the twentieth century or even by the modern church—things that could not be suddenly relinquished either by an individual or group decision. It was pointless to argue that not God but Gentiles had punished Jews through history, because the ideology of anti-Judaism was not amenable to evidence and observation; even with the best of will, before or after the Holocaust, no one could "disprove" the charge of deicide. It would not disappear through good intentions or any ethical impulse, including the Christian teaching of love for one's neighbor. This age-old belief continued to give sustenance to modern, "secular" hatred. Even the most determined Christian opponents of Nazism—including Dietrich Bonhoeffer—shared with the antisemites the basic belief that Jews lived under a curse for killing Christ. That robbed them of the language with which to speak unequivocally in favor of Jews during the Holocaust. Nothing in the Christian tradition permitted them to understand Jewish suffering as other than divinely willed. After the war, Christian thinkers—almost all of them converts—returned to St. Paul's letter to the Romans looking for signs that this greatest crime was not one more trial sent to the Jews in order to turn them to Christ.

To some readers, this book will seem an exercise in finding fault with the Catholic Church. Others may find it is apologetic. But the point of the book is neither to find fault nor to apologize. Many books of that sort exist, dwelling either upon moments when the bishop of Rome or other bishops spoke out against Nazism or moments at which they failed to speak out. But what were the constraints within which bishops and other Catholics *thought* about race or about Jews? Where did they have freedom to maneuver in their statements while remaining orthodox? Works that extract quotations from their historical context—in order either to condemn or exonerate the Vatican—leave such questions unanswered.

In seeking to re-create the mental horizons of the years before World War II, this book does not attempt to "explain" or account for the Holocaust. Clearly the Holocaust was unthinkable without the ancient Christian legacy of deicide as well as the related idea that Jews were cut off from divine grace, destined to wander the earth until they turned to Christ. Yet the recognition of the truth in these assertions does not constitute an explanation of why the Holocaust happened. Instead, this book has the more modest goal of answering the largely unexplored question of how the Holocaust changed the way Catholics thought about Jews. Contrary to widespread assumptions, the revolutionary about-face that took place at Vatican II did not flow "naturally" or "automatically" from reflection about the genocide, but rather resulted from struggle among theologians extending from the 1930s to the 1960s: about how to revise centuries of teaching on the crowd's self-deprecation in Matthew 27 ("let his blood be upon us and our children!"), or the place in the Epistle to the Hebrews declaring God's covenant with the Jews obsolete, or the idea flowing from Matthew 28:19 that Christians supposedly had no option but to proselytize Jews. How could a priest who had preached one interpretation of the New Testament for decades suddenly reverse himself and still seem a source of reliable understanding of scripture?

The story of this struggle depicts some courage and very much engagement, but it is not a simple story of heroism. The way to *Nostra Aetate* was not straight, but involved bends in the road, snags, and repeated detours along well-worn but ultimately circuitous paths of anti-Judaism. Even after World War II we read this story's protagonists calling the Jews Christianity's "enemies," infamous for killing Christ. The problem of the church's mission to the Jews, wrote one pastor in 1945, was that there had not been enough of it. The author was not an antisemite but a foremost opponent of antisemitism. Rather than force linear elegance upon a crooked historical path, the narrative that follows occasionally pauses to wonder about ideas that led nowhere or roads that were not taken. Most instructive and disturbing is how the way to the future of tolerance often emerged from a lengthy way station of intolerance. Historians looking for the origins of tolerance have no choice but to seek it in environments full of hatred, contempt, and suspicion. It is here that one sees the inadequacy of books that pluck either disturbing or exonerating phrases out of the church's murky past: they tell us nothing about how people lived in a past that exists beyond our mental horizons, nor do they tell us how ideas that we take for granted—like every line of *Nostra Aetate*, chapter four—first became thinkable.

1

The Problem of Catholic Racism

To understand how the Catholic Church has dealt with its ancient legacy of anti-Judaism, one must first question the widely held belief that the church—an ostensible "bulwark against the disorders afflicting the age"—opposed all racism, and thus also modern antisemitism. The point is not that Catholicism was especially racist. Indeed, probably no other institution more forcefully insisted on humankind's unity when racists doubted that unity early in the twentieth century. In the 1920s the institutional church stood farther above race and nation than did international socialism, and formed the strongest bulwark against race improvement—eugenics, a science that was extolled by right-thinking people across the globe.[1] The church never ceased welcoming converts throughout the world regardless of ethnicity or race, and from the 1920s, the Vatican began a drive to promote the formation of native clergies.[2] In October 1926, Pius XI consecrated the first six Chinese bishops, and between 1922 and 1939 the number of native priests in mission countries went from 2,670 to over 7,000.[3] In a move directed against the racism of fascist Italy, Pius XII elevated two black African priests to the episcopacy just after the outbreak of World War II. By that point, Japan had two bishops and over a hundred native priests.[4]

The point is rather that Catholicism can vary significantly across boundaries, and some national variants proved more open to racism than others. Before World War I, the Vatican had to prod the church in the United States to ordain African American priests, and even sent missionary priests to North America to achieve this purpose.[5] Yet this was more an intervention in practice than in teaching: no one questioned the legitimacy of sacraments extended to American blacks, either of baptism or ordination. No one claimed that blacks were excluded from Christ's promise of everlasting life. In German-speaking Europe, however, Catholicism opened itself to racist theology after World War I, and priests and influential intellectuals told the Catholic faithful that Jews—that region's "racial other" by common consent—bore a second original sin, an *Erbsünde* signaling special propensity to evil, transmitted from generation to generation and not erased by baptism. That sacrament was not pointless, but priests had to be careful when dispensing it to a people with an inclination to deceit. Once Jews entered the church, they had be kept from high offices and made to "work hard on themselves" over generations to undo the genetic inheritance of a supposed apostasy that took place hundreds of years earlier. In effect, a Jew could not become a full-fledged Christian in his or her lifetime.

This view will seem strange to contemporary Christians. Did not Christ instruct his followers to go and baptize all nations (Matthew 28)? Can a Christian remain Christian while claiming that Jews should be exempted from this mission?[6] Did not Paul write that after baptism there is "neither Jew nor Greek" (Galatians 3:28)? Yet German theologians of the prewar era believed they faced another "fact": that human races composed part of the natural order, and that these races consisted of persons having shared characteristics. Given that the church derives its ethics from natural law, the question then became how to adapt moral teaching to what seemed to be the realm of nature. Early church councils had rejected as heretical the claim that nature was a place of evil—this was Manichaeism. Thomas Aquinas later wrote that grace presumed nature. But what was nature? Because the Catholic Church was not a scientific institution, it relied upon

scientists for an answer. This continues to be true in our day when opponents of abortion depend on findings from microbiology. Science does not
always speak with a clear voice, but the church had learned from disputes
about heliocentrism the perils of ignoring scientific findings altogether.
Church leaders therefore proceeded with extreme caution during the
1920s when the scientific community declared "race" to be a reality in the
world of nature. Especially within Central Europe, Catholics speculated
about God's purpose in creating humans races. If races belonged to nature, which was essentially good, what duties did Catholics have toward
them?

In the years before 1945, German-speaking Catholics turned to two
priests for answers: the developmental biologist Hermann Muckermann
and the anthropologist Wilhelm Schmidt.[7] Muckermann was a Jesuit
who directed the section for eugenics at the Kaiser Wilhelm Institute for
Anthropology in Berlin, and Schmidt, a member of the missionary order
Society of the Divine Word, was a full professor at the University of Vienna. When Munich's Cardinal Michael Faulhaber met Adolf Hitler at the
Obersalzberg in November 1936, he confessed to having spent many hours
in the company of Muckermann in an effort to understand Catholics' duties to "protect the race."[8] In August 1943, at the height of the Nazis' racial
war, Germany's bishops met for a yearly conference at Fulda, and decided
to ask Hermann Muckermann how they might formulate views about race
that were scientifically and theologically accurate.[9] Muckermann had also
spoken at length on the question of race to Eugenio Pacelli—later Pius
XII—during the latter's time as Nuncio in Germany in the 1920s.[10] Schmidt
and Muckermann directed powerful institutions showcasing the life sciences to the world in the capital cities of Vienna and Berlin, and Catholic
publishers vied for the opportunity to spread their ideas about race. When
it came to the Jews, the two agreed with their secular counterparts that
baptism did not suddenly erase the Jews' genetic traits, and for them that
included the stain of having killed God.

By 1943 Hermann Muckermann had published over 250 works on topics including eugenics, the environment, healthy mothers and families,
the importance of breast-feeding, heredity, survival of the fittest, and "differentiated procreation." Thirty editions had been printed of his works on
race alone. By the time the Nazis ousted him from the directorship at the

Kaiser Wilhelm Institute in Berlin in 1933 for being insufficiently radical, Muckermann had done more than anyone to introduce Catholics to "moderate eugenics." But if one scrutinizes his works today, one finds little that seems inspiring, either as science or as Catholicism, assuming that one imagines science as involving the scientific method and Catholicism an appeal to religious ideas. In a popular book of 1928, Muckermann invoked the superiority of the "Nordic race" but made no mention of experiments or other evidence, let alone scripture. Rather than engender respect for the limits of the knowable, his knowledge of science gave him license to speculate. With no discussion of method, he averred that the Nordic race had more "creative initiative" than other races, which was shown in the "creation of states, the taming of nature, in science and in the arts." Anything of value in world cultures Muckermann credited a priori to Nordic influence. "The blood of the Lombards expressed itself in the Italian Renaissance," Muckermann wrote. Yet he made no effort to study the phenotypes, let alone the blood, of the "heroes" of that age. "Nordic" blood had not trickled into the Iberian peninsula, he speculated, and therefore the Spaniards had no Renaissance.[11]

Muckermann accorded to race the power to unlock secrets not only of European but also world history. "Mongolids," he wrote, were like "deep currents" in the sea, and "violent storms have to be unleashed in order to set them in motion, but once this is accomplished, then the mainland itself is not safe. A yellow danger is to be feared in the European world all the more, because the numeric superiority and the equally instinctual loyalty to nature preserve the primeval character and the power of life. The only really overcrowded country is Japan, which will perhaps unleash the yellow flood." Blacks were an inferior race with "modest" cultural contributions, more influenced by "direct sensory impulses" than other races."[12]

Because race acted as an incubator for things of real value, Muckermann opposed marriage between members of different races "unless a real enriching of the hereditary substance [Erbbestand] may be expected."[13] Although Muckermann claimed Jews represented a "racial mixture of Near Eastern and oriental genetic material," with "peculiar gifts" including "an ability to empathize with others at a spiritual level," he opposed marriages between Jews and Germans (the operative category was not "Christians"), because they would erode Germandom.[14] He explained why in a book published just as the Nazis were coming to power:

> Our first concern is to maintain the untouched, hereditary, elemental nature of the German people . . . The present age, which desires the renewal of the German people from its deepest biological sources, causes us to direct particular attention to this goal. One cause for concern is without doubt the swelling numbers of persons of Jewish origin in essential branches of our cultural life.[15]

Like Nazi thinkers, Muckermann assumed that race determined culture. "The bodily determines the spiritual," he wrote in 1928.[16] Until restrained by the Vatican in 1931, Muckermann advocated elements of negative eugenics, including isolation of persons deemed unworthy, that is, those who did not help "bear culture." Muckermann's efforts to register innate human quality involved measuring intelligence and also people's susceptibility to dental cavities. With the human soul a subordinate entity, Catholic sacraments came to seem a nonissue, and Muckermann warned against marriages between Jews and Christians, *even if the Jews were baptized.* "Let no one defend themselves on the grounds of baptism making a Jew a Christian," he reasoned, "baptism makes a person a child of God, but never changes his basic hereditary structure."[17]

Despite our difficulty finding anything recognizably Christian in such writings, Muckermann traveled easily in the Catholic elite of the interwar years, entertaining top politicians of the Center Party as well as Nuncio Pacelli in a well-appointed villa in the Schlachtensee section of Berlin.[18] The Jesuit met Pius XI in 1923 when in Rome to give a major address at a congress on racial hygiene sponsored by Benito Mussolini.[19] He secured a second appointment at the Vatican in the 1930s, in a time when Pius XI and state secretary Pacelli were viewed as staunch opponents of racial doctrines.[20] Why did they consult Hermann Muckermann to combat racism?

Answers are not easy. In his age, he was not seen as a racist. Far from sympathizing with Nazism, Muckermann had close ties to the anti-Nazi resistance, and he spirited two endangered German Center Party politicians across the border to the Netherlands after Hitler's seizure of power.[21] His brother Friedrich, also a Jesuit, directed Catholic resistance activities from Oldenzaal in the Netherlands. From the closing days of World War I, Hermann Muckermann had been a close friend of the Center Party's Erwin Respondek, an American agent who later informed the United States of Germany's plans to invade the Soviet Union.[22] Though careful not to get too involved in resistance activities, Muckermann secured contacts with General Franz Halder of the Wehrmacht General Staff for Respondek, from which he learned details of Hitler's meeting with army officers of July 31, 1940, on the planned attack on Russia.[23] A popular speaker on family and marriage, who "sought to define a middle course between Nazis' theories of racial superiority and traditional Church positions," Muckermann was considered a dangerous ideological rival by the Nazi regime and was kept under surveillance and forbidden to speak in public after 1936.[24]

After the war, Hermann Muckermann's star rose again. In 1948, at the age of seventy-one, he resumed his academic career at Berlin's Technical University.[25] He was charged with rebuilding the Berlin Institute for Anthropology and in 1952 received the *Grosses Verdienstkreuz* (Cross of the Order of Merit) of the Federal Republic. The popularity in German Catholic circles of this tall priest-professor with dark, piercing eyes lasted until his death in 1962. To historians, he remains an enigma, though he fits perfectly into Catholic discourse on race of the German lands.

The other great Catholic expert on race of that day, Father Wilhelm Schmidt of Vienna, supposedly represented a moderate Austrian approach to human sciences, emphasizing culture and spirit over physics and matter.[26] In 1923, Schmidt so impressed Pius XI that the Pontiff subsidized a museum of ethnology for Schmidt at the Vatican, and he gained a reputation as an opponent of racism. In the late 1930s, the American civil rights activist John LaFarge, S.J., cited Schmidt when arguing against "the inheritance of any fixed or stable mental traits."[27] Likewise, the editor of the Jesuits' *La Civiltà Cattolica*, Father Antonio Messineo, the most visible Italian Catholic critic of racism, used Schmidt to support his view that there was no such thing as a pure race.[28] Yet in fact these Jesuits had been reading Schmidt selectively.

Schmidt had all the scientific legitimacy of Muckermann and was equally racist. Before World War I, he established the premier Central European journal *Anthropos,*[29] and founded a chair of ethnology at the University of Vienna which produced disciples of his "cultural circle" approach to human development. He and his students controlled appointments in this discipline for decades. But Schmidt seemed more serious about Catholicism than Hermann Muckermann in Berlin. He was the confessor to the last Habsburg Emperor Charles, a man now a step from sainthood, and presumably he had attracted the pope's attention through his theory of monogenesis (supported with a twelve-volume study!), the view that there had been one original act of revelation.[30] Like the German bishops, the pope had deep faith in the powers of science to bolster religion.

Schmidt understood the potential of his dual credentials. "Race scientists," he wrote, "almost to a man educated as anatomists, physiologists, physicians, anthropologists—that is, as natural scientists—working with methods and means derived entirely from the natural sciences, suddenly make claims to talk not only of genetic attributes of the body, but also those of the soul."[31] For this they did not have the necessary training. Yet what was the substance of Schmidt's *Catholic* science?

One might have thought that Schmidt's advocacy of common human origins based in the Genesis creation narrative would have protected him from racism. Yet like Muckermann, Schmidt proceeded from an a priori belief in a hierarchy of human races. In his view races had arisen as a result of environmental conditions, and once they cohered in natural history they took on value that was transcendent. Schmidt opposed racial mixing in order to protect what was of value in a race. Like Muckermann, he assumed that Germans were the master race (*Herrenvolk*) in Europe and that Jews were a foreign race bearing markings of a historic crime, the killing of Christ:

This kind of transgression can by itself distort the being of a people; yet in the case of the Jewish people, the betrayal of its high calling has made this distortion go very deep. In punishment this people, as Christ himself predicted, was driven out of its homeland. Almost two thousand years of distortion and uprooting of its essence has then had a secondary but real effect on its physical race. These racial effects . . . are not neutralized by baptism. For that, Jews will have to work hard on themselves. [Converted Jews] may therefore belong to our number, but not in the same way as our German racial comrades.[32]

Like Muckermann, Schmidt wanted to keep Jews and Germans apart
by means of "robust racial hygiene" in order to "isolate and expel harmful
foreign bodies" from the German *Volk*.[33] And like his Berlin alter ego,
Schmidt did not explicitly endorse Nazi teaching (he called it "extreme"
and "pagan"), and the Nazis did not see him as an ally.[34] In fact, the Gestapo
arrested Schmidt the day German troops entered Austria in 1938.[35] Compared with theorists of the Third Reich, Schmidt preferred to speak of *Volk*
and not race, because the former word signaled the "sum of characteristics
called for by common fate, regardless of whether these are passed on gene-
tically or not."[36] But—characteristic for the time—Schmidt's *Volk* was not a
deracialized "cultural" category. The language spoken in German Europe
of that time did not permit a nonracial *Volk*. In the Central European mind,
race had a gravitational pull that no human community could escape. Despite his skepticism about the heredibility of certain characteristics, he
wrote that "that race is the most valuable which gives humanity the most
from its own inner strength."[37]

Schmidt occupied a contradictory place between the fronts of Catholic
Church and modernity. In early work, he expected to confirm the creation narrative of the Bible with scientific evidence.[38] Later, he felt a duty
to unite the Catholic teaching of the universal value of the human person
with findings from racial science, and this led him on a path of contradictions. His occasional insistence that "all people are brothers and sisters"
seems like an "alien element" on the background of his writings as a whole.[39]
In his overall vision, biological destiny had overwhelmed and crushed the
soul.

The French-American anthropologist Eduard Conte has described the
horror he felt when reading Schmidt's recommendations for dealing with
"racial aliens" in Central Europe. For Schmidt, the racially foreign "element" was "nothing other than an agglomeration of subversive products
of the dissolving bourgeois urban cultural intelligentsia in which Jewish
forces are strongly represented." The business of the day was to unmask
such elements as "enemies of the people, and then by means of conscious
and forceful racial hygiene to isolate and cut them off and then to expunge these harmful foreign bodies. In this way, those freed and cleansed
of their influence will themselves become more aware of their racial and

cultural peculiarity."[40] "From the mouth of a cleric," Conte comments, such words "sound disconcerting, indeed cruel."

Remarkable in the writings of the Catholic experts Muckermann and Schmidt is the anemic quality of Christian thought. They seemed to have subverted Christ's invitation: baptism had become not a gift to be shared or a duty of evangelization but a prerogative of blood to be protected. The question emerges as to whether science displaced theology because theology was powerless against the temptations of racism.

Let us consider the priest and professor Karl Adam, a theologian who might have provided evidence against this kind of proposition. Adam, "foremost German advocate of Catholicism," taught theology from a chair in Tübingen later held by Hans Küng.[41] In the years between the world wars, he seemed progressive, advocating ecumenism and opposing worn ideas of church hierarchy more compellingly than any other Catholic thinker of the first half of the twentieth century.[42] Instead of encrusted officialdom and stale precepts, he wrote, the church must be understood as a community that was alive and vital: the people of God. This anti-hierarchical understanding later animated many of the proponents of reform at the Second Vatican Council. Karl Adam did not limit the "People of God" to Catholics, and in 1924 he depicted the church in words that even today strike a reader as exceptionally tolerant: "Non-Catholic sacraments have the power to sanctify and save, not only objectively, but also subjectively. It is therefore conceivable from the church's standpoint, that there is a true, devout and Christian life in those non-Catholic communions which believe in Jesus and baptize in His Name."[43] Yet Adam did not live outside the racist age. The word *Volk* had the liberating power to expand the boundaries of the church by embracing Protestants, yet it also had the power to exclude because it signaled the ethnic unity of the German people. Karl Adam wanted to bring Protestants and Catholics together as a way of healing divisions among Germans, and in 1933 he considered Adolf Hitler as an ally in this quest, musing that Catholics must recognize the Führer as savior of the "diseased [German] national body," the man who could restore Germany's "blood unity."[44]

These were not retrograde, conservative views. Rather, as a modern theologian, anxious to keep pace with a Protestant-dominated scholarship,

Adam was transcending the dualism that had characterized stagnant scholastic theology, and making Christianity relevant in the modern age. He wanted to recapture the reality of Christ's humanity and sensuality—a quest that gained him a readership the world over—but he also wanted to fit into the racist spirit of Germany. In a 1935 lecture, Adam proclaimed that the "man of the future" was "not the man who has renounced sensuous life, who has been divided and torn asunder by the disastrous opposition of body and spirit, of Bios and Logos, but the man who has been restored to inner unity and wholeness."[45]

Unlike Hermann Muckermann or Wilhelm Schmidt, Karl Adam grounded his arguments theologically. He did so by resurrecting the Thomistic principle that "grace presumes nature" and in fact that "grace perfects nature."[46] Body and spirit were inseparable, and Christians were bound to venerate both. God expressed his will in nature through peoples and races. Like human bodies, the human species was "differentiated," working as "a unity through a diversity of organic functions."[47] The universal church recognized the natural divisions of humanity. Humanity depended not on "many single individuals" or "a sum of spiritual personalities," but rather on "the living national *Volkstum*."[48] According to Adam, discrimination against Jews did not contradict Christ's basic command to love one's neighbor as oneself. After all, love of the other assumed love of the self, and the self was German and Christian. He therefore portrayed Nazi orchestrated boycotts of Jewish businesses as the *fulfillment of Christian charity*, acts of "Christian-German self-assertion" aimed at stemming the "Jewish deluge":

> According to biological laws there can be no doubt that the Jew as Semite is racially foreign and will remain racially foreign. It will never be possible to integrate the Jew into the Aryan race: no "mixing of blood" would ever permit this to happen. Blood is the physiological basis of our intellect [*Geistigkeit*], of the special way that we feel, think, and want; it has given definitive shape to the Germanic myth, and to German culture and history. Therefore German self-assertion demands that we protect the purity and the freshness of this blood, and secure this through the force of law. This demand

springs from our well-ordered love of self: the love of self that for Christian morality is the natural prerequisite for love of neighbor.[49]

We see that ultimately Karl Adam had as much faith in "biological laws" as did the German Catholic hierarchy. He was a scientist (*Wissenschaftler*) like Muckermann or Schmidt, and science offered a cloak that fit the contours of his prejudices.

By 1943, Nazi authorities had violently removed Jews from the South German university town where Adam worked, but he continued to develop a theology aimed at dejudaizing Christianity. In peer-reviewed scholarship, he mused that Christ's "mother Mary had no physical or moral relation to those hateful energies and tendencies that we condemn in the full-blooded Jew. Through a miracle of God's grace Mary is beyond those characteristics that are passed by blood from Jew to Jew; she is a figure transcending Jewishness." Therefore Jesus was not a "race-Jew."[50] Adam's racism differed from that of Nazis for whom Jews could never, regardless of how many generations, lose their Jewishness. Yet the difference was more one of degree than of kind, because in the historical context of the Third Reich his views encouraged the intellectual ghettoization that proved a necessary stage in the destruction of the Jews. Theologians like Adam blurred the boundaries between Nazism and Christianity, making them invisible to many Catholics.

Like Muckermann and Schmidt, Adam was anything but an isolated figure in German or international Catholicism. His books went through dozens of printings in many languages and are influential to this day. Pope Benedict does not get two sentences into his first book on Jesus before noting the inspiration he received from Karl Adam.[51] Adam's notion of Christ as vitally human impressed readers as diverse as Edward Schillebeeckx, Bernard Häring, Yves Congar, George Orwell, Dorothy Day, Flannery O'Connor, Karl Rahner, and Karl Barth.[52] Liberals like Alec Vidler, Thomas Merton, Hans Küng, or James Carroll have recalled the profit and enjoyment of reading Adam in their formative years.[53] In the 1960s, Paul VI told Küng of his own early encounters with Adam, calling him "an exemplary theologian" who could reach "people today 'beyond the walls of the church.'"[54]

Hans Küng knows about Karl Adam's German nationalism but mis-remembers one thing. Adam was not cured of all attraction to Nazism by 1934. At worst, he suffered a minor setback that year after criticizing the German Faith Movement.[55] Küng also does not pause to wonder at the contrast: great modern theologian, trail-blazer for the more open church of Vatican II on the one hand, and enthusiast for Nazi racism on the other. How was that possible?[56] Of course, Küng was not alone in deceiving himself about Adam. With other members of the faculty, he trooped along to honor Adam's 85th birthday celebrations in 1961, just as Karl Rahner or Yves Congar had loyally contributed to a festschrift in his honor ten years earlier.[57] No work appeared in postwar Germany questioning Adam's views on the Aryan Christ, let alone censuring him for abetting Nazism. For all its diversity, German Catholicism was what Adam called it: a community with coherence. To disavow Adam, Muckermann, or Schmidt after 1945 would have been to raise the question of why they were not disavowed before 1945.

Perhaps we expect too much of German Catholics. After 1933, racism became a doctrine of a totalitarian state, and those publicly challenging it risked severe consequences. In 1934, Cardinal Michael Faulhaber of Munich reacted with lightning speed to deny reports from Prague that he had spoken out against racism.[58] No one forced Karl Adam to curry favor with the Nazis as he did, but many other German Catholics were simply frightened. What about their colleagues in Austria? Until the fiasco of Hitler's war most Austrians considered themselves ethnically German. The Nazis did not control this territory until the spring of 1938. Before that, Austria was ruled by a government that called itself anti-Nazi and "Christian corporatist," and it opposed Hitler as a way of keeping Austria independent. Because Nazism was identified with racism, Catholics could disparage racism in Austria with the state's blessing. The first journalist ejected from Hitler's Germany, the American Dorothy Thompson, por-trayed authoritarian Austria of these years as a bulwark against racism.[59]

Yet here too we see the massiveness of racist German nationalism pull-ing Catholics into its orbit, even some of those who opposed Nazism and suffered the consequences when Gestapo officers began hunting down critics after the *Anschluss* of March 1938. Take the Jesuit Georg Bichlmair, among the most gifted and influential Catholic preachers of the period. The hypercritical Hungarian social philosopher (and convert) Aurel Kolnai later described Bichlmair as "a born guide of men," for many years pastor to students at the University of Vienna, specializing in conversions and debates with anarchists and "other infidels."[60] Bichlmair was also a political player, who conducted talks with Socialists on behalf of the Christian Socials in 1927 and later adjudicated disputes within the Austrofascist governing coalition.[61] In November 1939, the Gestapo arrested Bichlmair for aiding Jewish converts to Catholicism, and shipped him off to exile in Silesian Beuthen for the rest of the war.[62] He may have known these "non-Aryan Catholics" from the early 1930s when he acted as director of the Viennese Mission to the Jews—a predecessor of Johannes Oesterreicher.

Nothing in this biography prepares us for a notorious speech Bichlmair gave in 1936. Echoing the sentiments of Schmidt and Muckermann, he declared that baptism was powerless to cure Jews of moral defects that they carried in their genes. The legacy of killing Christ had so diseased Jews as a collectivity that Jews entering the church would have to work for generations to undo the hereditary damage. The speech addressed a question bothering contemporaries: how the ancient church might respond to the peculiar challenges of secularization in an increasingly fascist Europe. Of particular concern to Catholics sensing pressure on the right were the new racial doctrines, especially from the Nazis, who contested ideological terrain with the church.[63] Unlike right-wing secular German nationalists, Bichlmair did not say that Jews could not be redeemed. If Jews continued to exist, that had to do with "God's wonderful Providence." Until Jews recognized Christ, however, they were condemned to wander through history "carrying their own corpse." He now injected insights from science into his argumentation. Admitting that shared biological traits need not be decisive, he nevertheless speculated about the presence of grace in the Jewish people: "At best one may say the following: because it persisted in religious apostasy this aimless and restless people does not possess sufficient salvific powers of grace in order to counteract its defective genetic material or to properly develop its valuable genetic material. This is especially true considering that this people has freed itself from belief in God and from all metaphysical connections." The momentum of his argumentation left him incapable of asserting the powers of baptism. Jews sprinkled with water did not suddenly become new human beings; the sacrament did not touch their "biological substance," and therefore Jews needed to work hard on themselves to remedy the weakness of their genetic inheritance.[64]

One Austrian Catholic who knew Nazism firsthand and might have been spared the illusions of Father Bichlmair was the medical doctor Albert Niedermeyer. Niedermeyer had practiced medicine for decades in German Lower Silesia, opposing Nazi racism until he was forced to close his practice in 1933. Among Reich Catholics he gained a reputation for fanatically rejecting eugenics, including all forms of sterilization. German Catholicism, even in the 1920s, was hospitable to "race improvement." In 1934, Niedermeyer returned to Austria, and as a leading Catholic physician composed books on pastoral medicine that are used to this day. The Nazi state did not forget him, however: hours after German troops entered Austria on March 25, 1938, he was arrested and sent to Sachsenhausen.[65] Yet before that he wrote a memoir of his years in Germany which tells us how he understood the battle against racism.

In early sections of the book, we see a steadfast opposition to the Nazis' instrumentalization of the human body. Niedermeyer's engagement with "the problems of racial hygiene" had led to a serious examination of the most central elements of Christian morality. In contrast to Karl Adam, Niedermeyer read the Thomist principle of grace presupposing nature in a way that permitted grace some independent power. Even those who were "severely retarded" could prevail over illness with the help of grace.[66] Yet he assumed that grace's workings should be visible to the naked eye, and soon he was writing of the importance of keeping the race pure: races were part of the "natural order willed by God."[67] When Niedermeyer's attention turned to the Jews, the racism he opposed in Germany suddenly gushes through narrow cracks left open for racist beliefs.[68] With his hostility to race science Niedermeyer had been an outsider among German gynecologists, but when he combined the languages of science and Catholicism he began propagating racist antisemitism, or more accurately racist anti-Judaism; like others in the Catholic camp, he portrayed his critique of Jews as superior to that of the Nazis.[69]

In Niedermeyer's view, modern antisemites erred by seeing the Jewish question as exclusively racial. A Christian had to place Christ at the center of any thoughts on the Jews. But that did not mean looking to the words of Christ, for example, on duties to neighbors; rather, it meant focusing on the circumstances of Christ's death. If one really believed that Christ was God, then the magnitude of Jewish guilt for his crucifixion was "beyond imagining." No other people had been as blessed with God's grace as the Jews, and thus their fall dropped them from a staggering height. By calling the blood of Christ upon themselves, the Jewish people had "frivolously sworn away their future." "How horribly this curse has been realized," he wrote. "One does not do Jewry a favor if one fails to make it look in a mirror," he continued, "in order to see why everything has happened as it has. The sign of Cain marks the awful treachery of this once noble people that is now despised among the peoples . . . even the most honest efforts cannot deny the basic fact that Jews have become repugnant, indeed frightening and sinister for other peoples."[70]

Now the anti-racist Niedermeyer, on the run from the Nazis, merged his racism with traditional anti-Judaism, which held that Jews lived under a curse and continued to be punished by God throughout their history. He thought it was a sign of divine justice that the Nazis launched a boycott of the Jews just as the Vatican proclaimed 1933 a holy year commemorating the crucifixion 1,900 years earlier.[71] "When one sees such connections one gains a better sense of the question of race," he surmised. Niedermeyer condemned Jews who tried to escape punishment for killing Christ by "dishonestly" becoming Christians, and he demanded special scrutiny for converts. It was a delusion to think that baptism could suddenly erase Jews' guilt for killing Christ.

Niedermeyer's attempt to introduce race as one desideratum in thinking about the Jews had now brought out in him full-fledged racism. Out of concern to respect the divine order—which included races—he warned Catholics against assimilation and demanded that Catholic marital counseling "express serious reservations about mixed marriage in every case."[72] If these were the sentiments of a self-described opponent of racism, one can imagine the views of those who actively espoused the teachings on race of modern science—which the church after all did not reject.

Better known than Niedermeyer, yet also concerned to fortify the Catholic world against racist nationalism, was the Austrian bishop Alois Hudal. Because he operated out of Rome as rector of the German college of the Anima, Hudal was among the visible Catholic prelates writing on race in these years. In 1937 he produced a book titled *The Foundations of National Socialism*, perhaps the most detailed study of the subject ever produced from a Catholic point of view.[73] Following St. Thomas Aquinas, Hudal believed "it is impossible that there is a point of view that is completely false, without some truth being mixed into it."[74] This was also true of National Socialism. In securing their own position in the German *Volk*, Catholics had to discern what was good about the Nazi movement and try to strengthen it. He called the "healthy" trends of the movement "pure Nazism" and identified them with Hitler, who supposedly opposed "leftists" like Goebbels and Rosenberg.[75] Some Nazis erred in making race the only criterion for judgment; in fact, race and spirit worked upon each other. In the case of the Jews, a historical act of will had left a deep imprint upon a people who were racially much closer to the Germans than were the Finns or Hungarians, thereby creating the special "Jewish problem."

Himself not a scientist, Bishop Hudal relied upon the experts Wilhelm Schmidt and Hermann Muckermann to compile a list of moderate, Catholic views on race: first, that the concept of race cannot be denied; second, that on the scale of values race is a good, but not the highest good; third, that humans' spiritual life is determined by blood and body, but only secondarily; and fourth, that races, like all life, are constantly changing.[76] He appeared to separate himself from Father Bichlmair by writing that the church could not discriminate against Jewish converts through an "Aryan paragraph," but then staunchly defended the German state's discrimination against Jews because of the dangers they posed for the "German *Volk* spirit."[77] Hudal's insistence on joining race and spirit made his racism all the more potent, because if race and spirit were inseparable, then each had to be protected. Like other German clerics, he enumerated the achievements of the German *Volk* as evidence of God-given spiritual substance that required aggressive defense. He welcomed Nazi racial laws because "this prevalence of Jews, easy to demonstrate statistically, could not continue in the cultural institutions of the German people . . . [especially] since young German men want to earn their living, have families, and place their abilities and gifts in the service of the *Volk* and the state."[78] Nazi Germany was effecting the will of the

Almighty through its racial laws, and Jews who were nonreligious had lost any right to defend themselves:

> Those non-Aryans who have a materialist view of the world and deny that human beings have an eternal soul have the least right to object to this legislation of the Reich. Jews such as these will have to get used to the fact that they are judged in purely racial-biological terms and can no longer have equal value and equal rights in our German people, because only the acceptance of the soul and faith in the supernatural order can protect one from such excessive interpretations.[79]

A few years later Johannes Oesterreicher was disputing that such a thing as moderate, Catholic racism could exist, and here we see why. To accord the subjective category of race any value, even in supposed relation to spirit, was to tie spirit to the interests of the author's purported "race." After the war, Hudal used his institutional power in Rome to smuggle Nazi war criminals to South America.[80] Yet before 1945 the Nazis rebuffed his efforts at reconciling their ideology with Catholicism; like Muckermann, Schmidt, and Bichlmair, he saw his works confiscated and censored.[81]

Can this handful of Catholic thinkers claim to speak for the German Church, or to represent millions of Catholics in Germany and Austria? We do not possess polling data to answer such a question definitively. We do know that save for a handful of émigrés at the heart of this book, no one rose to challenge Catholic racism, neither in the Catholic press, nor among the Catholic bishops, who had tremendous respect and influence, especially in Bavaria and the Rhineland. Decisive words from them would have made a difference. The bishops did not support the Nazi movement. Most found the brownshirts vulgar upstarts: brutal, revolutionary, and anti-clerical. Before 1933 the episcopate released numerous limitations: forbidding priests to join Nazi organizations, prohibiting uniformed Nazi party members from attending religious services, and on a case-by-case basis, keeping Nazi party members from the sacraments. In 1933 the bishops lifted the prohibitions in an attempt to find a modus vivendi with the regime. But before and after that year, bishops and priests showed that they agreed with the Nazi party on a core demand of its program: that the racialized German *Volk* be strengthened and protected. Race-thinking reached a high point of respectability in these years, and to most Central Europeans race was as real as water or air. If there was a problem with racism for the bishops, it was when it reached extremes. Race could not become a substitute deity.

In December 1930, over two years before Hitler came to power, Breslau's Adolf Cardinal Bertram—head of the German bishop's conference—wrote an extensive article on National Socialist ideology and condemned "exaggerated nationalism" and "glorification of the race" as "aberrations." At the same time he cited St. Thomas Aquinas to remind Catholics of duties to the state but also to forms of community grounded in blood:

> Various factors have created this community and the communal feeling of the national spirit. But the most basic is the community of blood. The extension of family to kinship, and kinship to ethnic tribe, and then ethnic tribe to nation, takes place unavoidably by laws that are encoded in human nature. It is willed by nature—or more accurately, by God . . . Thus according to Catholic teaching love of one's race, people and fatherland, this genuinely healthy nationalism, is not only licit and right, but a moral duty.[82]

But where exactly was the border between healthy and exaggerated nationalism? Did healthy nationalism involve rejection of all discrimination based on race? This neither Bertram nor any other bishop was willing to say. The following year, the Jesuit Jacob Nötges prepared a popular study explaining why the German bishops had condemned National Socialism, but in a section on "race and love" he wrote, "according to our holy Catholic faith the commandment of love puts order to our entire religious and moral life. It requires without doubt that the individual person and the individual race think first about itself and take care of itself."[83]

After the Nazis seized power, it became dangerous to speak out openly against racism because it was a doctrine of state. In 1938 the Gestapo interrogated the priest Wolfgang Lauen for simply invoking the equality of all races in a sermon at Berlin's St. Michael Church.[84] Still, that did not mean that Catholic prelates had to import assumptions of the racist worldview into religious teaching. Yet that is precisely what they did. In 1936, Germany's bishops published instructions for education of children stipulating that "race, soil, blood, and folk are precious values of nature created by God the Lord, and entrusted to us German people for conservation. The same God in his endless love has also left us the incomprehensible treasures of the supernatural."[85]

Priests colluded in spreading racist ideas, telling their flocks that Jews possessed a special disease contaminating their souls (the second "hereditary sin," as suggested by Schmidt and Bichlmair).[86] In November 1937, the Berlin diocese newspaper *Katholisches Kirchenblatt* took aim at the Nazi allegation that the Old Testament was the creation of a "Jewish race," making Christianity racially Jewish. Instead of saying that Christianity indeed rested on Jewish foundations, the writers took the argumentative steps recommended by Cardinal Bertram. The *"Judenvolk"* of the Old Testament was "joined in blood" yet lacked any "natural" relation to scripture. "Almost the entire history of the Old Testament," the authors contended, "is a struggle of the messengers of God against the natural-Jewish people." "If one wants to write of race religion among the Jews," they continued, "then this religion was one of idol worship." Living according to the law went against the grain of the Jews: "one hardly need stress that fulfilling the Ten Commandments did not flow naturally from Jewish blood."[87]

About the same time, Joseph Goebbels's *Der Angriff* mocked the church's claims to stand for human equality and published a collage of photographs showing State Secretary Eugenio Pacelli praying at the University of Notre Dame, Jesse Owens and Bill Robinson keeping the company of "Negro dancing girls" in Harlem, Mayor LaGuardia giving a speech in New York, and rabbis and pastors praying together in Riverside Memorial Church. "At God's Table All Are Equal," the caption read. Yet instead of defending Catholicism's interracialism, the Berlin Catholic diocese spoke of libel and objected that "every school child" could discern the supposedly obvious (but more subtle) Catholic beliefs on equality of nations (peoples).[88]

After the war, Germany's bishops claimed they had regularly taken stances against racism in their pastoral letters.[89] In fact, however, throughout the

Nazi reign they regularly condemned extreme manifestations of racism, and not racism as such. Shortly after Hitler's accession to power the bishops proclaimed that national unity was not achieved *solely* through uniformity of blood.[90] In a much-cited Advent letter of 1942 the bishops wrote that "the individual can and may never *completely* disappear in the state, people or race."[91] The following year they issued a pastoral letter warning against *killing* innocent people because of their race.[92]

In 1946, former mayor of Cologne (and future chancellor) Konrad Adenauer chided the bishops in a private letter for not speaking out more clearly against Nazism; they had missed a chance to reinvigorate the Catholic faith.[93] Perhaps the bishops did not speak out because of fear. Rather than confront the state doctrine of racism they spoke in general terms of the dignity of the human person and the need to respect the rights of one's enemies.[94] That was "structural" resistance, evidence that Christianity was incompatible with Nazism at the level of basic values, even when there was no conscious resistance of Christians.[95] But their internal deliberations suggest the bishops would not have spoken out against racial doctrines if they had been free to do so. In 1943, they were still struggling for clarity. As noted above, in August of that year the bishops decided to consult Hermann Muckermann to find ways of speaking about race that were theologically and scientifically accurate.[96] From today's perspective one wonders: why had they not learned that he was a source of the problem?

Before 1938, Austrian bishops could oppose racism and antisemitism with impunity, yet likewise failed to issue clear condemnations. The most outspoken was Linz Bishop Johannes Maria Gföllner, who released an encyclical in January 1933 proclaiming the impossibility of being "a good Catholic and a good National Socialist." Nazism was "deeply ill because of racial extremism [*Rassenwahn*]" and its racial ideology was "completely irreconcilable with Christianity and has therefore to be completely rejected." That was "also true of the radical racial antisemitism preached by the Nazis. To hate and persecute the Jewish people only because of its ancestry is inhuman and unchristian."[97] But why reject only "radical" racial antisemitism? Readers found an answer in the next paragraph: "Without doubt many Jews are strangers to God and exercise a very harmful influence in almost all fields of modern cultural life." Like Bishop Hudal, Gföllner was convinced that Jews were trying to "poison the Christian national soul [*christliche Volksseele*]."[98] Gföllner's letter thus not only failed to refute anti-semitism, it operated in racial terms. Some Jews were "degenerate," and "Aryans" were called upon to defend themselves.[99] "The family of nations contained differences both of bodily but also intellectual nature," he wrote.[100] His attempt to strike balance did the church no favor. The Nazis showed their disapproval of the bishop's letter by putting up posters around Linz showing Christ hanging on a swastika.[101]

Cardinal Theodor Innitzer of Vienna refused to support Gföllner's condemnation of Nazism in 1933 because he was conducting behind-the-scenes negotiations with the Austrian Nazi leader Theo Habicht.[102] In April he underscored his loyalty to the German *Volk* in its commonly understood racial sense, reminding Austrians that the Catholic Church recognized the "unspeakably high ideals and values that repose in blood and *Heimat*." These words gave Austrian Nazis propaganda with which to claim that the cardinal had recognized the Nazi program.[103] At the same time, Innitzer uttered words of sympathy for persecuted Jews in Germany and observed the plight of the church under Nazism with growing out-rage. He condemned racial antisemitism, and praised the anti-Nazi book of the courageous Viennese Catholic Irene Harand—while asking her not to make his views public.[104] He called Jews the "brothers" of Christ.[105] Yet in early 1938 he succumbed to wishful thinking, hoping the church would be left in peace if he declared loyalty to the new regime. He urged Austri-ans to vote for Anschluss as a "national duty" and affixed the words "Heil Hitler" before his signature, a gesture that enraged the Vatican.

Innitzer's attempts at appeasement achieved nothing. In the fall of 1938, Nazi rowdies entered his residence and destroyed furniture and windows while his aids kept the cardinal in a safe place. The Nazi party organized a massive demonstration against the Catholic Church in Vienna, and their Gauleiter Josef Bürckel read Innitzer's postcard to Irene Harand while tens of thousands jeered "Pfui Innitzer" and "Hand over the black dog."[106] The following year, Innitzer was pelted with eggs and potatoes while leaving a church in Königsbrun while the crowd taunted, "Give the black Cardinal a one-way ticket to Dachau!"[107]

Yet Innitzer continued to be plagued by allegations that he was less than loyal, and underscored his faithfulness to *Volk* and *Führer*, declaring after Hitler's occupation of the Sudetenland that he had "thanked the *Führer* and ordered thanksgiving services in the churches and the ringing of bells. I protest against the grievous allegations that I stood opposed to *Führer* and *Volk* in the great days of the German people."[108] At the same time, he took leadership of efforts of the Catholic Church in Vienna to aid so-called "Christian non-Aryans" after the arrest of Farther Bichlmair, and managed to secure the emigration of scores of people who otherwise would have been killed. His biographer calls Innitzer the most Judeophilic cardinal in greater Germany.[109] Innitzer wanted to resist Nazi racism, but failed to summon the language with which to do so.[110]

As members of the top church hierarchy, bishops Innitzer, Hudal, and Gföllner were conservative in every sense of the word. What about the more socially progressive forces from Austrian Christian Socialism, who tended to favor workers' rights, and democracy at the workplace and in the state? If anything, the picture there was bleaker. The closer the activist writer was to workers, the more insistent he became in vilifying Jews in a racist sense. These facts are not advertised in Austria of the present because some of these individuals stood at the foundation of the post–World War II order. Union leader Leopold Kunschak, the first president of postwar Austria, claimed he was not a "racial antisemite," yet referred to Jews as "locusts" and "pestilence," and advocated legal discrimination against baptized Jews as members of the Jewish nation.[111]

When we go further left in the Christian workers' movement, we encounter an even more radical antisemite in the social reformer and romantic anti-capitalist Anton Orel, a man who openly embraced Marx's labor theory of value.[112] Like Kunschak and many other leading Christian Socialist politicians, he suffered abuse after the Nazis entered Vienna, including arrest.[113] Yet a decade earlier Orel had been writing that the "baptism of a Jew is the baptism of a person who is infected with dangerous hereditary elements." There could be no community between "God and the devil, the mysterious body of Christ and that racial community, whose essence and race is the rejection of Christ."[114]

The picture does not change when we examine the political elite of the Austrian Christian corporatist state. Neither Engelbert Dollfuss nor Kurt von Schuschnigg refuted racism, though both came out against radical nationalism. The same is true of Prince Ernst Rüdiger von Starhemberg, that regime's most charismatic politician, who later flew missions for the French Air Force against Nazi Germany.[115] Emmerich Czermak, the last chief of the Christian Social party, wrote that "every honest Israelite must admit that his racial comrades are only a minority inside the German cultural area but take up far too many leadership positions."[116] In his view, "the Jewish rejection of Christ" had "weakened and deformed the Jewish racial character."[117] Czermak reached the same end point as the scholar-priests in his racist musings.[118] Members of two cultures should not mix any more than should two different varieties of flower, like carnations and roses.[119]

If we look to the Swiss lands where German is spoken, we find a thin book of Andreas Amsee entitled *The Jewish Question* appearing from the Institute of the Swiss Catholic People's Union on the eve of the war.[120] Amsee was a pseudonym for the Viennese Jesuit Mario von Galli, whom the institute had entrusted with informing Swiss Catholics about Nazism. Like his confrere Georg Bichlmair, von Galli sought to explain to Catholics why the "age-old problem" of the Jews was suddenly acute, and like Bichlmair he pleaded for a "sober" approach stressing Christian principles of love and justice. Reminiscent of Karl Adam, he portrayed justice as meaning "self-defense and maintenance of the goods of one's own *Volk*." All non-Christian attempts to "solve" the Jewish problem failed: emancipation, socialism, racism. Jews were not a race. Because of their rejection of the Messiah, the Jews had become a vermin-like destroyer (*Schädling*) of nations. Here the Jesuit's argument coincided with Adolf Hitler's. Only Christians really understood how to "solve" the Jewish question, and that was to convert Jews. Like Bichlmair and Wilhelm Schmidt, however, von Galli expressed doubt that baptismal waters could wash away the harmful characteristics that Jews had inherited.[121] His book was reviewed throughout the Swiss Catholic press, but with one exception, *no one uttered a critical word*. Instead, editors rejoiced that a priest had finally given a clear Catholic view, supposedly condemning modern antisemitism. Swiss historian Urs Altermatt concludes that these Catholics were too deeply imbued with centuries of Christian anti-Judaism to note Galli's theological "nonsense." After the war, using his real name, von Galli went on to a stellar

career in publishing and radio, reaching millions of German Catholics
with his reports from the Second Vatican Council, whose reforms he celebrated and projected as in keeping with everything the church had done
to date.

The racist and antisemitic language was so well established that even
after Hitler's defeat we hear its echoes. On May 8, 1945, the date of Germany's capitulation, Archbishop Conrad Gröber of Freiburg believed he
could criticize Nazism at last and told his flock that it was "wrong to succumb to an *extreme* antisemitism that knows no mercy." The following
month, Mainz Bishop Albert Stohr invoked the "divinely ordained community of blood and conviction uniting all German brothers and sisters."[122] The racism of Central Europe's Catholics went beyond what any
individual desired; even those who "meant well," like Theodor Innitzer,
reproduced it. We find it among people incarcerated by the Nazis and
among those who risked their safety to help "racial others." We see it
virtually any time a German Catholic opened his mouth to speak about
Germans, Jews, and race. We find it even in would-be condemnations of
racism by the German bishops, which remained superficial, touching the
words but not the underlying images and ideas. Technically, Jews were
supposed to convert for the sake of salvation. Actually, the church in Central and Eastern Europe was extraordinarily suspicious of those who tried
to enter it, never tiring of warnings.[123]

The bleak picture we have been sketching of the German lands is not
the whole story, however. From about 1933 a small band of Catholics,
mostly émigrés of Jewish or Protestant origin, began staging a vigorous
opposition to racism and racist antisemitism from outposts along the borders of Hitler's Reich: from Katowice, Olomouc, Basel, Lucerne, Strasbourg, and Oldenzaal (the Netherlands), and, still more significantly, the
intellectual and political headquarters of Vienna and Paris. These dissent-
ers produced the intellectual momentum that carried the church forward
to the Vatican II declaration on the Jews thirty years later.

Before we turn to their story, we have to explore where they stood
within the Catholic Church as an international institution, whose drive to
baptize all nations has historically stood in tension with the national par-
ticularism that reached an apogee in racism in the early twentieth century. Given that Fathers Muckermann and Schmidt knew and advised

several popes, one cannot presume their views were unknown in the Vatican. What did Rome make of the entry of racism into Catholic thought? Was it in fact orthodox Catholic teaching, or did the Vatican fail to silence voices it detested? And why did these Catholic voices propounding racism tend to emanate from Germany?

2

The Race Question

Those with basic knowledge of the New Testament must wonder how Catholicism could turn racist. In the Gospels of Mark and Matthew, Christ distilled all commandments into two: the first "to love the Lord your God with all your heart, with all your soul, with all your mind, and with all your strength"; the second to "love your neighbor as yourself."[1] Who was one's neighbor? Christ responded with the parable about a man left to die and brought back to life by a passerby of a different ethnicity: a Samaritan. The point was not to ask who was a neighbor but to be a neighbor. If loving one's neighbor was not enough, Christ went on to instruct his followers also to love their enemies. No human being could be excluded from the love of a follower of Christ.

Yet if Christ's words have been read for centuries, they have also been interpreted. Why follow Christ's command to love one's neighbor? The traditional answer was: in order to gain salvation for oneself. This ultimate goal had the effect of dividing neighbors from one another, a fact admitted by the Vatican's *L'Osservatore Romano* at the height of its battle with Benito Mussolini over race laws in 1938. The church, the editors wrote, had always "tried to demolish the barriers that divide humanity spiritually and to develop in all men sentiments of fraternity and love." But that was simply a preface to the actual message. Above all, the church had a duty to "shield its children from the dangers that threaten faith," and therefore its Teaching Office established canonical impediments to protect Catholics from intimate relations with "Jews and pagans" as well as "schismatic heretics."[2]

Throughout premodern Europe Catholics lived in closed communities that tended to restrict intimacies with non-Catholics. In much of Germany that insularity survived well into the Wilhelmine era, and in fact was reinforced by the anti-Catholic campaign under Bismarck, during which Catholics sought to protect themselves through networks of associations, including sports clubs, newspapers, mutual aid societies, trade unions, and fraternities. Catholics could keep to themselves from cradle to grave. Elsewhere, Catholics created their own schools in order to focus sociability upon themselves, so that Catholic families tended to reproduce Catholic families. Yet these calculations came under strain with accelerating urbanization of the early twentieth century, hence the concern expressed in *L'Osservatore Romano*. In 1916, the Vatican's Cardinal Secretary of State Pietro Gasparri described the problem for the freshly appointed Nuncio to Munich, Eugenio Pacelli—later Pius XII. Members of Bavaria's middle class tolerated "no restraints on their private lives," Gasparri wrote. "They enter into relationships with Protestants and persons of every other religion, so that mixed marriages in Bavaria have markedly increased, resulting in extreme harm to the Catholic Church."[3]

What happened when outsiders approached this well-fortified Catholic world hoping for assistance? For answers, generations of priests turned to the *Theologiae moralis* of the French Jesuit Jean Pierre Gury, printed from the 1850s in many editions and languages, and providing instruction for preaching but also for the confessional.[4] His work became the basis for half a dozen other manuals on moral theology over several generations, including the highly influential works of Hieronymous Noldin.[5] Gury portrayed the one-to-one relation of Christ's parable of the Samaritan as exceptional and wrote that love of neighbor must be "ordered." Neighbors differ, their needs differ, and the things we can do for them differ. The highest obligation was to love oneself, and one's prime concern had to be with salvation because of "the danger of eternal damnation or of death." Christians were obliged to risk their lives only when neighbors were helpless to attain eternal life, that is, when they were threatened with the fires of hell. In the case of Jews, that would mean that the mission impulse had to outweigh all other possible duties. If another's mortal life was in danger, Christians were not obliged to endanger their own lives.[6] What if one encountered demands on one's charity from more than one neighbor?

> If the circumstances are otherwise the same, persons are to be preferred who are closer to us: whether for reasons of blood relation, friendship, our office, our religious confession, homeland, or the like, because God has connected us to them through more intimate bonds . . .
>
> Therefore the following enjoy preference: 1) parents above others, 2) the spouse above one's children; one's children above one's siblings; one's siblings above other relatives, 3) Friends, benefactors, superiors, and those who are more useful to the public welfare above all others. However, according to general opinion, one's spouse is to be preferred to one's parents in cases of ordinary need.[7]

In the twentieth century, the German Capuchin Priest Heribert Jone (1885–1967) built upon the scheme laid out by Gury, who himself had developed teachings of saints Thomas Aquinas and Alphonsus Liguori. Jone, ubiquitous in seminary training in German and Anglo-Saxon countries, dwelt upon duties toward "blood relations" within and beyond the family:

> In case of the same degree of need, our relations to neighbors oblige us to help those who are more closely connected to us. Because these connections vary—for example we can be connected by membership in the same lineage, race, or religion, we must prefer neighbors in relation to the goods on which the respective connection rests. Yet because blood relations are the basis of every other connection, those related by blood (at least of the first degree) receive highest preference before all others, assuming the need is the same.[8]

Contemporary readers are shocked when they hear that Polish Primate August Cardinal Hlond supported a boycott against Jews in 1936, telling Catholics that "it is good to prefer your own kind when shopping, to avoid Jewish stores . . . and especially boycott the Jewish press." But he was well within the strictures of his time's moral theology. "One may love one's own nation more," Hlond asserted, "but one may not hate anyone, including Jews."[9] Indeed, a boycott might be considered a higher act of love, impelling Jews to recognize the hopelessness of their situation and accept Christianity—thus avoiding eternal damnation.

But Hlond was arguing in terms of love of Christians, Christians toward whom one had more direct duties, and fellow Poles with whom his congregations had "blood" ties. The highest Catholic authority in Hungary, Primate Justinian Seredi, likewise instructed his flock on their greater duties toward their own kind. "There can be and are degrees," he said, "because in the sense of natural law and positive divine laws we must love better those who are nearest to us than those to whom more distant ties bind us: family, nation, religious, etc."[10] In Germany—as the moral theology of Heribert Jone shows us—the idea of "nation" [*Volk*] soon became entangled with race. Cardinal Bertram, the head of the German bishops' conference, instructed German Catholics on their "moral duty" to "love race, *Volk*, and fatherland."[11] Leading theologian Karl Adam sharpened the point, writing that German Catholics had higher duties "on the hierarchy of love" toward unbelieving "racial comrades" than they had toward a "believing Hottentot."[12]

This reasoning seems strange when one considers that Christ chose an ethnic other in his example of how love should be extended to neighbors. He could have spoken of a hierarchy of love but did not. He could have spoken of the importance of "bonds of blood" but did not. Instead, he commanded his followers to abandon their families, and when he spoke of his own family, it was metaphorical: "whoever does the will of my Father in heaven is my brother and sister and mother."[13] Later in Matthew's Gospel, Christ speaks of the last judgment, at which the King tells the righteous: "as you did it to the least of my brethren, you did it to me."[14] Christian transcendence takes humans from their this-worldly family to the unity of the "kingdom of God," with conventional familial categories transported to all humanity. The vital distinctions are those of welfare, and these distinctions are to be effaced so that the last become first and the first last.

In more mundane terms, as in the parable of the Samaritan, Christ was warning against the egotism of the family, perhaps the most intense form of egotism because it is justified by love. In retrospect, one might add: justified also by Catholic casuistry in a period when critical study of scripture was frowned upon.[15] For good reason, Augustine had urged Christians to "stretch your love beyond your spouses and children–that love is found also in beasts and sparrows."[16] Yet, in more recent times, the concern with shielding Catholics from damnation produced a moral theology that instructed how to protect oneself from sin but not how to stretch love beyond blood relations.[17] In the racial age, Catholic teachers raised the family egotism Christ warned against to a new level, the would-be extended family of persons connected by "blood" in the modern tribe of the ethnic nation. Among German Catholics, the race feeling grew as the insularity of the Catholic milieu came under threat.

Regardless of how one understood neighbor, however, doing good was not necessarily its own reward, and moral theologians encouraged priests to instruct their flocks not to endanger their immortal souls—an activity that could become compulsive and distracting.[18] As summarized by Catholic sociologist Paul Hanley Furfey, a Catholic examined his conscience by asking, "Have I neglected my morning and night prayers? . . . Have I taken God's name in vain . . . ? Have I deliberately missed Mass . . . ? Have I taken pleasure in impure thoughts and desires . . . ?" Catholics were taught precisely what not to do, in what Father Furfey called "act oriented" theology, dominated by a "concern with concrete instances" that were condemned rather than by concern for promoting good behavior.[19] The prohibitions focused upon sex. Children were instructed in the sinfulness of sex, that all sins related to sex were mortal sins, and that these were far worse than other sins. Parents and priests told girls that the sexual act was "loathsome and degrading." Polish Catholic writer Irena Sławińska and her sister joked, "For mother the greatest sin was a kiss; nothing else was even close to it; but far, far beneath it she was willing to admit to the next gravest sin: premeditated murder."[20] The Austrian Catholic Friedrich Heer has traced such obsessions with concerns for "private salvation" and the resulting suffocation of "fleshly earthbound hopes" back to St. Paul.

The rise of this morality inflated negative images of the Jew as "lascivious, fleshly and sexually obsessed."[21] These visions were not new. For centuries, the Jew had concentrated Christian fears of contamination that endangered eternal life. In order to secure their own salvation, Catholics of the 1930s were told to keep Jews at arm's length, and they watched as others carried out a "judgment of God" upon the Jews. In 1936, the popular Catholic theologian Josef Dillersberger published a piece in the Austrian *Katholische Kirchenzeitung*—with the approval of Vienna's Cardinal Theodor Innitzer—encouraging Catholics to do just that:

All actions taken against the Jews are a continuation of the prophetic statements of the Lord. In the ancient world God used the Romans as an instrument of punishment, [and] now he uses the National Socialists. A Christian himself can never act as avenger and punisher. That we leave to the pagans! But we have to let happen what is happening because it is a judgment of God. Who can question God's decisions?[22]

If there was a neighbor needing a Good Samaritan in the 1930s it was the Jew, yet the day's moral theology placed Jews on the lowest rung of the "hierarchy of love": after family, after other Catholics, and after members of one's nation and race. This teaching was contained in manuals meant for the clergy, of special use when they were determining penance. Its impact on the Catholic conscience is difficult to gauge. What can be said for certain is that neither Catholic moral theology nor the natural law tradition acted to inspire resistance to racism. We can also conclude that racialist ideas about the German people, as constituting a substance of "value" that was important to cultivate and protect, made their way into Catholic teaching materials, popular books, and numerous sermons. For those who took theology seriously the ideas of "charity" and "neighbor" seemed inseparable from racialist concepts. Take the case of one of German Catholicism's foremost experts, Father Heinrich Weber, director of the Caritas Association of the diocese of Münster, and a "Caritas scientist." In *Essence of Charity* (1938) he wrote that "every person, even foreigners, indeed even enemies of the Volk fall under the concept of 'neighbor.'" Still, not everyone was "our neighbor to the same degree." Therefore, the unions of blood, of family, tribal identity, and membership in a race gave rise to "narrower and closer partnerships." One did not have to love all humans to the same extent.[23]

How such teaching might have limited acts of charity for the racially persecuted is difficult to know. But those who did the most seemed to know and care the least for that day's moral theology: they had not been to the seminary, had not read Heribert Jone, did not care about where Jews fit into Christian ideas about salvation, and were not concerned to convert Jews. If the Catholic opponents to racism tended to be converts, the most active and daring in taking help to Jews during the Hitler years were laypersons; indeed they were people who could not imagine becoming clergy: they were women. In Austria, Irene Harand set up her World League against Racial Hatred and Human Want in 1933 and became Central Europe's leading crusader against racial bigotry until, hunted by the Gestapo, she fled the continent in 1938; during the war years the Germans Margarete Sommer and Gertrud Luckner organized the support and rescue of scores of Jews, in part using funds provided by their bishops. In Hungary, Poland, and France, those who led Catholic relief efforts for Jews were also women.[24] For inspiration they fell back on their own unmediated readings of the Gospels, or teachings of "corporal mercy" they had learned as children, none of which involved concern about race or *Volk*. For them and the Jews they assisted, their ignorance of the theology of their day was a blessing.

Vatican and Nation, Vatican and Race

Now, as in the 1930s, many saw the popes as the firmest opponents of racism. Yet what indeed did Pius XI and Pius XII make of the racist thought making its way into Catholic teaching in this period? Did they point Catholics in different directions, toward love of the human family, without regard for boundaries of nation or race? The answer is: not with the certainty we might have hoped. The popes and their advisors were trapped in their time's moral theology and did not undermine its worries about personal salvation or the focus on one's own blood relations. They were also were bound to their time's understandings of race. Like contemporaries, they made no sharp distinction between "nation" and "people" and "race." Sometimes "race" signaled all humanity ("human race"), some-times it was equated with "people." The Holy See recognized the realities lying behind all these words, and, in the spirit of neo-scholasticism, it also drew conclusions by analogy. Just as human beings had rights, so did groups of human beings united in nations, peoples, and races.[25] Pius XI spoke of the "advantages" that God had "allotted" certain "ethnical com-munities."[26] Benedict XV said in 1915, "Let us take it deeply to heart: nations do not die."[27] God had bestowed nations upon humanity for its benefit. Of course, patriotism—favoring one's own group—had to occur within reasonable limits, as Pius XII argued in *Summi Pontificatus*, released shortly after the outbreak of World War II, when German and Soviet troops were consolidating their hold on Poland. Pius underscored the uni-versality of Catholicism:

A disposition, in fact, of the divinely sanctioned natural order divides the human race into social groups, nations or States, which are mutu-ally independent in organization and in the direction of their internal life. But for all that, the human race is bound together by reciprocal ties, moral and juridical, into a great commonwealth directed to the good of all nations and ruled by special laws which protect its unity and promote its prosperity.[28]

For Rome, nationalism became extreme when it denied the church free-dom "to exercise its mission."[29] Those who raised the nation to the level of a deity courted trouble.[30] Yet the church did not seek conflict. *Summi Pon-tificatus* strove for middle ground. On the one hand, the church fostered native clergy, and the pope appointed as bishops "twelve representatives of widely different peoples and races." He cited Colossians 3:10: "Where there is neither Gentile nor Jew, circumcision nor uncircumcision, bar-barian nor Scythian, bond nor free. But Christ is all and in all." Yet, on the other hand, Pius assured Catholics that the spirit of universal brother-hood did not stand in contrast to "love of traditions or the glories of one's fatherland." Christianity taught "that in the exercise of charity we must follow a God-given order, yielding the place of honor in our affections and good works to those who are bound to us by special ties." Christ had given "an example of this preference for His Own country and fatherland, as He wept over the coming destruction of the Holy City." Still, "legitimate and well-ordered love of our native country should not make us close our eyes to the all-embracing nature of Christian Charity."

In light of the extraordinary violence just unleashed on Poland, the pope's warning on the dangers of radical nationalism cannot be called vigorous.[31] He cited the Gospel but eschewed the Gospel's moral force, employing language that seems unnecessarily ethereal, even by Vatican standards. Enemies of racism labored in vain to find anything that might help their cause.[32] In fairness, one should acknowledge that Pius wanted to mediate peace and not seem inclined to the German side.[33] Yet, even that calculation failed. Although the encyclical was not read at German churches, Hitler Youth roughed up churchgoers.[34] Pius spoke out more clearly in his Christmas address, with the crisp statement that "one nation's will to live must never be tantamount to a death sentence for another."[35]

After the war, the Pontiff continued to seek balance. At Christmas 1946, he said that the "real supernationalism of the church, far from overshadowing particular nationalities and putting them all together in a gray uniformity, instead favors the characters and resources of each . . . and pays respect to their autonomy and originality."[36] The church's teachings on nationalism resulted from a view of the order of nature as seen from beyond nature, and directly subject to divine law. Into the era of decolonization, Pius and his successor John XXIII projected nations as possessing inherent value.[37]

In words and practices dating back to the sixteenth century, Pius's predecessors likewise strove for balance in the question of race. In the Bull *Sublimas Deus* (1537), Paul III rejected claims from among Catholics that the people of the new world were not fully human, and the church established missions to the Indians. Still, the church hierarchy in the New World remained European, and its discourse was pervaded by references to Native Americans' supposed proclivities toward lying, stealing, intemperance, and cowardice.[38] The Spanish realm was also witness to the challenge of blood purity laws that restricted the access of Jewish converts to public office in sixteenth-century Spain and seventeenth-century Rome.[39] Notions of blood purity accompanied Spanish missionaries to the New World and were applied against native peoples and African slaves. Originally, the Castilian crown considered converted inhabitants of the Indies to be of "pure blood" because they "descended from Gentiles who had not mixed with 'contaminated' or 'condemned' sects."[40] Yet during the seventeenth century a hierarchy evolved in New Spain according to which black "New Christians" were viewed as less pure than the native "New Christians."[41] The distinction was not tied to skin color but rather to the perception that blacks had entered the Christian faith and the Spanish realm as slaves, that is, against their will.[42] As a whole, these ideas of higher rank based in blood among Christians seem to have been limited to the Spanish realm and did not connect to modern racism: they were not cited as precedent in later racist tracts, and they lived on mainly in the practices of a religious order founded in Spain that was directly subordinated to the pope. Until 1946, the Society of Jesus excluded men of Jewish heritage from their ranks.[43]

The earliest allusion in church records to modern racist theories dates from the First Vatican Council of 1870, which condemned the fashionable idea of polygenesis, according to which human races were of various lineages.[44] In an interview given in 1892 to French journalist Caroline Rémy, Leo XIII condemned "race war." He went on to question the concept of race and asserted that "all are children of Adam, created by God . . . All people—all—do you understand?—are creatures of God! There are those who live in the blessed state of faith, and those to whom we are obligated to bring the faith. That is all that there is. They are all the same before the Lord, because their life is the work of his divine will."[45]

Papal statements from succeeding decades betray ambivalence because the Vatican shared the common attitude that "races" were as substantial as "peoples" or "nations." In May 1934, the Vatican secretary of State, Cardinal Eugenio Pacelli, wrote the German government a confidential memorandum affirming that

the Church recognizes race as a biological fact and does not deny the life values or the cultural stimulation that repose in race—when understood in certain boundaries, apart from all unscientific and ahistorical exaggeration. But she also knows that to make race thinking absolute, or to make it into a replacement religion—these are false paths, which lead quickly to disaster.[46]

Pacelli spoke out strongly in April 1935 before a quarter of a million people at the shrine of Lourdes. Targeting "those who are denying the fundamental dogma of sin and reject the idea of redemption," he said that it mattered "little that they mass around the flag of social revolution. They are inspired by a false conception of the world and of life. Whether they are possessed by superstition of race and blood, their philosophy like that of others rests upon principles essentially opposed to those of the Christian faith." An Associated Press reporter interpreted these lines as "indirect notice upon Chancellor Hitler of Germany that the church would never come to terms with him while the Nazis persist in a racial philosophy 'contrary to the Christian faith.'" And the *New York Times* ran the story under the heading "Nazis warned at Lourdes."[47] At this point, the Catholic Church in Germany had absorbed severe blows that shook sympathies of Catholic intellectuals with Nazism; still, a listener might have noted that Pacelli spoke of "superstition" whereas the Nazis claimed to represent science. Could the church contradict science?

Strong words such as those spoken at Lourdes were few. The Viennese dissidents Dietrich von Hildebrand and Johannes Oesterreicher had seismographic sensitivity for Vatican critiques of racism, and Oesterreicher's *Die Erfüllung* told readers in September 1937 that Pacelli had condemned the "bad sheep" of a nation who were causing it to "worship the false idol of race."[48] Yet if one looks to the American press, one sees that neither the *Los Angeles Times*, *New York Times*, *Wall Street Journal*, nor *Washington Post* picked this up. One newspaper that duly noted Pacelli's words was Joseph Goebbels's *Der Angriff*. We learn from the *Chicago Daily Tribune* that *Der Angriff*

> carried the report under a streamer headline: "Hatred at Pacelli demonstration. Only a Church festival?" . . . Commenting on Cardinal Pacelli's condemnation of "racial insanity" the correspondent asked: "Shall the Popular Front government of France undertake in the name of the church a punitive expedition against Germany? Is there already an alliance between Moscow, the Popular Front of France, and the Vatican?"[49]

The previous year, *Der Angriff* had ridiculed the church's assertion that all were "equal at God's table," placing Pacelli in a collage with African

Americans. Yet rather than confirming the church's universalism above races, the Berlin Catholic Diocese spoke of libel.[50] These reports return us to the perspective of the time and the dynamics of rhetorical battle with Hitler's Germany. Critiques of racism that seem mild today only increased Nazi abuse of German Catholics, at a time when dozens of priests and nuns languished in prisons for abuses against "morality." But there was more involved in such denials than fear. Even before 1933, German Catholics would have reacted defensively to such reporting. For decades, they had been suspected of softness on the national question. The Nazis made them squirm. Was the Catholic view not as the Nazis cynically proclaimed it, that all were indeed equal at God's table? How to reconcile this belief with the German patriotism that penetrated deeply into the institutions of German society, including the office of the Berlin Catholic Diocese?

The encyclical *Mit brennender Sorge*, read on Palm Sunday 1937 in almost all of Germany's 11,500 parishes, is often cited as a clear condemnation of racism.[51] Yet even here one finds latitude. Pius did not make racist thought anathema, but rather castigated extreme racist ideology, writing for example that "whoever detaches the race, the nation, the state, the form of government ... from the earthly frame of reference and makes them into the highest norm of all, higher than religious values, and worships them with idolatry, perverts and distorts the order of things provided and commended by God." He went on to condemn neo-pagan theories such as the "idolatric doctrine of the race."[52] The following year, the pope issued his most detailed statement on race, this time with little fanfare. In an instruction to Catholic colleges, he forbade "extreme racism," but not recognition of the existence of races and of their *value*. Just as nations were thought of as an undeniable aspect of creation, and thus part of God's plan for salvation, so were races.[53]

The "errors of racism" included the following propositions:

1. Human races, by their innate and immutable character, differ so greatly from each other that the lowest of them is further removed from the highest race of men than from the highest species of animals.

2. The vigor of the race and the purity of the blood are to be preserved and fostered by every possible mean ...

3. All the intellectual and moral qualities of man flow from the blood, in which the characteristics of the race are contained ...

4. The primary end of education is the cultivation of the racial character . . .

5. The instinct of the race is the primary source and supreme norm of the whole juridical system.[54]

These propositions aimed at extreme claims because only extreme claims might move the church to action, yet their usefulness diminished when Catholics encountered difficulties that had "less virulent roots."[55] According to South African Franciscan Bonaventure Hinwood, the following assertions remain permissible within the strictures of this "syllabus":

1. One should conserve "the vigor of the race and the purity of its blood within the limits of the moral order."

2. There exists a "limited and accidental gradation of races."

3. "Racial factors have some influence upon intellectual and moral qualities."

4. One should, within the scope of education, cultivate "a balanced love of one's race as one among the many good things of creation."[56]

In the summer of 1938, Pius XI emphasized the special value that derived from the "multitude" of peoples and races. "One cannot deny," the pope said, that within the "general" human race, there is "room for special races and many different varieties."[57] Still, there is no doubt that he detested modern racism. In these months, he sharply criticized the "Manifesto of Racial Scientists" and said that Italian imitations of Germany were undignified: "The Latins never used to speak of race, or of anything similar." Those words supposedly infuriated Mussolini. In July 1938, the pope told an audience of the Catholic Action that "Catholic means universal, not racist, nationalistic, separatist . . . this spirit of separatism, of exaggerated nationalism . . . precisely because it is not Christian, not religious, ends by being not even human." That same month he addressed students of the Collegio di Propaganda Fide. "In the human type [*genere*]," he said, "there is one single great universal Catholic human race, one single great universal human family, and in that, diverse variations . . . human dignity is to be one single great family, the human type, the human race."[58]

Such words stand out in accounts written decades after the fact. But one observer at the time believed the pope's "formal condemnation of racism" had failed to awaken Catholics from their lethargy.[59] Because it was not an encyclical, the syllabus on race was easy to miss, and even the Catholic press tended to ignore it. Major U.S. dailies instead dwelt upon the papacy's dispute with the Italian government as it adopted Nazi-style racial laws. Pius rejected attempts of fascist lawmakers to bar him from debates on race as supposedly beyond his competence in "religion or philosophy." Yet once involved, he unwittingly embraced the deeper assumptions of their racist legislation:

How can one say that relations between one race and another have no connection with religion and philosophy? Some races are more fitted and others less gifted, as may happen with members of the same family.

But when a race more richly endowed by Divine Providence comes in contact with a race less richly endowed, when it is a matter of countries that have or wish to have colonies, it is evident that a colonizing nation must be guided above all by the aim of civilizing, or, in other words, of communicating the benefits of its civilization to the country it wishes to colonize. This is the boast, and at the same time the duty of all civilizing countries.[60]

In part these comments signal the broad comprehension of race in that day, largely coterminous with "nation," but they also underscore the pope's reliance upon modern scientists like Fathers Wilhelm Schmidt and Hermann Muckermann who insisted that race science gave insight into the worth of human groups. Pius worried that any words he uttered casting doubt on the substance of race might tempt young Italians to turn their backs on the church: in the summer of 1938, fascist leaders pledged to purge members of Catholic Action because the pope had supposedly committed them to be "anti-racist."[61] Pius insisted upon his "right to a racist view" in order to spare these Italians a crisis of conscience.[62]

A special bone of contention concerned restrictions on marriage between persons of different "races." While the Vatican did not condone marriages between Catholics and non-Catholics—as we have seen, it discouraged them—it did not sanction an absolute prohibition of marriage between members of different races. Again striving for balance, Vatican writers noted,

> It is true that the church dissuades its children from entering such marriages, holding out the *danger of physically deficient offspring* and in this sense the church is disposed within the limits of divine law to support the efforts of civil authorities in reaching this most laudable purpose. But the church tries to achieve this object by persuasion, not by prohibition.[63]

The unnamed authors of this piece in the Vatican daily *L'Osservatore Romano* placed Jews farther from the Catholic flock than any other group by on the one hand affirming the Nazi understanding that Jews constituted a race, and on the other proclaiming one of the "greatest dangers for a believer" to be "marriage with a person not professing the Catholic faith."[64] The racially based caution against intermarriage is shocking but not surprising. The authors had attempted to merge the science of Hermann Muckermann with the moral teachings of the saints Thomas Aquinas, Alphonsus Liguori, and a host of their disciples. They neither advocated nor condemned "racially mixed marriages."

Catholics against Racism

The multiple qualifications of the Vatican's critique of racism derived from a failure to confront the scientific concept of race. Vatican writers had yet to discover a bridge of science to connect their moral vision on human unity to the world where humans lived. Yet they were not far from finding it. In 1938, Pius XI came across a book of the American expert and activist John LaFarge, SJ, entitled *Interracial Justice*, and in a private audience on June 22, he commissioned the Jesuit to prepare an encyclical on the race question, drafts of which were lost when Pius died in February 1939. If the Pontiff had studied the book carefully, he would have noted the following lines:

> No scientific proof appears to be available as to the deleterious effects from a purely biological standpoint, of the union between different

races of mankind. Were such proof forthcoming, it would fare hard with most of the civilized inhabitants of the earth, since few of them, least of all those of European descent, can claim any purity of racial stock.[65]

LaFarge was a pioneer, but he was not entirely alone. Deeply disturbed by Nazism, a handful of European Catholics and Protestants likewise set about unmasking the shoddy scientific foundations of Nazi and popular understandings of race. This was a moment between paradigms, when racist and anti-racist scientists struggled for influence in scientific institutes and international conferences, but neither could gain dominance.[66] In a sense, World War II itself settled the controversy by demonstrating the results of a consistent racist position: genocide.

For the time being, Christians in Central Europe chose the position that suited their prejudices against or for the targets of racial discrimination.[67] On one side of the debate, most German Christian thinkers regarded race as a force shaping the deeper character of human groups and guiding human history. We have seen their views expressed in the writings of Hermann Muckermann and Wilhelm Schmidt. The church's teaching office required only that they stop short of making race a cardinal value. At the opposite end, small handfuls troubled by the moral implications of racism investigated theories of cultural anthropologists like Franz Boas, who doubted the coherence of race as a concept. They needed scientific pioneers like Boas because ethical concerns alone did not suffice to overturn a concept still defended by most scientists in Central Europe. These Christians thus fell in line with ancient warnings against simple ignorance of scientific research. As early as the fourth century, Augustine had told Christians who disdained science that they made themselves and their faith ridiculous.[68] Church officials who later persecuted Galileo proved his point. Theories of evolution made Catholics of the modern age deeply uneasy, including Pius XII, who opined that humans did not come from animals.[69] Yet the Vatican was prudent enough not to say anything that science might prove false, and no teaching authority in the church ever contradicted evolutionary science.[70] In the 1930s, the church warned against making race a deity but could not forejudge scientific research that might locate some hidden value in racial groups.

The choice for or against racism therefore involved a leap of faith: faith in the power of science to back either prejudice or tolerance. Perhaps it is true that science cannot generate its own ethics, but those who claimed Catholicism generated eternally valid insights to which scientists were blind often deluded themselves. The influential Viennese Jesuit Georg Bichlmair self-assuredly proclaimed the superiority of the Catholic worldview over that of science in writings of the mid-1930s, but in retrospect we see that his Catholic ethics was powerless to correct his "scientific" belief that racial groups harbored special values. In his case, the leap from antisemitic prejudice to belief based in science was a short one.

And so we must ask about Christians in Central Europe who took an opposite leap, away from the attractions of racism that priests like Bichlmair found irresistible. In the 1930s, anti-racist science was relatively new, and those drawing upon it faced hostility and skepticism. As far as I could tell, Christian efforts to oppose race-thinking in Central and Western Europe added up to five books and scattered journal articles, some still collecting dust on the shelves of the library storerooms to which they were relegated generations ago, others long since destroyed. When German troops took Paris in 1940, the Gestapo located and pulped all the copies they could find of the two Catholic anti-racist books that had just come out in French.

Because of unresolved scientific questions, a certain ambiguity marks even works driven by disgust with Nazi racism. It was easy to show what science could not demonstrate: no researcher had shown a relation between genetic inheritance and the character of human groups. But genetics did give evidence that certain traits were passed from generation to generation, and even the most critical writers did not deny the possibility that human groups living in isolation came to possess shared characteristics. There was enough scientific research to refute the racists' claim to represent definitive knowledge, but not enough to present a new definitive vision.

Because of the censorship of the fascist regime, the most forceful Catholic anti-racist in Italy, the Jesuit Antonio Messineo (1897–1978), published his critique in the Vatican newspaper *L'Osservatore Romano*.[71] Messineo, a leading Catholic intellectual of postwar Italy and an internationally recognized expert in politics and law, edited the Order's *La Civiltà Cattolica* for four decades. After the war he was among the first prominent

Catholics to embrace religious tolerance, causing a minor sensation.[72] But Messineo got his start wrestling with the challenges that Italian fascism posed to Catholic understandings of nation and race.[73]

Like the popes he served, Messineo insisted on the dignity of "nation" as a locus for Catholic veneration, and therefore castigated German National Socialists for reducing nation to race. Race was a zoological term for dividing animal groups that anthropologists had transposed upon human life, thus "lowering thinking creatures to the level of animals."[74] Crucial to humans was their spiritual/intellectual dimension, something racism could not touch because of its attachment to "somatic characteristics," which had no demonstrable relation to "psychic" characteristics. Unlike German Catholic racists such as Muckermann, Messineo rejected all speculation on this matter.[75] Even anthropologists admitted that no definition of race had won acceptance, and they debated whether "race" should gauge people by place of origin, by skin color, or by cranial size. "Everything," he concluded, "remains uncertain."[76] Where other Catholic thinkers believed races were God-given, Messineo said the word "race" corresponded to nothing but a "vague formula."[77] Science therefore served Messineo as a basis for restoring a sense of mystery and dignity surrounding the human person.

Messineo launched his piece into the dangerous arena of Italian fascism—where the public could read only one side of the issue and that was not his.[78] In July 1938, a "Manifesto of Racial Scientists" had appeared, according to which there was a pure Italian race to which Jews did not belong.[79] "The Jews represent the only population that has never assimilated in Italy," the scientists wrote, "because they are constituted from non-European racial elements, absolutely different from the elements from which Italians originated." Messineo's piece boldly condemned such racism, but it did not represent unanimous opinion among Italian clerics.[80] The Jesuit Angelo Brucculeri argued that the Manifesto actually fit within the acceptable boundaries of Catholic thought.[81] And while the Vatican press may have permitted critiques of racism, it wrote of Jews with a certain callousness, tolerating condemnations of racism but not of antisemitism.[82]

In French-speaking Europe, the intellectually fiercest Catholic critic of racism was the Belgian Jesuit Pierre Charles, a liberal expert in mission work who often fell afoul of Rome.[83] The church had always taught that humans had one origin, he wrote. Augustine, for example, denied that "monstrous people" existed in Africa, writing that if there are people, they are from Adam.[84] Science supported this Catholic teaching. In 1911, luminaries such as Thomas Griffith Taylor, Franz Boas, Felix von Luschan (Berlin), and Charles Samuel Myers (Cambridge) had come together with Max Weber, Emile Durkheim, W. E. B. Du Bois, and many others at the Universal Races Congress in London to reject racism as a coherent theory.[85] Science gave no warrant to speak of inferiority of any human group, and Father Charles compared race science to medieval superstition. Optimistically, he wrote that no scientist took the race theorist Gobineau seriously. "It is difficult to understand," Charles concluded, "how a circumspect observer could accept a doctrine other than that of the substantial equality of different races." According to this Jesuit, racism drew its power not from science but from "political passion." When such passion found a weapon, it was difficult though not impossible for science to pry it loose. Still, neither Charles nor the scientists he cited had revealed race as a complete fiction, and part of racism's hold lay in the inability of scientists fully to deflate the concept.

"Lucien Valdor," pseudonymous author of the slim volume *The Christian in the Face of Racism*, joined Father Charles the following year in efforts to enlighten French Catholics. For many years, librarians believed the German/Italian Romano Guardini, one of the century's great theologians, stood behind the pseudonym, but recent research shows the author was Guardini's translator into French, Pierre Lorson, SJ, a Saarland native mobilized for Germany in World War I and France in World War II. Mostly destroyed by the Gestapo, Lorson's book is held in only four libraries across the globe.[86] Still, it has the honor of being the first book-length study of race from a Christian perspective written in French.[87]

As preacher at the Strasbourg Cathedral and with many relatives in Germany, Lorson focused his analysis on Nazi mythology, in particular the "Nordic myth," and he used the work of anthropologists to demonstrate that (1) the category of race was unstable, and (2) there could be no discussion of a hierarchy among human groups. Like Pierre Charles, he projected modern science as complementing holy scripture's verdict that all humans issued from the same couple.[88] Differences had developed among human populations over many generations, but one could not speak of superior races. Citing French scientists Paul Lester and Jacques Millot, Lorson rejected the idea that white stood above black or yellow. "No disciple of racism will convince us that the Mediterranean or the Semite has contributed less than the Nordic to enrich the higher human heritage," they had written. The American ethnologist Thomas Russell Garth had examined Native Americans living among whites and defused arguments about their hereditary inferiority. Intellectual capacities varied with education.[89] These findings were all the more convincing because Garth had started out a racist.

Christian teaching corroborated Garth's findings, but took them to a deeper level, undermining not only racial but national thinking. "The value of a group," Lorson explained, "even a racial group, depends upon the value of the individuals who make it up." And the value of individuals depended on their immortal souls: contrary to better-known German experts like Father Muckermann, Lorson said that soul, not body, determined personality. Racism involved the heresy of imagining that matter chained God's will, determining the character of souls destined to live for eternity. "Who will say that God is obliged to create identical souls according to whether he destines them for one race or the other?" Lorson asked. God was free to give a superior soul to a "Hottentot" and an inferior one to an Aryan of "pure blood."[90]

Lorson contended that his views represented those of the Catholic Church, and he did so by looking at how the church operated: everywhere on the globe, believers inclined toward the holy sacrifice of the mass, and the priests were "of every race, of every color, as in Jerusalem at the Pentecost."[91] The church believed in the primacy of the spirit and not of the blood, and did not recognize any racial, materialist, collective hierarchy, but only a "spiritual hierarchy of human persons."[92] Still, like Father Charles, Lorson did not entirely dispense with the concept "race," using it to designate human groups on one page ("look at the priests wearing the same vestments . . . they are of every race . . .") while unmasking it as a shoddy principle for constructing hierarchies on the next ("If there are no pure races, if there is no hierarchy among races, then one sees what to think of the pretensions of the Nordic, Indo-Germanic, Aryan race. It does not exist, and is therefore not superior to others").[93]

Some five hundred kilometers to the east, on an island of democracy amidst a sea of dictatorship, the leading Czech Catholic intellectual Alfred Fuchs linked his critique of racism to one of fascism. Fuchs, a convert from Judaism who died at Dachau in 1941, and an odd, self-proclaimed liberal in a mostly conservative Catholic world, published the only piece on racism to appear in the major Czech Catholic journal *Katolík* in the late 1930s.[94] He reasoned theologically. "Paganism begins when the nation is placed above humanity," he wrote, and "the denial of universalism means that people recognize only relative, partial values instead of absolute Being." Racism therefore was a rebellion against the first commandment and against the universal saving power of grace. Racists derived all morality from the blood and deified creation in place of the Creator. By contrast, Christianity assumed the "unending value of every single human soul." Anticipating changes in Catholic thought that would occur decades later, Fuchs envisaged a common cause among Christians, Jews, and liberals. Liberals had to oppose racism because it denied spirit as well as intellect—in German, *Geist* means both—and refused to recognize the universal application of reason.

Despite the word's murkiness, Fuchs did not think race was a fiction. Prague of the 1930s had filled with refugees from Germany, but the city also hosted scientific meetings featuring the day's leading anthropologists. Fuchs knew that science had neither confirmed nor denied the existence of race, and he assumed that races were like tribes and peoples and nations, and that God willed them to cultivate their peculiarities in virtue and in culture. But Christianity, unlike all preceding beliefs, connected peoples and tribes without distinction for the sake of a common goal which was eternity.[95] Christians loved their neighbors and did not discriminate by race. Fuchs knew that German theologians had questioned whether baptism could erase the "stain" of Jewish birth. Church teaching, however, left no room for debate. Catholics prayed and worked for the Jews' conversion.[96] He mentioned Opus St. Pauli in Vienna "led by the converted priest Jan Oesterreicher."

In November 1936, the Viennese Jewish weekly *Die Wahrheit* told its readers that another Jewish convert—Rudolf Lämmel—had just produced the first popular scientific work on the race question. Lämmel was a Swiss science writer who studied with Einstein and hailed from the Austrian branch of an old Hungarian Jewish family. He had been baptized Catholic as a child but then converted to Protestantism as an adult. Like other Christian anti-racists, Lämmel projected science as in harmony with scripture. Biology gave no evidence for the superiority of a "Nordic Race" and took the same view as the Bible: all humans were derived from one family. At some point in the deep past, pure races had emerged out of inbreeding and shared environmental conditions. Yet over time they had broken out of isolation and mixed with other peoples, so that present-day nations were racial mixtures.[97] Like other critics, he affirmed the possibility of acquired characteristics being transmitted from parents to children, yet he denied that the characteristics of race—real and visible in things like skull shape—affected intellect or character.[98] Lämmel believed that the mixing of races offered the best opportunity for humanity to develop to a higher stage, and mentioned the Jews as a racial mixture who continually brought forth extraordinary achievements and whose qualities did not deviate from those of "western humanity of white complexion."[99] He dwelt at length on the German dancer Vera Skoronel (1906–1932), who mixed "Nordic" and "Jewish" descent, and whose life's work had produced "great achievements, dispelling any doubt whether the part of white humanity that stems from the Jews is equal in value to the other white races." He did not mention that Skoronel was his daughter from a first marriage with Sophie Axelrod, daughter of Menshevik Pavel Axelrod, coeditor of *Iskra*, the official newspaper of the Russian Social Democrats.[100]

In July 1938, the Jesuits' *La Civiltà Cattolica* in Rome picked up on Lämmel's book, welcoming a non-Catholic's effort to assert the unity of the human race, yet arguing that Lämmel's Protestantism made the analysis insufficient. After all, Protestantism had spawned radical nationalism by dividing Europe, and only Catholics understood how to place the national question in the proper order of love: first God, then family, and finally country.[101] The Jesuit authors claimed that science could not do without Catholicism, though the truth also went in the opposite direction. Without evidence, they suspected Jewish traits in Lämmel, referring to a German-Jewish businessman to whom Lämmel might have been related.

It might seem strange that critics of racism could write in *Die Wahrheit*, a Jewish newspaper appearing in Vienna, the citadel of Austrofascism, after the collapse of the Austrian Republic in 1933, with a regime that was presumably racist and antisemitic. However, if we look to Vienna of the 1930s we find several Catholic publishing ventures devoted to anti-racism. In the fall of 1933, the young Catholic Irene Harand launched her World League against Racial Hatred and Human Want, as well as a weekly denouncing Nazi racism entitled *Gerechtigkeit* ("Justice"), from the Austrian capital. The following year, the émigré philosopher Dietrich von Hildebrand began publishing *Der Christliche Ständestaat*, which became the most sophisticated Catholic platform for critiquing Nazism. And in 1936, former Viennese vice-mayor Ernst Karl Winter, editor of the anti-Nazi *Wiener Politische Hefte*, printed one of three Christian critiques of racism (next to Lämmel's and Lorson's) to emerge in Central Europe of these years: Walter Berger's *Was ist Rasse (What Is Race?)*.

Like Lämmel, Berger had converted from Judaism to Protestantism, but his training was in philology, and he had no credentials to write on the race question. After fleeing the continent in 1938, he entered the British armed forces and then taught German literature in English public schools. He never wrote another work on science. In wartime correspondence with Ernst Karl Winter—who after 1938 was an exile in New Jersey—Berger recalled his work on race as opposing Nazi ideology.[102] Yet in fact his impact was more ambiguous. Like other critics, he took the leap of faith to anti-racism but never escaped the belief that race was real, reflecting a relation between individual and group characteristics. And so in 1936, while searching for literature that might support his own theses about the compatibility of Nazism and Catholicism, the Austrian titular Bishop Alois Hudal of Rome, later notorious for smuggling Nazi war criminals to South America, cited Berger's book to substantiate his view that "race" was much more than an imaginary abstraction.[103] Human and intellectual life were determined by "blood"—if only secondarily.

Despite his high rank in the church, Hudal was a frequent target of abuse for Dietrich von Hildebrand and his writers, one of whom despaired at the possibility of connecting race science to the broader public upon learning of the bishop's appropriation of Berger's book on race. Whether treated superficially or profoundly, the race question, at the borders of superstition and knowledge, was a danger to the faith, a "fashion" that Catholic intellectuals should refuse to indulge.[104] Yet Berger's book was reviewed favorably in yet another anti-Nazi journal to appear in Austrofascist Vienna, Johannes Oesterreicher's *Die Erfüllung*. And a second reviewer for Dietrich von Hildebrand appreciated Berger's centrist position.[105] Berger had written that neither environment nor heredity could account for all human variation. None of the reviewers concerned themselves with Berger's nonexistent credentials; the main point was that he could reach a broad audience.

The Czech-Jewish author Hugo Iltis (1882–1952)—a biologist of repute and author of popular works on the race question—likewise recommended Berger's book among a small handful of books on the subject. In the 1920s, Iltis worked in the anthropological mainstream and was on friendly terms with Fritz Lenz, later a leading Nazi race theorist. Yet after the Nazis assumed power in 1933, ethical revulsion prompted an evolution in Iltis's scientific views. Like other Central European scientists concerned with racism in Germany, he began taking more "Lamarckian" points of view, softening the hard facts of genetics by claiming that acquired characteristics could be inherited.[106] Still, even in 1936 he recommended a mishmash of authors to readers interested in the subject, including Berger but also the anti-racists Max Brod and Friedrich Hertz, the socialist Karl Kautsky, and the Nazi Egon von Eickstedt. Thus, in the confusion of the age, a brown Catholic (Hudal) read with profit a would-be anti-Nazi (Berger), while Iltis, at the forefront of the anti-racist campaign, found some usefulness in a Nazi.[107]

A similar combination of wishful thinking and opportunism characterized the work of an anthropologist Dietrich von Hildebrand engaged to write on racism, Hans Conrad Ernst Zacharias (1873–1953) of the Catholic University of Beijing. Zacharias had a Polish Catholic mother and Hungarian father who had converted from Judaism to Protestantism. During university studies in Jena, he became a positivist under the influence of the eminent naturalist Ernst Haeckel. Later, following years living in India, he converted to deism, then Free Masonry, occultism, Vedantism, high-church Anglicanism, and finally Roman Catholicism.[108] In a piece for Hildebrand written in 1935, Zacharias portrayed the race scientists Julian Huxley and A. C. Haddon as opponents of the concept of race. Animals may develop into racial groups, they had written, but humans did not because they never lived in isolation in a way that cut them off from other gene pools. Zacharias believed that human development possessed self-regulating qualities militating against the emergence of stronger or weaker groups. The greater the differences that emerged among human groups, the more humans were pulled back together through a kind of natural attraction. "All really great nations are a melting pot," he wrote.[109] However, Julian Huxley had not disavowed racial thinking entirely and in fact opposed interethnic mixing "on the ground that some ethnic groups possess a low average of innate intelligence."[110] Though he rejected Nazi eugenics, Huxley favored limitations on the breeding of less "valuable" strata of society.

In these years, Hildebrand allied with Hugo Iltis and his collaborator Ignaz Zollschan (1877–1948) to call for an international congress to test the ideas of racism. Zollschan, a Jew originally from Lower Austria, became involved in the Zionist movement while training as a physician in Vienna and came to figure among the most forceful opponents of the race idea in interwar Europe. From the 1920s, he tried to assemble an antiracist movement.[111] The Nazi press defamed Zollschan's plans for an international congress as a product of a Jewish-Catholic plot, something that caused schadenfreude among Hildebrand and his staff, certain that both nature and scripture were on their side.[112] They sensed that scientific grounds for race-thinking were dissolving, and that Zollschan was among those advancing arguments to make this happen.

But Zollschan was disappointed in his overtures to Catholics in general. He and Hugo Iltis had hoped to make systematic use of Christian arguments in their campaign against Nazism, during which Zollschan shifted his views to portray Jews as a cultural rather than racial group. Like Iltis, Zollschan developed a taste for Lamarckism because it softened the hard conceptual shells of biology and culture. Yet when reviewing Catholic statements—from the Vatican, from Hermann Muckermann, from cardinals Faulhaber and Innitzer, from Wilhelm Schmidt—they failed to find an unequivocal line against Nazi racial ideology.[113] Two audiences with Pius XI availed nothing.

Still, despite these sobering experiences and despite the failure of an international movement against racism to materialize, some Christian-Jewish collaboration against Nazi racism emerged at the Third International Conference on Population Science in Paris in 1937, where Zollschan and the American Jewish anthropologist Franz Boas joined forces with the (originally) Jewish Bohemian philosopher Maximilian Beck (1887–1950) to attack the German delegation.[114] They worked with the French *Races et Racisme* group, which included liberal Calvinist historian Edmond Vermeil, Durkheim's student Célestin Bouglé (expert in the "science of morality"), Marxist Georges Lefebvre, Catholic Jean de Pange, Jewish anthropologist Lucien Lévy-Bruhl (cousin by marriage to Alfred Dreyfus), the socialist ethnologist Paul Rivet, Protestant pastor and ethnologist Maurice Leenhardt, and Catholic peace priest Monsignor E. Beaupin. The purpose of their activities was to warn against pseudo-scientific racist theories.[115]

Dietrich von Hildebrand knew Maximilian Beck from Munich, where the two had belonged to the circle of Catholic phenomenologist Alexander Pfänder, and he published Beck's thoughts against racism early in 1937. The point was not whether science supported the idea of race, but that Nazi racism was a pseudo-science that drove people apart, thus opposing the Christian belief in all humans' likeness to God. Few people had understood the "monstrous consequences of this teaching," wrote Beck. All "morality and law" were based in the belief in human freedom. The humans who populated the world of racists, subject to "racial drives, instincts, and dispositions," could have no more responsibility than a stone pulled down by gravity. Such a world was hell on earth, in which people existed to serve the racial fantasy of a perverse God. In such a place, there would be no art, no beauty, no virtue: all would be a function of race. The only international relation would be war.

Converts, Border-Walkers, and Catholic Anti-Racism

In his study of the retreat of scientific racism in the United States and Great Britain, Elazar Barkan writes that the ultimate criterion for scientific allegiance in the interwar years was political.[116] Loren Graham asks whether the polemics surrounding evolutionary science in this time was an "entirely social and political phenomenon, essentially distinct from the scientific theories under discussion," or whether "there was something intellectually inherent in each of the competing theories of heredity which supported a particular political ideology."[117] Final arguments for speaking on race were not derived from science because science had not spoken a definitive word on inherited characteristics in human groups.

That meant that even anti-Nazis arguing against racism could not dispel all doubt. Who could tell whether scientists might indeed find a way to classify human groups by shared genetic characteristics? In 1938, Paul Rivet, a leading figure in the French struggle against racism, wrote that it was premature to draw ethnological conclusions about the Jews. At least another decade of "serological" studies was necessary.[118] In debates with Ignaz Zollschan and Maximilian Beck in Paris the previous year, German anthropologists claimed that studies of twins demonstrated that intelligence—and thus "intellectual and spiritual value" (*"geistige Werte"*)— was tied to genetic material.[119] This finding undermined Beck's claim that intellect (*"Geist"*) could not be linked with biology. Much conceptual and political untidiness remained among anti-racist culturalists like Lévy-Bruhl or Rivet who opposed the idea of "Nordic" superiority but were unwilling to apply principles of equality of races to peoples of color.[120] The leading anti-racist Ignaz Zollschan had vigorously propagated the idea of Jewish racial unity until the race idea began to be used against Jews. In 1937, he was calling for deeper study of racial theories and arguing that it would be wrong to dispute the role of race in creating aptitude, character, and talents in diverse groups of human beings.[121]

If Loren Graham is right, it is not clear what the social and political ideology motivating anti-racism might be called. Paul Rivet was a Republican, but Irene Harand and Dietrich von Hildebrand supported Christian corporatism, which stood to the right of socialism and somewhere to the left of Nazism. To them, liberalism seemed an ideology of the past. The political formation in which they worked, sometimes called Austrofascism, proved a short-lived alternative in dark years between paradigms, before the evident victory in Europe of cultural theories of race and of a liberal democratic practice of politics. Harand and Hildebrand would have called their engagement not political but ethical and religious: the point was to defend the dignity of the human person, and the anti-liberal regime of Dollfuss and Schuschnigg gave them a platform from which to do this.

Their ethical stance preceded but could not dispense with science. Still, it is astounding how little expertise was necessary to enter the conversation. Practicing anthropologists like Iltis or Zacharias were a small minority. Pierre Lorson, Antonio Messineo, Alfred Fuchs, Walter Berger, Maximilian Beck, and Johannes Oesterreicher wrote long tracts on race without any credentials at all. Rudolf Lämmel had the equivalent of undergraduate training in biology. Anti-racists had only to understand enough science to agree that scientists had failed to identify a principle of classifying humans that reflected anything definitive about human worth. The appeal to science was not so much to knowledge as to the insufficiency of knowledge.

If science was indispensable yet unreliable, what predisposed the diverse group of Christian anti-racists to place ethical certainties above scientific doubts? The answer is that the group was not as diverse as it seemed. They shared one basic trait: they lived along borders. The French for such people (applied to Father Lorson by his biographer) is *frontalier*, the German (used by Norbert Leser to describe the Austrians) is *Grenzgänger*.[122] Because it is impossible to walk, let alone live on a border, these people in fact were border-crossers who took ideas in both directions. Like Father Lorson, they spoke several languages while feeling rooted in diverse communities (Lorson called himself a "Franco-Saarois").[123] Because they never surrendered allegiance to one community in favor of the other, they wanted peace—while those opting for a single side often want war. The character of the borders and of the crossings differed. In some cases, like those of Fathers Lorson or Charles (a Belgian, also a missionary) it was ethnic, in others it was religious, but in most cases it was both. The borders they crossed tended to separate groups that considered each other enemies, and that made the acts of border-crossers subversive and destabilizing.

"Enemies" was a word used by many Christians, starting with St. Paul, to describe Jews. Albert Fuchs, Maximilian Beck, Johannes Oesterreicher, Hans Zacharias, Walter Berger, Rudolf Lämmel, and Dietrich von Hildebrand: all had come to Christianity from families that were Jewish in origin. Several, like St. Paul, never ceased seeing themselves as Jewish. The great majority of Catholics who wrote on the race question were Jewish converts, and virtually every figure of note in the Catholic battle against antisemitism was a convert. But once in the church, they were never entirely of the church. We see Catholic converts compulsively cooperating with Protestants and Jews in the would-be anti-racist movement of these years, practicing de facto ecumenism, an extraordinary phenomenon on the European continent of that time, when the church warned about the dangers of "indifferentism." But because these Catholics were converts it was difficult to tell them to shun contacts with the outside. The outside, after all, was their homeland.

But the irony of conversion, of crossing a border supposedly with no return, is that one never entirely leaves the point of origin. And the scandal of racism was that those expecting security in their new Catholic homes were told that they remained alien, "in fact" racially Jewish. In response, the neophytes first argued that nothing in their Jewish origin made them lesser Christians. This was the obvious point of Galatians 3:28. Under Christ, people ceased to be Jewish or Greek. Yet racism encouraged the converts to delve deeper and to reconsider St. Paul's sustained meditation on the Jewish people contained in his letter to the Romans, chapters 9 through 11. There they discovered that Jewish origin made a person a better Christian, because Jews stood "naturally" closer to faith.

Like all converts, they were carried into their new lives past boundaries that had seemed insuperable. They felt touched by grace because the border crossing had something miraculous to it. Such conviction helps account for the extraordinary missionary impulse in Johannes Oesterreicher. He wanted to bring his family, relations, and entire familiar world into his new home. But it also accounts for the extraordinary shock of the converts' encounter with racist Christianity in Germany. People who had freely chosen a new life in faith thus found themselves "predestined" to convert their new Christian world to a true lost faith; to move discussions about race and antisemitism beyond stale, self-contradictory patterns; to return to original texts and bring the fold back to original understandings; to invoke science despite a complete absence of qualifications. Conversion became the most powerful means of self-realization because it unlocked the force of a new self, permitting the exploitation of energies that one suspected but could never tap.

3

German *Volk* and Christian *Reich*

Christian anti-racists had one other group trait aside from being converts and border-transgressors: they tended to come from German-speaking Europe. We see this in the authorship of works refuting racism and antisemitism. In 1936, Ernst Karl Winter published the first systematic Christian critique of racism at his Viennese publishing house, Walter Berger's *Was ist Rasse (What Is Race?)*. Later that year, Rudolf Lämmel's lengthier and even more systematic critique appeared in Zurich. In 1937, Johannes Oesterreicher printed the first Catholic repudiation of antisemitism in his Viennese journal *Die Erfüllung*. The authors were Karl Thieme and Waldemar Gurian, by that point in Swiss exile. Two years later Peter Lorson, like them a refugee from Germany, produced the first Catholic critique of racism to appear in French, *Le Chrétien devant le racisme*. Soon after, Oesterreicher's own study—the first Catholic study repudiating racism and antisemitism simultaneously—came out in Paris, translated from the German original. The trend continued into the postwar years. In 1948, Europe's premier journal opposing antisemitism from a Catholic perspective—the

Freiburger Rundbrief—began publication from the southwest German cathedral town Freiburg, and through the 1950s the *Rundbrief* enjoyed the
protection of highly placed German Jesuits in the Vatican. Prominent was
the Bible scholar Augustin Bea, originally from a village directly across
Freiburg at the eastern edge of the Black Forest. In 1960, Pope John XXIII
charged Bea—now a cardinal—with formulating a statement on the church's
relation to the Jews. As theological advisors he took on three priests
originally from German-speaking Europe: Gregory Baum, Leo Rudloff,
and John Oesterreicher.

New ideas about Jews could have originated anywhere, but they tended
to come from the transalpine lands where German is spoken. These are
not the places with the highest proportions of Jews in Europe or the
largest antisemitic movements, and the question is why. Partly we are
witness to the strength of the German theological tradition, rivaled
only by that of France in the modern era. But more importantly the
prominence of German speakers in this struggle against racism and antisemitism reflects a special problem: a German Catholic racist syndrome. A response to Catholicism's age-old legacy of anti-Judaism grew
out of the German lands because a particularly virulent strain of racist
antisemitism had taken root in culturally German Catholicism in the
early twentieth century and had provoked a response. Before considering how Johannes Oesterreicher, Karl Thieme, and other Central European converts began formulating this response out of Vienna and other
outposts beyond Hitler's Reich in the 1930s, it is important to consider
what they were up against. What were the dynamics of this Catholic
racism? What in the culture of German Catholicism produced this
challenge, and what set German Catholicism off against other national
variants?

The word *syndrome* signals a set of conditions that occur in association
with each other, producing a potent and troubling shared mentality with
its own coherence and integrity.[1] A syndrome resists simple treatment.
But one can also use the less freighted concept "form of life" (*Lebensform*),
developed by Jürgen Habermas, to describe the distinctive ways of thinking that emerge within the discourses of national cultures. During the
historians' debate (*Historikerstreit*) of the 1980s, he reminded Germans
that they could not escape their history:

Our form of life is connected with the form of life of our parents and grandparents by a network of familial, local, political, and intellectual traditions, which are difficult to disentangle, and which have made us what we are today. No one can steal himself away from this milieu, because our identity, as individuals and as Germans, is indissolubly woven into it. This begins with facial expressions and bodily gestures and extends through language into the capillaries of our intellectual habitus. For example it is an illusion to think that while lecturing at foreign universities I could ever deny the mentality into which the very German intellectual movement from Kant to Marx to Max Weber are so deeply imprinted. We must stand to our traditions if we do not want to deny ourselves.[2]

Emerging from, as well as decisively shaping, the life form of German Catholics in the interwar years was a unique interplay of metaphors and symbols that had theological, political, and biological resonance: *Volk* (people, nation), *mystischer Leib Christi* (mystical body of Christ), *Blut* (blood), *Reich* (empire, kingdom), and *Erbsünde* (hereditary or original sin). Taken together, they produced a mindset that made the assumptions of modern racism all but irresistible. This conglomerate of symbols and metaphors did not float freely in Central European cultural space, but were deeply embedded in vital Catholic organizations of the time, above all the youth movements *Quickborn*, *Neudeutschland*, and *Neuland*, themselves subsets of the massive German youth movement (*Wandervögelbewegung*), whose enthusiastic, uniformed legions had no counterparts in Slavic or Romance Europe. While *Quickborn* was meeting for prayer and other communal activities at the castle Rothenfels in Lower Franconia under the guidance of Romano Guardini, one of the century's great theologians, their elders of the Catholic Academic Union met at the ancient Benedictine Monastery Maria Laach further west. Taken together, young and old were parts of the German Catholic "liturgical movement," which tried to inject life into stale ritual; anticipating the reforms of Vatican II, it demanded use of vernacular and more active participation in the mass of the people of God, the "*Volk Gottes*." Members of the movement sought deep experiences of "community," and were skeptical of the power of democracy to create a world worth living in. After years of denigrating the Weimar

Republic, the monks of Maria Laach, along with much of the mainstream Catholic intelligentsia, celebrated the accession to power of Hitler in 1933.[3]

Historians have long recognized an overlap of German Catholicism and Nazi racism that was grounded in joint concerns: anti-Marxism, anti-liberalism, anti-individualism, and the resulting attraction to a communitarian ethos.[4] But they have not pointed to a racist syndrome growing out of religiously based symbols and metaphors, nor have they understood it as a culturally German phenomenon on the background of international Catholicism. This syndrome grew within the most cohesive Catholic milieu in Europe, producing not only uniformed youth legions, but also newspapers and journals, trade unions, and the most powerful Catholic political organization in the world after the Vatican, the German Center Party. In other words, the Catholic racist syndrome was an exceptional combination of ideas, existing in an exceptional cultural and political context, and coinciding to an extraordinary degree with the National Socialists' own sacralized language, which "penetrated both the deep sensitive layers of man's emotional life and his conscious and intellectual activities."[5]

The most seductive element of the racist syndrome that took root in German Catholicism, the word *Volk*, evoked blood kinship dating back to time immemorial, and took on particular resonance during World War I; as the hold of throne and monarchy on the German people waned, *Volk* became a new locus of political legitimacy.[6] It grew especially dear to German Catholics who for decades were accused of loyalties divided between the Vatican and Berlin. Ironically, the freedoms of liberal democracy now permitted them to freely assert ethnic unity with other Germans. *Volk* stirred the Catholic imagination by mixing religious, ethnic, political, and cultural connotations in a radically new way.[7] More than that, it caused the political to gain transcendent meaning in a time of theological upheaval.

Liturgical Movement of the German Catholic *Volk*

The years following World War I saw the rise of a liturgical movement within international Catholicism, but the movement grew to particular

strength among German Catholics, who imagined the church no longer
as dusty doctrines, unquestioned hierarchies, or lifeless buildings but as
the organic, vital *Volk*, singing and praying in the vernacular, wresting
control of the mass from a Latin-mumbling priest. Indeed, the people of
God—*das Volk Gottes*—were the church. The idea of people as church was
inspired by the older idea of church as the mystical body of Christ. Read
in the racist spirit of the time, this meant that the church as the body of
Christ lived actually and mystically in a union of blood manifested in
God's *Volk*. Recalling Jeffrey Herf's notions of "reactionary modernism,"
the liturgical movement was anything but conservative, and it anticipated
reforms of Vatican II by calling into question ideas of church hierarchy.[8]
Yet in Germany the idea of church as mystical body of Christ also pro-
longed the sense of community that had emerged on the fronts of the
Great War by, for example, evoking a spirit of transcendence that refused
temporal compromises. It was not surprisingly intensely anti-liberal.[9] By
contrast, secular modernity seemed trite and obsolete. In the first issue of
the youth movement journal *Schildgenossen*, we discover the perspective of
one young enthusiast:

> The war and the events that followed have caused the boil that had
> grown in the big city to burst. In a society characterized by greed,
> affectation, hand-over-fist profiteering, the importance attached to
> money—once a symbol of bygone degenerate culture—is coming to
> an end. The fateful interconnectedness of all these things is our great
> sorrow, and the goal of our most secret longing is somehow to arrive
> on the opposite shore, where a new soulfulness has begun to shoot
> forth. That was my experience [at the 1920 *Quickborn* meeting] at the
> Rothenfels castle: this sublime isolation was life and meaning . . .
> here, so high above everything, the omnipotence of money was bro-
> ken. Here soul was pressed upon soul, will upon will and we could
> feel the life-pulse of the new spirit. The world had enough of half-
> measures: whole people were preparing to complete whole tasks.
> Everything had been drifting toward a solution which the World
> War brought. And now no one may continue working on the same
> level as before. Today, everyone who felt the want of the war years is
> compelled to draw from deeper sources in order to reach new heights.

We have been led into the wilderness and placed face to face against
life's deepest forces . . . we are mining beneath the deepest strata of
culture to a place where there is no compromise [*wir graben unterhalb
der Kulturschichten ins Unbedingte*].[10]

The passion of this generation was self-realization through a liturgy
experienced in massive gatherings but also with new intimacy, permitting
them to "shape their own lives with inner truth." Truth set young Germans
free of prior constraints. One of most popular Catholic authors of this time,
Breslau theologian Joseph Wittig, evoked the living presence of Christ on
the roads and byways of his native Silesia and was excommunicated for
suggesting that the ordinary believer might be as close to God as the top
church hierarchy.[11] The Italian-German theologian Romano Guardini formulated the period's memorable slogan: the "Church is awakening in our
souls."[12]

Liberation from the old meant surrender to the new. One of the movement's journals contended that "those who want to come alive in the liturgy must surrender their ego, they must cease praying only for themselves, must stop praying only their own prayers." Young Catholics had to
sacrifice individuality, "precisely that which the modern human believes
he cannot let go of. In the liturgy, one must bow in deep humility, rather
than assert one's own will."[13] Guardini, fired by the Nazis from his teaching post in Berlin in 1939, and in our day renowned for his moderation
and liberal attitude, shared the movement's ambivalence toward Weimar
democracy. In 1920, he addressed followers on the "sense of obedience" and
lauded the idea of "faithful trust." "Once more we are learning," he wrote
hopefully, "the royal virtue of giving of oneself and of having faith to take
risks, and that those to whom we give our obedience will use their power in
a way that corresponds to our willingness to show faith: they will lead cre-
atively, and exercise command with due reverence." In 1925, he revealed a
hesitation to pass judgment on political authorities. "The validity of order,
and therefore also of authority," he said, could "not be judged by the concrete qualities of those in whom rule is entrusted, but rather has its origins
in a separate sphere. Order is always in some way 'by the grace of God.'"[14]
He instructed his uniformed audiences that "a person is as free as he is
Catholic."[15] Guardini the moderate survived the Nazi years in painfully

private self-exile, making oblique but courageous critiques of a regime he grew to despise and fear, but Joseph Wittig became a (low-ranking) Nazi Party member.[16]

Heady ideas of the church as "people" or as "mystical body" encouraged a leveling of hierarchy, but they also focused attention on the supposed "leader." Scripture was ambivalent. Some passages refer to Christ as "mystical body," while others also call him the "head" of the body. Whereas the excommunicated Wittig spoke of a "general priesthood," other theologians like Karl Adam, Karl Eschweiler, and Engelbert Krebs became fixated upon authority. In Karl Adam's prose, Christ came to resemble a heroic figure of Germanic mythology, a "born leader [*Führer*]." Adam grew rapturous describing how this "fighter" and "master by nature" with "flaming eyes and burning cheeks" vanquished all obstacles on the way to Jericho. "In a six-hour march he had to surmount an upward grade of more than a thousand meters," Adam wrote, "despite the hottest sun, with no shade whatsoever—across the most barren and lifeless snarl of rocks. The amazing thing was this: Jesus did not tire . . . Only a top-fit human body could withstand demands of this sort."[17]

Seen from one angle, the German liturgical movement appeared to free young Catholics from concerns of the world and from political engagement, opening them to romantic ideology, which accented the role of interiority while calling for submission to authority.[18] But the religious also reinforced the political. The point of the new liturgy was to cause Catholics to experience themselves as unbounded within the whole. The Catholic mass thus allowed believers to transcend the alienating German city and to sense the ecstatic fulfillment of self-surrender. Not coincidentally, some of the movement's spokesmen recognized and praised the anti-liberal thrust. Ildefons Herwegen, abbot of the medieval monastery at Maria Laach, wrote in 1918 that the "individual, reared under Renaissance and under liberalism, has lived out its life [*hat sich ausgelebt*]. It demands community."[19] Herwegen's influence extended to France and the United States, where reforms from Maria Laach, like "dialogue masses" in which the congregation joined the altar servers in responses to the celebrant, "spread like wildfire."[20]

Youth movements sprouted in the German areas of former Habsburg lands, from right to left, also ironically emphasizing the ideas of "freedom" and "personal responsibility." For their adherents, ideology was "more than program," and leadership was to be "experienced and not decreed." The Austrian Catholic *Bund Neuland* exhibited the same willingness to abandon democratic norms that we see in Germany. Franz Kapfhammer, one of the movement's leading figures, wrote in 1932 that young people "suffered from the brutal devastation by party politics of all public and personal areas of life . . . we do not believe in the party-political and parliamentary solution of our needs. The becoming of a *Volk* takes place in more hidden, less hectic ways, at the level of cells."[21] As a whole, the group was devoted to strengthening the *Volk* (*Volkstumsarbeit*), and, with few exceptions, antisemitism.[22]

Activists of this period transmitted to posterity Catholic political ideas that promised to bring these various elements of desire, belief, and up-to-date scientific knowledge into unity. Best known was the "wholism" of Othmar Spann of the law faculty at Vienna, who became the most popular Catholic theorist of his age, commanding the loyalties of generations of students.[23] For Spann, the state would become the "natural body" of the *Volkstum*, and as such part of an "organically arranged international order," expressing an "essential spiritual and intellectual whole, and not the coincidental momentary will, either of the majority or some other sum of individuals."[24] "Governance had to go by stages," Spann postulated, "from above to below," and society had to be organized according to a hierarchy of corporations. The order was decided by the relative worthiness of the corporations: "the best form of state is that which entrusts rule [*Herrschaft*] to those who are the best [in a given society].[25] Spann preached his wholeness "Gospel" at meetings of the Catholic Academic Union at Maria Laach in 1931 and 1932, and he encountered but one lonely opponent, Munich philosophy professor Dietrich von Hildebrand, the unusual German intellectual who resisted German Catholicism's proto-fascist communitarianism. Instead of the *Volk*, Hildebrand invoked the worth and integrity of the human person.

Beyond Hildebrand, a man difficult to position politically, the only other Catholic resistance to anti-liberal, wholistic currents of thought grew among the left-liberal authors of the *Rhein-Mainische Volkszeitung* in Frankfurt. Yet for the majority of Catholic intellectuals young and old, parliamentary democracy held no intrinsic value.[26] Take one voice from 1922:

"Neither intellectually nor spiritually will we submit to the historically ob-solete formation which is called a [political] party . . . we do not believe in the *völkisch* healing power of parliamentarism that has been inherited from the liberal West, even when it clothes itself in the sparkling costume of a formally clean democracy."[27] Beyond Othmar Spann, the intellectual force in German Catholicism that tended to attract and gather such sentiments of skepticism toward democracy was the political theorist Carl Schmitt. Decades later Heinrich Lutz lamented Schmitt's "fateful role as destroyer of the faith of young Catholics in the rule of law and in parliamentary democratic forms."[28]

Yet Lutz cautions us not to presume the uniqueness of the German case. Democracy was under attack in other places as well. That is certainly true in the immediate neighborhood of Central Europe, where democratic rule survived only in Czechoslovakia. But the German case combined rhe-torical features in a way not witnessed elsewhere, making Catholics enthu-siasts for *Volk* understood as "mystical body" united in a "community" of "blood." "If the *Volk* was seen as the bodily unit of the race," Hermann Greive has written, "so the Church was understood as a bodily unit in Christ, not simply in a figurative, but rather in a supernatural and mystical way, which, because it was supernatural and mystical, was all the more real."[29] Greive called this mixing of supernatural and natural "theological physicism." "In the aftermath of political turmoil," he wrote, "political dis-orientation took hold of the broad masses of the German population, and caused many people to seek lasting solace in the Church while calling for the 'unity of the blood.' In this atmosphere traditional terms with new rac-ist overtones entered common speech with few people noticing; indeed this all happened at the same time that some Catholics took ostensible stands against race."[30]

Dramatic expression of this mix of biological, political, and theological can be found in the writings of Tübingen's Karl Adam, among the most influential theologians of the twentieth century and also a leading figure in the liturgical movement. Adam was particularly attracted to the notion of blood, which suggested to him the vital, living presence of God in human history. In a time of secularization marked by growing "disen-chantment," blood joined God and man mystically and actually, and made the message of Catholicism seem relevant. Racism provided modern, scientific theologians like Adam with a tool of reenchantment, a means of seeming relevant to the urbanized world in which they and their parishioners lived.

As a Catholic, Karl Adam could not dispute the unity of the church and the unity of humanity. Yet the idea of mystical body provided him with conceptual flexibility. The community of the church and the human community were by their "nature" "differentiated" like parts of the body. "The body works as a unity through a diversity of organic functions," Adam wrote.[31] Humanity's natural differentiation was by *Volk*—which in German means both people and nation. According to Adam, precisely the church's "internationalism requires the nationalism of her mission and her believers. A Catholic who denied his German blood and refused to see the *Reich* of God that appears before him in Church with his German eyes and to love this with his German heart; who affirmed some wishy-washy worn-out *natura humana*—and not his own German nature as the carrier of supernatural blessings, and who therefore wanted to cultivate some kind of cosmopolitan Christianity—this Catholic would be sinning against the essential relationships that, according to Catholicism, obtain between the natural and the supernatural, and thus against an essential part of Catholicism."[32] Sacred blood had to be protected. In 1933, Adam proclaimed Adolf Hitler the savior of the "diseased [German] national body," the man who could restore Germany's "blood unity."[33]

Before 1933 German Catholics may have voted for the Center Party, but like other Germans they felt attracted to Hitler for his promises to create a new *Reich*, a modern kingdom of God evoking the strength and harmony of earlier ages when a Christian German king ruled over Central Europe in a Holy Empire, fulfilling the will of God in history. Like *Volk* or "body," the word *Reich* was vested with political/racial as well as theological import. Germans called the medieval empire in which the Christian ideal reached its pinnacle the Holy Roman Empire of the German nation. And in German the Gospels call the Kingdom of God the *Reich Gottes*. No other concept was more central for Catholics trying to imagine God's will realized in the world, but also in the fullness of time. The idea of *Reich* became seductively evocative for Germans and Austrians living in hated republics of the interwar years, suggesting the potential greatness both of the united German nation and of a united Christianity.[34]

Shortly after Hitler's ascent to power in 1933, the Catholic Academic Union, the major organization in Germany for Catholic intellectuals, debated "The Idea and the Construction of the Old *Reich*," and historian Albert Mirgeler proclaimed that the medieval abbey at Maria Laach "symbolizes the Holy German Empire . . . The new epoch in which we live today can represent not only this Reich but also the Church of former times."[35] Influential Bonn historian Max Braubach asserted that the new Nazi order would "clear away the evil heritage of the past," and the eminent liberal (!) historian Franz Schnabel inveighed against the individualism that had undermined the idea of *Reich*.[36] Joining them in the months that followed were many other Catholic intellectuals who spoke on the virtues of a reawakened German empire.[37]

Beyond resonances with Hitler's state, or supposed recapturings of German Gothic Christianity, *Reich* also related to the Catholic concern for salvation of the world. In the Middle Ages, a strong and astute German king had secured peace and facilitated the flowering of Christian life. The defunct Holy Empire had thus played a key role in the "history of salvation" (*Heilsgeschichte*), helping to lead all humankind to the future willed by God. German Catholics believed a resurrected German-led empire in the center of Europe might play that role once again.[38] The old *Reich* therefore justified German nationalism in universal terms: when reconstituted, it would incorporate what God wanted for humanity, reinvesting German Catholics' lives with meaning.[39]

For theologians, the idea of *Reich* resolved the challenge of overcoming the dichotomy between matter and spirit, between "profane history" and the history of salvation. Influential theologian and priest Robert Grosche reasoned that just as Christ united humanity and divinity, so also history "moved from a beginning to the promise of fulfillment that was to be found in Jesus Christ. The unification of the two natures in Jesus was viewed as the proleptic anticipation of the end of history. Since the time of Jesus, all time was to be viewed as a historical transformation of the world that had already been spiritually completed in Jesus Christ." Grosche concluded that spiritual impulses would always anticipate secular events. He felt, therefore, that "this proper order of Christian history was becoming a reality with the establishment of the Third Reich."[40] History was revelation, and *Reich* was the crowning event. Far from being a Nazi,

Robert Grosche was the most prominent non-Nazi the U.S. occupation forces could find to help them set up municipal government in Cologne in April 1945.[41] In the 1960s, the left-wing Catholic Walter Dirks explained that *Reich* had been a "powerful political 'archetype,'" producing a "dizzy spell" among German Catholics like Grosche.[42]

If the theology of *Reich* was specific to Germany, German Christians did not succumb to it in equal shares. Though generally Catholic theologians tended to express racist views less often than Protestant counterparts, in one respect Catholicism proved more susceptible to Nazi racism than Protestantism, namely, in its rejection of the Lutheran idea of "two kingdoms."[43] In July 1933, deputy director of the Catholic Academic Union, Franz X. Landmesser, criticized Protestant theologian Wilhelm Stapel for portraying the state in metaphysical terms. To this, Landmesser opposed the Catholic idea of Incarnation: of God in Christ, of Christ in the church, and of the church in the Holy Roman Empire of the German nation. He imagined that currently the German political space had the task of assuming the historical "salvation mission" of the medieval *Reich*. This would form a realization of the "Christian West [*Abendland*]." Like Karl Adam, Franz X. Landmesser took the Catholic idea of incarnation into the symbolic complex of Nazi racial thought: just as God became human in Christ, so the "eternal soul" could find "bodily form" only in the *Volk*.[44]

German Christians wondering why dreams of *Reich* remained unfulfilled in the years between the wars quickly seized upon the figure of the Jew. Here all the heady imagery converged: with their foreign blood, Jews stood outside the mystical body, the people of God. But one last idea was needed to justify not only contempt for Jews, but passive acceptance of their suffering, and that was the German expression *Erbsünde*, which dictionaries translate as "original sin" but which literally means "hereditary sin," passed from generation to generation. If influential theologians preached that Jews could not become Catholic in a single generation, that had to do with the gravitational force of this idea of Jewish sinfulness, irresistible even for the German Jesuit Georg Bichlmair, who risked imprisonment for helping Jewish converts after the Nazis marched into Vienna in 1938. Two years earlier, the Viennese Jewish weekly *Die Wahrheit* observed in Bichlmair the dangerous powers that the notion of *Erbsünde* exercised upon the Catholic mind. In a public address in which Bichlmair "railed against the 'bad genetic make-up' of the Jews," the editors wrote, the Jesuit had presented "a classic case of the amalgamation of the Catholic concept of 'original sin' with the Nazi catchword of 'race.'"[45] Professor Alois Mager, who figured among the moderate voices in the Catholic milieu of Salzburg and openly criticized the Nazis, likewise invoked the "racial peculiarity" of Jews, whose rejection of Christ helped create a "spiritual attitude of radical denial and subversion."[46]

The racist syndrome could be found in people who took greater risks to oppose the Nazis than Father Bichlmair. Take the peace activist and priest Max Josef Metzger, arrested repeatedly by the Nazis and finally executed in 1944 ("in the name of the German *Volk*") for smuggling out of Germany Christian plans for the postwar political order, thus revealing his treasonous belief that the Nazis were doomed to fail.[47] Metzger took the *Grenzgänger* Johannes Oesterreicher and Annie Kraus into the church, and was himself an inveterate border-crosser into Protestant territory through the ecumenical organization Una Sancta, where he became the major Catholic figure, causing some consternation in the Vatican.[48] Shortly before his first arrest in 1934, Metzger eagerly conceded that Christianity opposed Nazism, but he thought active resistance by Christians to Nazism was pointless. Instead, he advocated "constructive and positive" cooperation in order to prevent "the worse," and argued that the regime might achieve something positive by forging a people's community (*Volksgemeinschaft*) through such activities as the winter relief (*Winterhilfswerk*). *Volksgemeinschaft* was a term of racial exclusion that might seem an odd goal for a Catholic priest, but for Metzger the ecumenist it had the allure of advancing unity of Protestants and Catholics within the German *Volk*.[49]

When we leave figures like Metzger and Mager, and enter the mainstream, we find Catholics not repelled by Nazism but instead intrigued by the possibilities it offered, even as they tried to keep a certain distance. For example, in 1933, members of the Catholic Academic Union endeavored to identify the "Catholic positions" that separated them from the Nazis.[50] Deputy director Franz X. Landmesser claimed that the Nazi "idea of *Reich*" did not "coincide" with the position of the Union. But what was that position? This he could not specify. He refused to make concessions to "some false form of Western democracy" or to validate "a nationalism which cannot hide its Hegelian origins." Landmesser and the monks

of Maria Laach had an easier time extolling an idea they shared with the
Nazis: namely, the vital importance of race.

Over the next twelve years, the Nazis showed Catholic enthusiasts of *Volk*
and *Reich* where the differences lay between the two sides, and how ultimately Catholicism and Nazism were not compatible. In a letter written to
Pius XII in 1944, Freiburg Archbishop Conrad Gröber, once among the
most vocal propagators of the virtues of *Reich*, admitted that the Nazis had
rebuffed his early overtures. Referring to the repression that set in after the
Concordat negotiated between the Vatican and Berlin in 1933, he wrote
that "we Catholics did nothing to cause this complete ideological turn
around." Not the Catholic Church but the Nazi Party had perceived the
ideological incompatibility between the two, and forced a break through
persecution of priests and other Christians.[51]

The boundaries between opponents and collaborators within the church
were fluid, however, and in the end German Catholicism remained one
church with one language. There is limited explanatory power in differ-
entiating Catholics according to progressive or reactionary stances. The
Catholic Karl Adam, who felt that the "driving spirit" of the Nazi movement was also his spirit, dedicated his first postwar book to the Catholic
Max Metzger, pacifist martyr of the Nazis.[52] Like Metzger, Adam is seen
today as a forerunner of ecumenism, and he did as much to break down
well-worn ideas of hierarchy as any other Catholic thinker of the first half
of the twentieth century. He showed remarkable tolerance toward German
Protestants. They, after all, were of the same race.

The International Context of German Catholic Racism

Jürgen Habermas felt his heritage as a German academic most keenly
when teaching at foreign universities, and we best discern the reality of
the German Catholic racist syndrome when we contrast it to other national cases. Though roughly translatable into other languages, the words
Volk, *Reich*, *Blut*, or *Erbsünde* possess a special resonance in their own
context. For no other national branch of Catholicism was the imperial
idea—the notion of *Reich*—remotely as central in the modern period as in
Germany.[53] There was no potentially political religious metaphor as evocative as *Reich Gottes* for non-German Catholics. In English one speaks not

of "empire" but of the "kingdom" of God. In France one has *Royaume de Dieu*. In neither France, nor the United States, nor any other place was the idea of the Kingdom of God linked for Catholics to any relevant political idea.[54] It is not even correct to call the English "Kingdom of God" a transcendent category: it was an abstraction, a vestige of ritualistic language that could be awakened to life only by religious inspiration. Countries of the historical Spanish realm produced potent political discourses of "blessed nation" and "mystical body," yet the idea was to forge new multiracial identities in order to unite rather than exclude. After countries in Latin American broke from the Spanish crown, the concepts were liberating rather than imperial.[55] In Europe, Hungary came closest to Germany in producing a racialized Catholic discourse, as we see in writings of the Jesuit Bela Bangha, a forceful advocate for a modern Catholicism in both Hungary and Austria, who suspected baptized Jews of being spiritually inferior or opportunistic. Not coincidentally, the two major figures in French Catholicism to oppose antisemitism in the postwar period were converted Hungarian Jews: they had been mobilized by the Catholic racism of their native lands. Yet the tradition of the Hungarian Kingdom of the Lands of St. Stephen seemed too inclusive to fully serve the purposes of those attempting to racialize Christianity.[56]

In countries where Jews were considered racial others, the local languages of Christianity did not conspire to make them seem to carry sinfulness encoded in their bodies. Neither English nor the Slavic and Romance languages suggest to believers that sin might be racially transmitted as *Erbsünde*. Other languages translate directly from Latin (*peccatum originale*) and speak of "original sin," not inherited sin.[57] Polish Catholic antisemites of the 1930s warned against pollution of Polish blood from the Jewish race—including converts—but did not attempt to square their prejudice with Catholic theology.[58] During the emergence of modern racist antisemitism in late nineteenth-century France, the seminary professor and *pasteur efficace* Canon Emmanuel Chabauty (1827–1914) identified Jews as allies of dissolution in league with Free Masonry, the forces behind all revolution, modernizing, and thus judafying the world.[59] By infiltrating Christian society, Jews subverted its norms. Jews had killed God and were more under the power of Satan than other peoples. Decades later, German theologians echoed Chabauty's belief that a second original sin rested upon the Jewish people. But the French language did not suggest to Chabauty or his allies that Jewish sin could be held in a person's physical self and then biologically transmitted.

The German idea of *Volk* suggests an exclusiveness not fully imaginable within French, American, or British discourses, and shows how embedded the Catholic Church became in regional contexts. The U.S. Christian press, whether Protestant or Catholic, and even at its most conservative, did not sympathize with racial antisemitism.[60] A British reviewer of a book by Karl Adam's student Hermann Franke (*The Salvation of the Nations* [London, 1938]) was bewildered at Franke's ability to "confuse the idea of a supernatural community, the church, with a natural community, the nation. His argument is tenuous to the last degree, and at the end of the book one is left wondering what it was all about." Franke's argument smacked of "some sort of Hegelian pantheism." Catholics must put aside this "dangerous little book," the reviewer insisted, and instead "in this age of rampant totalitarianism," stress the "worth of the individual soul and the sacredness of individual responsibility." Of course, the German edition had spoken not of *Nationen* but of *Völker*.[61]

The French nation is—in theory and largely in practice—a political community. For example, in 1991 the French Constitutional Council decided that the legislature could not speak of *le peuple corse* as part of the French nation because this would imply a distinction based upon ethnicity. The French political system does not legally recognize ethnic differences among it citizens. The German tradition is different, and from the early nineteenth-century programs of nation building have built upon romanticized ideas of a *Volk* united in ethnicity and culture.[62] Recent work has revealed limitations to the inclusiveness of French nationality laws, but still a crucial difference remains between a context in which tradition imagines ethnic others as co-nationals and one that does not. To put it another way: on the far right, France has had its supporters of Fichtean ideas of ethnic nation, yet after World War I they could be placed on the defensive as representing a Germanic racist idea. Even before the war there was agreement that the French nation was not characterized by race.[63] By contrast, it would have seemed absurd to argue in Germany that the *Volk* was a daily plebiscite; indeed it was a huge challenge in popular or scientific discourse to oppose the racialization of the *Volk* concept.[64] The issue was of special importance for the Jews, who could more easily claim during the racialized interwar years to belong to the French nation than to the German *Volk*.[65]

Racist ideas therefore had higher thresholds to cross before becoming part of French Catholic theology, and religious and biological/political idioms remained distinct. French Catholic racists tended not to invoke Catholicism in favor of their racism, and the odd practicing Catholic on the antisemitic right, journalist Édouard Drumont (1844–1917), took pains to distance himself from racism and called Jews the original racists who considered themselves a "privileged race" destined to "reduce other peoples to servitude."[66] In Drumont's time there were a handful of prominent racist clergymen, the best known being Father Pierre Baruteil, a doctor of theology at the Institut Catholique de Paris. In 1896, Father Baruteil won a silver medal in an essay contest developing practical thoughts on how to "annihilate Jewish power" in France. He entitled his piece the "Solution to the Jewish Question: The Race of Vipers and the Olive Branch."[67] Baruteil kept his identity as priest secret, however, because his racism brought him "to the borders of Marcionism"—the heresy according to which Jews worshipped a different God.[68] In fact, Baruteil's racism and Catholicism hardly intersected. He loathed the "Jewish race" but took little resort to scripture or theological tradition to support his views. Three other prize-winners in this competition were priests, but like Baruteil they concealed their identities behind pseudonyms, so incompatible did racism seem with the vocation of a Catholic priest in France.

Baruteil's case shows the conceptual difficulties of taking religious "anti-Judaism" beyond well-worn Christian stereotypes about Jewish accursedness into the dimensions of modern racism. His desire to racialize Catholicism pushed him to the edges of intellectual schizophrenia, giving "evidence of the discursive Judeophilia of Catholic Judeophobia: those non-Christians who were almost demoniacal become by their conversion almost angelic."[69] Perhaps Baruteil was not graced with powers of intellect to discern his own inconsistency; perhaps he represented a variation of the vaunted ability to hold two opposing arguments in one's mind at the same time.

In the decades leading to World War II, much of the French Catholic right resisted the temptations of racism, decisively aided by the Vatican's condemning of the nationalist *Action Française* in 1926, after which the center of gravity within on the right shifted to more moderate terrain. There was a *Ligue franc-catholique* of Canon Georges Schaefer (which replaced the *Ligue anti-Judéomaçonnique* founded in 1913 by right radical Monsignor Ernest Jouin), but it was politically and socially irrelevant, consisting of a small group of extreme aristocrats, haute-bourgeois, and ecclesiastics.[70] There was also the right-wing *Parti social français* (1936–40) that grew out of the *Croix-de-feu*, a far-right, paramilitary veterans' organization.[71] By 1938, the *Parti* had some 800,000 supporters and aimed to gain power through the parliamentary process. Historians are divided on the movement's antisemitism. In any case, it was qualitatively distinct from Central and East European counterparts on the Catholic right such as Joseph Eberle's circle or the Austrian Christian Socials Anton Orel and Leopold Kunschak, all of whom were openly Catholic as well as unrepentantly racist and antisemitic. Unlike French counterparts, they also had pretensions to contribute to "Catholic thought."

Following the rise of Nazism in Germany, French Catholics could become more aggressive in their argumentation, portraying racism as a danger to France that contradicted national traditions. In December 1937, the Jewish journal *Samedi* wrote that "one has to thank the racists for, in a sense, reunifying Judeo-Christian thought."[72] The only prominent Catholic racial antisemite active in France in the 1930s, Herman De Vries de Heekelingen, was not French. De Vries de Heekelingen held Swiss citizenship, and from 1923 acted as professor of paleography at the Catholic University in Nijmegen. Paris publishing houses brought out a number of his books, all suffused with Judeophobia and quickly translated into other languages. Like Catholic racists in Germany, De Vries de Heekelingen said that baptism had no power to affect the Jewish character.[73] He claimed that Jews hated the Catholic Church because it was the only obstacle to their efforts at world domination and represented the "supremacy of spiritual values above materialism."[74] He criticized Jewish "obsessions" with cleanliness, and he condemned the laws of Ezra-Nehemia taken to maintain genealogical purity, or as he put it, "to maintain the purity of their race."[75] Like Drumont, he portrayed racism as Jewish in origin. "If one criticizes German or Italian racism," he wrote, "one should equally criticize Jewish racism."[76] But De Vries de Heekelingen was such an odd figure in the

French Catholic scene that the literature portrays him as non-French and non-Catholic, in the company of secular racists and figures on the extreme right.[77]

There were prominent French Catholics who were racists, if less openly than De Vries de Heekelingen, but, as was the case with Drumont, their racism coexisted uneasily with their Catholicism, and it did not enter Catholic thought as such. Xavier Vallat, Vichy minister for Jewish affairs, called Jews a separate racial group that could not adapt to France. Louis Darquier de Pellepoix, likewise infamous for his service to Vichy, was truly racist and wanted to unite the French in their "race," claiming that French Communists might be saved but not the Jews belonging to French national parties. Yet as a French Catholic he felt constrained to deny that his antisemitism was racial:

> The Germans have made a religious myth of race, substituting it for all other belief. They pretend to a superiority of the race that is dominant among them: the Nordic race. Such a myth is the latest incarnation of the perpetual Germanic "evolution" . . . [This myth] has entered into an open struggle with the Christian religions . . . For us it is enough to consider Israel as a nation to be antisemitic. But to examine the racial problem gives us even more arguments against the Jew.

The French understanding of nation made this kind of division possible. Darquier de Pellepoix, sentenced to death in absentia for collaboration in 1947, insisted above all else that Jews belonged to a foreign nation. "I find my position not from the point of view of race but from the point of nation," he wrote. He claimed not to consider Jews an "inferior race." Important to him was to be French: "It is worth more in any case to be an imbecilic Frenchman than an intelligent Jew." Such views did not absolve Darquier de Pellepoix from implicit racism, however. Like others on the French right, he was obsessed by the weakening of French "blood."[78] Yet because he resisted calling himself or his ideas racist, he was not tempted to justify racism in Catholic terms, and rather than reconcile racism with Catholicism, he became involved in self-contradiction. He said at one point that German racism openly defied Christian religion, at another that "Aryan race" and "Christian civilization" were synonymous. Rather than redefine Christian love to make racism acceptable to the Christian as Karl Adam did, he proclaimed that hatred need not be foreign to the "Aryan race." As for his own commitment to the "precepts of love" of the church, Darquier de Pellepoix probably had more affection for his dog the "good Porthos" than he did for any Jew.[79] Karl Adam's type of Catholic, insistent on squaring racism with the central Catholic teaching of love of neighbor, was immeasurably more dangerous for Catholicism because it distorted Christianity's universalism. Vries de Heekelingen, Vallat, and Darquier de Pellepoix were not only not Catholic theologians, they were not concerned to be theologically orthodox.

Opposition to racism rhetorically governed the Catholic spectrum in France in part because of the growing tensions between the Vatican and Nazi Germany. There was little question where French Catholics should stand in an international dispute like this. The ultraconservative National Catholic Federation proclaimed repeatedly the "absolute opposition between Christian and racist doctrines." At the same time, young Democratic Christians who resolutely fought against antisemitism did so with the approval of the highest authorities of the church.[80] The anti-racist front included leading Catholic intellectuals like Emmanuel Mounier, Jacques Maritain, Stanislas Fumet, and François Mauriac as well as many bishops.[81] When the courageous Alsatian anti-racist Oscar de Férenzy methodically overturned the claims of antisemites in his book *Les Juifs et nous chrétiens* (Paris, 1935), this was well received in Jewish newspapers but also by liberal Catholics. Férenzy accused De Vries de Heekelingen of using "poor arguments," and Raymond-Raoul Lambert derided the Swiss professor's work as "a vapid summary of the attacks made by Hitler or Goebbels, with garbled quotes and a semblance of scientific research."[82]

In the French context, it was easy to delegitimize racist antisemitism with references to Hitler and Goebbels, and there were Catholics on the far right who tried to banish the evident associations. Charles Maurras maintained that Jews were not a race but a "people," and he chided Italian fascists for having followed the German model.[83] "Préjugé" was a dirty word, and the ultra-nationalist Robert Brasillach coined a phrase popular among French antisemites: "we have no prejudice and we are not racists."[84] Brasillach was executed in February 1945 for intellectual treason.

The point is not that France was without Catholic antisemites and racists, but that local languages of Catholicism and nationalism kept French Catholics from reaching the depths of alienation toward Jews that we see in Germany, Austria, and countries farther to the East. French Catholic opponents of antisemitism could argue from within the French tradition that what made France French was not racial, and in any case Jews were not a race. And because "racism" seemed delegitimized in French Catholic discourse, thinkers there were not impelled to ask whether indeed there was such a thing as "purely religious" antisemitism. The criticisms of racist antisemitism in France did not develop as sharp an edge as was the case in German Europe, where the widely accepted ethnoracial ideas of nationhood brought forth extensive, searching critiques of racism and antisemitism.[85]

Eugenics

The idea of *Volk* is not the unique property of Germany. It was absorbed into the local languages of Eastern Europe in the early nineteenth century (mostly as *narod*), and to the east of Germany ethnic understandings of the nation still hold sway. Yet the racist syndrome of German Catholicism did not develop as fully in Poland, Hungary, or Czechoslovakia. We see this most clearly in the peculiar attraction to eugenics among German-speaking Catholics of the 1920s and 1930s.

Ultimately, the Catholic Church did more to oppose eugenics than any institution, but its opposition took time to stir. From the late nineteenth century, when the science of eugenics first emerged, Catholics struggled for orientation with limited guidance from Rome, and some prominent theologians went so far as to support "negative eugenics," including sterilization. In December 1930 the Vatican finally spoke out in the encyclical *Casti Connubii*, rejecting the ideas that humans served scientific "conjectures" or that the family was subordinate to the interests of the state. Pius XI told believers that governments that kept persons from marrying for fear they might generate "defective offspring" had lost sight of the "fact that the family is more sacred than the State and that men are begotten not for the earth and for time, but for Heaven and eternity." He condemned sterilization, birth control, and abortion.[86] *Casti Connubii* left room for inveterate eugenicists, however. The original Italian said that "hygienic counsel in order to procure more certainly the health and vigor of future offspring" is not "contrary to right reason." Similarly, in Polish, Spanish, and German translations the equivalent of "offspring" or "issue" was used rather than "child," and the eugenic implications were clear. The general point is that the Vatican did not rule out concern for the health of the race; it simply warned against making race into a deity.[87]

German theologians became adept at interpreting Catholic teaching to accommodate popular ideas of a racialized *Volk*, and before *Casti Connubii*, a number of influential figures advocated sterilization, including Hermann Muckermann, Joseph Mayer, Fritz Tillmann (moral theology, Freiburg), Franz Keller (moral theology, Bonn), Georg Schreiber (Center Party politician and priest), and Ludwig Ruland (pastoral medicine, Würzburg).[88] Hermann Muckermann provided the general racist vision. But in 1933 the Nazis rejected collaboration with Catholic racists because the Catholics were unwilling to countenance the total devaluation of the human individual. Muckermann was suspected of watering down race science and was expelled from directorship at the Kaiser Wilhelm Institute for Anthropology in Berlin. The Nazis had again clarified where the borders ran between the two worldviews.[89]

Catholics elsewhere did not match the Germans in their enthusiasm to improve the human body. Like the Vatican, French Catholicism did not condemn all eugenics.[90] At the eighth congress of the Association for the Christian Marriage in 1930, Maurice-Louis Dubourg, Archbishop of Marseille, said that "Christian morality constitutes a eugenics which no other would know how to replace." Yet *this* eugenics focused on the environment rather than the body and recommended marital fidelity to strengthen the family, chastity before marriage to prevent syphilis, and temperance.[91] French Catholics opposed euthanasia and sterilization, and contended that "positive" eugenics must address humans' spiritual dimension.[92] When judging whether a young person should marry, they worried less about inherited physiological imperfections and more about whether matrimony was the path leading to that person's eternal destiny. One popular preacher informed his listeners that human society was not a "stud farm." French Catholics rejected the "marriage certificates" (permitting access to marriage to those judged biologically fit) that German experts like Hermann Muckermann found an acceptable part of "positive" eugenics.[93]

At a deeper level the struggle was not about arguments, it was about identity—whoever embraced eugenics did not understand what it meant to be Catholic in France. A person's stance on sterilization or abortion was part of a cultural "code" signaling membership in a particular milieu. Those who argued for eugenics were seen as threatening "others" situated beyond the cultural divide, sworn to weakening Catholicism. Like counterparts elsewhere in Europe, French Catholics suspected an unholy alliance of eugenicists and neo-Malthusian advocates of birth control, conspiring to reduce the rural and working-class populations who supported Catholicism.[94] To favor eugenics in France was to be un-Catholic, whereas to oppose eugenics in Germany was to be un-German.

Similarly, in Poland concerns about German neo-paganism, seen as modern and hostile to Catholicism, intermingled with arguments about national identity, and Poles embracing racism were projected as both un-Catholic and antislavic.[95] If in Germany mainstream Catholic opinion was open to the eugenicists' belief that the race needed protecting, this attitude was less convincing among Slavic neighbors. Still, even in East Central Europe race-thinking was not rejected completely, and Catholic writers sought Thomistic balance by speaking of race as part of nature with a legitimate role in God's plan. Leading Polish authority Father Józef Pastuszka wrote that racism had healthy elements, including the emphasis on state authority, the idea of leadership, and the rejection of democratic ideas of equality.[96] Polish Catholics translated a rare Catholic tract on eugenics in which Hungarian Bishop Tihamer Toth concurred with the Vatican that Catholicism offered the "best positive eugenics." If there was a problem, it was not the increase in numbers of the "degenerate" but the "artificial limitation of healthy families." "The future," Toth argued, "belongs to those courageous races who have held their own in the battle for life by producing a robust and abundant progeny." Protecting the race was fine as long as one avoided pure materialism. The individual, Toth wrote, possessed a "natural right" to marry which no state could infringe, yet he cited *Casti Connubii* to the effect that it was correct to advise such people against marriage. In a balancing act typical of the moral theology of that age, Toth condemned those who would deny absolution to persons who entered marriage despite "hereditary illness," yet he refused to say that those who knowingly entered such unions were without all sin.[97]

Though acceptable among Hungarian Catholics, who came closest to Germany's racist syndrome, Toth's advocacy of positive eugenics seemed highly unusual on the background of Polish Catholicism. More common was the view expressed by the Jesuit Stanisław Podoleński, who died in the *Pfarrerblock* at Dachau in 1945, according to whom science had nothing to say about the value of a human being. Rather than embrace the "positive" eugenics allowed by the church, he and other Polish writers tended to assemble arguments against the neo-Malthusian stance of their secular opponents.

In Czechoslovakia as well, Catholics fit their argumentation into the overall political context. If the national (and secular) gymnastics society Sokol promoted improvement of the body, their Catholic rivals (Orel) accused them of promoting an "anti-Christian ideology" based in Darwinism, which ignored the human's spiritual side.[98] The Slovak biologist and neo-Thomist philosopher Josef Florian Babor identified the word "race" as Germanic in origin and predicted that Nazi pseudo-science would lead to violent measures against humans.[99] The major Czech Catholic antifascist, Jewish convert Alfred Fuchs, was more consistent in his rejection of racism than his Polish counterpart Father Pastuszka, and he confessed no attraction to antidemocratic models of racist regimes.[100] In Poland as well as Czechoslovakia, racial ideology and eugenics were branded as typically German. Much as German nationalism caused some German Catholics to embrace eugenics for fear of not fitting in, in Slavic East Central Europe it had the opposite effect.

Internationally, the eugenics movement fared best where Catholicism was weakest: Norway, Estonia, Sweden, Denmark, Finland, several American and Canadian states, and then finally Germany. In Germany, Catholics were on the defensive against majority Protestants but also against secular ideologies such as socialism and liberalism. Therefore, a look at the United States—where Catholics were also a large minority in a majority Protestant culture—tells us more about what made Germany distinct.

Like co-religionists in Germany, American Catholics lived in a society that embraced eugenics. Still, they kept their distance. That was not for lack of intellectual temptations. In the 1920s, the American Eugenics Society made overtures to the leading Catholic social thinkers John A. Ryan, S.J., and John Montgomery Cooper, both professors at the Catholic University in Washington, DC.[101] Neither was immediately skeptical. They shared the belief of the Europeans that "true" eugenics had to be formed according to Catholic principles, based in the insistence on healthy families. Cooper, an important anthropologist in his own right, wrote in 1928, "While the Catholic may and does disagree with some of the proposals made in the name of eugenics by the radical left wing of the eugenics movement, he may and should be in hearty sympathy with conservative and scientific eugenics as such." Cooper therefore advised students searching for partners to avoid marrying people from families with a reputation for emotional or mental problems.[102] Cooper also voiced respect for the race and its maintenance: "Just as death is, humanly speaking, the greatest harm that can befall the individual," he wrote, "so death is, humanly speaking, the greatest harm that could befall the race. And were no more children born, the race would die. Love of neighbor, therefore, in its Christian and Catholic sense, is deeply interested in birth."[103] In Germany, too, Catholics were arguing that Christian charity implied duties to one's own race. But here the parallels cease. In 1929, Cooper wrote that "neither the cultural nor the psychological evidence is sufficient or even near-sufficient to establish the superiority of Nordics or of any other racial group."[104] In the context of German culture, this would have seemed an extraordinary statement from a professional anthropologist. Likewise, any sympathy for eugenics on the part of John A. Ryan soon faded. Also in 1929 he dubbed eugenics a "pseudoscience" and posed questions about how its categories were constructed: "to subordinate the weaker groups to the welfare of society means simply that some human beings are to be made instruments to other human beings . . . One who does not identify right with might can produce no cogent reason for treating the weak as of less intrinsic worth than the strong, even though the former may be in the minority."[105]

The following year, the American journal *Eugenics* misleadingly informed readers that Ryan supported eugenics. The source of this information was not Ryan himself but rather Germany's leading Catholic advocate of eugenic sterilization, Father Joseph Mayer. In an article entitled

"Eugenics in Roman Catholic Literature," Mayer argued that the Catholic Church did not oppose "well-founded principles or policies of modern eugenics."[106] This was indeed true before *Casti Connubii*'s release in December 1930, when a wide range of Catholic thinkers embraced "positive" eugenics. Ryan himself had established two principles by which the Catholic Church might condone the "negative" measure of sterilization as a legitimate function of the state.[107] First, the population of "unfit persons had to be so high as to constitute an imminent danger to the public welfare," and, second, "the state had to have exhausted all other feasible methods of dealing with the situation." Yet he also made clear that such conditions were not met in the United States, and he encouraged American Catholics to resist the sterilization laws on the books in their states. Joseph Mayer portrayed other Catholic authorities as enthusiasts of eugenics when in fact they, like Ryan, had severe difficulties with programs of race improvement.[108] In an even more ambitious review of that same year, the Austrian priest Josef Grosam, an expert on Christian marriage, chided Mayer for exaggerating Catholic support for eugenics and wrote that no Catholic theologian found sterilization justified as part of a eugenics program or as punishment of a criminal.[109]

The historian Ingrid Richter has discovered that within Germany and Austria most Catholic theologians came to oppose sterilization. Yet, including Grosam, they still tended to favor the lifelong quarantining of the mentally ill, thus settling any need to sterilize them.[110] This option of compulsory detention does not appear to have won adherents outside culturally German Europe, and again it appears to signal a German peculiarity. Also noteworthy is that even Josef Grosam was willing to make unequivocal statements only about the immorality of sterilizing people who were healthy, thus admitting that there was a grey area on the eve of the papal pronouncements.

Why was Germany so different from the United States, even though in both places Catholics felt uneasy about the eugenics projects dear to liberals, socialists, nationalists, and Protestants? In large part, American Catholics intuited the incompatibility of Catholicism and eugenics sooner than their counterparts in Germany because of the way they were integrated into their society. They had their own professional organizations, hospitals, schools, and universities to mediate a gradual incorporation on their own terms. German Catholicism, despite its vaunted milieu, had nothing like this dense network of protection and influence peddling. The majority Protestant culture battered German Catholics for decades with allegations of treason, creating a trauma of otherness that had no parallels in the American context. The defeat of 1918 finally connected them with other Germans in shared loss, and at the dawn of the Weimar Republic they were desperate to fit in and be recognized as belonging to nation and people. To reject eugenics would have made German Catholics seem unenlightened, medieval, anti-modern, and unconcerned with the welfare of the *Volk*— precisely the stereotypes they wanted to defuse.

Because of their "negative integration," American Catholics were not as concerned as German counterparts about such allegations. Their isolation was not a cause for concern but a source of security. Fathers Cooper and Ryan worked within Catholic institutions of higher education and made careers insulated from—but not independent of—the pressures and expectations of the mainstream. Germany lacked Catholic universities and a network of Catholic secondary education that might have eased the entry of Catholics into modern society, including the world of modern science.[111]

Concerns of an immigrant church in the United States also created a special wariness about eugenics among American Catholics: from the late nineteenth century, the dominant Anglo-Saxon culture had portrayed mostly Catholic immigrant groups as deficient and targeted them for reduction. Birth control, viewed as a further stage in human progress by the establishment culture, was seen by Catholics as a threat.[112] Concerns of this sort then merged with a general alarm at the perils of modern ideologies like materialism, socialism, liberalism—and the Darwinism that stood behind eugenics. Germany, however, was not a society of immigrants, and the standards for loyalty were drawn more stringently within a framework of ethnic nationalism. If Germany was a society strong in regionalisms, these regionalisms were self-contained and not continuing challenges to each other.

In sum: the Americans had built their own institutions and gradually entered an increasingly open civic nation on their own terms. The point is not that American society was free of ethnic or religious exclusion, but that rhetorical means existed for contesting such exclusion; in the 1920s

Catholics, Protestants, and Jews founded societies opposing prejudice.[113] As Johannes Oesterreicher discovered in 1939 during his Parisian exile, American conditions produced the strongest response to racism in international Catholicism.[114] In Germany, after decades of discrimination and under the trauma of a lost war Catholics were desperate to be seen as fully German, and did not question the common assumption of the *Volksgemeinschaft*: that they were united racially with other Germans, and that the race was worth protecting.

The case of eugenics explodes the idea that we can speak straightforwardly about "the Church." In 1930, the Vatican had come out against eugenics more forcefully than any institution, but it still left plenty of room for Catholics in France, Germany, or the United States to reach differing conclusions on "bettering the race." The Vatican also moved slowly, having debated eugenics for more than a decade before releasing the encyclical *Casti Connubii*. And despite intense debates in the Roman Curia that began shortly after the Nazis seized power in Germany, the popes never released an encyclical on race. The universal church confronted believers from within national contexts, and comparative studies of the church's universalism press home the power of the local. They tell us things about contexts otherwise difficult to perceive, such as the strength and texture of a nation's discourse about itself.

The historian examining the Catholic racist syndrome in Germany finds little guidance from within existing literature, however. Specialists on Germany have studied the milieu of political Catholicism and the ferment of youth movements like *Quickborn*, yet none has remarked upon or tried to account for this syndrome in a European context. What about German modernity produced this mass attraction to racism, even in a local entity of the universal church? How did German ethno-nationalism make for a particular kind of antisemitism? The recent turn among historians to "transnationalism" only sublimates these issues by placing Germany in larger contexts that do not account for the German specificity.[115]

But the attraction among Germans to racism was not only Catholic: if anything, it was even stronger among Protestants, some of whom severed all connections to Judaism and the Hebrew scriptures, and preached a Gospel of the Aryan Christ.[116] They represented the majority culture that

Catholics wanted to belong to. In a controversial book, influential despite criticism heaped upon it, Daniel J. Goldhagen argued that something was special about the racism and antisemitism produced in the German context before World War II.[117] Rudimentary comparative study suggests that his basic insight was correct. The German lands produced the *ideologically* most potent strains of antisemitism seen in Europe and probably the world. They contaminated Christianity but were virulent within a political movement that claimed to transcend Christianity as a "Jewish religion": namely, the National Socialist German Workers Party. Yet the German lands also generated a response. In the 1930s, German-speaking Europe became an epicenter for Catholic (and Christian) debates about central ethical questions: who is the other, what is race, how should one look upon a racial other, and how should Catholics behave toward Jews? This anti-racism in the German lands was potent and forceful because it faced antisemitism at its most extreme and because it was carried by Christians whom the racists considered Jews.

4

Catholics against Racism and Antisemitism

Books about Catholic opposition to Hitler tend to focus on the Vatican or the bishops of Germany, but that was not where the action was. Those wanting to learn how Catholicism as an intellectual tradition confronted Nazism must instead look at the Catholics who became politically active during the 1930s in places far from the Vatican and beyond Hitler's reach, above all in Vienna, but also in Salzburg, Lucerne, Basel, and Paris and along the German border in Alsace, Polish Upper Silesia, and the Netherlands. These Catholics, mostly German émigrés, mined Christian thought as well as modern science for arguments that would upset the intellectual bases of Nazi rule. Their most immediate enemies were not Nazis but rather other Catholics drawn to Nazism, such as Bishop Alois Hudal and the major Catholic publisher Joseph Eberle, whose racist ideas were viewed as urgent challenges because they risked hollowing out the faith from within and because they appealed to German Catholics, among whom nationalism tinged with racism was rampant.

Against attempts of Catholics like Hudal and Eberle to build intellectual bridges to the Nazis, the émigrés argued that Catholicism and

Nazism were incompatible. The former taught salvation of all human beings through a Gospel of love, the latter the elevation of one *Volk* over all
others. In the white heat of this internal Catholic dispute we see the begin-
nings of the new teaching about the Jews promulgated by Paul VI in 1965.
Yet given the Vatican's equivocal language on race and its silence about the
Jews in this period, these émigrés worked out their arguments with little
guidance from above. In 1935, Vatican Secretary of State Pacelli confided
to Dietrich von Hildebrand that he hoped moderate strains in Nazism
might win out.[1] Hildebrand replied that moderate Nazism did not exist.
Two years later, members of the Roman Curia were debating whether to
join the Fascist Bloc—a move Pacelli considered potentially "useful."[2]
Johannes Oesterreicher or Dietrich von Hildebrand never saw any usefulness in Nazism. The latter found it so corrupting that he imagined alli-
ances with virtually everyone—including the left—as worth exploring.
That was an extraordinary position for a Catholic to take in starkly polar-
ized politics of the 1930s.

Following the German occupation of Austria in 1938, the center of gravity of Catholic opposition to Nazi racism began to shift westward from
Austria and Switzerland as Dietrich von Hildebrand, Johannes Oesterreicher, and Waldemar Gurian joined thousands of Central European
thinkers seeking refuge first in Paris, then in New York City. After the
war, with intercontinental communications reestablished, the debates of
small groups of Catholic intellectuals continued and developed, connecting Central Europe to the United States in a special way, linking an argument about anti-racism to one about tolerance. America was perhaps the
one place in the Catholic world where the word "tolerance" was not exclusively pejorative.

But the world within which intellectual resistance to racism took root
and flourished was culturally German. Just as German-speaking Europe
produced a racist syndrome challenging Catholic universalism so it generated a response through a campaign of anti-racism. The story of its
evolution defies expectations we might have for Catholic opposition to
Nazi antisemitism. For one thing, opposition to racism did not lead directly to a refutation of antisemitism because it did not explain why Nazi
racism had focused on the Jews. The Jews were not a race, after all, even
anthropologists admitted as much. In addition, this German Catholic opposition to Nazism was especially strong in Austria, usually not considered

part of Germany. And finally, the political order from which it gathered strength was not a bulwark of liberalism, like France or Great Britain, but the anti-liberal corporatism of Engelbert Dollfuss and Kurt von Schuschnigg that historians call "Austrofascist." How could a fascist state produce opposition to racism?

Anti-Racism and Anti-Nazism

Jews like Hugo Iltis believed that anti-racism would naturally translate into opposition to antisemitism because they understood modern antisemitism as a kind of racism. Catholics who opposed racism—like Johannes Oesterreicher—tended to agree, but they had the problem of specifying the relation between modern antisemitism and the traditional Christian beliefs about Jews that we now call anti-Judaism. To what extent did a renunciation of racism imply a renunciation of that ancient legacy of contempt based in the Jews' rejection of Christ as Messiah? And contrariwise: to what extent was modern antisemitism bolstered by anti-Judaism?[3] Many Christians claimed that they practiced a "moderate antisemitism" in order to nullify the spiritual dangers that emanated from Jews, and that this "purely religious" discrimination was qualitatively distinct from modern racial antisemitism. By 1940, Johannes Oesterreicher forcefully rejected the possibility of "moderate" antisemitism, but this point of view took years to consolidate in the émigrés' writing, and was not evident to many other Catholics who attempted to oppose racist antisemitism in the early 1930s. If God had placed Jews under a curse, then did not the Church have to protect the faithful from them through some kind of discrimination?

We see the difficulty Christians had in specifying the relation between antisemitism and anti-Judaism in an effort the Vatican undertook to condemn racism and modern antisemitism in 1938. This was the so-called lost or hidden encyclical, commissioned by Pius XI but never issued after he died in February 1939. Its drafting followed years of debate within Vatican walls about how to respond to the challenge of Nazi "neo-paganism" which officials feared might uproot Christianity from Central Europe. In Germany, the government was shutting down Catholic youth groups and gaining uninhibited access to young people's minds. It was true that Pius XI had spoken out against antisemitism in 1928, but he had done so after banning a group in the church that worked for improved relations between Catholics and Jews. This group, formed in 1925 by two Dutch priests and the Dutch convert Maria Francesca Van Leer, called itself "Amici Israel," and demanded an end to affronts to Jews, such as the Good Friday prayer that called them "perfidious."[4] By 1928, this association counted as members several thousand priests around the globe, including nineteen cardinals.[5] Its strength alarmed members of the Holy Office, and they recommended suppression.[6] Pius XI followed the recommendation, but then appended a condemnation of antisemitism in order not to seem antisemitic.[7] The public was told only that the group had "adopted a manner of acting and thinking that is contrary to the sense and spirit of the Church."[8]

With the ascent to power of Hitler, Pius received letters from Catholics demanding a clear condemnation of Nazi racism. In April 1933, the Jewish convert Edith Stein (now a saint of the Catholic Church) impatiently addressed the Holy Father. "For weeks now," she wrote, "not only the Jews, but also many thousands of loyal Catholics in Germany—and I believe in the entire world—are waiting for the Church to raise its voice . . . Is not this war of destruction against the Jews a cruel insult to the most holy humanity of our Savior? All of us who are true children of the Church and who see the situation in Germany with eyes fully open, fear the worst for the reputation of the Church if the failure to speak out continues."[9] Two years later, the priest, missionary, and papal biographer Joseph Schmidlin, like Stein a border-crosser later murdered by the Nazis, took pen in hand and wrote a fierce protest to the Vatican, urging Pius to break completely with the Nazis:

> The church has recently been the target of diabolic attacks, dripping with hatred, launched by the German government. They have been increasing in number and cannot leave Your Holiness in any doubt that everything in Nazism and in the neo-pagan camp is preparing for battle.
>
> But people are asking why instead of simple speeches the Church does not move to unequivocal actions, for example canceling the Concordat, which the Nazis have broken a hundred times . . . what damage this feeble appeasement is causing us, which lulls our friends to sleep and emboldens our enemies![10]

The Roman Curia was not deaf to these pleas and studied how to make a response. But it moved slowly. By 1938, the text for an encyclical was ready, but because of the pope's death in February 1939 and his successor's policies of appeasement, it was never issued. Both critics and defenders of the church regard this lost text as a missed opportunity for the church to condemn racial hatred as well as antisemitism, and it was much anticipated at the time. Johannes Oesterreicher grew lyrical at rumors swirling in Paris after New Year's 1939, and wrote to encourage his friend Karl Thieme. According to French newspapers, "the Holy Father, troubled by the pressure Hitler is exerting upon Europe, has spelled out his policies in a new encyclical addressed to all the Catholic bishops of the world, in which he underscores the church's opposition to the new Nazi paganism, which will be officially condemned and placed on a par with Bolshevik atheism. The encyclical will also denounce the persecutions against the Jews and the laws on racism that have been passed by totalitarian countries."[11]

Within weeks, Pius XI was dead and the initiative stashed away in Vatican archives. Yet the drafts that have recently surfaced suggest that the encyclical's suppression was not such a bad thing. Had it been issued, the pope would have reinforced traditional anti-Judaism, and in the pervasive racism of that day, that meant bolstering antisemitism. One could not shun the Jews "religiously" without marginalizing actual Jewish human beings. But the draft was not entirely the work of the pope. As was the case with most encyclicals, he had not produced the original text. In early 1938, alarmed at the turn to racism by Italian fascists, the Pontiff had begun reading everything he could on the subject, and came upon the book *Interracial Justice* by American Jesuit John LaFarge. In June of that year, LaFarge fortuitously visited Rome, and the pope asked him to draft an encyclical against racism during a hastily arranged audience.[12]

John LaFarge, son of the eminent stained-glass painter of the same name, had grown up amongst Boston Brahmins and been educated at Harvard and Innsbruck before going off to work with African American Catholics in Maryland and then at important positions in the Catholic publishing world, where he became the American church's most prominent opponent of racism. Yet he felt inadequate to the task the pope had requested of him. Jesuit General Włodimierz Ledóchowski therefore arranged for the assistance of two confreres with greater expertise, the French Gustave Desbuquois and the German Gustav Gundlach. The latter, a prominent authority on Catholic social teaching, drafter of the encyclical *Quadragesimo Anno* (1931), and author of the entry on antisemitism in the German Catholic encyclopedia, was thought to tower above LaFarge in intellectual capacity, yet his contribution falls far behind the Catholic critiques of racism we have already encountered.[13] Gundlach failed to argue consistently either in terms of science or morals, in part because he—like other prominent German Catholics—succumbed to the temptation to translate ancient Christian stereotypes about Jews into the language of the racist age.

Gundlach contended that only the church properly understood the Jewish question, because this was a question of religion and not of race. But as a modern theologian he—like the racists—drew conclusions not from scripture but from history perceived through modern Catholic lenses. Who were the Jews? They were a "basic human group" who had "gambled away their exalted historical calling once and for all" and been separated by an "immovable boundary" from the rest of humanity. By turning "against their own blood and calling vengeance upon themselves and their children," Jews had sacrificed their "communal life as a race."[14] Thus, the Jews were a race after all, and through the ages the church had permitted the Jews to survive in segregation in order to remind Christians what happened to those who "abandoned the gift of the grace of true faith."[15] Nothing short of mass conversion could solve the "Jewish problem."[16] He claimed to oppose all discrimination directed against Jews, but rather than consider how the church might ameliorate the lot of victims of racism—which after all was supposed to be the critical focus in the encyclical—Gundlach dwelt upon the church's own victimization.[17] "No one," he proclaimed, "has suffered more from this Christian-Jewish indifferentism in this and the last century than the Church itself."

Sobering as Gundlach's descent was from anti-Judaism to racism, less edifying still were the contributions of John LaFarge, who spent much of his life advocating the rights of African Americans victimized by discrimination. Yet when he turned to Catholic writings on the Jews, LaFarge drew upon the same anti-Judaic tradition as Gundlach and like him read it through the *Geschichtstheologie* (historical theology) of the racist age.

The basic "fact" was that Jews were a chosen people who had refused their calling, "blinded by a vision of material domination and gain."[18] As a result,

> this unhappy people, destroyers of their own nation, whose misguided leaders had called down upon their own heads a divine malediction, doomed, as it were, to perpetually wander over the face of the earth, were nonetheless never allowed to perish, but have been preserved through the ages into our own time. No natural reason appears . . . to explain . . . this indestructible coherence.

One purpose of the Jews' survival was to remind Christians "who live in presumption and blind self-confidence [that they] can perfectly well share the unhappy lot of the fallen branches."[19] "Fallen branches" was a reference to St. Paul's notion of the Jews having been the trunk of the olive tree from which the New Israel of the church had grown. In contrast to Gundlach, LaFarge noted that "Israel remains the chosen people," and when Jews did "come back to Christ," either as individuals or as people, they would "find themselves wholly at home in their own house, more than any other people in the world."[20] But until that day, Jews and Christians had to be segregated, for the church could not be blind to the "spiritual dangers to which contact with Jews can expose souls, or to make her unaware of the need to safeguard her children against spiritual contagion . . . The Church has warned against an over-familiarity with the Jewish community that might lead to customs and ways of thinking contrary to the standards of Christian life."[21] To readers of such lines in 1939, Jews would have seemed carriers of illness to be shunned at all costs. Forced emigration would have seemed the logical prescription.

LaFarge did not see himself as an antisemite, and he warned against the evils of antisemitism, which he understood as involving actions rather than attitudes. The church condemned "persecutory methods" in order to "preserve faith and morals of her members."[22] He cited the 1928 papal condemnation of antisemitism as directed against "hatred," but argued not in terms of a command to love Jews as neighbors, but rather in terms of their utility in a Christian view of history. "History's long experience," LaFarge wrote, "has repeatedly shown that persecution, instead of obliterating or lessening the harmful or anti-social traits of a persecuted group, merely intensifies the tendencies that gave rise to them."[23] Antisemitism might redound to the harm of Christianity, becoming "an excuse for attacking the sacred Person of the Savior Himself." "Those who suffer injustice themselves," he continued, "not infrequently become the devotees of injustice. Their bitter resentment against their own pitiable condition leads them to wreak or attempt to wreak their vengeance upon those who appear to enjoy a more fortunate position."[24] Even as victims Jews were a danger.

Perhaps Pius XII chose not to publish these words because they would have frozen antisemitism into the teachings of the church. Scholars have described him as a careful strategist, with a predilection for diplomacy.[25] Yet had he ventured forth on his own with a bold initiative, it is not clear what language he would have used. Neither he nor his predecessor had independent expertise. At the beginning of their deliberations on Nazi racism in 1934, Pius and his state secretary Pacelli regarded the titular Bishop Alois Hudal—later infamous for smuggling Nazi war criminals out of Europe—as a source of enlightenment on the race question. By 1936, Hudal had disappointed them as an avid bridge-builder to Nazism. LaFarge must have seemed a godsend when he surfaced in Rome two years later. Yet he too possessed no transcendent insights. Similar to Gundlach, when LaFarge attempted to refute racist antisemitism from within standard Christian understandings of the Jews, he found himself entangled in a web of anti-Judaic assumptions, and powerless to undo the prejudices of modern antisemitism.

Meanwhile, north of the Alps, Johannes Oesterreicher and his comrades in Vienna, Basel, and Paris were scouring the Catholic tradition and modern science to find arguments against racism. They did not suddenly jump ahead to insights proclaimed by the church in the 1960s, and in many ways they remained mired in the same anti-Judaic view of history we see in Fathers Gundlach and LaFarge. For them, Jews continued to be deficient, destined to suffer divine punishment until they turned to Christ. Yet because many of these émigrés were of Jewish origin, racism—even implicit—was not an option. And because they lived in the shadow of Nazi Germany, ignorance was also not an option. They knew well the trajectory of Nazi racism from refugees crossing the border, but also from their own families. Adding to this existential sensitivity were the racist ideas entering their own Catholic world, compelling them to contend with Nazis and would-be Nazis for cultural influence in their own cafés, parishes, salons, government offices, and academic institutions. These circumstances made the arguments between racists and their opponents more direct and serious than elsewhere.

They could also be quite violent, for example when Hildebrand and his friends portrayed church dignitaries as traitors to the faith. For this and similar indignities the émigrés were portrayed as upstarts who exploded the cozy insularity of Viennese Catholicism. Yet rather than be ostracized, the newcomers (though always fully orthodox) sought allies beyond the boundaries of the church. By 1934, Catholic émigrés in Austria were practicing ecumenism in a time when ecumenism was viewed with deep disfavor in the Vatican.[26] The list of Jewish and Christian authors published by Dietrich von Hildebrand and other anti-Nazis included Martin Buber, later management guru Peter Drucker, historian Felix Gilbert, novelist Joseph Roth, philosopher Hans-Joachim Schoeps (who wrote anonymously for Johannes Oesterreicher), the Orthodox philosophers Nicolas Berdyaev and Vladimir Solovyov, the Protestant Karl Barth, and very many lesser known figures. This early Catholic ecumenism anticipated a question that hovered over the deliberations at the Second Vatican Council: to what extent should the church draw upon tradition or scripture as it sought inspiration to move forward in the modern world?

Dietrich von Hildebrand, the most influential figure of the Catholic emigration, perfectly captures the émigré personality as it contemplated this choice. As a person with a Jewish grandmother, who grew up in a cosmopolitan artists' home in Florence and Munich, he was not tempted by racism. As a former Protestant, he thought it natural that Christians should respond to racist Christianity by turning to scripture *and reading it for themselves.* Yet independent forays into original sources had the potential to unsettle Catholicism at its deepest moorings, and Hildebrand projected his views as in perfect accord with the teachings of Rome. He knew top church officials like Pacelli intimately and was happy to conclude his condemnations of racism with the old formula *"Roma locuta est, causa finita est!"* The problem was that Rome rarely spoke out, and the Catholic cause in an Austria, dominated by German nationalists, often seemed lost.

Austrofascism as a Platform for Anti-racism

If the struggle that took place in Vienna of the 1930s prefigures postwar dilemmas about change within the church in some ways, in one way it does not: this struggle was launched from a state we know as fascist, more precisely, Austrofascist. One expert has called the Austrofascism of Engelbert Dollfuss one of three genuinely fascist regimes to seize power anywhere in the world in those years. Yet after World War II, fascism was passé. Among other things, it had generated extreme national chauvinism, including racism. We would have expected Catholic anti-racism to emerge from a free country like France with its strong Catholic intellectual traditions, or from Hungary and Poland where the regimes were authoritarian but did not strive for the total reorientation of society we associate with fascism.

Yet if we look at the map of Europe in the 1930s, Austria was clearly the point from which new energies propelled innovation in Catholic thought. The first systematic Catholic critique of antisemitism in history appeared in Vienna in 1937. By that point, readers examining Vienna's newsstands could find four Catholic journals opposing Nazism: Irene Harand's *Gerechtigkeit* [Justice], Dietrich von Hildebrand's *Der Christliche Ständestaat* [The Christian Corporatist State], Ernst Karl Winter's *Wiener Politische Blätter* [Viennese Political News], and Johannes Oesterreicher's *Die Erfüllung* [Fulfillment]. Harand targeted broad audiences of Christians and Jews while Hildebrand and Winter focused on the Catholic elite. Oesterreicher hoped to inform Christians and Jews about Christian-Jewish relations, but also to interest Jews in Catholicism.

Austria of the mid-1930s lacked none of the fascist trappings: the charismatic if small dictator Dollfuss had crushed democracy and sent political opponents to concentration camps. He was called "Führer" and proclaimed himself anti-liberal while donning military uniforms beneath a Tyrolean feather cap. Carried to power by self-described fascist paramilitary units funded by Mussolini, Dollfuss created a national unity front as well as a constitution modeled on the Italian fascist variant, emphasizing "corporatism."[27] Yet in one important way Austrofascism defies expectations. According to sociologist Michael Mann, fascism involves extreme nationalism, yet Austria had two fascist movements competing for the

same nation. For one of them, Adolf Hitler's Nazism, Austrians were ethnic Germans, and "Austria" did not exist; while for the other, Dollfuss's
Austrofascists, Austrians were a German tribe, constituting not a racial
but a political entity following the tradition of the Habsburgs. The Austrofascists paid lip service to the idea of *Anschluss*, (the political union of Austria and Germany) but, as Nazi Germany increasingly revealed itself as
anti-clerical and totalitarian, many Austrians imagined Austria as a state
with a special mission in southeastern Europe. In fact, Austrofascism—far
from openly espousing racism—was not even nationalist, let alone involved
in missions of "national cleansing."[28]

As for "paramilitarism"—another of Michael Mann's criteria for
fascism—Austria indeed had right-wing militias that formed after World
War I to put down revolution. By the late 1920s they had solidified into an
anti-democratic movement. Some of their members called themselves
"fascist" and wanted to make common cause with the Nazis. Prince Ernst
Rüdiger von Starhemberg, their most visible leader, ominously spoke of
the "Jewish-Marxist betrayers of the workers" and promised to "fight on
to victory even at the cost of a few Asiatic heads rolling in the sand."[29] Yet
Starhemberg had a choice: either to band with the Nazis, who indeed
would have sent heads rolling—perhaps his own, or with the Christian
Socials who needed Heimwehr support to build a stable coalition. He
chose the latter, and entered Christian Social governments in 1930 and in
1932. After the civil war of February 1934, he advanced to vice-chancellor
and took an important role in building the supposedly fascist "Fatherland
Front," which fell under his leadership.

During the civil war, Starhemberg's militia helped crush the socialist
Schutzbund, thus providing Dollfuss with the "bottom-up" violence that
fascist movements require. Yet after that, the paramilitaries fell into dis-
use, and in 1936 were quietly folded into the government's Fatherland
Front. Despite calls from the base for a "putsch," Starhemberg acceded to
his organization's destruction and resigned from the cabinet of Kurt von
Schuschnigg, the businesslike Catholic conservative who assumed power
after Dollfuss was assassinated. If Starhemberg was interested in "party
life," it was of the festive sort: he had to be summoned from the exclusive
Kobenzl Bar in the wine hills above Vienna to be informed of his own
dismissal.[30] The Austrofascist Schuschnigg did not put this rival up

against a wall but rather offered him work as plenipotentiary for child welfare ("*Protektor des Mutterschutzwerkes der Volksfront*"), a role the Prince enjoyed. He had just had a child of his own with the Austrian Jewish actress Nora Gregor, who later, when both were in exile from the Nazis in Paris, starred in Jean Renoir's *Rules of the Game*, which critiqued a decadent society on the verge of fascism.[31] In the fall of that year, the Prince climbed into the cockpit of a fighter plane to fly missions against Nazi Germany.

Starhemberg signals a further difficulty with standard ideas of fascism applied to Austria. Without a heroicized figure to serve as the central font of knowledge and charisma, someone hungry for and able to wield power, fascism remains only energy and idea. Starhemberg was not interested in ruling. He possessed the charm and popularity, bold daring, and connections to have seized power more than once. Whether one considers him a bon-vivant playboy or anti-Nazi devoted to the people of Austria, the fact remains that he lacked a consuming desire for self-assertion.[32]

Starhemberg's example tells us that Austrofascism was about contradictory forces that produced change, including evolving insights on the nature of fascism. Starhemberg learned what the word meant by watching what the Nazis made of it. By 1938, fascism meant racism, and Mussolini fell in step by aping Germany's Nuremberg laws of three years earlier. At the same time, the word "totalitarian" emerged to describe something new in the regimes of Hitler, Mussolini, and Stalin. But Austria's leaders never aspired to total rule. Though they adopted fascist forms—the Fatherland Front had a forced greeting (*Front Heil!*), banners, uniforms, mass rallies, membership cards, and dues—their regime came increasingly to resemble the authoritarian states that dotted the region, evidently lacking fascism's revolutionary dynamism.[33] Austrofascism moved not toward revolution but toward "a more uniform bureaucratic authoritarianism," evolving into a conservative caretaker regime, a development cut short by the German invasion of 1938.[34]

Austrofascism was an epithet used against Dollfuss by his enemies to the left, and many reject the term as vilifying and inaccurate. Still, critics and defenders agree that Austrofascism denotes the regime led by Dollfuss and Schuschnigg. Its contradictions propelled an increasingly radical parting of the ways after 1935. If Starhemberg and Dietrich von Hildebrand moved toward the political center, others on the Christian Socialist right, sensing the pro-Hitler mood among compatriots, evolved toward radical nationalism, though logic of state kept them from openly embracing Nazism as that meant the end of Austria.

Because Nazism was racism, some interpreted Austrofascism as involving hostility to racism and ethnic nationalism. In Austrofascist Vienna there was no limit to how far one might push arguments against racism, and anti-racism became a kind of political correctness, reflected in the 1934 census which forbade counting by race.[35] Before the *Anschluss* of March 1938, the Natural History Museum in Vienna rejected entreaties to hold a "Jewish exhibition" with the argument that "Jews are not a race."[36] Austrofascist officials rebuffed efforts of the Nazified Austrian anthropological community to interest them in questions of racial biology.[37] Lamenting the regime's hostility to racial doctrine, the Viennese Society for Racial Hygiene refused to join the Fatherland Front in 1935, and instead became the Viennese Chapter of the German Society for Racial Hygiene—in effect a cover organization for the Austrian Nazis.[38] After the Nazis consolidated power in 1938, their leader Alois Scholz called Austrofascism a time of oppression.[39]

Not coincidentally, the Austrofascists' godfather, Monsignor Ignaz Seipel, had written at length on the national question, asserting that Austrians uniquely intuited the difference between state and nation.[40] In the mind of Engelbert Dollfuss, tiny Austria continued to bear the multinational mission of the Habsburgs, who had intended their state to be a beacon radiating multinational culture to eastern and southeastern Europe. Landlocked Austria was in reality unbounded; and if it was German, it was also more than German. A renewed federal Austria would resurrect the Habsburg community of fate by peacefully uniting Slavs, Romanians, and Magyars with Germans.

But these sentiments stood against other equally urgent sentiments. Austrofascists could not escape a Christian Socialist past where political success built upon the antisemitism of the middle classes; indeed, competition with Nazi Germany to be the more truly German state tempered critiques of racism. If they seemed philo-Semitic or anti-German, Austrofascists risked losing support to Austrian Nazis, even if the Nazi party was illegal in Austria. This tension marked the work of Austro-Catholics.

Against the efforts of Dietrich von Hildebrand to undermine racism stood the concern of the Viennese Jesuit preacher Georg Bichlmair that the church not leave itself defenseless against nationalism. Within Austrofascism there was also space for Catholic Judeophobia, and if neither Dollfuss, Schuschnigg, nor Starhemberg were antisemites, close to them stood Viennese Vice-Mayor Josef Kresse and union leader Leopold Kunschak, both visceral haters of Jews, with organizations full of boastful antisemites, prolonging legacies of Christian Socialism.[41]

Western journalists hardly knew what to make of Austrofascism. Two of the most astute, Shepard Stone of the *New York Times* and G. E. R. Gedye of the London *Times* castigated Dollfuss's regime as fascist.[42] Yet the first American journalist expelled from Hitler's Germany, the polyglot sophisticate Dorothy Thompson—who reputedly socked another woman for making pro-fascist remarks—considered Austrian leader Kurt von Schuschnigg a hero in the struggle against fascism. In her introduction to Schuschnigg's *My Austria*, Thompson took Austria's mission to involve "bringing together various nationalities, their civilizations and languages, for the purpose of achieving political and economic welfare." For these ends, Schuschnigg wrote, "not force, not the instruments of war, but rather the spirit and work of culture discharge the task of the mediator." The tasks facing Austria could "never be discharged by a power, living under a system of ideas so exclusive, so atomizing and explosive, as German racialism."[43] By the time Thompson's book appeared, Schuschnigg was languishing in a Nazi camp.

Whatever it was, Austrofascism became a staging ground for the most violent clash on the European right about politics adequate to the time—with arguments for racism deriving from Christian Social antisemitism as well as mass sympathies for Hitler, and arguments against it building on revulsion over news from Nazi Germany as well as hope for an alternative befitting a Catholic Austria, most eloquently expressed by non-Austrian émigrés. Austrofascism was destined to bring forth new Catholic insights on Jews and race because its survival depended upon seeming non-Nazi— therefore anti-racist—while successfully competing with the Nazis on the platform of German nationalism. Both tendencies could flourish within a "Christian corporatist" state that vowed to realize Catholic social principles, probably more fervently than any regime in Europe.[44] In this context, racists and anti-racists, Catholics, Jews, and atheists profited by associating their arguments with Catholicism. These arguments were open-ended because Catholicism had not answered basic questions about race or how it related to the status of the Jewish people.

Recovering Saint Paul

The layout of central Vienna predestined unplanned encounters, with streets and alleys lazily converging upon public squares and their popular cafés, places where would-be opinion makers and their associates gathered for lunch and gossip. People who refused to speak with each other were constantly crossing paths, and nothing remained secret for long. When handfuls of exiles began trickling in from Nazi Germany in 1933, the routines of this cozy place were suddenly disturbed. Under the looming threat of its northern neighbor, Austrofascist Vienna slowly transformed into a camp under siege, an increasingly claustrophobic space where one could escape neither enemies nor the unpleasant questions they might pose.

Prominent among the newcomers was the Munich philosophy professor Dietrich von Hildebrand, son of Adolf von Hildebrand, a cosmopolite sculptor who designed monumental fountains in Munich while dividing time between his villa there and the former convent San Francesco di Paola in Florence. Hitler, who had lived in Munich on the eve of World War I, called Adolf von Hildebrand his favorite sculptor. He did not know of the artist's Jewish mother. The Nazi leader grew to despise Adolf von Hildebrand's son Dietrich, whom he called a "pest" [Schädling] who should be "eliminated."[45] Hitler knew about Hildebrand junior from reports written by his ambassador to Austria, Franz von Papen—a Catholic who thought that Christianity could be reconciled with Nazism. Other Catholic bridge builders to Nazism, such as editor Joseph Eberle and Bishop Alois Hudal, joined von Papen in lamenting the unsettling effects Dietrich von Hildebrand and his band of émigrés had upon the traditional anti-semitism of Vienna.

Benedict XVI has described Hildebrand as "most prominent" among the intellectual figures of modern Catholicism, and Pius XII called him "Church Doctor of the Twentieth Century." He has become a favorite of the Catholic right. Yet conservatives of his day reviled Dietrich von Hildebrand for his opposition to nationalism and for the unsettling questions he posed about age-old institutions such as marriage. As the first major Catholic thinker in history, he contended that "'the act of wedded communion has the end of propagation but in addition, the significance of a unique union of love.'"[46] Yet this cosmopolitan advocate of peace and love also confounds expectations held on the left: though no one outdid him in opposition to Nazism, Hildebrand questioned liberal democracy and had positive things to say about Mussolini, Dollfuss, and Starhemberg—whom he preferred to Schuschnigg.

The ideological latitude of Austrofascism provided Hildebrand with excellent conditions to develop his ideas, but he did so from a trajectory well established by 1933. Above all, he was concerned to protect the "human person" against the depravations of the modern nation state. In 1921, he followed a handful of German Catholic intellectuals, including the peace activists Franziskus Stratmann OP, and Max Josef Metzger (who later baptized Johannes Oesterreicher), to Paris at the summons of Marc Sangnier, founder of the progressive Catholic Sillon movement, which was dedicated to workers' rights and international peace and an important part of the French reaction to antisemitism.[47] Deepening his contacts to French Catholics in the following decade, especially the circles around Jacques Maritain, Hildebrand acted as a conduit to the Austrians for impulses from French Catholic thought on the Jews—especially the ideas of Maritain's godfather Léon Bloy—while at the same time transmitting innovations from German Catholicism, where Erik Peterson was building upon the revolutionary ideas of Bloy.[48] At the meeting with Sangnier Hildebrand he revealed the depths of his hatred of nationalism, doing something unthinkable even for moderate Germans, including socialists: blaming Germany for the Great War, and calling the attack on Belgium an "atrocious crime."[49] Upon his return to Munich, Hildebrand was branded a traitor, and two years later he evaded a Nazi assassination squad during the "Beer Hall Putsch."[50]

In 1928, Hildebrand refined his critique of nationalism in response to a piece by fellow Catholic Carl Schmitt, arguing for the paramount value of the "person," followed by collectivities such as family, church, diocese, and parish—and only after them, the nation. Far from being "perfect societies" (as Aquinas had claimed), states had no independent worth. They had the right to exist, but this right did not lie "at a higher level than the right of the individual human being to his earthly life." Confronting sacrosanct scholastic political philosophy, Hildebrand rejected the idea that states might be considered equivalent to the whole of the humans who lived in their boundaries. States came and went, and had value only insofar as they "served humanity."[51] The early death of Beethoven or Goethe would have been an "incomparably greater evil" than the demise of the rotting Holy Roman Empire in 1803. The same was true of national communities (*Volksgemeinschaften*). A person's death might cut off his potential to save eternal souls, but "values of this order are never impinged by the life or death of an individual *Volksgemeinschaft*."[52] Such ideas were extraordinary in a place where Hegel's apotheosizing of the state pervaded thought of right and left, and where Catholic theologians turning to Patristics or the well-ordered schemes of Aquinas found little to refute the arguments of nationalists.

Hildebrand reaffirmed his outsider position shortly before Hitler's ascent to power when, as the lone intellectual of repute, he challenged the wholistic nationalism of leading Austrian Catholic Othmar Spann at meetings of Germany's Catholic Academic Union.[53] Beyond Hildebrand, the only other intellectual resistance to the anti-liberal mainstream of German Catholic thought came from the left-liberal authors of the *Rhein-Mainische Volkszeitung* in Frankfurt. For the majority of Catholic intellectuals young and old, however, individual rights held no intrinsic value.

Hildebrand's followers trace his personalism to philosophical training in the phenomenological school of Edmund Husserl—who awarded Hildebrand *summa cum laude* for his dissertation on the "Idea of a Moral Act"—as well as to his close friendship with the "Catholic Nietzsche" Max Scheler. In response to popular communal tendencies, Scheler had posited the "person" as a category possessing its own being, a "prototype of substance," theologically the image of God.[54] Yet prior to philosophy came Hildebrand's upbringing on both sides of borders: between northern and southern Europe, between Catholicism and Protestantism, and between Italic and Germanic cultures. He spent his young years in lavishly appointed villas, surrounded by a Jewish grandmother and agnostic Protestant father and siblings, learning never to feel many kinds of foreignness as foreign. The man who matured into a prominent Catholic philosopher was unthinkable without the rights accorded to him as a human person to develop according to whim and desire, against all provincialism let alone the demands of modern states or national movements. Hildebrand fiercely defended his ideas. Joseph Ratzinger, who knew Hildebrand from southern German parish life, recalled stories of violent arguments that fourteen-year-old Hildebrand had with his sister and father against the proposition that "moral values are relative . . . completely determined by our circumstances."[55] Although stubborn, Hildebrand was not severe, and he always showed interest in new thought. He had the elation of spirit that one finds among the pious and manifested his independence in Austrofascist Vienna with blithe disregard for his personal safety, despite threats from the Nazi underground.[56]

On a Saturday morning in the fall of 1933, Hildebrand visited Engelbert Dollfuss in the chancellor's private quarters. Both were interested in the ideological direction of the new Austrian state, and they chatted for half an hour before the chancellor was called for an outing in the countryside with his wife and two children. Hildebrand's abandonment of a tenured position at Munich just months earlier suggested to Dollfuss a more general "solution" to the intellectual problems confronting corporatist Austria and Nazi Germany: the two rival states should exchange professors. Nothing came of this idea, but Dollfuss did bless Hildebrand's plan to found a journal to argue in favor of a Catholic Austria and against National Socialism.[57]

Early columns in this journal—*Der Christliche Ständestaat*—denounced well-known Nazi collaborators such as Franz von Papen, Martin Heidegger, and Carl Schmitt, but Hildebrand's associate Klaus Dohrn also directed attention to lesser known brown Catholics such as theologians Joseph Lortz and Karl Eschweiler.[58] At this point, however, the approach of Hildebrand and his friends to the conflict with Nazism was more intuitive than carefully reasoned. Dohrn—after the war an advisor to Henry Luce of Time/Life, with easy access to the offices of Konrad Adenauer—had felt aesthetic and moral revulsion from personal encounters with storm troopers in Germany, but he was unable to specify why Lortz or Eschweiler promoted Nazi ideology, and simply recommended "deeper study."[59] Similarly, the attraction the younger generation felt for Nazi and illiberal icons like Othmar Spann was often emotional and difficult to counter with reasoned argument. The Austrian Franciscan Zyrill Fischer tried to refute Nazism in a pioneering brochure of 1932, but failed to specify what distinguished Nazi from non-Nazi thought. He ridiculed Alfred Rosenberg's *Myth of the Twentieth Century*, but he expected Catholic readers to sense the incompatibilities on their own. To Rosenberg's idea that the humiliated Christ should be replaced with a spear-carrying god, Father Fischer pleaded simply: "Is that not too much?"[60]

The threat of racism focused the minds on Hildebrand's staff, however, especially when they saw its flames jumping the firewalls of Catholic teaching and entering their own camp. In December 1933, Father Wilhelm Schmidt, the century's leading Catholic anthropologist, told an audience in Vienna that a "perversion of the Jews' inner being," was "punishment" for killing Christ. "Two thousand years have had a psychological effect on [Jews'] being," intoned Schmidt, and that could not be "undone by baptism."[61] To refute such ideas, Hildebrand chose the Jesuit theologian Ferdinand Frodl, who, as Hildebrand later recalled, understood the "absolute unchristianity" of antisemitism, "something that even the opponents of Nazism in Austria did not always comprehend." Frodl's article "Nazi Bacillus in the Baptismal Font" appeared in the edition of December 17, 1933.[62]

Though he lacked formal training in biology, Frodl took on the famous anthropologist with skepticism based in science, thus revealing the crucial importance as well as the ultimate insignificance of scientific expertise.[63] "Nothing can be said about the gifts possessed by varying races," he wrote, "because we know nothing at all about the extent to which biophysical racial characteristics relate to psychic peculiarities." For Frodl, such epistemic uncertainty extended to the idea of "people." What held the Jews together was unclear, and therefore the "Jewish question" remained open, resistant to simple clarification. The indistinctness of "race" and "people" suggested the untenability of any generalizations about Jews.[64]

So far, these ideas were in keeping with the Catholic critiques we have seen. Frodl broke new ground by tapping the Bible for its abundant racialist metaphors—like blood, seed, flesh, root, grafting, stock, nature, tribe, and kin—and using them against the racists. In his letter to the Romans, St. Paul emphasized two facts: the cohesion of the Jews as a people existing through history, and the special favor the Jews enjoyed with God regardless of their rejection of Christ. Comparing an olive tree to the people of God, Paul had likened Israel to the root (Romans 11). Whereas Christians had to be grafted on as "wild branches," Jews would be "grafted onto their own olive tree" when they turned to Christ.[65] The most "natural" Christians were therefore Jewish Christians. Frodl lightly ridiculed Schmidt's un-Christian statements: "According to Father Schmidt," he wrote, "we from the wild olive tree are in a better situation." If Schmidt or anyone else invoked the ideas of race and *Volkstum*, then Jews *had* to be seen as especially suited for Christianity. Frodl had begun to unlock the potential of the Apostle Paul, racialist *avant la lettre*, to refute Christian racists of the twentieth century. For Christians there could be no problem with a Jewish "race," however that was understood.

After 1938, the paths of the Fathers Schmidt and Frodl diverged. Schmidt, fired from his teaching post in Vienna, found comfortable refuge in Fribourg, Switzerland, while Frodl maintained his professorship in Klagenfurt and got drawn into anti-Nazi conspiracies, despite concerns about his collaborators' amateurism. In 1944, the *Volksgerichtshof* convicted Frodl to three years prison for failing to report the anti-state activity he knew about to the authorities. His co-conspirators went to the guillotine.[66]

In the spring of 1934, a second article appeared in Hildebrand's *Der Christliche Ständestaat* that continued breaking open the ground Frodl had loosened.[67] The title might have seemed a paradox: "religious antisemitism." What was religious about antisemitism if the church had condemned antisemitism, as Pius XI did in 1928? And who had the authority to address the subject? Hildebrand revealed little about his authors. Many were pseudonymous, and this one was identified simply as "A. G. Kraus." Readers would have been surprised to learn that "A." stood for "Annie," that Annie was a Jew from Berlin who had studied philosophy with Husserl, and that she moved in the company of converts like Waldemar Gurian, Erik Peterson, Gertrud von Le Fort, and Dietrich von Hildebrand while acting as secretary to Carl Schmitt. Though Kraus was baptized in 1942—also by the priest who took Johannes Oesterreicher into the church two decades earlier, the martyr Max Metzger—after the war Schmitt still believed that Kraus looked down upon him as a "stupid goy."[68]

In 1934, the not-yet-Catholic Kraus began working out for the church why Catholicism—unlike Protestantism—was "absolutely resistant" to antisemitism. Perhaps her thinking was wishful, but new ideas often begin as wishful thinking. From the early church's vilification of Marcion as heretic, Annie Kraus reasoned that Catholicism could never separate Old from New Testament. The Old was fulfilled in Christ but not abolished. Luther, by contrast, had placed a wall between law and the Gospel, thus inviting believers to denigrate the former. Like the Amici Israel initiative of the 1920s, Kraus stressed Catholicism's Jewishness as a way to protect it from antisemitism. In subsequent issues, Hildebrand published further articles emphasizing the Jewish contribution to the church. In 1935, he printed Karl Rahner's brother Hugo's idea that Catholics had to agree with the Nazis that the church was unalterably "judafied."[69] Yet unlike the Nazis he celebrated this fact. That same year, Hildebrand quoted the (Protestant) convert Theodor Haecker's belief that Judaism was one of the foundations for "the existence of western man."[70]

Though little known in the Anglo-American world, Haecker deeply imprinted the anti-Nazi resistance in Germany with his views on the power of God in history and the human destiny of freedom. Upon attending one of his secret lectures in Munich, Sophie Scholl wrote, "No one has convinced me with the simple gestures of his face as he has."[71] A plaque on Haecker's birth house describes him as "resolute Christian, master of the word." But what attracted Annie Kraus to Catholicism was more deed than word. In her view, its emphasis on good works made Catholicism less potentially antisemitic than Protestantism. She did not doubt that Catholics succumbed to antisemitism, but for Protestants the problem lay in basic principles. Those who thought that faith alone could secure salvation despaired at the possibility of acting, and because they believed that sin transformed humans beyond all hope of effective action they became tempted to racialize Original Sin (Erbsünde). Catholics, by contrast, thought that human freedom permitted humans to repair faults while God remained free to transform human reality through grace. Kraus found the origins of this Catholic disposition in its Judaic heritage, which stressed the active fulfillment of God's will in the law.

Judaism was not simply a religion of the past, however. Like Father Frodl, Annie Kraus discovered in Paul's letter to the Romans signs that Jews still had a role in bringing about salvation. She cited parts of the epistle that soon attracted the attention of Johannes Oesterreicher and his friends. If the Jews' rejection of Christ was salvation for the Gentiles, then what would be the effect of their final entry into the Messianic Kingdom? "Jews are the last hope of the world," Kraus concluded. But that did not mean that Christians should go out and massively convert Jews in order to bring about this end. She saw in proselytizing an attempt "willfully to anticipate the plan of the Almighty, which is hinted at in the letter of Paul to the Romans," only accentuating the proselytizers' poor faith.[72]

If the Jews were the last hope of the world, why did Kraus ultimately convert? We know that other Jews with Christian leanings, like Simone Weil or Franz Werfel, refused to take that step out of solidarity with their people. But she idolized the man who baptized first Johannes Oesterreicher then her, Father Max Josef Metzger, a peace priest in contact with numerous opposition groups who was finally caught and executed in 1944. Hildebrand, who first met Metzger in 1921 in Paris, recalled how "consoling" it has been to know a German priest completely free of "confusion" regarding Nazism.[73] From the moment a deportation order ("to the East") arrived for Kraus in 1942 until Germany's defeat three years later, she took shelter in dozens of hiding places in an odyssey that led from Berlin to northern Italy. Once during this ordeal, the German police arrested Kraus for aiding Russian slave laborers but released her before they discovered her identity.[74] After the war, Kraus worked for Bavarian Radio and corrected manuscripts for Karl Rahner while writing theological studies of *Arrogance* and *Stupidity*, things she knew much about from her environment.[75]

The essay Kraus wrote for Hildebrand summarized views expressed in a much longer study that has survived as a yellowing carbon copy in the papers of John Oesterreicher at Seton Hall University, among the few things he salvaged from his former life while fleeing the Gestapo in 1940. Kraus's essay was important to him because of her thoughts on mission and on Paul's letter to the Romans, but also because of her harsh treatment of Martin Luther. Though Oesterreicher's personal role in promoting this work in the higher chambers of the church later in the century is unquestionable, he was also willing to borrow substantially from anyone whose work he found valuable: above all, fellow converts Dietrich von Hildebrand, Karl Thieme, and Waldemar Gurian.

Oesterreicher and Hildebrand had exchanged a few letters in the 1920s, and they finally met in the fall of 1933. First impressions proved deceiving.

Hildebrand later recalled Oesterreicher as a young priest with a handsome face, of medium height and blond hair. But he was incredibly self-conscious: "one of those people who don't know where to put their arms and legs." The meeting inaugurated a friendship that lasted decades, waning only after Vatican II, when Hildebrand faulted Oesterreicher for losing interest in converting the Jews.[76] As the two became prominent in the Catholic intellectual scene of Vienna, Hildebrand discovered in Oesterreicher a man of "iron will, able to put people under a pressure that they could hardly withstand." Hours after Engelbert Dollfuss was shot by Nazi assassins in July 1934, Oesterreicher insisted that Hildebrand go without delay to Austrian president Wilhelm Miklas and plead that Kurt Schuschnigg become chancellor and not Prince von Starhemberg.[77] Oesterreicher would not relent, and Hildebrand managed to press his way forward and successfully argue the case. Yet given Schuschnigg's mild character (when compared to Starhemberg), Hildebrand later regretted that he had listened to the young priest.

Oesterreicher had been born in February 1904 into the home of the Jewish veterinarian Nathan and his wife Ida in Stadt Liebau, a German language community in northern Moravia at the southern edge of what became known as the Sudetenland. At age ten, he began attending the *Gymnasium* in nearby Olmütz, and it was here that his lifelong interest in Christianity began. One day in 1917 or 1918 young "Hans" Oesterreicher happened upon a thin volume excerpting the Gospels (*Words of Christ*) in a bookstore near school and took the book home, where he read it in secret. Many decades later, he recalled being "captivated by the majesty and gentleness of Christ." The editor of this compilation was Houston Stewart Chamberlain.[78] But Oesterreicher's conversion was not sudden. At this point, he was the elected representative of the Jewish boys at his school and an enthusiastic participant in Zionist scouting, the only member of his group to complete lessons in Hebrew.[79] In 1920, he went to study medicine at Vienna and continued his exploration of Christianity, chiefly through the works of Søren Kierkegaard. It took Cardinal Newman's *Development of Christian Doctrine* to break his skepticism regarding Christian dogma, which he took to be a corruption of the Gospel. Yet decisive for his subsequent path was the priest he happened to hear preaching in Vienna, the great Catholic missionary of ecumenism, pacifism, and temperance, Max

Josef Metzger. In 1924, Metzger baptized Oesterreicher in the sacristy of the gothic cathedral at Graz. Soon Oesterreicher abandoned medical school for the seminary, from which he graduated in 1927, a year ahead of his class (ordination took place in Vienna on July 17). Metzger began familiarizing Oesterreicher with the workings of Catholic publishing, making him editor of his ecumenical journal *Missionsruf* (9,000 subscribers).[80]

By the time Metzger was called back to Germany in 1929, Oesterreicher was working as a priest in Gloggnitz, a town in the mountains south of Vienna where he founded a scout group. His next station was the *Paulanerkirche* in Vienna's fourth district, where he founded groups for girl scouts and continued to draw upon his experience from Zionist youth in Moravia. In 1933, alarmed by the rise of Hitler, he approached one of Vienna's foremost Catholic preachers, the Jesuit Georg Bichlmair, with the idea of publishing a journal on the Jews that would challenge Nazi antisemitism from a Catholic point of view. Work as a priest of Jewish descent had alerted Oesterreicher to the influx of racist ideas among Catholic Austrians. When hearing Oesterreicher's ideas, Bichlmair supposedly responded, "You're a godsend. I always wanted to publish a periodical on the Church and the Jews, but I've never been able to find an editor."[81] Bichlmair and Oesterreicher became *"Duzfreunde"*: sharing intimacy of the informal *"Du,"* something close friends often never achieve, especially if they are intellectuals.[82] Yet two years later Bichlmair plunged Oesterreicher's ministry into its deepest crisis by asserting that Jewish converts were not equal to "Aryans" because of "bad genetic material." Like Father Wilhelm Schmidt's lecture of late 1933, this talk had an electrifying effect on the anti-Nazi émigrés. It also made waves through the international press and caught the attention of Franz von Papen, Nazi legate in Vienna, who called it "sensational" in a report for Hitler.[83] Papen listed this speech along with rallies of the paramilitary wing of the Christian trade unions as evidence that radical nationalist thought was winning over the masses of Austrian Catholics.[84]

The incident was all the more shocking because Bichlmair, a man of learning and science, did not figure among the open antisemites of his day, very unlike the Jew-baiting Austrian priest Gaston Ritter or the shrewd Christian Socialists Anton Orel and Josef Leo Seifert, who hurled racist calumnies at the Jews with little concern for Catholic teaching.[85]

Bichlmair, by contrast, carefully weighed his words for their orthodoxy, and the Jewish community felt scandalized precisely because he had seemed moderate, indeed critical of Nazism; in 1932, the National Socialist Press had attacked Bichlmair, alleging a "fraternization" between Jesuits and Jews in the wake of a radio address he gave reiterating the Holy See's condemnation of antisemitism from 1928.[86]

If Bichlmair's foray surprised people at the time, it continues to resist efforts at explanation in our day. After the Nazi invasion of Austria in 1938, Johannes Oesterreicher took refuge in Switzerland, leaving Father Bichlmair behind in Vienna where he built an office to aid Austrian Catholics of "non-Aryan" descent, the very group he had spoken against two years earlier. So tireless was Bichlmair in aiding these converts that the Gestapo arrested and deported him to Silesian Beuthen. In 1946, probably buoyed by his reputation as victim, the originally German Bichlmair returned to Vienna and was made the head of the Austrian Jesuit Province, an extraordinary honor.

If we examine the recollections of the Hungarian Jewish convert Aurel Kolnai, whom Bichlmair baptized, we begin to sense why Bichlmair felt compelled to speak out on the "Jewish question." In Vienna of the 1920s and 1930s, Bichlmair functioned as "official Catholic debater with anarchists and other infidels, a stout, jovial, energetic middle-aged man of peasant stock, learned and of wide interests, but thoroughly practical, a man of firm certitudes but ready to ponder counter-arguments."[87] Bichlmair, as much as any German Catholic of that time, wanted to bridge the gap between modernity and the church, and in Austria that meant confronting a nationalist language dominated by National Socialism. His compulsion to protect the church led Bichlmair to address all conceivable questions before all conceivable audiences. For many years pastor to the University of Vienna, Bichlmair also traveled in the Austrian political elite, reaching out to the Socialists (on behalf of Christian Socialists) in 1927, and later smoothing out disputes within the Austrofascist governing coalition.[88]

Bichlmair did not believe that central church authorities had spoken out clearly on the church's relation to the Jews, and he feared Catholics were unnecessarily ceding ground to modern nationalism. Aiming to protect the church and the immortal souls of uncounted Austrians and Germans, Bichlmair prepared a lengthy talk for Austria's Catholic Action that was reprinted in a popular brochure entitled *The Church in Struggle*.[89] Other articles in the brochure give a sense of the challenge perceived by Bichlmair: three dealt with race, another was entitled "The Religious Choice—A Demand of the Time," and still another "Mystery—Not Myth!"[90] By laying claim to ultimate questions of worldview, the Nazis had launched a battle for souls. Yet Father Bichlmair asserted no special right to speak on the Jewish question. Driven neither by prejudice, interest, or even knowledge, he intended to show "in a purely academic sense the principles in Christian ethics upon which a solution to the Jewish question in Austria . . . must be formulated." He added that "every Christian is obligated to assume this point of view if he wants to make the principles of Christianity a reality." Bichlmair was simply a sound recorder of eternal truths. Though his superiors in Rome were not happy with this talk, no bishop or church censor rose to counter his interpretation: indeed, high prelates packed the rooms in which Bichlmair, Wilhelm Schmidt, or titular Bishop Alois Hudal spoke of race, presumably eager to learn what the church indeed thought.

According to Bichlmair, the new era imposed a new point of view upon Christians, one that was more difficult to arrive at than views of earlier times. Paradoxically for someone claiming to speak for a religious faith, Bichlmair said the "Jewish question" had become relevant because it was no longer religious. "We sense it," wrote the priest, "above all as a national and ethnic [*volklich*] problem." In contrast to Christian Socials such as Lugmayer or Czermak, Bichlmair said that the essence of the "problem" lay not in Jews' "heretical influence" but rather in the fact that Jews "belonged to a particular *Volk*, to a different race. It is from this point of view that the Jewish question enters the terrain of Christian ethics."[91] By addressing a burning question of contemporary life, the churchman thus turned his back on theology, ignoring the question of why a religion of love need concern itself with ethnicity and noting simply that even Jews favoring assimilation considered themselves a *Volk*.[92] According to Bichlmair, Christ had presented self-love as love's highest form, and that was also true for ethnic groups. When Germans started thinking of themselves first, they would see that the Jewish question was a "question of right"—their right.[93] In fact, readers of the Gospel will note that Christ did not speak of self-love as a higher form but placed it on a plane with love of neighbor. His command to love extended to individuals and not to groups. But Catholic audiences of the time had little exposure to scripture with which to confront the Jesuit. Priests told them that biblical interpretation was risky business best left to the church's teaching office.

Bichlmair's racist conclusions followed logically from his assertion that ethnic groups were moral actors. The Jews had once been God's instrument for bringing the world its redeemer, yet they had rejected him. Their "disloyalty toward their divine calling can be called a kind of *Erbsünde* [original sin] of the Jewish *Volk*." To this Bichlmair added that "commonalities of racial-biological genetic material need not be decisive," yet then he backtracked, writing that religious apostasy had given the racially "alien" Jewish people a dangerous, subversive character, from which Christian Germans had to be protected. Bichlmair could not disavow the sacraments, but he claimed that Jews resisted their promises. "Over time the effects of the saving graces of Christ can rectify the weaknesses of character in the Jewish people stemming from religious apostasy," he wrote. Yet he was not optimistic. Baptism's grace, dispensed to individuals, was a thin reed against the mighty currents through which God shaped history, enveloping and molding whole peoples, with little concern for the acts or desires of single persons.

We are tempted to ridicule his idea that Jews needed salvation "like any other race." Yet Bichlmair, later prisoner of the Gestapo, was not an opportunist. To seem credible to German Christians in a racist age, Bichlmair could not claim that rejecting Christ meant nothing for a people's character. Otherwise, Christ had made no difference to human history. Bichlmair, intrepid evangelist to heterodox audiences, wanted to speak a language that would be heard and understood by those who took Christian faith seriously and were unwilling to glorify either the "here and now" or the transcendent but rather sought a compelling new synthesis. Christ may have said nothing about races and spoken of love of neighbor in the singular, but the Bible speaks of "priestly people" and sins visited upon many generations. In Bichlmair's time, race had become synonymous with people. He was refining views that we also find in the writings of scientist Wilhelm Schmidt, Austro-Hungarian Jesuit Bela Bangha, publisher Joseph Eberle, and many others.

Unlike other racist Catholics, Bichlmair had unimpeachable authority, and if Oesterreicher and Hildebrand attacked Schmidt, Eberle, or even

Bishop Hudal in print, they had to be careful with him. "The brown Catholics," Oesterreicher wrote to one confidant, "will fashion a hangman's noose for us from any direct attacks on Father Bichlmair, costing us the sympathy of the Cardinal, and perhaps making our work impossible."[94] But Oesterreicher was determined to organize a response nonetheless. The church could not capitulate to "racist insanity."[95] There was also reason for hope. Oesterreicher knew that the Jesuit General in Rome, Włodimierz Ledóchowski, himself a reputed antisemite, would have preferred that Bichlmair drop his piece altogether. And indeed Bichlmair was prevailed upon to relinquish directorship of the board of the Viennese Mission to the Jews, the *Pauluswerk*, which he and Oesterreicher had founded in 1934.

Because he could not criticize Bichlmair directly, Oesterreicher turned to the Catholic intellectual Karl Thieme for assistance, sparking a difficult and formal but very productive friendship that lasted over a quarter century. Like Hildebrand, Kraus, Oesterreicher, Haecker, and Gurian, Karl Thieme had recently converted to Catholicism, like them he was an amateur theologian, and like them he occupies shadow spaces in European intellectual history, all but invisible beneath the soaring reputations of his friends and acquaintances such as Walter Benjamin, Karl Mannheim, Theodor Adorno, and Alfred Döblin.[96] Yet ultimately the Protestant convert Karl Thieme became the most influential Catholic writer on the Jewish question in the twentieth century.[97]

Like those who combatted racism from within Austrofascism, Thieme's early trajectory makes little sense within conventional political categories. Scion of a Protestant theologian family from Dresden, and a believing Christian all his life—indeed religion teacher as a young man—in 1924 Thieme shocked his milieu by joining the Social Democratic Party of Germany, despite its "vulgar Marxist" anti-religious propaganda and during a time when Christianity and Marxism were viewed as enemies.[98] Three years later, after finishing studies at Leipzig in history, theology, and philosophy, he followed his teacher Hermann Heller, a Jewish legal scholar from Austrian Teschen, to Berlin's Deutsche Hochschule für Politik, a private, eclectic, cosmopolitan school that taught an innovative curriculum and featured a staff of republicans and skeptics that included Theodor Heuss, Franz Neumann, Ernst Niekisch, Eckart Kehr, and Albert Salomon. In 1930, Thieme took a job as professor at the Pedagogical

Academy in East Prussian Elbing (today Elbląg, Poland), and his interests migrated rightward, involving explorations of "third way" politics, in particular the ideas of conservative revolution propagated by Otto Strasser and the *Neue Blätter für den Sozialismus* as well the Catholic Ring Movement of Heinrich Brüning.

How he managed to keep these commitments together is a mystery. In these last years of Weimar, Thieme was also busy trying to join Protestantism and Catholicism as an editor at *Religiöse Besinnung*, the lone journal promoting dialogue among Christians of all stripes in Germany— something the Vatican strongly opposed. As was the case for the circles around Dietrich von Hildebrand, it took the Nazi seizure of power and the self-revealing violence that followed to provide clarity for Thieme as to where he must stand with his political and theological engagement.

On March 14, 1933, shortly after Hitler's accession to chancellorship, Elbing's Social Democrats chose Thieme to give an address celebrating Karl Marx on the fiftieth anniversary of his death. The event never took place. Instead, during the previous night the Gestapo hauled the city's Marxist politicians out of bed for all-night interrogations. They caught up with Thieme the following week and placed him in protective custody. Upon his release, Thieme's boss at the Pedagogical Academy informed him that he no longer had a job: a new law forbade Social Democrats from holding any position in the German state. Wondering how to care for a young family, Thieme considered joining the anti-republican *Stahlhelm* as a demonstration of political loyalty, but this group had just been absorbed into the SA (paramilitary organization of the Nazi Party), and his wife Susi refused to be seen in the company of a man wearing a "black spider" (i.e., a swastika) on his sleeve.[99] Thieme then waited to see what course the Nazi regime would take, hoping the "left" would gain ascendancy. The waiting ended on July 17, 1933—Thieme later noted the date precisely—when he visited Berlin and received firsthand information about the "Köpenick blood week," an orgy of torturing and killing carried out by the SA, mostly against Social Democrats, costing scores of lives. After this point, there could be no doubt that brutal disregard for life was at the heart of Nazism.[100]

Thieme decided to go into opposition against Nazism, but his first "battle" was waged within Christianity. In the fall of 1933, Karl Thieme witnessed the Nazi cult of death exerting control over the German Protestant churches as one *Landeskirche* after the other—first in Prussia, then Thuringia, Saxony, Lübeck, and Wurtemberg—voluntarily accepted the Nazis' *"Arierparagraph"* and excluded from church offices persons of Jewish origin. This was *precisely* the kind of reasoning (by Father Bichlmair) in the Catholic context that had provoked the ire of Johannes Oesterreicher. Like Oesterreicher, Thieme was horrified to see his church abjectly denying the power of God's grace and blaspheming against the Holy Spirit.[101] The shock caused him to look to Rome: as a place where Christianity might be shielded from desacralizing servitude to politics. In late October, he and his Protestant friends (the "Thieme circle") addressed a letter to Pius XI requesting admission to the Catholic Church. At issue was not attraction to any particular aspect of Catholic teaching, but the simple belief that a "new church" had supplanted Christ's church in much of Protestant Germany: a church worshiping not God but race. "Our Lord said not only, give Caesar what is Caesar's," they wrote the pope, "but also give God what is God's." Jesus had not repulsed, but rather "loved his Jewish people, even if unbaptized, with burning heart, as we love our own." Thieme was probably the first Christian theologian in modern times to state that Christ the Jew loved the Jewish people of the postbiblical era.[102]

The pope never responded to Thieme's letter. One admirer of Karl Thieme's later compared him to another great Saxon, the writer Gottfried Lessing, also a "champion of lost causes."[103] Though he had hoped to take entire Protestant communities, parishes, and pastors with him, at most forty pastors (not the anticipated six hundred or more) followed Thieme into the Catholic Church. Thieme himself converted on January 30, 1934 in the *Liebfrauenkirche* in Leipzig-Lindau. In retrospect we might say that he was too skeptical about Protestantism; ultimately many Lutherans and Calvinists rose up and confronted the brown Protestants with their own countermovement, the Confessing Church.

We know how many Protestants converted with the Thieme group because Nazi officials registered the quiet protest of conversions to the Roman Church. Alfred Rosenberg, the chief of Nazi ideology, condemned Thieme and his friends for their treasonous "pilgrimage to Rome."[104] As it happened, in February 1934 Karl Thieme indeed journeyed to Rome, where he encountered German Catholics who felt as he did about Nazism: Josef Höfer of Paderborn, a priest and ecumenist; Hermann Joseph Schmitt of the Catholic worker movement; and the Catholic trade unionist Bernhard Letterhaus, later executed for his role in the plot against Hitler. He also met up with an old friend from Leipzig, Johannes Schauff, expert on agricultural affairs and at the center of Rhine resistance circles.[105] Thieme was astounded to find in Catholicism—a world apart from the Protestant milieu he knew in Saxony—so many men like himself, attuned to what he called the "signs of the times."[106] Robert Leiber, a German Jesuit and secretary to Cardinal Pacelli, was informed of Thieme's visit, and this contact would also prove useful in the years to come.

Armed with superb recommendations, Thieme now moved to the Rhine city of Düsseldorf, where he took a job as coeditor (with Johannes Maassen and Waldemar Gurian) of the weekly *Junge Front*, a forum for Catholic opposition to racism and materialism. Despite harassment, *Junge Front* continued publishing until liquidation in January 1936, increasing circulation to over 350,000—a feat that Thieme took as evidence that much of Germany stood against Hitler.[107] By this point, Thieme no longer lived in Germany, however. He had expended much of his energy in Düsseldorf supporting Catholic opposition initiatives that extended from his friend Schauff to activists of Catholic worker associations, trade unions, the Center Party, and young men's associations.[108] Just after Easter 1935, Thieme and Schauff met at the Cologne apartment of Edmund Forschbach, a conservative politician who had become disenchanted with Hitler; Thieme, possessing "excellent information," called for active resistance because Hitler was seeking a revolution in the European state system that would lead to war.[109] One of the more concrete ideas to emerge was to use Catholic hunting clubs to seize power throughout the Rhineland.[110] Informed that he faced imminent arrest, Thieme slipped across the border to Switzerland in August 1935, and he settled at his mother's home at Läufelfingen (near Basel), making this the base for the next decade.[111]

Shortly before this escape, Thieme wrote a letter to Johannes Oesterreicher pleading confusion as to his own political identity. He confessed to sitting somewhere "between all chairs."[112] Thirty years later, Walter Dirks, next to Heinrich Böll Germany's premier left Catholic intellectual, gave an obituary for Thieme on West German radio, telling listeners that Thieme had a "very personal position that did not fit easily among the categories used to divide parties and political religions."[113] Dirks hinted at the integrity of Thieme's confusing commitments. He was basically irenic, wanting to unite ideologies, whether political or theological, and always seeking unity as a way of realizing God's kingdom. Never far from Protestantism, Thieme took "an *active* sense of biblical eschatology" into his life as a Catholic. Marxism and Christianity met in his eschatological hope, and he could no less stop working toward a classless society than he could for Christ's second coming. Another old friend, theologian Ernst Wolf, added one more idea that fascinated Thieme: the belief that salvation was achieved through nations, *Völker*. Connecting everything—the ecumenism, eschatological hope, and fascination with the history of nations—was his abiding sense of the mystery of the church, which according to St. Paul was a church of Jews and Gentiles.[114]

The blasphemous antisemitism that he saw entering the Protestant churches in 1933 injured each of these concerns: it made the *Volk* not a basis of salvation but an idol; the churches profane rather than holy; and German Christianity a pagan cult rather than *Una Sancta*. The battle against antisemitism drew him like a magnet to Oesterreicher, who also worked in ecumenism (as editor of *Missionsruf*), and believed that God carried out his plans for humanity through the nations. Like Thieme, he read the signs of the times, hoping the end was near. If Thieme and Oesterreicher were attracted by the likeness of their interests, they were also repelled by the likeness of their personalities: opinionated, difficult, intellectually capacious, vulnerable but absolutely certain in moral judgments, tireless, and by turns flexible and uncompromising.

Karl Thieme was not quite as focused on Jewish-Christian relations as Oesterreicher. He took an interest in pedagogy throughout his life and after the war French occupation authorities called upon him to reorder the education system in Baden. In 1953 he became professor for European history, philosophy, and German studies at the University of Mainz. While combatting antisemitism with Oesterreicher before and after the war, Thieme was also contributing regularly to the Swiss press and writing several books, including a layman's translation of the Bible. He maintained vigorous correspondence with individuals across the political spectrums, who tended, like him, to bridge the otherwise unbridgeable. It is no coincidence that Thieme's friend Johannes Schauff later helped form West Germany's first "grand coalition" of Christian and Social Democrats in 1966; or that Schauff worked closely with another friend from student days in Leipzig, the Social Democrat Herbert Wehner, whom he and Thieme had known as a Communist. The circles of Karl Thieme had begun intersecting with those of Johannes Oesterreicher and Dietrich von Hildebrand in 1932 when Engelbert Dollfuss called Schauff to Vienna to address a rally of Austrian farmers (agriculture was his specialty) against National Socialism. Two years later, Schauff was in Rome visiting Joseph Wirth—once German *Reichschancellor* for the Center Party—and got to know Klaus Dohrn, Hildebrand's cousin and closest collaborator.[115]

The collaboration between Oesterreicher and Thieme lasted until 1960, when the two men who devoted their lives to dialogue found they could no longer speak to one another. Though subsisting on complexity, they became obsessive about nuances of interpretation, and disagreement became unbearable when their convictions all but overlapped: by 1960 both had broken through to the belief that the church's relation to the Jews should be ecumenical, not missionary. Still, neither of these converts ever lost his missionary fervor, though it was now directed to Christians. In his seventies Oesterreicher continued turning out book reviews, dozens of pages in length, to counter what he viewed as false Christian theology on the Jews.[116] Karl Thieme's energy was hardly sapped even by inoperable cancer. He began the week of July 21, 1963, giving two scheduled lectures for young theologians at a meeting on Jewish-Christian relations at the Abbey in Swiss Einsiedeln, speaking from a couch because he could no longer stand. On the third day of the meeting, medics evacuated Thieme to the *Bürgerspital* in Basel, where he died two days later.[117]

When Oesterreicher appealed to Karl Thieme for help in 1936, Father Georg Bichlmair's influence was spreading through Austrian Catholicism. Leaders of the Catholic youth group *Neuland* were planning to segregate the "nationally other"—in other words, to make separate spaces in their organization for Jewish converts. All the errors of Bichlmair and "many other Nazi Catholics" came together in discrimination against Jewish converts within the church, Oesterreicher wrote, and that was the best place to attack them.[118] "Would you be so kind," he asked Thieme, "as to discuss in *Die Erfüllung* the opinions lying at the bottom of Father Bichlmair's talk—namely the attempt to reconcile nationalism with the Church?" The issue was urgent. Word of Bichlmair's Catholic racism had traveled as far as the United States, with devastating effects upon Oesterreicher's target audiences.[119] Identified only as an "important Catholic writer in Germany," Thieme made two points. First, the question of whether or not to support the "antisemitic spirit of the time" was a decision for or against Christ. One could not reject Jews and accept Christ. "Tell me what your attitude is toward the Jews," he wrote, "and I will tell you what kind of Christian you are!" Second, Christians' primary task was not to proclaim Jesus to the Jews. Rather, their task was to tell Christians that "the Jew in their midst expects the fulfillment of the main command of Jesus, the 'new commandment' (John 13:34), the command of love, with an urgency that has never before existed."[120]

Oesterreicher himself took on one of Bichlmair's admirers, namely, the prominent Catholic intellectual Joseph Eberle, publisher of *Schönere Zukunft*, the most widely read Catholic journal in German-speaking Europe, and among the most determined bridge builders from Catholicism to Nazism. Like Bichlmair, Eberle exploited Rome's silence on the Jews to produce authoritative sounding articles. As universal outsiders, Jews had developed "unheard of solidarity throughout the world," Eberle wrote in the summer of 1936. Evidence could be seen in the worldwide echoes of Bichlmair's talk. Hardly had he "held a talk on the Jewish question in Vienna," Eberle continued, "than Jews in Czechoslovakia, France, and England are threatening to boycott the Austrian tourist industry, and American Jews are making protests."[121] Over many centuries, Eberle alleged, the Jews had disturbed the natural relations among Christians and thus kept the supernatural from "developing as it should." He therefore wanted first to exclude Jews from the professions, then from the Christian world.[122] Was that possible? Oesterreicher related with horror to Karl Thieme an exchange he had with Bichlmair in April 1936. To the question of what would become of Jews who had been denied property and work the Jesuit had answered simply, "they will have to emigrate."[123]

Like Bichlmair, Eberle demanded restrictions upon Jewish Christians because "blood and race are not erased by baptism." "As a whole," the publisher wrote, "the church is true to St. Paul's phrase: No neophytes! In other words: whoever came to the church yesterday should not want to play teacher today."[124] He fumed over "a group of freshly arrived émigrés and Jewish Christians" who propagated philo-Semitism, and he branded as "unchristian any opposition to the peculiarities and activities of the Jews." For the newcomers, even "to ask about the Jewish question seems strange."[125] In fact, the neophytes were undermining walls of antisemitism that some hoped would protect the church from the challenges of modernity. Eberle was not alone with concerns about the converts. After discovering that Hildebrand had a Jewish grandmother, the editor of Vienna's Catholic daily *Reichspost*, Friedrich Funder, called him simply "the Jew Hildebrand."[126] The *Reichspost* told readers that Oesterreicher meant well, but he was too concerned about antisemitism and had been distracted from the task of winning Jews for Christ. "A need for increasing the volume of literature opposing antisemitism, already available in abundance, hardly exists," the paper wrote.[127] Funder, like Eberle, was smarting from attacks the newcomers made upon his favorite authority on the Jews, Austrian titular Bishop Alois Hudal. Hudal was outraged that Catholics would dare question the wisdom of a bishop, and he informed Vatican State Secretary Pacelli in the fall of 1936 that the émigrés were harming church interests and were intriguing against him personally.[128]

In Oesterreicher's view, the *Reichspost* had become deaf to Christ's words. Those who said that enough had been done to stop antisemitism, he wrote to Karl Thieme, had grown tired of "all this talk of sermon on the mount, of a command to love, and similar unpleasant things."[129] Oesterreicher's sources for discovering Christ's words continued to be unorthodox, however. If he had been drawn to Christianity by Kierkegaard, now he found inspiration from the (Protestant) German Confessing Church. Yet Oesterreicher could not advertise the non-Catholic sources of his thought in polemics with Eberle. He therefore covered himself by citing sermons of Munich's Archbishop Michael Faulhaber before getting to his real inspiration: a secret memorandum of German anti-Nazi pastors according to which all humans needed salvation equally. Against Nazi glorification of the Aryan man, the Protestant authors had argued that Christ's command of love of neighbor made antisemitism impossible. The memo was supposed to be a secret communication to the German government, and two of its authors landed in Sachsenhausen when it was leaked to the press. One, Friedrich Weissler, from a patriotic Prussian family, was identified by the Nazis as a "full Jew" and died in a Nazi camp in February 1937.[130] Perhaps Oesterreicher and Weissler found it easier to preach Christian charity for Jewish neighbors because the Nuremberg laws had made them the neighbors.

Oesterreicher then cited Russian Orthodox thinkers Nicolas Berdyaev and Vladimir Solovyov to make the point that Christians should concern themselves with the faults of other Christians before looking at the Jews. According to Solovyov, the Jewish question was in fact a Christian question: Christians had to behave like followers of Christ before Jews could even imagine becoming Christian.[131] "How should the Jews turn to the Good News of Christ," Oesterreicher asked, "when they see the famous Catholic writer Dr. Eberle constantly writing about the Jewish question but never speaking a warm and human, indeed a Christian word?" Like Karl Adam, Joseph Eberle projected self-love as the highest form of love, and the self as coterminous with "nation."[132] Yet here we see that even for Oesterreicher the adjective "Christian" had been reduced almost to an afterthought, buried deep within a paragraph somewhere in the middle of a lengthy polemic with a "Christian" author.

From the standpoint of scripture, Eberle proved an easy target. The more he argued out of a theological vacuum for racist exclusion, the more he drew Oesterreicher, Thieme, or Hildebrand to an appreciation of neglected biblical texts. They were inspired in a special way by the French mendicant Léon Bloy, who had recovered St. Paul's prophetic writings on the Jews while opposing Christian antisemites during the Dreyfus affair of the 1890s. In Paul's letter to the Romans, chapter 11, they soon discovered the untenability of Eberle's idea that the Jewish people had "turned to stone, against Christ and Christianity." To the question of whether the Jews had stumbled beyond recovery Paul had answered, "Not at all!" (Romans 11:11).

For evidence that God had "not rejected his people" (Romans 11:2), Oesterreicher took the logical but unprecedented step of looking at Judaism since the time of Christ. Anyone who knew the "postbiblical religious writings of the Jews knows how much the spirit of faith dwells there, what longing there is for the one true God; he knows that in Jewry distant from

Christ, next to stiff-neckedness there is also a remnant of what was most profound in the old Israel: and that this remnant is actively at work. How could it be otherwise? How can the Jewish people return to Christ if it is consigned to perdition?" Christians should worry about faithless Christians. "Jews may misunderstand scripture," he wrote, "but they maintain it, whereas the apostates among Christians reject God's word. The apostate Jew is closer to Christ than the break-away Christian."[133]

Hildebrand's Personalism

In the spring of 1937, Oesterreicher arranged for Dietrich von Hildebrand to expand upon these Pauline thoughts at a talk at Vienna's *Pauluswerk* entitled "Jews and the Christian West." Oesterreicher hoped to counter the racism of the Austrian Catholics, about which Franz von Papen was reporting enthusiastically to Adolf Hitler, and Hildebrand's thoughts were soon filtering through discussions in Vienna's Gentile and Jewish press. Although one cannot cleanly separate Oesterreicher's and Hildebrand's ideas on the Jewish people, one does detect a boldness to Hildebrand's writing deriving from his philosophy. His ideas about Jews' role in postbiblical history were new strains of Catholic thought, interesting because Hildebrand combined his universalistic personalism with an appreciation of one ethnic group.

Before taking recourse to scripture, Hildebrand started with a first principle. What stood out for this unorthodox yet ultramontane Catholic against the maze of abstractions beloved by Bishop Hudal, Joseph Eberle, and the nationalist Christian Socials—like nation, state, or *Volk*—was the *human person*. Hildebrand rejected all discrimination. "I may feel the same toward an unbaptized Jew that I feel toward a non-Christian Aryan," he wrote, "but Jewish descent as such may not prejudice my attitude in any way."[134] To judge a person by descent was to treat him as an "animal." A Christian was bound not only to forsake discrimination but also to show solidarity for discrimination's victims. Echoing Karl Thieme, he wrote that the persecutions of Jews in Germany had to trigger solidarity with the "least of my brothers."[135]

If papal pronouncements condemning racism had existed, the ultramontane Hildebrand would have cited them. Yet there was little from the

Vatican to draw upon. Hildebrand hastily mentioned the little-known 1928 statement of Pius XI condemning antisemitism, but then elaborated his own philosophy to refute the Nuremberg laws—something the Vatican never did.[136] "When seen from a Christian perspective," he told his audience, "the so-called Nuremberg racial laws are outrageous and barbarous, not only because of the childish claim that Jews are the root of immorality, but above all because of how they are practiced. It stands to reason that the people behind these laws are also the bitterest enemies of Christianity. They deny of the intellectual/spiritual character of the human person."[137]

Former Protestant Hildebrand then delved into scripture for further inspiration. "Austria's Catholic mission," he wrote, "means that as a Christian state it must stay free of all the miasmas of blood material-ism . . . flirting with antisemitism means not only betrayal of the spirit of him who said: 'Whoever does the will of my father in heaven is my brother, sister and mother' [Mark 3:35] but also a betrayal of Austria's mission for all of Europe."[138] Hildebrand had made the groundbreaking assertion that Jews *of that time* were doing the will of God *as Jews*. Like Oesterreicher—and in contrast to virtually all other Catholics writing on the issue—Hildebrand was saying that no break separated the Jews of now from the Jews of the Bible. According to St. Paul, Hildebrand instructed his readers, Jews were the "first ones," the "root" that carries the branches, and non-Jews are "wild twigs" that have been "grafted in." Judaism there-fore remained the living source of "noble juices" of faith. Furthermore, Jesus was a "bodily" descendent of Jews, and therefore racial antisemitism denigrated the "race" of the savior. Here, Hildebrand refuted the view popular among Catholic antisemites that Christ did not belong to the Jewish people. Joseph Eberle, for example, had written that the Virgin Mary, freed from original sin, was "removed as it were from the natural context of the Jewish people."[139] Against Eberle's contention that Jewish converts should mind their place, Hildebrand argued that their *Volk* heri-tage gave them exalted status. Jews' descent through their families from Abraham was an "advantage" that must fill Christians with special rever-ence and joy—"once community with Jesus has been established."[140]

If as a personalist Hildebrand opposed prejudice against members of other ethnic groups or nations, as a Christian he thus argued for prejudice in favor of one ethnic group. Citing nineteenth century French Catholic

Ernest Hello, Hildebrand wrote that "Israel is God's favorite. Whoever blesses it is blessed, whoever curses it is cursed."[141] He recalled St. Paul's words that "the gifts of God are irrevocable." Christians, by contrast, had to be on their guard. "For if you were cut off from your native wild olive and *against all nature* grafted into the cultivated olive," he told his audience, "how much more readily will the natural olive branches be grafted into their native stock!" The malady of this age had afflicted not Jews but Christians and former Christians: the racist antisemites. As Hildebrand interpreted Romans 11:24, faith went "against the nature" of Gentiles but not of Jews.[142]

Like Oesterreicher and Thieme, Hildebrand found special inspiration in the nineteenth-century French thinker Léon Bloy, who had called antisemitism blasphemy because it attacked Christ's family. How would we feel if people constantly spoke about our father and mother with the greatest disdain, Bloy had asked. That was how Jesus felt listening to antisemites who could not accept God's choice to become human as a Jew. Antisemitism, "a completely modern affair," was, in Léon Bloy's words the "most terrible blow to the Lord, because it strikes the face of his mother, and comes from the hand of Christians. In the time of the early church, people hated Jews and beat them to death, but never insulted them as a race: instead the church feared and prayed for them, well aware that St. Paul had promised them everything: that they should be the light to the world."[143]

The turn to Paul (following Bloy) made Hildebrand—like Oesterreicher—reflect upon the riches of postbiblical Jewish culture and thought. He told his listeners at the *Pauluswerk* that "an unprejudiced look at the Jewish literature of the many centuries since Christ shows what a reverent, classically human, deeply religious spirit can still be found there." As evidence, he related a story from Hassidic literature about humans' need to rely upon God's grace in order to do good and subdue lower instincts.[144] "Whoever has maintained a sense of the world of the religious," he argued, "cannot read selections from postbiblical writings without being moved, whether it is the 'Dudele' or the words of the Talmud about the Just One or the story of the shepherd in the 'Book of the Holy' by Yehuda Hachasid. Everywhere we find traces of the spirit which lives in the Old Testament."

Because he viewed Jewish culture as crucial to the formation of Europe, Hildebrand rejected suggestions that Jews settle elsewhere. Israel's role in forming the West was so crucial that Europeans could not look upon Jews as they did other peoples. This people "beloved because of their fathers" (Romans 11) was so woven into the history of salvation that even if separated by religion the Jews belonged to the Christian West. Hildebrand cited words spoken in 1933 by Toulouse Archbishop Jules Gérard Saliège instructing Christians on the bonds linking them to Jews. "I cannot forget that Jesse's root blossomed in Israel and carried fruit there. The Virgin, the first apostles were of the Jewish tribe. How should I not feel one with Israel [*mit Israel verwachsen*], just as the twig does with the tree from which it has sprung."[145] Compare these words to those prepared for the never released encyclical of Pius XI. There, one reads that "the Jews are separated from the rest of humanity by an immovable barrier" and that "Jewry . . . has frivolously sacrificed its exalted historical calling once and for all" and "lost the enveloping communal life in race by turning against its own precious blood and calling it in vengeance against itself and its children."[146] Intellectually speaking, the Vatican was not where the action was.

A Growing Schizophrenia: History and the Jews

Hildebrand had gone further than any Catholic thinker in developing Paul's thoughts to produce a new appreciation of the Jewish people. Jews possessed a special calling, never broken. Hildebrand also applied his personalist philosophy: like all human beings, Jews should not suffer discrimination. But where did they fit into God's plan for the world? This urgent question went to the heart of what believers call Providence. Of what use was religion if it did not give hints about God's design for the world? The godless were precisely those who refused to acknowledge that God gave humans signs that they might detect and read about his will in History. The problem for Catholics arguing against antisemitism was that to think about the Jews historically returned them to the heart of anti-Judaism, to the belief that God had destined the Jews for suffering.

To appreciate the pressures felt by Christians in this time and place to invest everyday history with transcendent meaning we may take the case of Karl Borromäus Heinrich. Before World War I, Heinrich was a close friend of Austrian Protestant expressionist Georg Trakl and an editor at the satirical German weekly *Simplicissimus*. After having worked as a diplomat during the war, he entered the abbey at Swiss Einsiedeln, where he lived with his wife as a secular monk and wrote tracts against the Nazis. In November 1936, Johannes Oesterreicher published Heinrich's reflections on the psychology of antisemitism. Seeming to digress, Heinrich wrote that "if God permitted the World War to take place, that was not the simple result of a divine whim."[147] He reasoned in terms familiar from the Old Testament. The Great War and its conclusion were punishments that were supposed to "lead us back to God." Oesterreicher also printed reflections of the German convert Theodor Haecker, later an inspiration to Munich's White Rose student resistance, who described the Old Testament as a guide to the "relation of peoples and politics to God." Yet it was a "mysterious guide," Haecker wrote, full of admonitions to "repent" and "change one's ways," often better at showing what not to do. It was easy to learn the wrong things. According to Haecker, "heretical 'Christian statesmen'" had taken wisdom from the Old Testament in order to pronounce their own people elect in a "direct, unblemished, naturalistically brutal and biological form."[148]

Oesterreicher's collaborator Karl Thieme agreed that there was "something awkward about applying biblical categories to phenomena outside the bible," because "by the power of the Holy Spirit these categories have a uniqueness that cannot be replicated." Still, Christianity looked anxiously for signs because Christian hope was always hope for the end of the world.[149] Like Oesterreicher, Thieme was deeply influenced in his apocalyptic musings of the convert beggar-prophet Léon Bloy, who had taken Jacques Maritain and his wife Raïssa into the church in 1906. Thieme also drew inspiration from the skeptic Karl Kraus, who like the Catholic émigrés had admired Engelbert Dollfuss. Kraus focused attention on the "signs of the end of time and of the state of affairs that is promised to follow beyond the end of the world," and unlocked a special category: "the absolute readiness of this world to disappear and fade away."[150] Or, "more precisely, he rediscovered this category, independently of the Christian apocalypsts Léon Bloy and Ernest Hello." Kraus "knew that for those who believe in a better existence beyond this eon, to know for sure it is going to end is not a reason for despair, but rather for hopefulness."[151] Kraus had been baptized in 1911 (sponsored by Adolf Loos) but left the church in 1923.

Prophetic statements from Léon Bloy, Karl Kraus, and Ernest Hello combined with selected passages from the Bible to strengthen Catholic émigrés in Vienna in their belief that the Jewish people continued without interruption from biblical times. Now came the problem: the history of Israel in the Bible was one of trials and punishment and repentance. Was not the recent history of Israel also one of trials and punishment? And would not the trials end only with the Jews' conversion to Christ? For the time being, this seemed the implication of Romans 11:25–26. According to John Oesterreicher, this kind of questioning was a legacy of Judaism. The Jews had been the first people to realize the "absolute value" of history. "For them there was not the return of all things in an eternal cycle of cosmic events," he posited in an article of 1936, "because the essential thing of their teaching of a divine plan for the world was its uniqueness." From the Jews Christianity had assumed this "prophetic and apocalyptic" approach to history, although a "new creation" had been established in the "historical personality" of Jesus of Nazareth.[152]

Hopes of grounding his historical vision inspired Oesterreicher to reproduce writings of the Jewish thinker Martin Buber in his journal *Die Erfüllung*. At Rosh Hashanah in 1933 Buber wrote that the Almighty was "calling to judgment all forms of life."[153] German Jewry faced special challenges and Buber asked, what "are the German Jews doing? Will they change their ways? Or will each content himself by saying: I am blameless?" Buber specified what he meant by "the guilt" of the Jews: "lukewarmness in being Jewish, casualness in communal life, industrious obsessiveness with ends, an empty lust for life, non-committal smart-talk . . ." In the pen of Johannes Oesterreicher, Buber's word *"umkehren"* (to change one's ways) became *"bekehren"* (to convert). He issued the following commentary on Buber, presuming to specify what God desired for the Jewish people:

One country after the other falls to the embrace of Antisemitism. What are the Jews doing to repulse this danger? They hold congresses, set up law offices, speak, write, make complaints and accusations, and so on. Certainly, all of this must be. But this will not bring forth help. This is not what our current predicament requires. That is not what God requires. He wants real renewal and He really wants people to change their ways. For Antisemitism, as suffused as it is with the meanness and vileness of people, in the end remains a judgment of God.

In fact, Buber had wanted to communicate something very different. If he called Jews to change their ways, that was to make them united because the "modality of their existence . . . the symbiosis with the German people has been destroyed."[154] The point was not conversion to Christianity. Furthermore, Buber was immensely skeptical about humankind's ability to discern the meaning of God's judgment.

Oesterreicher, like Karl Thieme, did not use the word *deicide* to explain the trials sent to the Jewish people. In March 1937, Oesterreicher asked Thieme to write on a sermon by the Apostle Peter that showed that the Jews' guilt was not in crucifying Christ.[155] Yet both men also held that the Jews would continue to suffer until they recognized Christ as Messiah, and in effect they affirmed the teaching (associated with deicide) that the Jews lived under a curse. Karl Thieme had embraced Jacques Maritain's idea that Jews should "understand persecution as visited upon them by Providence because of the rejection of Jesus." Maritain derived this view from Genesis 42:22, which tells of the moment when Joseph's brothers understood they were being punished for their misdeed. "Reuben said: Did I not tell you not to do the boy a wrong? But you would not listen, and his blood is on our heads, and we must pay." Thieme read the persecution of Jews in Germany as analogous, reflecting the guilt shared by Israel for rejecting Jesus. But if one reads the entire passage today, one might draw very different conclusions—if one assumes that Jews and Christians are brothers:

> They said to one another, "No doubt we deserve to be punished because of our brother, whose suffering we saw; for when he pleaded with us we refused to listen. That is why these sufferings have come upon us." But Reuben said: "Did I not tell you not to do the boy a wrong? But you would not listen, and his blood is on our heads, and we must pay." (Genesis 42:21–22)

In the 1930s, the assumption that Jews and Christians were brothers did not apply, and in effect, Thieme and Oesterreicher in part legitimated modern antisemitism by "reading" it as a sign that Israel should repent.

The philosophers Dietrich von Hildebrand and Jacques Maritain sensed the problems of this logic but felt powerless to resist it. Hildebrand rejected the idea that Jews carried a special stain from biblical times to the present. Everything that Israel did it did as a representative of humanity. "Every other people would have mocked, stoned, and crucified Christ," he wrote.[156] Yet things were not so simple. He balanced reverence for the Jewish people with the belief that Christians constituted the "new Israel." If Hildebrand called Jews the "people of humanity" (*Menschheitsvolk*), he also added that "the function that Israel once had as representative of humanity . . . has been assumed by the Church of Christ." What then was the role of the Jews? Hildebrand gave the only answer Christianity of that time possessed: it was to one day "recognize Christ." Until then they would suffer tribulations.[157] Hildebrand did not explain why Jews were punished if every other people would have acted as they did. He denied that any particular sinfulness applied to the Jews and affirmed that there was but one original sin. Yet he also implied that a spiritual deficit was passed from generation to generation of Jews.

Such was the spirit of a time when religious believers were desperate to show their relevance in history. Yet Hildebrand was troubled by his own conclusions, and in 1936 he printed a rare condemnation of the faith in Providence that he himself had embraced. "The Jewish question," the French Franciscan B. Lacombe had written, "is exclusively a this-worldly concern . . . Therefore Catholic theology in the strict sense and the Jewish question of today have nothing to do with each other." Lacombe—probably a pseudonym—relegated all discussions of antisemitism to the realm of moral theology. In moral theology one could discover "binding church decisions." Rather than speculate on the place of Jews in God's plan, Lacombe wrote that "antisemitism belongs in the confessional booth—that is its relation to theology." "To treat the Jewish question as 'punishment of God,'" he said, "is not some mystical way to gain a profound understanding of the 'problem,' but rather a shallow mystification of sins we ourselves have committed."[158] Hildebrand seconded this sentiment by writing of the hypocrisy of "today's antisemites," supposedly "outraged" that Jews had nailed Christ to the cross, ignoring the "host of baptized Catholics who nail Christ to the cross every day . . ."[159]

For the time being Hildebrand and other anti-Nazi Catholics in Vienna could not ignore "this worldly concerns." Alienation from "this world" was driving many other Christians toward Nazism, a movement that political philosopher Eric Voegelin—also an émigré in Vienna—had likened to a modern Gnosticism. It was also alienation of co-believers from "this world" that led Karl Borromäus Heinrich or Karl Thieme to scriptural passages suggesting that a resolution to the growing power of evil in the world somehow lay in the "Jewish question." Thieme seized upon Maritain's idea that antisemitic persecution was visited upon Jews "because of the rejection of Jesus" precisely because it fit his eschatological mindset, his ostensible witness to the "apparently unstoppable apocalyptic dissimilation on the entire globe."[160]

Had they been speaking to Martin Buber rather than citing him for their purposes, Johannes Oesterreicher and Karl Thieme might have wondered at the perils of gnosis. Buber spoke of judgment but not judgment of God, and he did not believe that humans should try to gain insight into God's designs.[161] If Buber had spoken to the Catholics he might have said: it is a mistake to compete with the Nazis on the field of esoteric knowledge rather than of duty to God, to the heritage of law given to Christianity from Judaism. But a conversation with Buber began only after the war, when he helped convert Karl Thieme to a new way of looking at history and God's role in it. Contrary to what Karl Kraus or Léon Bloy had suggested, there was no "certain" way of reading history's meaning. By the 1960s, the Catholic Church followed suit, shifting to the view advocated by the Jewish philosopher, reading the "signs of the times" in terms of ethical imperatives and not as a curse willed upon anyone, Jewish or not.[162]

For the time being, Catholic intellectuals who used the lenses of their faith saw things that were deeply unsettling. Take Jacques Maritain, often considered the most progressive Catholic thinker on relations to Jews in the past century, who remained in close contact with Hildebrand and Oesterreicher from the 1930s through the 1950s. In an essay written in 1937, he apologized for the conclusions he felt compelled to draw from the drama of Calvary regarding the relation of Israel to the world. "Such words as 'penalty' or 'punishment' which we are obliged to use when we seek to elucidate human matters from the viewpoint of divine conduct of history, must be deprived of any anthropomorphic connotations," he wrote. At a crucial moment the Jews had chosen the world, and "their penalty is to be held captive by their choice. Prisoners and victims in this world which they love, but of which they are not, will never be, cannot be." If Jews were to read these words, they should understand that "as a Christian I could only try from a Christian perspective to understand the history of their people."[163]

Maritain's embarrassment stemmed from the evident schizophrenia. On the one hand, the persecution of Jews in Germany was supposed to arouse a Christian solidarity with Jews that was unprecedented. On the other, this persecution was one of a series of signs: the uncanny rise of Hitler (a man Oesterreicher called an anti-Christ), the irrepressible success of "neo-paganism," and the failure of anyone in power to oppose it. All of this pointed to a cataclysm, the final step of the unfolding of God's plan for humankind. Maritain's solution to the riddles of Providence was to reiterate Christianity's distinction between the theological "mystical Body" of Israel and the historical Jewish people. The former was unfaithful and "repudiated," the latter was not.[164]

In Dietrich von Hildebrand we have the fullest record of this growing tension in the Catholic mind on the eve of the Holocaust: excruciating because the hope for final reconciliation of God with man seemed to require the crimes of the anti-Christ. Within the views offered by Hildebrand we find the claim that Israel was separate yet not foreign; part of the West yet with little part in making it; a people who could not be understood in *völkisch* terms, but a *Volk* beloved because of its fathers. As a personalist opposing all discrimination, he refuted racism by employing language replete with racialist metaphors such as "stock" or "progeny." He said that Israel had failed in its mission but continued to have a mission, that it should convert but still maintain its special "Jewish" character among Christian nations in the present and foreseeable future. He insisted that Christians see Israel as a people enveloped in mystery, yet he claimed to have certain knowledge of this people's ultimate destiny to turn to Christ. The Jewish people was alive yet cut from its roots. Hildebrand talked about Israel falling away from faith—united above all by rejecting Christ—but he also celebrated the evident faith of postbiblical

Judaism, while writing that it was the rejection of Christ that held them together. He insisted that "blinded" Jews must turn to Christ, but he also said that they must not assimilate—that is, they must remain Jews.[165]

The story of the Catholic opposition to Nazism in Austria, Switzerland, and France reveals much courage but also reminds us of the power of commonly shared assumptions—in this case anti-Judaism—to limit thought and action. The certainty that the fist step to any improvement of the lot of Jews must be their conversion to Christianity forestalled active charity. One of Vienna's leading rabbis, Armand Kaminka, was quarreling with Johannes Oesterreicher in these years over his decision to expand the Catholic mission to the Jews in Vienna, the *Pauluswerk*. Would the effort not be better spent in improving the welfare of suffering Jews, Kaminka asked? He noted the irony that representatives of a faith "in whose religious ethics there is not a single sentence that does not derive from our Hebrew literature are doing us the favor of offering us the salvation that we ourselves have drawn forth."[166] But at a more fundamental level Kaminka reflected upon the self-defeating nature of Christian missions to the Jews. "There is a visible measure to judge the eminence of a religion and that is the kindness and compassion that it fosters," he wrote. "If the rich missionary societies in England, Holland, and other countries would simply use their means to lessen the physical need of persecuted Jews and to give refugees a home, then they would, following the ways of God, not only be practicing true love and compassion, but they would also cause the strength of their faith to shine forth in brilliant light."[167]

Was it possible for Catholic opponents of Nazism to show solidarity of that kind, unconcerned with making Jews into Christians? The Swiss historian Urs Altermatt speaks of two groups among Catholics in these years: a milieu of right-wing integral nationalists for whom modern antisemitism was a constitutive part of their worldview, and the mainstream Catholics for whom it was accidental. Christian thought did not necessitate the antisemitism of the former, but it did make anti-Judaism all but inescapable for those who took Christian thought seriously. Exceptions prove the rule. If we look across continental Europe in the 1930s, we see two initiatives of Catholics to fight antisemitism without the presumption that Jews must become Christian.

From 1936 to 1939, the Alsatian Oscar de Férenzy (1869–1942) published the bimonthly review *La Juste Parole* out of Paris, defusing the lies and distortions of the antisemitic right, in and beyond France, and reaching a print run of 6,000 issues.[168] He received financial support from the French bishops as well as Jewish organizations (such as the Consistory).[169] Férenzy's inspiration was Christian solidarity, and to reach the Catholic masses he did not worry about the fine points of Catholic theology the way that Karl Thieme did. Though fervently Christian, he denied any desire to proselytize, and indeed he harshly criticized *convertisseurs* who tricked young people into secret baptisms.[170] For his target audience of average French readers, Férenzy reprocessed the findings of progressive theologians such as the French Jesuit Joseph Bonsirven, reaching conclusions that they never stated as bluntly—for example, that Judaism was a "living" tradition.[171] Though opposing a massive front of Christian and non-Christian antisemites, Férenzy undoubtedly had an impact. His book *Les Juifs et nous chrétiens* (1935) was not only well received in Jewish newspapers (the editorial writer of the *L'Univers Israelite* declared he had read it in single night) but also by liberal Catholics: he received a letter of "felicitations" signed by sixty bishops.[172]

Férenzy in turn modeled his operation on that of the extraordinary Austrian activist Irene Harand, who published the anti-Nazi weekly *Gerechtigkeit* (Justice) out of Vienna from 1933 to 1938.[173] She likewise cared little for limits that theology set on Christian solidarity, and devoted issue after issue to commonsense refutations of stock antisemitic lies: about "Jewish cowardice," about Jews' links to Free Masonry, about Jewish plans for world domination, about Jews' refusal to do agricultural work, and so on.[174] She short-circuited rather than confronted the Catholic discourse of the time, refusing to take seriously eschatology (*Geschichtstheologie*) or the natural law tradition; at times she simply ridiculed Catholics' concern to validate suffering as supposedly necessary for redemption.[175] Like Férenzy, Irene Harand dismissed the charge of deicide as logically flawed. The Pharisees who demanded Christ's death may have been Jews, but so were his Apostles and most of the early Christian communities. Clearly "the Jews" did not kill Christ. "How absurd it is to make today's Jews responsible for the crucifixion of Christ 2,000 years ago," she wrote, "is something everyone will understand who has even an iota of intelligence or conscience."[176]

Yet in the Catholic camp those considered most intelligent thought precisely that.

Harand was content to think of Jews as Jews, and to defend their civic and religious rights without preconditions. More important than worrying about "grace of baptism," she wrote, was "to make sure that all people, whether Jews or Christians, put into effect love of neighbor, which both religions regard as *the most essential thing*."[177] She knew something about the Jewish tradition from her collaborator at *Gerechtigkeit*, the Jewish lawyer and senior citizen advocate Moritz Zalman. Those who wanted to convert the Jews could not write a sentence in her publications:

> I will never allow in my paper even the shadow of a suggestion that it is somehow Christian to threaten Jews or others with the fires of hell, from which they can only free themselves by baptism. Fighting antisemitism has nothing to do with baptism, but is the duty of all genuine and true Christians who feel love of neighbor for the people in their community . . . We must practice this love without condition, regardless of whether our brother or sister has received the grace of baptism, and we must act as true Christians.

She quarreled with Johannes Oesterreicher in public and of course did not print him.

Though not concerned with conversion of non-Christians, Harand was anything but an unfaithful Christian, and she appeared year after year on her front pages with young people for whom she acted as confirmation sponsor. Yet she believed that faith was revealed in acts rather than avowals. Jews who lived good lives could be justified, but Christians could not be justified by grace alone. The "baptismal certificate alone is not sufficient to give people the right to call themselves Christians," she wrote, "but rather they become Christians only by practicing love of neighbor, justice, and mercy toward their neighbors, regardless of what religion or race they belong to."[178] Harand spoke and organized tirelessly within Austria for five years, and took her message on the road as well, giving hundreds of talks from Vienna to Norway, Warsaw to Prague, and finally London, where she received news of the German invasion of Austria in March 1938.

Back in Vienna, Gestapo agents ransacked the offices of her organization (The World League against Racial Hatred and Human Want), and hunted her with orders to shoot to kill. Her friend Moritz Zalman tried to escape but was dragged off a train about to cross the Austrian-Swiss border. He died at Dachau in 1940. Lacking Zalman's encouragement and stimulation, Harand withdrew from activism during her exile in New York City, where she and her husband Frank kept up with activities of the Austrian Cultural Federation and exchanged cordial visits with Ernst Karl Winter, the former Viennese vice-mayor and staunch anti-Hitlerite, who in the postwar years was productively quarreling with Karl Thieme from his home in Teaneck, New Jersey.

What set Férenzy and Harand apart from other Christian activists against Nazism was that they talked to Jews. Like the important Anglican foe of antisemitism James Parkes and the American councils of Christians and Jews, they gave early evidence of the fruits of Jewish-Christian dialogue.[179] Direct conversation demanded a new language, and it also opened persons of extraordinary empathy—like Harand, Férenzy, and Parkes—to a new quality of solidarity. A figure from an earlier generation who might be counted in this tiny group was the Catholic poet and philosopher Charles Péguy, who died fighting for France in 1914. Péguy's personal affection for the Jewish writer Bernard Lazare caused him to resurrect a neglected teaching of the Council of Trent from the sixteenth century. "Should anyone inquire why the Son of God underwent His most bitter Passion," the bishops had taught, "he will find that besides the guilt inherited from our first parents the principal causes were the vices and crimes which have been perpetrated from the beginning of the world to the present day and those which will be committed to the end of time."

Péguy's statement was written in private to a friend and did not enter the Catholic conversation of the interwar years. It indeed represented orthodox Catholic theology, but, largely ignored, managed to coexist with a "historical" teaching according to which "the Jews" had killed Christ.[180] It was this latter teaching that gave answers to a question that bothered many Christians: why God permitted the Jews to continue to exist as a people though they had failed to accept their Messiah. In varying degrees, both Johannes Oesterreicher and Dietrich von Hildebrand took on board the Trent teaching, acknowledging that Jesus had died for

the sins of all humans, but still they insisted that Jews bore special responsibility, perhaps not so much for Christ's death—here they agreed
that all humans were responsible—but for continuing to fail to accept him
as Messiah.

Catholics could maneuver beyond these assumptions, but they did so at
the price of irrelevance. Because of her scorn for mainstream Catholic
thought, Irene Harand had no visible impact upon it and remained largely
unknown to historians until the late 1990s when the young Austrian Kurt
Scharr stumbled upon her organization's records while doing civil service
in Moscow—where the NKVD (The People's Commissariat for Internal
Affairs) had deposited them in 1945 after confiscating them from the
Gestapo. Harand had leapfrogged the intellectual quarrels of her time and
began speaking a language of tolerance that other Catholics learned only
after the Second Vatican Council. We see more evidence of the consequences of leaving behind mainstream assumptions in words spoken by the
Catholic Priest Dr. Bartolomaus Fiala (b. 1899), and reprinted by Harand in
the late winter of 1937. In an address to the Union of Jewish Front Soldiers—
something unheard of for a priest—Fiala emphasized the Jewish origins of
Christian beliefs, for example, that one should love one's enemies and worship only one God. He pointed to the sources in Judaism of many Christian
prayers.[181] On a podium that included a Zionist editor as well as the Communist Bruno Heilig, Fiala expressed doubts about baptism as a method of
fighting antisemitism. The "great intellectual and spiritual [*geistig*] power
of Judaism and its religious mission," Fiala noted, could "not be esteemed
highly enough." Fiala argued that Christianity and Judaism complemented each other. "There are no two world views or religions that have
as much in common as Judaism and Christianity," he asserted. "Jewry
which rests upon Moses and the other writings of the Old Testament cannot be in hostile conflict with Christianity, because the Old Testament is
the preparation of the New Testament: the root, the stem from which
Christianity proceeds as the fruit . . ." The morality of Judaism stood
above that of all other peoples, not only "in theory but in realization."
Fiala's scheme recognized no break between the faith of "Ancient Judaism" and the faith of Jews of his age.

Within days of this talk, Vienna's Cardinal Innitzer got on the phone
to Fiala's order (the *Kalasantiner*) demanding they declare publicly that

Fiala had not spoken in the name of the church.[182] What caused Fiala to express his radical views in Christian-Jewish understanding is unknown. No other Catholic priest went on record projecting Catholicism and Judaism as complementary, mutually supportive faiths, such that Jews did not need baptism. Fiala scandalized Catholic Vienna by projecting Jews as holy regardless of baptism.

If they are exceptions that prove one rule, Harand and Férenzy, along with the Anglican James Parkes, conform to one other: they lived on the boundaries of their communities and dared crossing into foreign cultural, ethnic, and religious terrain. Férenzy, who died in 1942 at age seventy-three after torture by the Gestapo, was born of Protestant parents of Jewish heritage in Bern (as Oscar Fraenzel de Ferenzy), and as a young man edited the pro-French radical right-wing Catholic paper *Voix d'Alsace.* Having been an insider, he understood the dangers of extreme nationalism. In 1933, he wrote a piece arguing that Nazi antisemitism and anti-Catholicism were two sides of the same coin, and he feared that regional antisemitism might lead Alsace into the embrace of Nazi Germany.[183] Irene Harand's mother was Protestant and her favorite relations were Jewish.[184] At an early age, she had been taken across a boundary that was normally unbreachable. Like other "bourgeois" Viennese, her parents rented summer quarters at a spa in the Austrian countryside. One afternoon Irene and her sisters were harassed by local boys, who chased them shouting "Jews, Jews, Jews!" In their minds, well-to-do people from Vienna were Jews. Almost sixty years later, Harand wondered, "Why does an experience that I had as a five-year old remain in my memory to the present day? One never forgets the first time one is scared to death, and feels surrounded by a world of enemies." The first time she experienced antisemitism it was "on the receiving end."[185] James Parkes, a native of trilingual Guernsey in the Channel Islands, had his empathy awakened as a young Anglican priest when he saw a close Jewish friend moved to tears at the idea of Christian missions.[186] Parkes became an outsider in his church with the view that Christians must surrender all efforts to convert Jews, and by the mid-1930s he was the first serious Christian theologian who denied that there should be a mission to the Jews.

After World War II, Catholic theologians found inspiration in the "humanity" of James Parkes as well as in his fresh exegesis of St. Paul, yet they also lamented the Anglican's openly unorthodox theology and his "superficial" historical analysis.[187] In a move impossible for a Catholic theologian, Parkes simply disregarded the Gospel according to John as "a canker on the body of Christianity."[188] But the Catholics Fiala, Harand, and Férenzy, operating beyond the boundaries of Christian orthodoxy in their day, failed to exert any influence in debates on Catholic-Jewish relations after World War II. It would be uplifting if the church could look back upon these heroic figures as sources of the change that emerged at Vatican II, but that was not the historic truth. In fact, the revolution in Catholic teaching on the Jews came from Catholics and other Christians who remained deeply mired in anti-Judaism.

5

Conspiring to Make
the Vatican Speak

When he looked upon the Europe of his era, Johannes Oesterreicher saw
signs that God wanted humanity to repent. Often hundreds of years passed
"where contradictions lie slumbering beside one another" he wrote, "but
then come times when the accounts are presented and the forces of hell
find air to breathe . . . the frightful challenge that comes from evil is also
a challenge that comes from God to his servants on earth . . . these are the
times when the lukewarm are spit out."[1] In late 1938, Karl Thieme watched
as Jewish refugees desperately escaped Germany across the Swiss border
at Basel, and he confided to Oesterreicher that this was "only the 'beginning of the birth pangs'. Next year they will come in earnest . . . what we
have before us is 'advent' after all! Therefore stand up and lift your heads
because your redemption is near! We cannot repeat this often enough!"[2]
"Birth pangs" was the expression used by Christ in Mark 13 to signal the
end of time. Relief over an approaching world-historical "decision" was
general among Catholic opponents of Hitler. When Ribbentrop and
Molotov signed their pact in August 1939, Jacques Maritain wrote his

friend the later Cardinal Charles Journet that the "beast is revealing itself more and more." He knew that the pact meant "war and catastrophe" but "from a spiritual point of view it will illuminate the consciences and gain the Church fighters for liberation." Journet told Maritain of a visit he had just received from Dietrich von Hildebrand. Despite the impending war Hildebrand was not "dejected."[3]

Johannes Oesterreicher admitted that scripture did not provide transparent vision for those trying to make sense of these events. "Certainly the history of the world is not a court of judgment for the world," he wrote Thieme. But if one could not have certain knowledge of what the coming catastrophe meant, one could have some knowledge. "The judgment of God," he wrote, "not for the natural human being, but for the Christian— even if without absolute certainty—is becoming clearer all time." Oesterreicher recalled a passage in Cardinal Newman's *Grammar of Assent* describing how Napoleon had mocked the pope for excommunicating him. "Will the weapons now fall out of my soldiers' hands?" the Corsican had wondered. "Two years later they did indeed," Oesterreicher commented, "from the hands of the bravest and the most robust."[4] In a similar way, Hitler the Austrian was bound to fail.

But how the Nazi leader failed depended upon other Europeans. Thieme and Oesterreicher worried that the continent would incur the wrath of God for failing to stand up to Hitler, whom they called the anti-Christ. "The real historical-theological question is this," Oesterreicher wrote his friend, "whether there are more just men in Europe than once in Sodom and Gomorrah, who might put off judgment."[5] He and Thieme had frightening premonitions of events on the horizon, but they believed that cataclysm might be averted if righteous Christians confronted Nazism at its core teaching of racism, which they took to be synonymous with antisemitism.

Beyond Genesis and the Gospel of Mark, the émigrés were also reading sections in Paul's letter to the Romans that assigned the Jews a key role in the coming denouement. Thieme and Oesterreicher hoped to redirect the apocalyptic energies of the age by triggering a mass conversion of Jews and ushering in the messianic age vaguely foretold in Romans 11:25–26, perhaps bypassing the fire and brimstone of an apocalyptic struggle. "Lest you be wise in your own conceits," the passage read, "I want you to understand this mystery, brethren: a hardening has come upon part of Israel, until the full number of the Gentiles come in and so all Israel will be saved; as it is written, 'The Deliverer will come from Zion, he will banish ungodliness from Jacob' . . ." (RSV). Clear from this statement was that Jews would not turn to Christ before the Gentiles did. And clear from observations from their time was that Jews would not turn to Christ until Christians abandoned the racism that made the church a place few Jews contemplated entering. "To the extent that we fulfill the command of Jesus and love the Jews," Thieme wrote, "we may hope they will find in Jesus the messianic hope fulfilled."[6]

He and Oesterreicher thus launched a campaign against antisemitism in the church, but this campaign was always driven by a certain utilitarianism. Yes, Christians should respect and love Jews, but the ultimate point was that Jews drop their resistance to seeing Christ as Messiah. When the "stiffneckedness of Israel toward Christ is broken and it speaks its faithful 'Yes,'" Oesterreicher wrote in 1937, "a springtime of joy will come over the earth."[7] If Israel had only accepted Christ during his time on earth, then God's Kingdom would have been realized then and there.[8] Citing Rabbi Eliezer (A.D. 90–130) Oesterreicher wrote that the coming of Isaiah's kingdom—where the lamb lay next to the wolf—"depended entirely upon the repentance of Israel . . . everything depends upon whether our generation, in particular Israel, understand the signs of the time . . ."[9]

Opposing racist antisemitism and working to convert Jews were therefore always two parts of the same act for the émigré Catholics, but in the eyes of Jews the latter vitiated the former. In Vienna Oesterreicher was known as an inveterate proselytizer, and in the spring of 1936 Head Rabbi Dr. David Feuchtwang warned Jews of the dangers they faced from "open enemies" who wanted to "physically destroy us," but also from people like Oesterreicher who offered "sham friendship" but want to "destroy us spiritually by converting us." "Not our power and perhaps also not our knowledge stands in the way of our enemies," Feuchtwang wrote, "but rather our tradition, our good moral qualities. Our religion means love of human beings, love of peace, and mercy; that is why we are a thorn in the side of those who possess none of these virtues. They want to destroy us, because we are a living admonition to the consciences of the nations." Feuchtwang compared the situation of the Jews in Central Europe to that of the Jewish people leaving Egypt: they faced dangers on two sides. Oesterreicher in turn castigated the rabbi for failing to rise to the stature of a "leader like Moses":

> It is difficult for us to say this in light of the venerability of his office, but it must be said that the religious leader of Viennese Jewry speaks to his community not of God, but only of the good moral qualities of his people: He does not tell them to change their ways. Yet one must be deaf to the voice of God if one does not understand that with all the suffering he has let come over Israel he wants to pull it toward him.[10]

This was the most offensive part of Oesterreicher's message to the Jews: that Hitler's persecution would persist until they accepted Christ as Messiah. It also reminds us of the schizophrenia we see throughout the Catholic response to antisemitism in these years, namely, the belief that it was the work of the anti-Christ yet also the will of God.

Only after World War II did Catholic theologians, led by Karl Thieme, confront and fully reject this view, opening the way for the new vision of Vatican II. But in these years they took first steps. The eschatological stood in uneasy tension with the ethical as Thieme and Oesterreicher labored to change Christian ideas about Jews in three major efforts: first, a Catholic Memorandum against antisemitism published in German, French, and English (1937); second, an attempt to have the pope make an appeal to Catholics for the Jews (1938/1939); and, finally, a book-length refutation of racism and antisemitism from a Catholic perspective, Oesterreicher's study *Racisme—antisémitisme, antichristianisme* (1940). While writing his book, Oesterreicher also used an émigré Austrian station in Paris to speak out over the airwaves to listeners in Germany, employing Catholic apocalyptic language to associate Hitler with the ultimate forces of evil.

For the first effort, Oesterreicher called upon two foremost students of the issue, Karl Thieme and Thieme's close friend Waldemar Gurian, both collaborators in anti-Nazi polemics at the German Catholic weekly *Junge Front* (1932–1936), and now émigrés in Switzerland.[11] Gurian (1902–1954), also a friend of Hannah Arendt and a meteoric talent on the tiny

Catholic left in Weimar Germany, published the relentlessly anti-Nazi *Deutsche Briefe* from Lucerne in the mid-1930s, then went on to help found the discipline of political science in the United States from the University of Notre Dame. The collaboration between the sensitive intellectuals Gurian and Thieme soon faltered, however, with each suspecting the other of unfair criticism. By the time they finished co-authoring the Memorandum the two émigré friends were communicating only through Oesterreicher in distant Vienna. In addition, Gurian complained about honoraria never received. That may have had to do with Joseph Wirth, the erratic former German Reich Chancellor also living in Swiss exile who had commissioned the statement from Oesterreicher in the first place. Aside from being a bon vivant and man of multiple loyalties (later a Stalin-prize laureate), Wirth was notoriously penniless.[12]

After *Kristallnacht* of November 1938, Thieme began wondering whether it was enough simply to reach out to Catholic intellectuals. With Wirth, Oesterreicher, former Danzig mayor Hermann Rauschning (author of *Hitler Speaks*), and a handful of other German Christian émigrés, he tried to get the pope himself to appeal to Catholics throughout the world on behalf of Germany's Jews. The émigrés used contacts in Rome like the pope's secretary, Jesuit Robert Leiber, to circumvent the venal Vatican bureaucracy. The effect of an appeal for the Jews would be so miraculous, they believed, as to stimulate a mass conversion of the Jews and trigger the Messianic age.

At the same time, Oesterreicher, by this point in Paris, worked on his study of racism, a final gesture of activism in Europe before he fled to New York and became John M. Oesterreicher, American Catholic expert on the Jews. Using the French capital's libraries and supplied with references by Thieme, he culled the entire Christian tradition—including copious condemnations by U.S. bishops of the German regime after *Kristallnacht*—in an attempt to portray the Catholic position against racist antisemitism as clear and unwavering. Knowing that in fact the church's position had been more ambiguous, Thieme voiced skepticism: "I find all the pieces of evidence you have sent me proving that the church has 'not been silent' a travesty," he protested. Rather than an "unending cascade of general statements," Catholics needed "very concrete" instruction, and Rome was not providing it.[13] Oesterreicher attempted to fill the gap. His book remains the most extensive and serious critique of both racism and antisemitism from a Catholic point of view ever issued. It also gives a sense of the mental horizons of the time.

A Catholic Memorandum on the Jews

As intellectuals, Thieme and Oesterreicher believed in the power of the printed word, and they were happy to accept Joseph Wirth's idea to produce a Memorandum on the Jewish question in 1937, with Thieme addressing the theological and Waldemar Gurian the scientific and historical sides of the question. Former Chancellor Wirth believed the Catholic Church was doing too little to combat antisemitism and demanded that Thieme and Gurian show the "courage, to reveal Church measures [in the Jewish question] as serious mistakes, as actions taken against the spirit of the Gospel."[14] Gurian, however, rejected this "extreme" demand as "nonsense" and threatened to withdraw his contribution if words to that effect were included in the forty-page Memorandum which appeared in Oesterreicher's *Erfüllung* in 1937, then as a booklet from the Paulist Press in New York, and finally in Paris.

Because its primary purpose was to cause "Christian antisemites" to reassess their ideas about the Jews, the Memorandum projected Catholicism and antisemitism as irreconcilable, and like all work of the émigrés in this period, it failed to question the church's own record, about which Oesterreicher and Thieme expressed doubts in private.[15] Both knew well the failure of the hierarchy to speak out in favor of Europe's Jews, and it was precisely Catholic racist antisemitism that drove them to action. But they also believed that this Catholic contempt was a deformation and not a natural outgrowth of Christian teaching, and thus branded their cradle Catholic opponents "heathens" and "neo-Pagans."

Gurian and Thieme insisted on anonymity, partly out of concern for Thieme's relatives in the Third Reich and partly because of Gurian's Jewish ancestry. Oesterreicher figured openly as editor, but launched the Memorandum into a hostile environment, a fact reflected in the difficulty of getting signatories from the upper clergy of the church. For example, the otherwise sympathetic leading French Catholic expert on Judaism, Joseph Bonsirven, S.J., refused to sign on because he was ill, an "excuse" that Oesterreicher questioned. Yet in fact repression at the hands of his own order had incapacitated this scholar. In July 1936, Bonsirven had organized a conference on the "the Question of Israel among the Nations," which was well-received among the French public but caused the Vatican to demand a "review."[16] According to Bonsirven, "the only thing one could reproach him for was not having said that Jews are malefactors and corrupters."[17] After this, Jesuit General Włodimierz Ledóchowski in Rome forbade Bonsirven to study contemporary Judaism, and forced him to cancel a collaborative work with Father Charles Devaux, Superior of the Notre Dame de Sion fathers (and later rescuer of hundreds of Jews), that had already been commissioned. The shock was so great that Bonsirven required two months of "*repos absolu*" at Montpellier. The only sense in this muzzling, as Bonsirven wrote the Jesuit provincial, was "not to offend a General who is an antisemite." This was "opportunism and nothing else . . . a wound to religious life." "I have promised obedience," Bonsirven wrote, "but not to a capricious will."[18]

Besides intellectuals like Bonsirven, Oesterreicher had hoped to attract European bishops to a condemnation of antisemitism. "We would like to present the Memorandum to the bishops after it has appeared," he wrote Thieme in 1937. "Could you act as mediator with the present bishop of Basel?"[19] In the end, not a single bishop supported the undertaking in print. The American publisher noted that other Catholic intellectuals endorsed it but had been unwilling to sign, presumably because they lived in Nazi Germany or Fascist Italy.[20] Among those who did sign, only the first three are well known today: Jacques Maritain, Maritain's friend (later cardinal) Rev. Charles Journet, and Dietrich von Hildebrand. The other signatories included the Rev. Dr. Silvester Braito, O.P., and Rev. Basilius Lang, O.S.B. (Czechoslovakia); Prof. Edgar de Bruyne (Belgium); Rev. Charles Devaux, and Stanislas Fumet (France); Rev. Zyrill Fischer, O.F.M., and Rev. Alois Wildenauer (Austria); Rev. Benoît Lavaud, O.P. (Switzerland); Dr. Eduard Pant (Poland); Rev. Franziskus Stratmann (Germany; Italy), and Rev. Johannes B. Kors, O.P. (Netherlands). The Czechs, leading figures in a Catholic intellectual renaissance, were known to Oesterreicher because of his occasional work in Bohemian and Moravian seminaries; Pant, Stratmann, and Fischer were prominent Germans who attacked Nazism in Dietrich von Hildebrand's publications; and

Kors was a convert who served as president of the Catholic University in Nijmegen.

Because it was directed at Christian antisemites, the Memorandum argued that discrimination against Jews could not be defended through Christian teaching. The God of the Old Testament was not a "Jewish" God separate from the God of the New, Karl Thieme wrote, and Israel was the people of the one God. Thieme reinterpreted New Testament passages that were frequently used to provoke hatred of Jews. If Christ called anyone "sons of the devil," it was sinners who happened to be Jewish—and not Jews without distinction. Far from being set against the Jews, Jesus "loved his people," confining "his mission specifically to the 'lost sheep of the House of Israel'." Waldemar Gurian probed other religious sources used by antisemites to justify discrimination. He admitted that church authorities confined Jews to ghettos during the Middle Ages, but with the passing of medieval society along with that society's "public morality" based in faith, so had passed any justification for special laws against Jews.[21] In any case, church discrimination against Jews was abolished with the unified and updated Canon Law of 1917.[22] Gurian rejected popular calls for quotas that would limit numbers of Jewish students or lawyers to the percentage of Jews in their society: such discrimination was based in a racist worldview incompatible with Christianity, which saw the value of humans in reason and spirit and not in "blood." Those concerned by unfair business practices—which antisemites associated with Jews— should demand legislation against those practices and not against human beings.[23] Gurian warned that any act of discrimination would establish racism as a general principle and demoralize public life.[24]

Gurian and Thieme recognized that Christians bowed to racial hatred, but thought that its sources lay outside the church in a secular worldview that promoted a "naturalistic picture of man." Gurian cited an extreme, but logical, outgrowth of this view in a Nazi commentary on the Nuremberg laws according to which "the difference between the lowest so-called humans and our highest races is far greater than that which exists between the lowest humans and the highest apes."[25] If modern antisemitism was derived from Christianity, it was by way of secularized religious tropes. Gurian introduced readers to yet another German refugee working out of Vienna—the political scientist Eric Voegelin—who had just published a study arguing that "race" was a pagan substitute for the lost conception of the Mystical Body of Christ. Voegelin traced the genealogy through the philosopher Johann Gottlieb Fichte, who had secularized the binary opposition "Christ-Antichrist" by applying it to the relation of the German people to Napoleonic France. In the place "of the Kingdom of God he set the Nation."

Far from a source of antisemitism, Christianity was the only defense against it. "Insofar as the Church ultimately interprets the Natural Law and guarantees it respect," Thieme wrote, "she will unceasingly demand that the rights of the Jew as a human being shall not be violated. The Church defends the rights of man and must defend them because she knows that they are not human but God-given rights, even if all nations of a secularized 'Christianity' should join in the cry: 'Down with the Jews!' The Church, which is named after Jesus, the Christ of the House of David, cannot do otherwise than exclaim: 'Peace upon Israel.' "[26] By contrast, people with secular worldviews were powerless to craft laws to protect people whom science had deemed "racially" disruptive.

In retrospect, this kind of approach may seem triumphalist, an attempt to direct attention away from the church's own troubled past. But if Thieme had affirmed that the church once stoked antisemitism, he would have justified the antisemites' claim that Christianity and antisemitism were compatible. Instead, he presented Catholic teaching as unchanging, derived from eternal truths. But this was not only a strategy: Thieme did not believe there was a problem with Christianity. The deeper strata of Christian anti-Judaism did not trouble Catholic opponents of Nazism. For them, Jews were the people of God, but they lived under divine punishment for rejecting their Messiah. "For the very reason that he called Israel to His own sonship out of all the nations of the earth," Thieme wrote, "God also punishes it all the harder, according to Amos, for all its sins."[27] He chided "secular" Jews for seeing in the "happenings since 1933 nothing more than a materialistic, nationalistic self-determination." "No one can approach the Jewish question of our day," he continued, "without expressing disappointment and sorrow that, by and large, Judaism did not see in the persecutions of recent years—in harmony with the constant warnings of the prophets—a reason for self-examination and conversion to God *and* His anointed.[28]

As terrible as the persecution was, for Christians it was not incompatible with the idea that God still favored the Jews. "All the unspeakable misery of Israel only arouses God's irate love," Thieme wrote, "which grows the greater the more Israel becomes, in part, obdurate against Him in arrogant pride or bows in false humility to the letter of His Law whose spirit and meaning it continues to deny. The word of the Lord is still true: 'Thou art My servant Israel, for in thee will I glory. Can a woman forget her infant, so as not to have pity on the son of her womb? And if she should forget, yet will not I forget thee."[29] Such was the inspiration from Christian tradition available to avant-garde opponents of racist antisemitism. The difference between them and their opponents at this deeper level of belief was that their opponents thought that Jews were damned beyond redemption, while the émigrés were confident that was not true. To his own question of whether God had "rejected his people," St. Paul had answered no, "God has not rejected his people whom he foreknew." Thieme also quoted Breslau theologian Friedrich Maier (later teacher of Joseph Ratzinger), who warned against "sitting in judgment over Israel."[30]

The Memorandum instructed Catholics to use all their influence to combat anti-Jewish measures "because they are neither protective nor justifiable defensive measures; they are aimed only at defamation and destruction."[31] Oesterreicher and Thieme followed their own advice, and decided to go to the top of the church hierarchy, using connections from the émigré circles to cause the pope speak out in favor of the German Jews. One might wonder that they had not lost faith in top church officials. Oesterreicher routinely complained of the preponderance of "Nazi Catholics" in Central Europe; the installation of clericofascist Father Josef Tiso as head of the Nazi puppet state of Slovakia darkened his already sinister premonitions. "Therese von Konnersreuth," he confided to Thieme, "once had a vision. Looking in the great crowd that walked sneering and mocking past the cross at Golgotha, she saw many dressed in red capes: Prelates of the Church. May God grant that soon the cup of sinfulness will be full, so that the mercy of God will run over."[32] Thieme registered even greater skepticism about Catholicism's supposed opposition to racist antisemitism: "the unending cascade of general statements—like the one made by [Paris Cardinal Jean] Verdier—cannot replace the very concrete things about which the people ought to be instructed . . . because they no longer know about them!"[33]

Still, belief in one holy Catholic and apostolic church was an article of faith, and from the time he arrived in Paris, Oesterreicher and his motley group of exiles and other anti-Nazis—including Thieme, Hermann Rauschning, Joseph Wirth, Waldemar Gurian, Jacques Maritain, Karl Barth (known among the conspirators as the "Rabbi"), as well as others whose names we do not know—attempted to make the men in red capes act on behalf of Germany's Jews. In December 1938, Thieme described to Oesterreicher the first stages of a "utopian" plan. Oesterreicher would ask Paris Cardinal Verdier to assemble Catholics for a meeting with the pope proposing a collection in the churches to alleviate the plight of the Jews, showing that "we as Christians can no longer stand aside and look at what is happening to them." Traumatized by *Kristallnacht*, Thieme insisted that persecuted Jews become the church's top concern. Pius should "call upon Catholic Christians, above *everything* else, to do all they can for the Jews, with the last measure of their energy."[34] His draft letter for the pope showed that Thieme had arrived at a new solidarity with the Jews, brothers in two senses: stepbrothers of Christians but also "blood brothers" of Christ:

When was it ever more necessary than now to prove ourselves as neighbors to our stepbrothers in Christ—just as the merciful Samaritan did for his stepbrother in Moses who had fallen among thieves?

And which moment could be more suitable to summon Christians to a Samaritan act for the blood brothers of our savior than the celebration of his birth *ex radice Isai*?

Therefore we request, if possible, that the Christmas address of Your Holiness contain a word for the persecuted Jews. We are certain that such a word would be epoch-making: in the history of the holy Church, in the history of humanity and not least in the history of the conversion of Israel. And even if it should serve as pretext for new persecution of the Church in Germany and Austria—which is certain to happen in any case—this would be borne with a lighter heart in the knowledge that it was suffered for the witness of merciful love.[35]

For Oesterreicher and Thieme, solidarity for Jews was never distinct from the conviction that they were living at the end of time, and that conviction was never distinct from the idea that Jews should be led to Christ. Thieme hoped that gestures of sympathy for Jews from the Vatican would be so miraculous as to cause a mass conversion and usher in an age of peace and harmony. "The question," he wrote, "is only whether God will make a miracle happen and permit a sign to take place toward Israel whose effectiveness would surpass all efforts directed at the conversion of Israel since the Pentecost."

Letters and entreaties from highly placed contacts failed to move the pope to action.[36] As Oesterreicher explained many years later, Pius XI was in ill health, having suffered two heart attacks in November 1938, and the Vatican was concerned not to worsen the situation for the church in a time of approaching war. Papal secretary Montini—later Paul VI— told Oesterreicher that it was "not the custom of the Apostolic See to offer a blessing before something has happened, but only after it has happened."[37]

From the start, Oesterreicher had been less optimistic because he knew Vatican officials were "full of worry because of the threatened confiscation of all church properties in Germany and Austria." A sign of solidarity with Jews might provide the Nazi state with a welcome pretext for attack. Oesterreicher sympathized. Where Thieme thought a Christian act of solidarity for the Jews would make the Christianity of the church more attractive than ever, Oesterreicher feared it would make the visible church disappear because Hitler would destroy it. Yet Oesterreicher was filled with optimism when rumors circulated through Paris on the Vatican's plans to issue an encyclical "underscoring the Church's opposition to the new Nazi paganism and denouncing the persecutions against the Jews and the laws on racism that have been passed by totalitarian countries."[38]

Oesterreicher refused to let matters rest when the encyclical was buried in early 1939. He and Thieme expected a European war, and believing that most Germans opposed Hitler, the two planned to use Vatican connections to provoke an uprising within the German military. Though Oesterreicher described Pius XII—elected in March 1939—as "timid" and "fearful," he and Thieme schemed to have Vatican radio release Catholic German soldiers from their oath to Hitler just before a German attack.

"According to tradition," Oesterreicher wrote, "the Catholic is not bound in obedience to his ruler if the ruler launches war in criminal fashion."[39]

In order to make the new pope "cooperate," Karl Thieme used Swiss Catholic politicians with direct lines to Pius's German secretary Robert Leiber, S.J., thus bypassing the Vatican's state chancellery. In the meantime, Oesterreicher composed a radio message while the group fashioned sound recordings.[40] In late April, Thieme informed Karl Barth of the initiative in order to make Protestants jealous of Catholics, and then perhaps "Rome jealous of Geneva."[41] Oesterreicher wondered whether they should not simply tell the pope that Geneva was about to "speak clearly, and that it was necessary for Rome to do the same." "I think it unlikely," Oesterreicher concluded gloomily, "that the somewhat apprehensive Pius XII will make his mind up to do the only right thing, namely to release German soldiers from their oath, maybe even to pronounce a 'general' condemnation of the person who is inciting war."[42]

News from the Vatican under Pius XII continued to disappoint Oesterreicher. Was it true that the pope gave the order to ring church bells on Hitler's birthday (April 20)? Did he want to "negotiate" with Hitler about infractions against the Concordat? "It is enough to make one cry and laugh at the same time!" he wrote Thieme. The pope needed instruction: "we cannot say too clearly what needs to be done."[43] Even after the Führer sent his troops into rump Czechoslovakia in violation of the Munich agreement, Pius continued to appease Hitler. A week later, Oesterreicher expressed relief mixed with disgust. "The political situation is not the way we would like," he wrote his friend. "The Pope's offers to mediate have been rebuffed, thank God. Hopefully Pius XII has learned from this. Supposedly an encyclical is being prepared in which the pope takes issue with the international situation—hopefully in a different way than the unfortunate Duke of Windsor. *He who does not have the courage to accuse should spare us and himself any appeal to morality.*"[44]

By June, Oesterreicher had given up on the pope, who had just welcomed over three thousand soldiers of the Italian-Spanish Arrow Division to the vestibule of the Hall of Benediction and blessed their rosaries.[45] "It is beyond understanding," he wrote Thieme, "that Pius XII, after all his diplomatic experiments as Cardinal State Secretary have failed, is still attempting diplomacy, and not preaching the truth." After war broke out,

Pius issued the encyclical *Summi Pontificatus* which suggested not even mild rebuke of the Germans and offered only vague consolation to the Poles, couched in the equivocal language that infuriated Oesterreicher. In a meeting on September 30, 1939, Pius spoke of the tears Poles were shedding for the horrors visiting their homeland: Christ recognized the special value of these tears, which held their own "sweetness."[46]

No wonder Europeans of that time failed to hear the pope. In June 1940, French Cardinal Eugène Tisserant lamented the pontiff's failure to issue an encyclical "on the duty of the individual to obey the dictates of his conscience, because this is a vital point of Christianity." "I fear that history will have reason to reproach the Holy See for a policy that suited its own ends and not much more," Tisserant concluded.[47] Oesterreicher stressed similar points just after New Year's 1940. The Germans retained a feeling of obligation to state authority that is "completely false," he wrote Karl Thieme. They would never rise up against Hitler because they loved death more than life. He pointed to a dramatic case just making headlines. The British Navy had trapped the German pocket battleship *Admiral Graf Spee* at Montevideo, giving its captain Hans Langsdorff a chance to turn against Hitler and fight for Germany. Instead, Langsdorff scuttled the ship and killed himself. "There is no other way," Oesterreicher explained, "than the collapse [of Hitler's regime] to liberate the German people and the entire world from Hitler: that is, not only from the person, but also from the spirit which made him and placed him on his throne."[48]

Oesterreicher was demanding unconditional surrender years before this became the policy of any state. But his attention was shifting elsewhere because the spirit of Hitler went beyond Europe. One task remained for Oesterreicher before his hair-raising escape from France in June 1940, and that was to present a Catholic refutation of racism to an international audience, confronting Hitler's spirit with Christian truth. "I am of the firm conviction" he wrote to Thieme, "that Hitler stays in power because nowhere on earth is anyone resisting him from their innermost being, because no one is atoning or doing penance. What happened in Sodom and Gomorrah is being replayed: there are too few just men."[49]

Preaching to Catholics in the Reich

News of the Nazi attack upon Poland reached Johannes Oesterreicher as he was conducting a retreat somewhere in the Swiss Alps. French authorities canceled reentry visas, and Oesterreicher became desperate to get back to Paris where he was to make radio broadcasts into Nazi Germany. Trusting Providence, he boarded the express in Basel. When the train reached the border, a customs official looked suspiciously at Oesterreicher's papers then permitted him to continue for no obvious reason. From September 1939 until shortly before the German conquest of Paris, Oesterreicher broadcast Sunday sermons into the Reich that could be heard as far as Vienna but were also intercepted at the listening stations "Landhaus" in Stuttgart and then at "Seehaus" in Berlin, both under the direction of Joseph Goebbels.[50] Though Oesterreicher left his transcripts behind during the mad rush out of the capital in June 1940, the records kept by Nazi snoopers have survived in the German Federal Archives, and therefore we know what Oesterreicher said. In contrast to Pius, Oesterreicher left no doubt as to the identities of the war's victims: Poles, Czechs, and Jews, with the highest death totals among the last group.[51] He told listeners of mass executions of men, women, and children; the unleashing of typhoid among Warsaw Jews; arrests of Catholic priests; long-term plans to sterilize Polish boys and girls and starve the Polish population.[52] He branded leading Nazis "enemies of the Cross" and went beyond prayers and condemnations to instruct listeners to "stand up" and oppose the "heathens" and "enemies of their Lord," who had "plunged Europe into war" and made love a crime of state.[53] He called Hitler the anti-Christ.

Oesterreicher's radio messages feature the combination of apocalyptic vision and intense political engagement that we know from the anti-Nazi plotting he did with Karl Thieme. Speaking of the destruction unleashed by the "men of disaster"—gas and fire bombs, microbes, pestilence, and the fear they generated—he urged his audience not to forget what the Lord promises, that "amidst suffering and fears new things are born, that the horrors are not something final, but a sign of coming joy, signs of the wonderful return of the Lord himself . . . we are in the Advent, the time of waiting and hoping . . ."[54] The opportunity to speak directly to Germans living under totalitarian rule also brought forth the "personalist" sensitivity that Oesterreicher took from the company of Dietrich von Hildebrand. In mid-February 1940, he told listeners that

> every person is and remains unique. Every one is of unending worth, every one is called to his own task, every one a thought of God. None is the copy of another, none will ever come back again . . . the more a human being lives in spirit and in love, the more evident it becomes that he is not simply a species exemplar [*Gattungsexemplar*] but a personal being. God's word pertains to everyone: "I have ransomed you and called you by name and you are my own." [Isaiah 43:1][55]

The turn to personalism was also stimulated through friendship with Jacques Maritain, participant in the conspiracies of Rauschning and Thieme. Maritain's notion of human rights had evolved through confrontation with the new evil called "totalitarianism," and, as Samuel Moyn argues, "there is no way to fathom Maritain's conversion to rights and that of the whole Continent without looking to the larger Catholic Church's conversion to personalism. How this happened was unexpected and dramatic, and due above all to events in the mid-1930s that decided Pius XI to commit the Church to antitotalitarianism."[56] Oesterreicher specified the source of the threat with a frankness the popes avoided, telling listeners in the Reich that "Brown Bolshevism" wanted to "destroy the individual."

The Gestapo discovered Oesterreicher's identity after it was mistakenly divulged in the October 27, 1939, broadcast, and instructed Munich's Cardinal Faulhaber as well as the Catholic authorities in Vienna to stop the priest—or else.[57] News of the ultimatum reached Oesterreicher in Paris, and he adopted the "compromise" of continuing to write the sermons but asking someone else to read them. During and after the war, he occasionally heard from people who had heard the sermons, once as far away as Rome. He learned that a landlady in Vienna called him a "*Hetzpfaff*": a "rabble rousing priest."[58] His broadcasts reveal that it was possible for Catholics to make devastating critiques of the war-mongering Nazi elite, but also that the Gestapo did not hesitate to threaten consequences for such words. They make one wonder what would have been the effect of even a single bishop calling Hitler an "unclean spirit" then beseeching God to make him disappear. Oesterreicher told listeners in November 1939 that the German Dominican Franziskus Stratmann had prayed for Hitler's exorcism while the Führer sojourned in Rome. Hitler was "not simply a loud speaker, or an irresponsible statesman," Oesterreicher instructed, "he was archenemy and antipode in human form." Oesterreicher told Germans that the behavior of their army in Poland was "devilish."[59]

Against Racism and Antisemitism

Like Christian works on racism by Rudolf Lämmel, Erich Voegelin, Pierre Lorson, Irene Harand, or Walter Berger, the book that Johannes Oesterreicher published in Paris in 1940 has become a collector's item, available in a half-dozen libraries worldwide and rarely on the international book market. It is part of a buried past of theological and sociological reflection from Central Europe issued on the eve of the Nazi assault and represents a high point in Catholic thought about the racism of antisemitism. It was also an end point. After the war, the conviction rose that antisemitism and racism were separate things because Jews were not a race. After leaving Europe, Oesterreicher never again wrote on the race question.

He composed this book at the urging of acquaintances in Paris. "Again and again all kinds of people ask that a book be written on the race question," Oesterreicher confided to Karl Thieme in February 1939. "Bishop [Roger-Henri-Marie] Beaussart also told me not long ago how necessary a book is against racism."[60] Hermann Rauschning wrote a positive review of Oesterreicher's manuscript for the publisher, and the prominent French Catholic expert on German affairs (and close friend of Dietrich von Hildebrand) Robert d'Harcourt penned the introduction for the book's first edition, which appeared in Paris in the spring of 1940. Three years later, a longer version appeared in New York for which the philosopher Jacques Maritain added a preface.[61]

The book's point was not originality. To the displeasure of Rauschning and other reviewers for the press, Oesterreicher mainly reproduced opinions with commentary, on the one hand, of experts on the race question including scientists and Catholic thinkers, and on the other, of the racists themselves. He was convinced that Catholics were ignorant on both

counts, especially the latter, not having read Rosenberg or Hitler in the
original. To critics, he responded that few Catholics would read the
thoughts of a little-known priest, but very many wanted to know what
the church thought about racism. Rauschning called the book the first
"real criticism written from a Catholic position."[62]

Former medical student Oesterreicher first poked fun at Adolf Hitler's
inability to distinguish race from species and Julius Streicher's notion that
it was dangerous to introduce sperm from one race to another because "foreign albumin is the sperm of a man of another race . . . a single cohabitation
of a Jew by an Aryan woman suffices to ruin her blood forever." "Can one
enter into a discussion with such nonsense?" Oesterreicher asked.[63] Yet he
did enter into a discussion, showing that racial scientists could identify no
races with certainty. Anthropologists of all persuasions employed inconsis-
tent criteria to classify races, especially where Jews were concerned. In fact,
Oesterreicher wrote, Jews had the hair and skin color and cranial dimensions of the places where they lived.[64] Though blood supposedly united
races, no supposed race could be identified with blood type, including the
Jews. No one could identify any principle that would indicate where boundaries ran between races. If there were races, Oesterreicher wrote, it was in
their nature to "disappear."

At its core, racism was not about science, but rather about belief in racial "superiority."[65] Such belief was groundless. Some researchers claimed
that persons of African descent had "a lower intellectual level," yet such
findings were due not to consubstantial inferiority, but rather to the treatment Africans had suffered, or the climate in which they lived. Furthermore, it would be "incorrect to maintain that the civilization of white
people was superior in every regard to that which blacks would have created if they lived in the same geographic conditions and received the same
intellectual nourishment as white peoples."[66] Racism was not only a belief,
it was part of a system of beliefs that arose from the ruins of Christianity
through the efforts of man to rid himself of God and any morality beyond
human will. "Modern times began with the struggle against God," Oesterreicher maintained, "and they now culminate in the brutal destruction of
everything that is human. Racism is anti-humanism, a consequence of anti-
Christianism." Oesterreicher had an easy time showing that this belief
system struck at the heart of the Church's universalism. For Aryans there

was "no communion of saints, no communal life, no solidarity," indeed there was no sin, because Aryans' blood was pure, their race "good."[67]

Throughout the book, Oesterreicher treated racism as if synonymous with antisemitism, one implying the other, each suggesting the "question of questions" that Karl Thieme had formulated several years earlier: "tell me what you think of the myth of blood and of race, tell me your attitude toward Jews, and I will tell you who you are."[68] Yet he also made clear that Jews were different, and he said nothing about Nazi anti-Slavism or hatred of other racial groups. "It is obvious," Oesterreicher wrote, that the hostility to the Jews "does not, as the racists argue, grow out of the 'racial instinct.' Spokesmen for the Nordic myth have friendly relations with the Japanese, Armenians, Hungarians, and Arabs—thus to people who are much further away from the Germans in regard to race than are the Jews."[69]

Hitler's antisemitism differed in one important regard from racism: it was concerned not with inferiority but with dangerous powers. It did not battle ostensible Jewish faults or shortcomings, but rather constituted a strategy of "cultivating" such things. Jews were "dirty," so one denied them sanitary facilities; Jews were "dishonest," so one denied them protection by law.[70] Oesterreicher cited a piece from a magazine of the Nazi storm troopers (SA) saying that the "good Jew" was a German's worst enemy because he provokes pity and "paralyzes our struggle." Here one saw that even the Nazis intuited some enduring value attached to the Jewish people because of their divine vocation. The challenge was to locate Catholic sources making that point.

Even when he republished the book in 1943, Oesterreicher could find no words of defense for the Jews coming from the papacy. He did print the little-known remarks of Pius XI uttered to Belgian pilgrims in 1938. "It is not possible for Christians to participate in antisemitism," the pope had said, moved to tears. "We recognize everyone's right to defend himself, to equip himself with the means necessary to protect against anything that menaces his legitimate interests. But antisemitism is inadmissible. We are spiritually Semites."[71] Oesterreicher portrayed these words as exemplifying the pope's solidarity, and argued that Pius had gone beyond biblical language to turn explicitly against the racist formulation. Otherwise, he might have said: spiritually we are Israelites. But Oesterreicher also noted less-known segments of the pope's statement that cast doubt on his own interpretation. "The promise was made to Abraham and his progeny," Pius had continued. "Paul's text does not say to the descendants, it does not use the plural, but rather the singular, to his descendent. This promise is recognized in Christ and by Christ in us we are members of his mystical body. By Christ and in Christ we are the spiritual progeny of Abraham."

Pius's references were to Paul's letter to the Galatians, in part a polemic with the Jews [Galatians 3:16]. A question Oesterreicher did not pose was this: if Christians spiritually are Semites, who are the Jews? By implication, it would seem they are "ethnic" Semites, outside the body, disinherited, and if they evoked solidarity in Pius, it was the solidarity of a lost kinship. Christians were spiritual, but Jews, in accordance with anti-Judaic stereotypes from time immemorial, were carnal. Jews as a living people were absent from the words the pope uttered to the Belgians, as they were from every Vatican statement from 1933 to 1945. Some historians now project the words of Pius XI as an important statement in defense of the Jews, but at the time they were not published in the Vatican press, nor read on Vatican Radio.[72] Karl Thieme accused Oesterreicher of wishful thinking. "Impromptu statements made to pilgrims, regardless how heartfelt (as shown by the [pope's] tears) are no substitute for a statement by the [Church's] teaching authority!"[73] For his book, Oesterreicher was thus left clinging to papal citations hundreds of years old. In 1247, after pogroms had swept through Central Europe, Innocent IV ordered that German bishops "reestablish the previously existing situation and cease importuning [Jews] in any way." Innocent's proscription was renewed by Gregory X in 1273, and constituted, in Oesterreicher's view, the "eternal voice of the Church."

Oesterreicher found but one statement of solidarity made by a continental European bishop in November 1938, when the synagogues smoldered across Germany and Austria, namely Marius Besson of Geneva, who asked that his flock pray for those persecuted either for "profession or race." Oesterreicher also reprinted words spoken by the remarkable Archbishop Jules Saliège of Toulouse over five years earlier. "How can one ask me not to feel connected with Israel," Saliège had asked, "as the branch does with the trunk out of which it grew?" Oesterreicher added that a "true Christian" felt the kind of "solidarity" Saliège was referring to. From careful study of the British *Catholic Herald*, Oesterreicher discovered that Vatican Radio had not been silent after *Kristallnacht*, but its editors had not found a pope or bishop to stand up in defense of Jews. "We can hardly do better than to repeat the words of the Jewish Rabbi," the station broadcast on November 18, "who declared in sympathy with priests persecuted in Mexico and Spain: 'let us count their victims among our own victims and beg God that he shed his grace and mercy on them as well as us!' "[74]

Oesterreicher had better luck when he consulted American newspapers in the French libraries where he worked on his book. "The protests against racist barbarism in the United States were stronger than any where else," he conceded.[75] Not only that, American Catholics were probing the events of November 1938 for deeper meaning. Perhaps the most famous protest came from Catholic University Professor Fulton J. Sheen—later a bishop, television personality, author of dozens of bestsellers (including cookbooks)—who said on November 24, 1938, that the racial myth of "superior" German blood had a basic flaw: no blood is more dignified than that of the Jews, because it was the blood of the Redeemer. He also argued for Jews' human rights. Even if Jews were not "joyous" at their special connection with Jesus, "we Catholics protest passionately against their persecution, because as *human persons* they posses inalienable rights."[76] Archbishop Michael J. Curley of Baltimore likewise protested against *Kristallnacht* over the American airwaves. The "Jewish people were victims of savagery without precedent in history," Curley said, "and to be silent now is an offense against God and humanity, a cowardice that would abase us." If the Jews had committed a crime, it was "to belong to the race which Jesus, the founder of our Church, the savior of the world, belonged to."[77] In the same radio program, Fordham University President Robert J. Gannon said that Nazism was the worse for springing from Christian soil. It was a "new rupture with grace," superficially similar to the barbarism of Attila or Alarich, but far more dangerous because they were "never Christians, had never taken the sacraments." Other bishops registering outrage after November 9, 1938, included those of Boston (O'Connell), Milwaukee (Stritch), Westminster (Hinsley), Liverpool (Downey), and San Francisco (Mitty).[78]

We can speculate that the greater degree of involvement of U.S. bishops had to do with the more advanced state of interfaith relations in a more religiously tolerant society. Perhaps they and their British colleagues had a greater feeling of impunity far from Hitler's reach. Yet within Europe, the activist stance of Thieme and Oesterreicher was unusual for Christians—not only because of the pervasive absence of solidarity with Jews across the continent, but because of the general deference of Christians to Providence. One prayed for peace without telling God the precise way He should effect it. In the summer of 1939 Thieme and Oesterreicher, having given up on the pope and bishops, tried to stimulate a massive "crusade of prayer" of Christians across Europe asking God not only to grant peace, but to aid the German people in causing the "criminal" Hitler regime to "disappear." Karl Barth and Jacques Maritain refused to support this appeal, however. Barth claimed that as an evangelical Protestant he could not endorse the intention of placing "supernatural means in the service of natural purposes," and Maritain wrote that "God knows better than we do what is right for the world."[79] This was very similar to the logic given by the pope for not condemning the German invasions of the Czech lands in 1939: he did not want to "intervene in historical processes," and thereby question the will of the Almighty as exemplified in History.[80]

Oesterreicher and Thieme had a very different perspective: they felt the crime of antisemitism openly defied the will of God as exemplified in History. This conviction had brought them together in 1934. The issue was so clear that what seems to us a pipe dream appeared to them fully realistic: of course millions of Christians would pray publicly for the Hitler regime to disappear from the face of the earth; Hitler claimed to be God and was an enemy of God. "The Aryan man feels himself to be the creator and master of the world which he imagines exists to glorify him," Oesterreicher wrote in his book. "Racist madness is a rebellion against God who on Sinai gave his commandment to the people of Israel and to all humanity: 'I am the Lord your God. You shall not have other gods before me.'" Therefore, "the myth of the superiority of the 'Aryan' race . . . is in the last analysis a protest against the election of Israel."[81] The Nordic man could not bear a God who had placed the key to history in the hands of small desert people and given this people the vocation of bringing humanity "fullness." (Romans 11:15). Those denying the Jews a role in bringing this "fullness" to the world had resurrected an ancient heresy: "an invisible line leads from Marcion to the partisans of the racist myth."[82]

If antisemitism was rooted in blasphemy, how did that involve Christ? According to Oesterreicher, both the election of Israel as well as the birth of Christ in Israel scandalized a world that could not accept "that God became man and *our brother* as a member of the Jewish people, of his people." Therefore, all persecution of Jews "touches" Christ. "Whoever insults Jewish blood insults the blood of Jesus." Oesterreicher gave many examples of Hitler's regime striking out against Christ the Jew. In Linz, Nazis portrayed Christ as a Jew hanging on a swastika, and in Cologne they smeared the words "*Christus verrecke*" on churches. In 1938, the Nazi Women's League issued a circular comparing the "Jew Jesus" moaning on the cross to the heroine Planetta who managed to utter "long live Germany!" before dying. There was also the story of a German boy refusing to genuflect at a cross. "First get rid of the Jew!" he demanded.[83] "These are the fruits of racist education," Oesterreicher concluded, "the hate of Jews always degenerates into hatred of the Old and the New Testament." Oesterreicher's deepest inspiration on the anti-Christianity of antisemitism came from the American Jewish author Maurice Samuel, according to whom,

> We shall never understand the maniacal, world-wide seizure of antisemitism unless we transpose the terms. It is of Christ that the Nazi-Fascists are afraid, it is his omnipotence in which they believe, it is him that they are determined madly to obliterate. But the names of Christ and Christianity are too overwhelming, and the habit of submission to them is too deeply ingrained after centuries and centuries of teaching. Therefore they must, I repeat, make their assault on those who were responsible for the birth and spread of Christianity. They must spit on Jews as the "Christkillers" because they long to spit on the Jews as the Christgivers.[84]

Samuel's analysis tended to discourage deeper reflection on the Christian origins of antisemitism, however, and such analysis is largely absent from Oesterreicher's treatment. Like Fordham President Gannon, he identified antisemitism as a revolt against Christianity from within Christianity: Goebbels and Hitler were baptized Catholics. Christian origins gave Nazi antisemitism a particular savagery, but also triggered Oesterreicher's apocalyptic perspective. The National Socialists, while not faithful Christians, did have faith in Christ—faith of a special kind, faith of the anti-Christ.

Still, Oesterreicher's critique fostered solidarity. The reference to the heretic Marcion made clear that Christianity must be linked to Judaism. The question was how. As recently as 1928, Vatican Cardinal Secretary of State Merry del Val was dictating that the relation between Christians and Jews must be negative. "Hebraism with all its sects inspired by the Talmud continues perfidiously to oppose Christianity," he wrote in an internal opinion, accepted by Pius XI just before he banned Amici Israel, the group calling for friendship with Jews. Individual Jews might convert, but the Jewish people were damned.[85] Worse: they were a danger from which Christians must be protected. The French author Sr. Cécile Rastoin connects this religiously based attitude to the Vatican's failure to condemn the Nuremberg laws. Though based in racism, these laws had the unintended positive effect from the Vatican's perspective of segregating Jews from Christians and shielding the latter's immortal souls.[86]

Oesterreicher's emerging perspective was pushing aside these ancient ideas, calling for Christians to feel solidarity with Jews, first because they are persecuted (whatsoever you do . . .), second because as Christ's kin they are our brothers, and third because they, like Christians, give witness to God. By 1940, three guiding images of the Jews were converging in the Christian imagination: Jews as brothers, witnesses, and priests. What had not changed was the view that Israel was fated to suffer: "Israel is proscribed and persecuted because God is merciful."[87]

We see in Oesterreicher the same theological schizophrenia that we witness in Dietrich von Hildebrand and Jacques Maritain in these years. He contradicted himself within the book on racism, warning at one point against "antisemitism" as a "horrible danger" because the "hatred against the people of Israel becomes hatred against Old and then New Testament."[88] Therefore, antisemitism should disappear. Yet forty pages later he wrote that "antisemitism, sated as it is with the meanness and malice of the human being, remains a judgment sent by God. Would that Jewry understood this judgment."[89] For the time being, the tension found uneasy resolution in a core Christian belief, dating back to the earliest thinkers, namely, the virtue of suffering. If people suffered—Jews or anyone else—that was to be understood as divinely willed and not without meaning. Humans had to reconcile themselves.

To say that Jews were destined to suffer did not necessarily imply contempt. After all, Christ had been destined to suffer a horrible death. Without suffering the world could not heal.[90] Catholicism is deeply marked by the Pauline view that suffering can redeem sin.[91] Not only that: suffering was a sign of election.[92] Léon Bloy, a major inspiration to Oesterreicher and his friends, had felt (in Stephen Schloesser's formulation) that suffering was "not merely a *privileged* path of redemption, but in fact the *exclusive* mode of participation in the supernatural."[93] Antisemitism, a trial sent to the Jews, was part of their destiny of contributing to humankind's redemption. This gives a new twist to Saul Friedländer's notion of "redemptive antisemitism." The point for Christians was not that they should participate in acts of hatred against Jews—according to the teaching of the day, that was forbidden—but that they expected others to take part in such acts and therefore validated them.

In *Racisme*, Oesterreicher told of a Jewish woman who learned to bear the suffering she was subjected to after the Nazi occupation of Austria. Though previously a-religious, she now grasped the deeper meaning of the painting *Mater Dolorosa*, understanding when she herself felt torture that the "tortured creation" longs for redemption. The following day she went to the church where this picture was hanging and asked to be baptized. Oesterreicher concluded that "the Martyrdom of all those who suffer under racist despotism will not have been in vain."[94]

How did Jews suffer for humanity? Unlike earlier generations of persecutors, the Nazi "beast" was not content with the physical destruction of Jews. Through the Jews, Oesterreicher believed, the Nazis hoped to strike a lethal blow to the "human person, to the inalienable dignity of the human being."[95] While he advocated charity for Jews of the sort exemplified by the Good Samaritan, Oesterreicher also felt reminded of Christ's passion:

The Jews too give witness today for Jesus of Nazareth. The Jews, who have not roof over their heads and soon will have not ground beneath their feet, may say with Christ: "the foxes have their dens and birds of the air nests, but the Son of Man has nowhere to lay his head." How they are mocked, flogged, killed. Have they not received a "crown of thorns"? Don't people spit in their faces? Are they not numbered "among the evil doers"? What do they receive to quench their thirst but a "sponge soaked in sour wine"? Israel, indissolubly linked to Christ, is similar to him. Because of the cross Israel kept its distance from Christ: now this cross has been placed upon its shoulders. His life is suffering and martyrdom. Today the Jews, without knowing or wanting it, in a certain sense are giving testimony of their king who is also king of the entire world.[96]

Did these lines evince contempt for Jews? This is a more general question that can be posed of the Catholics of that time. Can one speak of contempt for Jews among Christians when most kept their mouths closed and did not participate in acts of persecution? Is passivity the same as hatred? Perhaps not. Most German Catholics had limited personal contacts with Jews, and their political organizations are on record as opposing antisemitism before 1933, both as discrimination and as violence. But when French-Jewish historian Jules Isaac later wrote of *roots* of contempt, he meant a latent force, not necessarily visible in acts or words. And that is what we have here. The point is not that the Catholics of Central Europe were called upon actively to aid the perpetrators. The point is that Catholics could look at the perpetrators' deeds and find them justified. Oesterreicher wrote that "antisemitism . . . remains a judgment sent by God." Where the Jews were concerned, Catholics shared the basic assumption of the Nazis that Jews were fated to suffer punishment. The assumption remained even after the Nazis incarcerated priests, shut down Catholic organizations, and preached hatred of Christ the Jew. The Nazis arrogated to themselves the "world historic task" of exacting punishment while Christians watched, perhaps asking, with theologian Josef Dillersberger of Salzburg, who can argue with God? [*Wer darf rechten mit Gott?*][97]

As Léon Bloy had suggested regarding the phenomenon of antisemitism, the issue was not whether a Christian subscribed to six or seven or eight stereotypes about Jews, it was about the deep sources of a criminal perspective, the old anti-Judaic vision, which made sense of the world for perpetrators but also for onlookers. That vision remained even when one "absolved" the Jews of deicide, because the idea of Jews living under punishment was untouched. Therefore, Hitler could—and did—claim to be doing a service to Christianity by persecuting Jews, and Christianity did not have a language with which to oppose him. No matter how much Christians objected to violations of human dignity, the human person, or the sanctity of life, they were for the most part left speechless when it came to Hitler's target—the Jewish people.[98]

Only after the fact did Christians wonder more deeply about the "service" done for Christianity. Was the Holocaust a punishment sent by God? If not, then they had to break with the belief that Jews lived under a curse. In the postwar period Christian theologians did this, developing the contrary view that Jews were loved by God. This went along with a new way of reading the signs of the times: of rejecting as presumptuous the idea that any human can know whether and how God might punish humanity. One therefore sees at the Second Vatican Council several things not coincidentally coinciding: a positive vision of the Jews (*Nostra Aetate*), a way of reading the "signs of the times" as ethical imperatives and not insight into God's designs for history (*Gaudium et spes*), and an understanding of the church as not the sole locus of grace in the world (*Lumen gentium*).[99] In some way, all of these changes took place under the impact of the Holocaust.

6

Conversion in the Shadow of Auschwitz

Auschwitz had little immediate impact on Christian thinking about the Jews, though basic facts were available during the war. From the fall of 1942 at the latest, Americans could read in daily newspapers that the German regime was killing millions of Jews. The press told readers about death camps and also about the killing operations of the SS in Eastern Europe. Yet it also reported the deaths of untold thousands of human beings of other groups whom the Nazis considered subhumans.[1] Americans and Europeans did not see how the crime we call the Holocaust towered out of the landscape of Nazi crimes until decades later. A first history detailing the event's systematic planning and execution did not appear until 1961. Only in the 1970s, partly under the influence of the American television miniseries *The Holocaust*, did the singularity of the destruction of the Jews establish itself in Western consciousness.[2]

Yet even if Christians had immediately recognized the unique character of this crime, that would have meant little for the anti-Judaic components of Christian theology. Christians could not suddenly rewrite the

Bible or reinvent centuries of tradition. They could neither expunge the Jewish crowd's wish from Matthew's Gospel that Christ's blood be poured upon them and their children, nor could they excise sections of the epistle to the Hebrews that called the covenant to Israel "obsolete." Paul's claim in Thessalonians that Jews were "heedless of God's will" and that "retribution has overtaken them for good and all" remained, regardless of how ugly those words sounded, as did his reference to Jews (in Romans) as "enemies" (sometimes translated as "God's enemies").[3] Christians could not suddenly close their eyes to teaching dating back to the second century according to which Jews were fated to suffer until they turned to Christ. With the exception of the Anglican minister James W. Parkes, no Christian theologian of note dissented from this point of view before 1945: not Charles Journet, Jacques Maritain, Karl Barth, Martin Niemöller, or even the martyrs Dietrich Bonhoeffer and Bernard Lichtenberg. Though horrified by Nazi antisemitism, leading Catholic theologians Romano Guardini and Erich Przywara—both inspirations to the White Rose resistance group in Munich—remained silent. The prominent French anti-fascist theologian Henri de Lubac said nothing publicly against anti-Judaism before 1945. Those few Christians who opposed antisemitism in the interwar years, such as Maritain, Karl Thieme, or Dietrich von Hildebrand, still said to Jews, in essence, "The Jew Jesus of Nazareth has become my savior, redeemer and King; and because of that, I would like that he finally be recognized by his own people as their redeemer, because then they will be saved."[4]

During the war the French-Jewish historian Jules Isaac began formulating a pathbreaking and influential analysis of the "sources of contempt" contained in Christian thought. But for the time being, anti-Judaism remained intact, and Christians saw no reason to examine Christianity for its support of antisemitism. For one thing, Nazi violence went beyond the Jews, and even if the Nazis used Christian arguments for measures taken against Jews, that could not explain the killing of millions of other human beings, for example, the Gypsies.[5] For another thing, the Nazis had sought to destroy Christianity, and from the moment the European churches emerged from the war, they portrayed themselves as victims, even in Germany. Like the Jews, they suffered the violence of the pagan juggernaut and sacrificed priests and pastors in the Nazi camps.

Strange as it sounds, it was *this* sense—the sense of common suffering of Jews and Christians—and not witness to Auschwitz that gave impetus to the remolding of Christian thought.[6] It did so because it opened channels of communication between Christians and Jews who were concerned about a resurgence of racial and religious bigotry after the war. This was a revolutionary development. With the possible exceptions of the Mendelssohn/Lavater and Rosenzweig/Rosenstock-Huessy disputes of the eighteenth and early twentieth centuries, it was the first time since the days of Justin Martyr that Jews and Christians had discussed any theological matter other than whether or not Christ was the Messiah.[7] Once Christians began talking to Jews about theology—whether to the French thinkers Jules Isaac and Edmond Fleg, Swiss rabbis Eugen Messinger and Lothar Rothschild, or German-Jewish intellectuals such as Martin Buber or Schalom Ben Chorin—they began to realize how obscene much of their own teaching sounded when spoken in the shadow of the war's crimes. Such conversations opened their minds to the possibility that anti-Judaism in Matthew or Thessalonians formed the deeper wellspring of contempt that made Auschwitz possible.[8]

This conclusion, fully developed by the American theologian Rosemary Ruether and others after Vatican II, was still inconceivable to Christians of the early postwar years.[9] But in their first conversations with Jews, they began inching their way toward it. They did so within meetings of councils of Christians and Jews that emerged to combat religious and racial bigotry, first in the United States in 1928, and then in the United Kingdom and France (1942) and Switzerland (1946).[10] Representatives from these single-country organizations came together to form an International Council of Christians and Jews that met in Oxford (1946), and then in the Swiss towns of Seelisberg (1947) and Fribourg (1948). In 1948, U.S. Occupation authorities transplanted this kind of organizational form to Germany, making the theologian Karl Thieme their deputy for religious questions the following year.[11]

Activism against Antisemitism

The organizers called the crucial meeting at Seelisberg an emergency meeting, because they knew that antisemitism had retreated but was not dead. One had only to look at Poland, where hundreds of acts of anti-Jewish violence were breaking out, including full-fledged pogroms. In France, the political right gradually reemerged, and so did the old vocabulary of hatred, more cleverly disguised than in the past but no less ominous. Even in Germany, despite the military occupation, anti-Jewish violence occasionally burst to the surface. Of 500 German-Jewish cemeteries, some 200 had been desecrated by 1950. In 1949, cattle dealer and World War I veteran Gustav Steigerfeld (in Wiesenfeld, Lower Franconia) found a note on his gate threatening lynching—for no reason other than that he was Jewish. Steigerfeld had returned to Wiesenfeld from killing camps that had consumed his only daughter, nineteen-year-old Berta, in 1942. He and his wife were the sole survivors of a community of twenty-two.[12] The "denazified" hotel owner Hans Rief broke into the synagogue of Markredwitz (Bavaria) and destroyed prayer books and Torah scrolls. The city government of nearby Offenbach refused to appoint Dr. Herbert Lewin as director of the gynecological clinic in the municipal hospital because of resentment he allegedly bore as the sole survivor of his family. According to mayor Karl Kasperkowitz, "no woman could feel safe in his care."[13] And so on. American occupation authorities feared a resurgence of antisemitism that might extinguish the small remainder of German Jews.[14]

Well-informed of this continuing violence—indeed, convinced that Nazi education had deeply rooted Jew-hatred in German society—the Seelisberg organizers created a subcommission on the tasks churches faced in combating antisemitism as an ideology that was sustained partly by religion. It produced ten landmark theses that are now recognized as the first important fruit of the dialogue between Christians and Jews:

1. Remember that One God speaks to us all through the Old and the New Testaments.

2. Remember that Jesus was born of a Jewish mother of the seed of David and the people of Israel, and that His everlasting love and forgiveness embraces His own people and the whole world.

3. Remember that the first disciples, the apostles and the first martyrs were Jews.

4. Remember that the fundamental commandment of Christianity, to love God and one's neighbor, proclaimed already in the Old Testament and confirmed by Jesus, is binding upon both Christians and Jews in all human relationships, without any exception.

5. Avoid distorting or misrepresenting biblical or post-biblical Judaism with the object of extolling Christianity.

6. Avoid using the word Jews in the exclusive sense of the enemies of Jesus, and the words 'the enemies of Jesus' to designate the whole Jewish people.

7. Avoid presenting the Passion in such a way as to bring the odium of the killing of Jesus upon all Jews or upon Jews alone. It was only a section of the Jews in Jerusalem who demanded the death of Jesus, and the Christian message has always been that it was the sins of mankind which were exemplified by those Jews and the sins in which all men share that brought Christ to the Cross.

8. Avoid referring to the scriptural curses, or the cry of a raging mob: "His blood be upon us and our children," without remembering that this cry should not count against the infinitely more weighty words of our Lord: "Father forgive them for they know not what they do."

9. Avoid promoting the superstitious notion that the Jewish people are reprobate, accursed, reserved for a destiny of suffering.

10. Avoid speaking of the Jews as if the first members of the Church had not been Jews.[15]

Jules Isaac worked on this subcommission, and we now know that its theses anticipate ideas expressed in his pioneering work *Jesus and Israel* (1948), save for the crucial thesis nine.[16] Because Isaac met with John XXIII in 1960 and successfully urged the pope to commission a statement on the Jews, some historians have assumed a direct link between his ideas and the Vatican II document *Nostra Aetate* of 1965 in which the church formally broke with anti-Judaism and condemned antisemitism.[17] Yet the story is more complicated. If the conversations with Jews in the postwar years opened Christian minds to new ideas, they did not necessitate their acceptance. The ideas had to be tested for theological soundness.

This testing occurred in tiny groups of theologians who wrote and debated out of offices in France, Germany, and the Netherlands between the end of the war and the opening of the Second Vatican Council seventeen years later. In 1947, Seelisberg participant Father Paul Démann, a converted Hungarian Jew, began publishing the review *Cahiers Sioniens* from Paris, and, with the help of fellow converts Geza Vermes and Renée Bloch, he refuted the anti-Judaism in Catholic school catechisms, especially the idea that Jews lived under a curse. Everywhere they looked in popular Catholic teaching in France, Démann, Vermes, and Bloch found evidence that the Shoah had done nothing to revise thinking about Jews. The following year, concentration camp survivor and Seelisberg participant Gertrud Luckner founded the journal *Freiburger Rundbriefe*, a German counterpart to *Cahiers* with a more theological bent and wider readership. As advisor, she took on Karl Thieme, like her a convert from Protestantism. Three years later, Miriam Rookmaaker van Leer, likewise a convert (from Protestantism), founded the Dutch Catholic Council for Israel (Katholieke Raad voor Israel) and engaged the priest Anton Ramselaar as her theological advisor.[18] Ramselaar had known the founders of the Amici Israel initiative of the 1920s, which included the convert Sophie van Leer.

In 1958, Ramselaar, at the suggestion of Ottilie Schwarz (a convert from Vienna), convened an international symposium in Apeldoorn, the Netherlands, which brought together the leading Catholics thinkers from France (Paul Démann), Germany (Karl Thieme, Gertrud Luckner), Israel (Abbot Leo Rudloff, Father Jean-Roger Hené), the United Kingdom (Irene Marinoff), and the United States (John Oesterreicher)—all converts. At its third meeting in 1960, this group produced theses that were passed on to John XXIII—along with a letter from Jules Isaac and a recommendation of Oesterreicher's Institute for Judeo-Christian Studies at Seton Hall University in South Orange, New Jersey. Oesterreicher founded this institute in 1953 with significant help from the Benedictine Abbott Leo Rudloff and the eminent Chinese legal scholar John C. H. Wu, professor at Seton Hall and, like Rudloff and Oesterreicher, a convert to Catholicism.[19]

Beyond these small groups, few Catholics wrote about Jews in the years leading up to the Vatican Council.[20] Through the 1950s, the Catholic press—whether the French *Études*, the American *Commonweal* and *America*, the British *The Month*, the Polish *Tygodnik Powszechny*, or the German

Stimmen der Zeit and *Hochland*—featured next to nothing on the Shoah, let alone suggested that this event should unleash soul-searching within the church about its past. Take *Commonweal*, the liberal lay magazine of American Catholics: famously independent, a forum for the writing of Dorothy Day and Graham Greene, courageously outspoken against Senator McCarthy, and a reliable source of information on Hitler's crimes in the 1930s. In June 1949, John Cogley, former editor of the *Chicago Catholic Worker*, praised the "modern liberal secularist mind" for the "rash of 'tolerance' novels, plays and movies" that had continued the "good fight" against murderous antisemitism in the past decade. "But when one considers the enormity of the Nazi blood-carnival," he wrote, "it never ceases to be amazing that the Christian conscience has been so slightly disturbed." Cogley had never heard a single Catholic sermon on the evil of antisemitism. Yet because it was a sin, Christianity could not remain silent: "it is religion alone that can make the final and effective appeal to conscience." Cogley reprinted the theses of Seelisberg in the hope that they might "act as guide for the conscientious mother or father intent on keeping children safe from the poison of antisemitism."[21] Children's author Claire Hutchet Bishop praised this act, but noted that "you can look around with a magnifying glass for the Catholic publications which are going to reprint them." "The last cold blooded murder of six million Jews," Bishop continued, "has shown that it is impossible to get a Christian reaction from Christians."[22]

As if to vouchsafe this prediction, *Commonweal* remained virtually silent on Christian-Jewish relations through the 1950s, save for briefly reprinting some of Paul Démann's suggestions for catechetical reform in 1950 and reporting the recognition received by Pius XII for standing up for the Jews upon his death in 1958 ("there was probably not a single ruler of our generation who did more to help the Jews in their hour of greatest tragedy than the late Pope").[23] Under the impact of the Eichmann trial three years later, editor James O'Gara finally broke the ice with a painful reflection upon the failure of Christians to oppose Hitler: "for every Christian voice that was raised against Hitler, there were hundreds which were not, and this not only in Germany." O'Gara recalled that during Hitler's reign American Catholics were amazed that a German priest had chosen to flee Germany: they believed there was "something wrong" with him.[24] In the early 1960s, such soul-searching was exceptional for the U.S. Catholic press, which tended to "ignore the long history of Christian anti-semitism when discussing the phenomenon of Nazi antisemitism and to emphasize the aid and assistance given to Jews by Catholics."[25] After this opening, *Commonweal* produced numerous pieces on Judaism and Jewish-Christian relations, devoting the entire issue of September 28, 1962, to "The Jew in American Society."[26]

The other well-known U.S. Catholic journal, *America*, a Jesuit weekly, devoted the barest of attention to Christian-Jewish relations in the 1950s, the exceptions often featuring something about John Oesterreicher.[27] In France, the *Documentation Catholique*, which featured highlights from the Catholic press across the globe, likewise had next to nothing to report about Jewish-Christian relations through the 1950s, save the occasional mention of Oesterreicher and his counterpart on the French scene, Paul Démann.[28] Between 1945 to 1962, the French Jesuit monthly *Études* carried a single brief piece on Christian-Jewish relations, its aim being to uphold anti-Judaic views through a polemic with Jules Isaac.[29] Its German counter-part, *Stimmen der Zeit*, featured nothing on Christian-Jewish relations through the 1950s (also nothing on Judaism), though there was one brief article on the issue of Jewish collective guilt. Germans, the author of this piece noted, had learned the injustice of accusations of collective guilt, not from the Holocaust, but from having the world apply them to the Germans in 1945.[30] In 1959, Oskar Simmel closed a discussion in *Stimmen* on the tragic fate of Jewish converts in wartime Vienna with the promising but elusive words: "we will not get past working through some problems that have not been worked through."[31] Likewise, the German Catholic monthly *Hochland* featured nothing on Jewish-Christian relations (or antisemitism) until 1959.[32] *The Month*, a British Catholic publication going back to the 1880s, featured frequent coverage of antisemitism during the Nazis' reign, but, similar to *Commonweal*, it fell silent after the war and failed to probe the deeper sources of the tragedy, let alone how they might relate to Chris-tians or Christianity.[33]

Historians surveying Catholic opinion of the postwar years register embarrassed silence: disappearance of overt hostility but an absence of ideas of how to relate to Jews. Even in the few pieces reflecting upon the events of World War II and antisemitism, there was virtually no questioning of the role of the Catholic Church. Catholics took for granted that that the Nazis—enemies of Christianity—bore responsibility for the crimes committed. When John XXIII announced in 1959 that an Ecumenical Council would meet in Rome, only a handful of the hundreds of proposals for agenda items (*vota*) mentioned Christian-Jewish relations. In over 800 pages of notes sent from Dutch, Belgian, French, English, German, and Polish bishops, not a single suggestion was made to consider Christian-Jewish relations at the Council. Many bishops wanted discussion of relations with other Christians and even with atheists, yet none intimated that antisemitism within the church was a problem.[34] "It took the will of John XXIII," Giovanni Miccoli concludes, and the "perseverance of Cardinal Bea to impose the declaration on the Council."[35]

The Troubling Origins of the New Vision

Bea and John XXIII did not create this declaration out of intellectual thin air, however. They drew upon the work of the handful of Catholics activists who cared about relations to Jews and had gathered for yearly meetings at Apeldoorn, and they took Fathers Oesterreicher, Rudloff, Ramselaar, and their friend the convert Bruno Hussar on as advisors at the Council. These activists in turn were drawing upon a tradition that stretched backward in time, through the Catholic anti-Nazi opposition that had assembled in Austria and Switzerland of the 1930s, to the international Amici Israel movement in the 1920s, and finally to France of the 1890s, where a small but important group of Catholics had opposed racist antisemitism during the Dreyfus affair. This was an origin story the pioneers agreed upon. When contemplating the deepest roots of the Apeldoorn theses, Ottilie Schwarz placed her finger squarely on French Catholic Dreyfusards: Jacques Maritain, Charles Péguy, and their teacher, the antimodern apocalyptist Léon Bloy, an essayist and novelist who shunned the material world and lived as a beggar, losing two children in the process. Other pioneers from the anti-Nazi struggle concurred.[36] Waldemar Gurian cited Bloy as his source for the Pauline idea that that God's promises to the Jews were irrevocable, and Karl Thieme said that "the most important specifically Christian . . . statements [on the Jews] almost all go back to Léon Bloy—directly or indirectly."[37] In 1963, John

Oesterreicher wrote that only "rarely in the decades before the appearance of National Socialism did a voice make itself heard that came from the depths of faith." One such voice belonged to Léon Bloy with his *Le Salut par les Juifs*.[38]

Yet this was an origin story pointing to dark and troubling sources. If Bloy astounds for the horrible penury he imposed upon himself, he also repels for the anti-Jewish remarks that laced his writings. In *Le Salut* (1892), Bloy referred to Jewish fishmongers he encountered during a visit to Hamburg as "horrible traffickers in money" who "sicken the universe."[39] He described other Jews as "bloated holders of parasitic capital" who kept Christ on the cross: "They have nailed him strongly enough that He cannot come down without their permission."[40] Pierre Birnbaum, a foremost student of French Antisemitism, has called Bloy "one of the most extreme and vociferous antisemites of turn-of-the-century France . . . activated by an obscene and unnatural antisemitism which no theological dialectic, however subtle, can render legitimate in any degree whatsoever."[41] Yet in his time Bloy was considered antisemitism's enemy—indeed, he wrote *Le Salut* against the racist antisemitism of Édouard Drumont, and sent copies to rabbis. The Dreyfusard Bernard Lazare reviewed Bloy's work in a piece entitled, "Un Philosémite," and the Zionist André Spire cited Bloy to support his view that "the tension which Israel raises among the nations may not disappear."[42] In Prague, Franz Kafka had read Bloy with profit, claiming that with *Le Salut* Bloy offered Jews protection as one might one's "less fortunate relatives."[43] The Viennese Catholics who opposed Nazism in the 1930s mined Bloy's writings for two pathbreaking insights. The first was simple: a Christian could not think of Jews as "racially" inferior. After all, the Jewish "race" had produced Christ, his family, as well as the apostles. Dietrich von Hildebrand cited at length from Bloy's *Le Salut* in his landmark speech at the *Pauluswerk* of 1937. "What would our feelings be," Bloy had asked, "if those around us were constantly talking about our father and mother with the greatest disrespect? Exactly this is constantly befalling Jesus Christ, our Lord. People have forgotten that God made man was a Jew, indeed, by His human nature, the Jew *par excellence*, the Lion of Judah. People further forget that His mother was a Jewess, the flower of the Jewish people, that almost all of His ancestors were Jews, that the apostles were Jewish, as well as the prophets, and finally, that our entire holy liturgy is rooted in the sacred books of Israel."[44]

There was more than the obvious family connections. Bloy was the first influential Christian thinker to affirm that God had not rejected the Jews (Romans 9:1) but rather continued to love them. Yet the nagging question pressed itself all the more urgently upon the Christian mind: how could a people most naturally drawn to faith be resistant to Christ?

Bloy resolved this tension in a dialectical vision whereby Jews moved history forward, even when they were persecuted. He believed that the salvation of the world could spring only from extreme degradation, which explains his fascination with the poor traffickers in Hamburg but also his own choice to live as a beggar.[45] In an influential image, he wrote that "the history of the Jews dams up the history of the human race, as a dike dams up a river, in order to raise its level." Metaphysically desperate Jacques and Raïssa Maritain found this vision so intoxicating that they abandoned a suicide pact and entered the Catholic Church with Bloy as their godfather in 1906. "At that time we knew nothing about the Christian faith," Jacques later recalled. *Le Salut* was "for us like a storm of supernatural thunderbolts ... *the revelation of the divine meaning of human history* ..."[46]

Bloy became an inspiration to Catholics opposed to antisemitism because he provided a vision of history rooted in faith, and not simply reasoned argument bolstered with facts. A few other courageous individuals from Bloy's time, like Anatole Leroy-Beaulieu or Charles Péguy's friend Bernard Lazare, had carefully refuted antisemitic stereotypes in volumes full of data, and Jacques Maritain or Waldemar Gurian were happy to augment these catalogues in their writings of the 1930s. Yet showing that Jews did not form conspiracies upholding Communism or international finance, or that many were pious and faithful rather than subversive was relatively straightforward. One had merely to fight ignorance. Bloy, however, argued in different dimensions, unlocking mysteries of God's designs in a world that had seemed irremediably disenchanted. Bloy's "supernatural thunderbolts" gave people starved for meaning—like the Maritains—energy to speak out amidst a secular mainstream that lacked appeal to transcendent visions. The point in arguing that there was nothing deficient in Jews' "nature" was to say that nature was not the point. As Bloy wrote, "mystery calling for boundless worship" was hidden beneath the outward history of a persecuted people, who survived the "merciless tutelage of several millions of Christian princes" through God's grace.[47] Jacques Maritain concurred, writing that Israel presented an "astounding interweaving of the natural and the sacred, of the supernatural and the temporal."[48]

Bloy's epochal achievement was to alert Catholics to untapped meanings in St. Paul's letter to the Romans, chapters 9–11, and it is no exaggeration to say that the path to Vatican II begins with him. Despite the deeply troubling stereotypes he shared and advanced about Jewish persons, Bloy was the first major Catholic thinker of the modern era to state clearly and irrefutably that the Jewish people had a salutary influence upon history. Secular opponents of antisemitism could argue for the rights of Jews as individuals, but they lacked a language with which to defend Jews' existence as a people. Bloy accorded himself a prophetic role, and wrote that he was the first Catholic author since the church's earliest days to understand the Jewish people through the prism provided in the Epistle to the Romans.

For many, however, Bloy pushed his sense of paradox beyond the limits of the tolerable.[49] Jacques Maritain's friend (later cardinal) Charles Journet called the shortcomings of Le Salut par les Juifs "considerable." "Five or six affirmations will remain completely original," he wrote. Yet because the book was not a "common treasure," it was "well worth the trouble to extract them."[50] From the 1930s, Catholics seeking new ways of thinking about Jews took what they could from Bloy, but began looking elsewhere for fresh, theologically sound exegesis of Paul's letter to the Romans. They found it in Erik Peterson, a theologian who, like Bloy, had converted from Protestantism and spent his life in poverty. For Bloy's godson Jacques Maritain, the discovery of Peterson's thin book The Church of Jews and Pagans (1934)—a detailed analysis of Romans 9–11—was providential, and he wrote a preface for the French edition, which made a deep impression upon French Catholics.[51] In 1935, Karl Thieme called Peterson "the greatest living Catholic theologian."[52] Peterson had been a brilliant student of the leading Protestant theologian Adolf Harnack, and was also close to Karl Barth. In the late 1920s, he comfortably held a chair in Protestant theology at Bonn, where he frequented intellectual circles that

included Carl Schmitt and Annie Kraus. At Christmas 1930, he caused a
sensation by suddenly converting to Catholicism, in part stimulated by
the words of the Harnack: that scripture lives through tradition, and
tradition through the living form of succession. Failing to find academic
employment until after World War II, he spent the 1930s as a part-time
teacher at the Vatican while his family grew to number two adults and
five children. In recent years, the German theologian Barbara Nichtweiss has rescued Peterson's writings from obscurity, and in October
2010 the Vatican sponsored a commemorative session, with Benedict
XVI giving the introductory address and several of Peterson's children
in attendance.

Peterson's journey away from Protestantism had tempered his eschatology, and he warned against the "speculative way of looking at things,
in which Christianity was a historical phenomenon that needed to be
embraced conceptually." In lectures on the church, Peterson argued that
"there was no guarantee to find the internal meaning of historical events."
In Peterson's view, the "solution of the puzzle of history was suspended
eschatologically until the end of time, when God will reveal it."[53] He
took particular issue with the tendency of Protestant history writing in
his day to "spinelessly bow before everything that has ever existed," and
to draw the unwarranted conclusion that the Jews had forfeited their
God-given vocation. In a piece published in Oesterreicher's *Die Erfüllung* in 1936, the priest Thomas Michels drove home a thought of Erik
Peterson's: "It is one of the stupidities of modern thinking to imagine
that a decision of God's (like the election of Israel) could be corrected by
so-called 'History.'"[54]

Before, during, and after the war, Thieme, Oesterreicher, and Journet
routinely cited Peterson's exegesis of Paul to defend their own recentering
of Catholic thought in Romans. But neither Peterson nor Léon Bloy had
fully opened Paul's letter to the Romans. Yes, the Jews were a people specially blessed, and yes, they moved history forward, but still only to point
humanity toward Christ. Israel remained, in the words of Bloy's disciple
Jacques Maritain, "blindfolded, and dispossessed through its lapse and rejection of the Gospel." Its role was to bear permanent witness to the authentic-
ity of the church's message.[55] One implication of this view was that Jews
continued to suffer until the end of time. No would-be philo-Semite dared

utter such words publicly after Auschwitz, but they remained an implication of the basic viewpoint.

No one believed more fervently in Christian eschatology than Karl Thieme, and ironically but logically, Thieme came to incorporate the tension in Christian thought that grew unacceptably painful after World War II. He preached love for Jews with his heart, while dictating with his intellect that Jews remained the enemies of Christianity. Such words reflected the spirit of Léon Bloy, who had called for a truce between Christians and Jews but never denied that they were set against one another. Bloy knew that such words sounded harsh, but he believed he had to be absolutely true to Christian teaching.[56] Perhaps Thieme's dilemma in the postwar years was similar to that of faithful Marxists confronted with logical extremes of their ideology within Stalinism. Like Marxist revisionists, Thieme faced the challenge of trying to restore the original faith, yet unlike them he did not have the option of abandoning the eschatological vision and opting for pragmatism like Social Democracy. Christianity was always a religion of hopeful anticipation of Christ's return. But, very much like a Marxist revisionist, he continued to scour original texts for suppressed meanings, and by 1950 he was arguing for placing one set of texts above others. If revisionists favored the early Marx, Karl Thieme favored Paul's last epistle, written around A.D. 56 to the Christian community in Rome but now read in a way that was unprecedented.

When Karl Thieme revolutionized his thinking about the Jews around 1950, the effect was so overwhelming that he confessed to undergoing a "conversion." This conversion story is of absorbing interest to those interested in the journey taken by Catholic thought over the past century because Thieme was the first major Catholic thinker to grasp in St. Paul's letter to the Romans the view that Jews remained beloved by God as Jews. *They* did not need conversion—but the Catholic Church did. We see Thieme's pioneering role by looking at other Christians who had struggled against racist antisemitism under the shadow of the swastika. After 1945, Dietrich von Hildebrand and Jacques Maritain went onto other pursuits, as did Waldemar Gurian, who wrote on the Soviet Union from a teaching position at Notre Dame. Other allies from the 1930s, such as fathers Ferdinand Frodl or Franziskus Stratmann, likewise never again publicly addressed Catholic relations to the Jews. After surviving the war hiding in Berlin and southern Germany, Annie Kraus turned to other topics: the theological meanings of stupidity and arrogance, while working as an assistant to Karl Rahner. The most active French Catholic opponent of antisemitism in the 1930s, Oscar de Férenzy, an Alsatian convert from Protestantism, died after torture by the Gestapo in 1942. Irene Harand, whose Viennese work against racism inspired Férenzy, survived the war, but lived her remaining years with her husband Frank, the former Habsburg captain, in happy domestic seclusion in New York City.

What about Johannes Oesterreicher? His engagement in Christian-Jewish relations continued from the early 1930s to the early 1990s. It is true that several years' hiatus ensued in June 1940 when Oesterreicher was forced to flee his office in Paris and seek shelter with Dominican priests at Toulouse before being smuggled across the Pyrenees with other refugees, including the Dietrich von Hildebrand family. Bearing a Czechoslovak passport issued at Marseilles, he traveled under the name Jan Maria Oesterreicher. In Lisbon, Oesterreicher joined an effort organized by Otto von Habsburg to get Austrian and Jewish refugees overseas, and was among those who secured transit visas through the United States based on entry visas issued by the embassy of China. (Later it emerged that the Chinese visas were invalid.) After landing in New York in November 1940, Oesterreicher—a recommendation in hand from the Brazilian ambassador he met on the *S.S. Exeter*—applied for permanent residence (granted in 1942). Now known as John, he was giving sermons at the Church of the Assumption on West 49th Street in New York City within six months of starting his English lessons. In the summer of 1946, Cardinal Innitzer of Vienna extended his "leave of absence" so that Oesterreicher could devote himself to the "conversion of Jews," a task he believed God's grace had preserved him for through dozens of miraculous coincidences.[57] He made vigorous efforts—in close consultation with the missionary order Notre Dame de Sion in Paris—but the results were meager. The overwhelming majority of people who attended his courses on Catholicism at St. Peter's Church at 16 Barclay Street in New York City in the early 1950s were Catholics, and he counted only two converts who might not have come into the church if it were not for these courses.[58]

Hoping to intensify his "special work" with Jews, Oesterreicher opened an Institute for Judeo-Christian studies at Seton Hall University in 1953, and launched a quasi-scholarly journal on Jewish matters (*The Bridge*), where some authors refuted antisemitic stereotypes while others quarreled with Jewish authors about their faithfulness to Judaism.[59] During the 1950s, no Jews wrote for him, and if there was interest at Seton Hall in Jewish thought, it was mainly to suggest that Jews were "awakening" to Christ.[60] Yet by the late 1950s, Oesterreicher called the institute's mission "ecumenical": it was about fostering knowledge of Judaism among Catholics and assisting the church in the rediscovery of its Jewish origins proclaimed at Vatican II.

His lifetime journey back to Jewish roots embodies the journey taken by the church back to its own Jewish heritage. But Dutch priest Anton Ramselaar, who knew Oesterreicher from work at the Second Vatican Council, wrote that Oesterreicher was always "more a fighter than a thinker."[61] He had a gift of getting other people to work together, and propagated their ideas. In the 1930s, Oesterreicher had organized the first Catholic statement against antisemitism (the "Memorandum" written by Thieme and Gurian in 1937), and tried to get the pope to speak out for the Jews. Then, in Parisian exile he compiled all Catholic statements opposing antisemitism and racism in a single volume. This book was interesting not for original thought, but for the way it reflected the possibilities and limits of Catholic opposition at that moment. Oesterreicher later drew important advocates of better relations with the Jews—for example, Sister Rose Thering and Fathers Edward Flannery and Lawrence Frizzell—to his institute at Seton Hall. In the late 1950s, his yearbook *The Bridge* began publishing pathbreaking work: refutations of the Elders of Zion myth, Charles Journet's ideas on Israel's destiny, an exposé on antisemitism in the Soviet Union, and essays on contemporary Jewish thought. Oesterreicher continued to be Karl Thieme's important sparring partner, and though the two fiercely disagreed, Oesterreicher found himself relying upon Karl Thieme's work when it came time to draft and redraft statements on the Jews at the Second Vatican Council.

Karl Thieme, the Forgotten Pioneer

It was thus left to Karl Thieme to incorporate the evolution in Catholic thought about the Jews that began with Léon Bloy's turn to Paul's letter to the Romans in 1892 and culminated in the statement *Nostra Aetate* at Vatican II in 1965, which placed inspiration from Romans at the center of Catholic understanding of the Jewish people. There is more to this claim than the simple fact that he survived and struggled for clarity in an engagement that stretched from the 1930s to the 1960s. He also assumed singular institutional influence. From 1948 until his death in 1963, Karl Thieme acted as theological advisor at the *Freiburger Rundbrief*, the major German-language forum advocating reconciliation between Christians and Jews. Though Cologne's Cardinal Frings—Germany's most powerful bishop—disapproved of the *Rundbrief*'s work, by 1953, 20,000 copies were going out to "priests and religion teachers" throughout German-speaking Europe with the "explicit approval of the [Freiburg] Episcopate."[62] If the journal was orthodox, it was not narrow, and it regularly printed contributions of Jewish and Protestant authors; by 1953, German Protestant bishops were circulating the *Rundbrief* to their own flocks. Because of Freiburg's location a stone's throw from Swiss Basel and French Strasbourg, Thieme acted as synthesizer and propagator, a kind of clearinghouse for new Catholic ideas about the Jews, whether they emerged in the United States, Paris, London, or at his own desk.

Nowadays Thieme is all but forgotten, and histories of the Vatican Council trace the development of the statement on the Jews in *Nostra Aetate* without mentioning Thieme even in a footnote. Those concerned with relations between Jews and Christians in our day rarely cite him as an inspiration.[63] In a retrospective written shortly before his death, Thieme accorded to himself the origin of not a single idea. His many books are long out of print, unknown even to specialists. Yet Thieme was highly regarded in his day. At his death in 1963, the Dutch Catholic Council for Israel commented that "no one else can fill the empty space he leaves in Germany as well as the international arena."[64] The German-Jewish thinker Ernst Ludwig Ehrlich called him "a lonely voice in the wilderness," who was "granted the knowledge shortly before his death that leading representatives of his Church have made his view of things their own for the next phase of the

ecumenical council."[65] Gerhard Riegner, the man who had relayed news of
the Holocaust to the Allies in 1942, and later acted as Secretary General of
the World Jewish Congress, knew Thieme well from visits to Basel, and he
described him as a pioneer of a new Christian vision of Judaism, among
the "very first to contribute to a deepened reflection" on Jewish-Christian
relations.[66]

The word "pioneer" fits Karl Thieme. He signaled to other Catholic
theologians where the road ahead was sound, and his role at the *Rundbrief*
assured that many were watching. Yet beyond this, he took the pivotal
role as field agent for the Societies for Christian-Jewish Cooperation that
American occupation authorities set up across Germany in 1948, and thus
had close personal acquaintance with all those across Germany involved
in Christian-Jewish discussions. He also traveled abroad, acting as a German participant at the international meetings in Strasbourg and Apeldoorn
in the 1950s, and kept close contacts with the *Cahiers Sioniens* initiative in
Paris as well as Catholic and Protestant groups in the Netherlands. From
1949, Thieme's travels also took him to Rome, where he built upon contacts from the prewar years with the pope's German secretary Robert
Leiber, S.J., as well as the Bible scholar Augustin Bea, confessor to Pius
and consultor at the Congregation for the Propagation of Faith. Throughout the 1950s, Bea collaborated in censoring theologians who fell astray of
church teaching, but he protected the Freiburg group, initially as an in-
vestigator for the Holy Office. Karl Thieme kept in close touch with Bea
and others in "Vatican Circles."[67] In 1959, John XXIII made Bea Cardinal, then the following year the president of the newly formed Secretariat
for Promoting Christian Unity. In this position, Bea shepherded *Nostra
Aetate* to its promulgation, and thanks to the hard labors of theological
advisors like John Oesterreicher or Gregory Baum, helped make two of
Thieme's revolutionary ideas church teaching: that the Jews were not only
a religion but also people ("stock of Abraham") and that Catholics hoped
for a "day of the Lord," when all peoples will address the Almighty in one
voice, and "serve him shoulder to shoulder" (Zephaniah 3:9).

The politically astute Thieme and the *Rundbrief* editor-in-chief Gertrud Luckner used adversity to their advantage. Opposition from Cardinal Frings caused them to establish relations with individual bishops and
pastors, which in the long run produced grassroots support down to the

parish level.[68] Gertrud Luckner made a point of sending personal notes to newly appointed bishops along with the *Rundbrief* itself. Prominent theologians Romano Guardini and Karl Rahner supported the circle's work, and with time the *Freiburger Rundbrief* gained adherents among the younger generation of Catholic intellectuals.[69] Ten days before Thieme died in the Basel *Bürgerspital* in July 1963, the young theologian Joseph Ratzinger wrote him that "we all too often forget the third dimension of the ecumenical conversation, that of the encounter with Israel, and therefore require again and again to be reminded of this biblical foundation."[70] From the start, the *Rundbrief* enjoyed support among Jewish leaders, for example, Leo Baeck, who in 1949 encouraged Luckner's "meaningful and significant work," and wrote, "I can imagine how difficult your work is and how you meet not only with indifference or opposition but also with enemies. However, you are working for a future, for a blessing."[71]

Gertrud Luckner and Karl Thieme incorporated two tendencies among Christians interested in bettering relations with Jews: the ethical aiming at solidarity with the "least of my brethren," and the intellectual hoping to bolster faith with understanding. Over time, their collaboration helped close a gap between the two, resolving an ancient schizophrenia between the call to love Jews as neighbors and a belief that God had singled Jews out for punishment. During the war, moved by Christian charity, Luckner used her graduate training in social welfare to organize an "Office for Religious War Relief" at the Archdiocese of Freiburg, and with funds from Archbishop Conrad Gröber aided beleaguered German Jews, helping some escape to Switzerland. Just as she was about to distribute 5,000 marks to the last Jews of Berlin in November 1943, she was hauled off a train and arrested by the Gestapo, ending up at Ravensbrück.[72] Upon liberation, Luckner sought out Jewish survivors, and she worked until her death in 1995 at improving understanding between Christians and Jews. She was the sole German present at the 1947 Seelisberg meeting, and she was the first German officially invited to Israel in 1951. She, Irene Harand, Czesław Miłosz, and Pope John XXIII are the only persons discussed in this book who are honored as "righteous" at Yad Vashem.

After the war, Luckner resolved to continue her work against antisemitism, yet she lacked the theological training to discern how she might use Christianity for this purpose. That is why she turned to Karl Thieme. He knew that the Seelisberg theses could not serve as a foundation for Catholic thought, no matter how much goodwill stood behind them, because theses six through nine still represented important elements of Catholic teaching. St. Paul had called Jews "enemies" in his letter to the Romans, and the belief that Jews had known a "destiny of suffering" for the "death of Jesus" was not "superstition"—as the theses claimed—but a pillar of Catholic faith, perhaps the most solid pillar remaining among "historical" arguments for Christianity in a time of rampant secularization. Thieme's conundrum as theologian was this: the teachings on Jews by the Christian churches seemed based on unchanging truths. To deny them was to deny the faith itself, faith in the divinity of Christ, among other things. Could a people destined to receive Christ as king reject him with no consequence at all?

Thieme claimed to have shown passion for the Jewish people since 1934, for example, by coauthoring the 1937 Memorandum condemning Nazi antisemitism that might have endangered his family in Germany.[73] Yet passion could not justify a change in theology. In fact, Thieme feared that his reputation as "philo-Semite" weakened the impact among Christians of anything he wrote. "What one does not find in my writings, despite Léon Bloy," he wrote John Oesterreicher in 1946, "is even the most gentle weakening of the reproach against the Jews, which also runs through the Old and New Testament."[74] Thieme's deep concern for biblical sources, a legacy of his Protestant upbringing, was proving a stumbling block. Yes, according to St. Paul, "all Israel would be saved," Thieme admitted. But not, he argued, by some "magic trick" effected by the Almighty at the end of time. If God had wanted to, he could have caused a mass conversion of Israel at the time of Christ. Converting Jews was work Christians had to do themselves. "God's word tells us that we decide our 'eternal' destiny by what we do here below," he wrote in lines full of reproach to Swiss-German theologian Hans Urs von Balthasar, one of his many correspondents, who was also intrigued by eschatology but less concerned with making Jews Christians.[75]

The insular character of wartime Switzerland had created hothouse conditions that gave this anti-Judaism an extended lease on life. Yet as the Swiss borders reopened to the world, Karl Thieme's moral and intellectual security attracted scrutiny, first from Oesterreicher, by then a parish priest on New York's Upper West Side. In the summer of

1945, he received a book Thieme had completed the previous year entitled *The Church and the Synagogue*, which interpreted the first postbiblical evidence of the split between Christians and Jews. Oesterreicher noted with disapproval Thieme's belief that God was meting
out punishment to two peoples, Germans and Jews, in order to lead
them to Christ. Of the two, Thieme believed, it was the Jews who were
the more "infamous" because of the crucifixion of Christ.[76] He called
Jews "enemies of the Christian name."[77] From his years spent as missionary in Vienna and New York, Oesterreicher knew how the words
"enemy," "infamous," or "mission" sounded to Jewish ears, and he refused to employ them. He accused Thieme of carrying a Lutheran
disdain for Jews over into Catholicism. The "humiliations and sufferings of the last several years," Oesterreicher instructed his friend,
combined with the persecutions of Jews throughout the ages to cause a
"tensing up" of the hearts of Jews, making any conversation, let alone
missionary work, impossible.[78]

Thieme was unmoved. Paul had written "as concerning the gospel,
they are enemies for your sakes: but as touching the election, they are
beloved for the father's sakes." (Romans 11:28). Even today, translators
unnecessarily make the passage even more anti-Judaic by transposing
into English a parallelism they believe exists in the original Greek between the words for hate and love. Thus, in many editions of the New
Testament, the Jews become "enemies of God" in this passage. According
to this reasoning, if Paul wrote that the Jews were beloved by God for the
sake of their fathers, "enemies for your sake" implies hated by (and thus
enemies of) God.[79] Oesterreicher favored a contrasting interpretation
that placed the accent on love. God loved Jews although they were enemies *of the Gospel*. Furthermore, the entire section of Romans (esp. 11:25)
suggested that Christians should imitate God by loving the Jews in a special way.[80] Yet the original Greek does not call Jews enemies of God.

Calling Jews his "blood brothers," Oesterreicher described the approach he used on the streets of New York: he no longer argued with
Jews, but appealed to them in Christian charity. After the "torment of
these past several years, which every Jew has suffered in one way or the
other," Christians could not call Jews enemies.[81] No doubt he was thinking of his father who died at Theresienstadt, and his mother murdered at

Auschwitz. Thieme lacked this elemental sympathy, and Oesterreicher chided him for it. "You point out very well Israel's stubbornness," he explained, "but I think you do not sufficiently stress Israel's great trial, the immense sacrifice Our Lord demanded of His people—a sacrifice which cannot be compared to that demanded of pagans. Therefore you do not give full justice to the mysterious words: 'forgive them they know not what they do.' "[82] In other words, Christ himself had absolved Jews of any guilt for the crucifixion, and it was not necessary for Christians to imagine Jews as their opponents.

Still Thieme did not waver. "God is an enemy to them," he wrote, "only because they were hostile to him and are hostile to him and reject his witnesses as incorporated in Christians to the present day." For Thieme, the question was not about an opportunity to communicate with Jews but about strict faith. Perhaps Jews were "brothers," but in rejecting Christ they became God's enemies. Or was Oesterreicher denying that Christ was God? One could not *sweeten these elementary facts with pretty words.*"[83] As a dialectician, he noted that the Gospel's call to love enemies assumed the existence of enemies. "But even when the Jew is our enemy we may not forget," he explained in his book, "the command of Jesus: 'Love your enemies, do good to those who hate you, pray for your persecutors . . .' Ultimately Jews should learn from Christians what love really is, see that only in Jesus is their justice, and finally be 'converted.' "[84]

Oesterreicher was troubled by the moral ramifications of Thieme's formula. Christians who called Jews enemies fostered visions of Jews as vengeful and dangerous, and placed themselves in the company of antisemites. To call Jews enemies was to imply that the synagogue was Satan's instrument. Oesterreicher worried that Thieme's religious reasoning had the objective function of fostering hatred of Jews among people who had no concern with religion but used the charge of deicide to further racist prejudice. Christians had absolutely no reason to take offense at the rejection of Christ by his people. Oesterreicher pleaded with Thieme to consider Jews not as enemies and brothers but only as brothers. Not simply brothers, of course, but "lost brothers" who were "astray, stubborn, stiff-necked."[85]

Though he never confessed to it, Oesterreicher's thinking had begun to undergo a change. Before the war, he had shared Thieme's point of view. "Antisemitism remains a judgment sent by God," he wrote in 1936.[86]

Yet now, emotionally if not geographically closer to Europe's killing fields, Oesterreicher was scrutinizing Christians instead of Jews. By contrast, Karl Thieme had been insulated from the turbulence of his time in a Swiss hamlet called Läufelfingen (*Land* Basel), and continued calling the Jews' denial of Christ the "most scandalous thing" in history. The worldlier Oesterreicher retorted that Christians' "thousandfold" denial of Christ was at least as scandalous. In this new age, Oesterreicher also questioned the apocalyptic obsession he had shared with Thieme in the late 1930s. After Auschwitz, one simply could not claim that it was God who was punishing Jews. Indeed, those who called Jews enemies aided antisemites who claimed to act in God's name. Yet Thieme remained wedded to a hope that God would redeem the world in the near future, and he continued to cite a "Jewish friend" who told him in 1933 that "the eschatological perspective" was correct, "at least for the Jews."[87]

At the time of Vatican II, many involved in Christian-Jewish dialogue held John Oesterreicher in suspicion because of his work as missionary to the Jews. When Oesterreicher was called to be an advisor to Cardinal Bea, Karl Thieme voiced desperate concern to Gertrud Luckner.[88] Yet in the early postwar years Oesterreicher's function as a missionary was a saving grace, opening his ears to a new language. "When Jews hear the word 'enemy,'" he wrote Thieme, "they are no longer able to question what is meant, and a conversation with them becomes impossible."[89] Thieme, the convert who had put behind Lutheranism for a supposedly truer form of Christianity, felt his old friend was an opportunist. Faith was not a set of interpretations one could pick up and put down as one liked; it was not an interpretation at all, but an inspiration for discerning meaning in the world that had developed over many centuries. In the 1930s, he and Waldemar Gurian had used Christian inspiration to refute antisemitism as a form of racism, and nothing had happened to change the validity of their conclusions.

We see Thieme's continued confidence in the old formulations in an unpleasant exchange he had with the Jesuit Hans Urs Von Balthasar in the last years of the war. Balthasar was academic chaplain in Basel, and Thieme paid regular visits to him for theological disputes on matters like eschatology and the mystery of the Jews. Balthasar went on to become one of the century's foremost Catholic theologians, a favorite of John Paul

II among many others, influencing virtually every branch of Christian thought. Yet during the war, he reasoned that the Jews must be a "race" because they were a *Volk*, and race was the basic ingredient of *Volk*.[90] "The Jewish people is a people made by God," he wrote, "because its role is to act as the flesh and blood representation of the covenant with humanity, a real human race."

Early in the twentieth century, many Jews had used the word "race" to describe what united the Jewish people, yet, as we have seen, by the 1930s Jewish writers found other terms: of course "people," but also "tribe." Karl Thieme warned Balthasar not to use "race" to describe the Jews: this "biological concept assumes purely natural characteristics like white, yellow or red skin color, while any visible characteristics of the Jews have emerged through history, and have a mimical [i.e., nonessential] character." Jews could not be a "real human race," as Balthasar contended because Jews were "racially mixed like all of us Europeans." Thieme felt secure on this bedrock of arguments he had used against antisemitism from before the war. Balthasar feebly defended himself in a postcard. "By race I understand a human type that is partly caused by somatic factors deeply rooted in a Jew's being," he insisted. "A people remains a people and that comes from the blood."[91] That Balthasar, whom French Cardinal Henri de Lubac has called the most cultivated person of our time, could insist on the hard category of race to describe Jews in October 1943 tells us something about the power of the racist syndrome among German-speaking Catholics. But after 1945 Balthasar sensed the inappropriateness of this word and, like other European intellectuals, ceased using it to describe Jews. The article that Thieme attacked does not appear in the great theologian's collected works.[92]

Perhaps Thieme felt a sense of triumph after such an exchange. Yet the anti-racist argument had done nothing to weaken his commitment to Jewish mission because this argument implied that Jews were "naturally" more suited to faith than Christians. In the summer of 1945, Thieme turned to the first issue of *Judaica*, a journal of the Swiss Christian missions fostering study of Judaism, and found his views confirmed. Robert Brunner, the journal's editor, published a piece entitled "Mission to the Jews after the Second World War?"—asking whether evangelization of Jews should continue after the deaths of "six million defenseless human beings." His answer was yes, it should. In fact, Christians should feel shame that they had not devoted even more resources to making Jews Christian before the war. That might have saved lives. And to those who thought that mission endangered the "existence" of Jews he said: Christians cannot be Christian if they ignore Christ's "command" to do missionary work. Those who forsook mission were denying that Christ was God.[93] Such views proliferated throughout postwar Protestantism, and were precisely those of Karl Thieme.[94]

All the while, Brunner insisted he opposed antisemitism. As evidence of his good intentions, he printed an essay by Basel Rabbi Lothar Rothschild entitled "A Jewish View of the 'Jewish Question.'" Rothschild reached diametrically opposed conclusions from Brunner, reminding readers that Christians' desire to baptize Jews had been historically inseparable from the threat of punishment, for example, medieval tortures and death at the stake. He zeroed in on the problematic nature of Christian eschatology. Christians had become obsessed with baptizing Jews because they believed there could be no redemption of the world until Jews converted to Christianity. Rothschild did not dispute the Christian justification for this belief in Paul's letter to the Romans 11:25–26. He wondered simply that Christians made an act of God dependent upon the behavior of Jews, and he noted that according to the Jewish view the world would be redeemed when God and not man desired that to happen. In the meantime, every religious community should try to educate its members to the highest ethical rigor.[95]

Midway through this essay, Thieme noticed something that made him cringe. In a footnote, the rabbi discussed Thieme's book *Church and Synagogue* and urged his readers, whether Christian or Jewish, not to read it because it was the work of an "antisemite." Rothschild cited the passages in which Thieme called Jews "enemies" and "infamous." If Thieme claimed to love Israel, argued Rothschild, it was not for the sake of the Jews but for the sake of the church and its vision of the end of time. The point was not love but the gaining of converts. Thieme's idea that Jews were Christians' "enemies" made any discussion with him impossible.[96]

Rothschild had plunged Thieme into a crisis of conscience that lasted until 1950, when he confessed to Ernst Karl Winter, once vice-mayor of Vienna, of having undergone a "conversion."[97] Suddenly Thieme was writing that Christians must abandon their mission to the Jews, and that they were more guilty than Jews of Christ's time for the crucifixion.[98] He spoke of the churches' "guilt" for failing to instruct their "members about the special Christian duties toward Jews and about God's continuing salvific intentions for the Jews."[99] Now he urged Christians to imagine their relation to Jews as ecumenical, like that of younger to older brother. "Israel is God's 'special property',," he wrote to Martin Buber, with whom he conducted a lively correspondence, "and remains sanctified in a way that is hardly accessible to us 'believers from the peoples of the world.'" He no longer portrayed Jews as "enemies" or even potential Christians, but rather as "comparable to our clergy."[100] Antisemitism, therefore, could not be dealt with as racial hatred. It was, instead, like anti-clericalism. To slander Jews was to curse God, to "blaspheme."[101] As a good academic, he supported all these ideas with sources. *Scripture* spoke of Jews as a holy priesthood, and it instructed Christians to "revere" the Jewish people (Romans 11:13–24).[102] Most important, he no longer read Romans 11:25–26 as necessitating the conversion of Jews to Christianity before the end of time.

Conversions always have an element of the unpredictable. Perhaps Thieme used the word "conversion" to describe his radical shift in views because of its flexibility. On one level, he had taken a turn that made sense—he could now speak about Jews in a way that seemed appropriate to the time—but on another level, this turn could not be explained by reason alone. It was true that one could read Paul in a new way. But why do it now? The Holocaust had not had a direct, immediate impact on Thieme's thought—or indeed on the thought of other Christian theologians. What about the founding of the state of Israel? This world historical event had important implications for Christian theology. Karl Barth pronounced it as providential, and in 1949 it probably loomed large in Thieme's mind.[103] Church historian John Conway has noted that the new state defied the ancient belief that God had dispersed the Jews as punishment. Now, the Christian "theological myth of Jewish national demise" had become untenable.[104] The Freiburg Circle took the state's founding as a sign that God was permitting part of the Jewish people to settle once more in the "promised land."[105] Yet they were not uncritical. Each issue of the *Rundbrief* brought news of achievements in Israel, but Karl Thieme

wondered about the relation a secular state might have to Israel's transcendent mission.

More basic to his conversion was the constellation of the postwar years
when Protestants, Catholics, and Jews concerned about religious bigotry
suddenly began speaking to each other. Thieme began hearing what
Christian entreaties to conversion sounded like to Jewish ears, and he
found them unbearable. Still, he worried about intellectual consistency,
and told Theodor Adorno that he dreaded the unexplored theological territory ahead, likening his journey to a walk onto a "razor sharp ridge"
from which he could tumble, either back into anti-Judaism or into heresy.[106] But two forces gave him confidence to move forward: first, the
simple moral conviction of Jewish interlocutors that Christian missions to
the Jews were inappropriate after Auschwitz and second, the relief he felt
after decades of growing tension between the Christian ethics that instructed him to love Jews as neighbors and the Christian eschatology that
told him Jews must cease being Jews.

The mass and velocity of the insights propelled Thieme forward. From
late 1949, just as Thieme began advising the council coordinating the
work of Societies for Christian-Jewish Cooperation, and having dozens of
meetings with German Jews, new ideas began supplanting old ones, even
though some of his interlocutors (like Rabbi Wilhelm Weinberg of
Frankfurt) were skeptical about the chances for Jewish life in Germany.
Among these encounters two stand out, one with the well known philosopher Martin Buber, then in Jerusalem, the other with a long-forgotten
rabbi who worked in German Silesia in the 1840s.

Karl Thieme stumbled into a furious exchange with Buber by publishing what he felt was a defense of Jews in the first edition of the *Freiburger
Rundbrief* (1948). Christians must not think of Jews as forever abandoned
by God, Thieme wrote, and to make the point he appropriated a story
from Mark 5:42 in which Christ treats a dead girl as if she were sleeping
and tells her to get up. Similarly, Thieme reasoned, Jews were not spiritually dead, and would awaken when Christ came and commanded them to
arise.[107] This was a rebuttal to Christian antisemitism: no one could say
the Jews were rejected for all time. The proof that they were alive was that
they could become Christian. Up to this point, Thieme and Buber were
having a friendly exchange of views, but now Buber asked whether the
contact was not based on hypocrisy:

I had been persuaded up to now that you were interested in real understanding with those religious Jews who have understanding for people acting as faithful Christians. But how should such understanding be possible if you identify spiritual life for the Jews with their readiness to be converted? I have my spiritual life in a direct contact to God and myself, and in addition I have my bodily life. I cannot believe that God would allow a Christian to question this fact, and equally I cannot believe that God would allow me to act this way toward a Christian. Judaism and Christianity stand united in the mystery of our father and judge: and therefore the Jew can speak of the Christian and the Christian of the Jew only in fear and trembling before the mystery of God. On this basis alone can there be genuine understanding between Jew and Christian.[108]

Buber was saying that Thieme's anti-racism was insufficient. Before the war, to say Jews could be "converted" was to undo the racist idea that they were forever lost. Now this argument revealed the persistence of a deeper problem: the belief that Jews were deficient. This in turn was connected to the old anti-Judaic idea that, to use Jacques Maritain's formulation, one could separate "carnal" from "spiritual" Israel, and that Jews of the present no longer represented the promises God had made with Israel in the Pentateuch. Those promises had supposedly been transferred to the "New Israel" of the church. No wonder Buber found Thieme's references to Israel "inconceivably abstract." They did not involve actual Jewish persons. The problem, he suggested, was not Judaism but Christianity that had been deformed. How could Jews be the neighbor Christ told his followers to love if Jews were enemies of God? In representing Jews as spiritually dead, Christians distorted their own spiritual lives, disconnecting action from belief.

Thieme called to his defense the Jewish thinker Jules Isaac, the driving force behind the Seelisberg theses, who had said in a radio interview that being Christian involved "a missionary task" that could not be abdicated. "One had to have always in front of one's eyes the famous verses of the Epistle to the Romans of St. Paul," Isaac explained, "that the joining of Israel will be resurrection from among the dead." This seemed to Thieme a Jewish voice absolving Christians who imagined that Jews needed awakening.[109] Moreover, Isaac's comment had been directed at Christians and not at Jews, and therefore only Christians could understand them. Yet then Thieme confessed explicitly the tension besetting his entire construct by saying that his allusion to the sleeping girl should be understood at the level of spirituality and not morality.[110] The Christian thus spoke one language to other spiritual Christians, and reserved another for carnal Jews.

After Auschwitz, this kind of duplicity could not hold. Yet simultaneously Thieme worried about what Christians would say to the idea that conversion to Christianity would mean nothing for Jews. But if it meant anything, did it not mean new life? Thieme pleaded that Buber had misunderstood him, thinking he had accused Jews of "contemptible vulgarity," when in fact he had simply written that Jews were tragically blind in turning away from Christ. Surely Jews would understand that Christianity required Christians to believe this. But Thieme also signaled that it was no longer what he believed. New words now make an appearance. Oesterreicher had insisted that he call Jews brothers, and here he does. That was not revolutionary. What was new was his insertion of the word "older" before the word "brother." The few Christians who called Jews brothers in the prewar years—like Dietrich von Hildebrand—had assumed Jews were the younger, prodigal sons, who must somehow return to their patrimony.[111] If Jews were the elder son, then they were the loyal son who stayed home while his brother went and squandered the inheritance. The new understanding implied—as Thieme wrote to Martin Buber—that Jews were the son to whom the father says *"you are always with me* and everything that is mine is yours." This statement and others, Thieme pointed out, [John 1, 17, 12, 29ff] represented the "legitimation of Jewry," of all times, until the end of time.

Buber tried to wean Thieme from his eschatological perspective, writing that no believer must feel a compulsion to "hope for the end of time." No one therefore had to imagine that Christians were meant to be Jews or Jews Christians.[112] Buber thought that in the end questions about the relation of God and man would wither in the radiance of God's mystery. All human communities would be dissolved. In the meantime, he saw the world as unredeemed—regardless of whether Christians called him "stubborn."[113] Thieme assented in part. "We see the world becoming less redeemed by the day," he wrote. But we also see the good seeds maturing for the harvest—in many different fields, "also in God's favorite garden Israel."[114] Israel was not deficient but favored, and producing good fruit. That also was new.

The eschatological perspective had not disappeared: for Karl Thieme, Christ had inaugurated the end of time. But now passages from Romans, passages he had read scores of times, were telling him new things:

> And even the others, if they do not persist in their unbelief, will be grafted in, for God has the power to graft them in again.
>
> For if you have been cut from what is by nature a wild olive tree, and grafted, contrary to nature, into a cultivated olive tree, how much more will these natural branches be grafted back into their own olive tree.
>
> Lest you be wise in your own conceits, I want you to understand this mystery, brethren: a hardening has come upon part of Israel, until the full number of the Gentiles come in, and so all Israel will be saved; as it is written,
>
> "The Deliverer will come from Zion,
> he will banish ungodliness from Jacob;
> and this will be my covenant with them
> when I take away their sins." Romans 11:23–27 (RSV)

Previously he and other Christian readers had focused on the idea that Jews—the "others"—would be joined with Christians in the final days. But now, inspired by Jules Isaac, Bern's Rabbi Eugen Messinger, and perhaps others, Thieme noted that Paul had indeed prophesied that "All Israel will be saved," but only *after* the "full number" of Gentiles had come into the Messianic Kingdom. If the salvation of Israel was certain, then missionary activities should focus on those whose salvation was not certain. This new reading had already become popular in the emerging Christian-Jewish dialogue in France, where Jules Isaac was arguing that the meaning of mission had to shift in a post-Holocaust world.[115] Thieme embraced this understanding in his correspondence with Martin Buber, writing that the final "reconciliation" of church and synagogue could not happen until "those Christians of Pagan origin have given evidence for their faith through a practical life of love." Only in this way, Thieme continued, could there be a "fundamental *revision* of the relation of all serious

Christians to the Jews." Bern's Rabbi Messinger had accepted this understanding as a "useful foundation for promoting friendship between Christians and Jews."[116]

At some point in late 1948, Thieme found himself reading the letters of
Israel Deutsch, a rabbi who had ministered to the Jews in the German-
Polish borderlands a century earlier. The new reading of Paul's letter to
the Romans opened his mind to the revolutionary idea that God had
meant Jews to continue as a people after the time of Christ. Suddenly he
was projecting the Jewish decision not to follow Christ as perfectly understandable. Not only that, but the Jews' refusal seemed justified, because
for Jews to accept Christ would have meant the end of the Jewish people.[117] These ideas accorded with a message that Rabbi Deutsch had
wanted to impress upon his friend Abraham Pless, a leading proponent of
emancipation among Silesian Jewry. Thieme reprinted excerpts from
their correspondence in the left-liberal *Frankfurter Hefte*.

> 12 November 1839: Just as Providence is happy to distribute physical
> and moral gifts unevenly among people, so it was also happy to raise
> a little band of outcasts from the dust and to elect it as bearer of truth
> in order to edify the nations, until the promised time should come . . .
> If the Israelites living in Egypt had been merged with the natives
> then the intention of God to raise them up to a priestly kingdom
> would have been frustrated.[118]

If God meant the Jews to continue, then these Jewish perspectives
could become Christian perspectives. In August 1950, Thieme announced
major planks of his new understanding in a public letter to the Jewish
émigré and socialist historian Helmut Hirsch, at that point teaching in
Chicago. Hirsch, later a biographer of Rosa Luxemburg, supported the
work of the Freiburg Circle, but doubted whether there could be real
friendship between Christians and Jews, given the dialectical conflict of
ideas between both the two sides. Thieme saw a chance to explain how it
had been "given" to him to understand revelation in a new way. Without
surrendering the belief that Jews would recognize Jesus, he now reached
the "conviction that a Jewish person not only as an individual person, but
also in a certain sense precisely as '*Jew* can be pleasing to God [*Gott wohl-*

gefällig].'" "Precisely for the Jews according to the entirety of divine revelation certain promises continue to be in force," he wrote, "so that one
can assume that even in distance from Christ the Jewish people enjoys
special guidance and special grace." "I am certain," he continued, "that if
God's grace permits 'Israel according to the flesh' to continue to exist to
the end of time, and *then* made recipient of very great compassion, then
their character as chosen people has not been abolished, but only suspended in some of its effects."[119]

With the exception of the Anglican James Parkes, this was the most
sudden and radical shift in a Christian theologian's view of the Jews in
modern history. Yet no sooner was Thieme "converted" to a view uniting
previously irreconcilable facts than he was attempting to convert others.
From that point on, Thieme's appeals to Jews were geared not to making
them Christian, but to convincing them that Christians love them as the
Gospel demanded. Before Christians could extend mission to anyone,
they faced the task of living lives in accord with the teachings of Jesus.
That was Thieme's message to a young German who believed that Christ
had made Jewish morality obsolete. All religious communities, Thieme
responded, have adherents who fail to live up to their calling. But in
people like Martin Buber, Leo Baeck, and many others, Christians could
see Judaism producing teachers whom Jesus would have admired. Furthermore, Jesus had first "cleaned in his own house," and likewise
Christians—especially those in Germany—should condemn the sins of
their own people "which cry out to heaven" before worrying about the
"splinter" in the eye of their brother.[120] In a private communication to
the International Missionary Council in London, likewise concerned
that Christians not surrender their mission to the Jews, Thieme wrote
that today's task—in the post-Holocaust era—was evangelization by
"deed rather than by word."[121]

In these years of revolutionary transformation in Christian ideas, Israel was not only a people but was also a state. In Thieme's eyes, Israel's
transcendent vocation should carry over to the new state, for which he
envisioned a role as spiritual and intellectual center, similar to the Vatican for Catholics. Thieme worried that the new state might be carried
away by a nationalism of the sort that Jews had learned in the "host countries" of Europe, but he did not think that Christians could presume to

give instructions to Jews on this score.[122] They should tend to their own house.

At the same time, like Dietrich von Hildebrand in 1937, Thieme and others in the Freiburg Circle hoped that Jews would continue to enrich European societies. Rabbi Deutsch had unlocked a metaphor from the book of Exodus that Christians and Jews could share when reflecting upon Israel's vocation: "And you shall be to Me a kingdom of priests and a holy nation."[123] Thieme used this phrase in a broadcast of Bavarian Radio in 1950. "This people and every one of its members," Thieme wrote, "has an indelible character irremovably stamped onto it just like those who receive the Christian sacrament of Holy Orders."[124] To secular opponents of antisemitism, the idea that Jewishness was stamped on each individual Jew could of course seem problematic. But as a Christian veteran of the struggle against racism, Thieme had no qualms. Jews were not a race, but that did not rob them of the coherence of a people, possessing what we now call ethnic identity, passed from family to family over many generations. The legacy of anti-racism therefore involved not only the conversion of Christians to a new point of view; it pivoted on the very idea of the Jewish people. The point for Christians was not to subvert the family-like coherence of the Jewish people, but rather to convert it to a positive valence.

Thieme's conversion of 1950 lived up to John Oesterreicher's definition of the word: a total reorientation of one's existence.[125] It involved not just refuting this or that belief, for example, about deicide or covenant, but taking a new outlook on the world. Karl Thieme had always read current history in terms of two fixed points: the church and the Jews. Their fate signaled the will of God for humanity. Now he was content imagining that Jewish history provided no signs that he or anyone could read clearly, and he advised Christians who wondered about the vocation of Israel to heed the words of former Berlin Chief Rabbi Leo Baeck, who said in 1948 that "Jewry is *the mystery*, and not simply one mystery among others." This phrase, anticipated before the war by Jacques Maritain, became a mantra for the Freiburg Circle, signaling that the old speculative dialectical theology was itself a hindrance to the understanding they sought with Jews (also a lesson from Erik Peterson).[126] For Christians concerned about the relation between faith and history, Baeck's words meant that "Jewry represents the most mysterious aspect of the mystery of the presence of God among human beings."[127] Into 1949, Thieme had thought the world stood on the verge of redemptive cataclysm. Now he soberly wrote to Martin Buber that it was becoming less redeemed by the day. He denied the eschatological assumptions lying behind everything he had written for twenty years, in the process helping deconstruct an intellectual edifice Christians had constructed over centuries.

Karl Thieme was not the only Christian intellectual abandoning old positions in those years. As early as 1942 Karl Barth rejected proselytism toward the Jews, though he still insisted that Israel was "rejected" by God.[128] In 1948, the converted Hungarian Jew and Notre Dame de Sion priest Paul Démann was writing an incisive refutation of the idea that God had cursed Jews, and he went on to produce groundbreaking critiques of the anti-Judaism of Catholic catechisms. In 1949, the Dutch Reformed Church asserted that Christians should abandon attempts to convert Jews and instead understand themselves as the "younger sister entering dialogue with the older brother." The church and Israel were parts of a divided "people of God."[129] The following year, the Berlin-Weissensee Synod of the German Evangelical Church declared "we believe God's promise to be valid for his Chosen People even after the Crucifixion of Christ."[130] Thieme participated in a panel on Judeo-Christian relations of the Evangelical Church at Kassel in March 1950 at which, for the first time, German Protestants failed to use the word *mission* to describe the Christian task toward the Jews.

In part, these new understandings grew out of ecumenical discussions with Jews, the likes of which were unthinkable before the Holocaust. Joining Thieme at the Kassel panel was the Protestant pastor Karl Janssen and the Jewish rabbi (and Holocaust survivor) Hugo Nothmann.[131] From 1949, the *Freiburger Rundbrief* had Jewish collaborators such as Hans Lamm, Rabbi Robert R. Geis, and later Ernst Ludwig Ehrlich. Besides Karl Thieme, at least one other prominent Catholic—Henri Daniel-Rops, Catholic writer in postwar France, and like Thieme a would-be philo-Semite—was shamed in private correspondence by a Jewish intellectual with whom he sought friendship, and as a result renounced New Testament anti-Judaism. For Thieme, that intellectual had been Martin Buber; for Daniel-Rops, it was Jules Isaac.[132]

Nowhere did Karl Thieme make pretensions to originality. His discussion of Paul's letter to the Romans drew in everything that had been written up to that point, and was ecumenical, holding Anglo-Saxon Protestants W. D. Davies and James Parkes above German Catholic counterparts when the latter suffered from petty consistency that kept them from seeing in Paul's letters "what really is written there."[133] As his thought advanced in the early 1950s, Thieme drew upon the revolutionary New Testament studies of Davies, Marcel Simon's work on the coexistence of early Christian and Jewish communities, and Gerschom Scholem's on Jewish mysticism.[134] For the latest revelations on the medieval papacy and its hostility toward Judaism, he turned to the Jesuit Peter Browe.[135] Readers of the *Rundbrief* discovered via reports of Paul Démann what had been said about Israel among Protestants at the international Ecumenical Conference in Evanston, Illinois, in 1954.[136]

Karl Thieme composed Catholic theses for Evanston, several of whose formulations later entered the Vatican II document *Nostra Aetate*. These in turn would have been unthinkable without the theses of Schwalbach, for Catholics a theologically sounder version of the Seelisberg theses, which were released in 1950 after consultation with Protestant theologians throughout Germany as well as intensive engagement with societies of Christian-Jewish cooperation in Stuttgart, Offenbach, Berlin, and Frankfurt.[137] Among those sending in ideas were left Catholics such as Walter Dirks and Eugen Kogon, but also members of the Frankfurt Society of Christian-Jewish Cooperation such as Max Horkheimer, Theodor Adorno, and Dolf Sternberger (later editor of *Frankfurter Allgemeine Zeitung*).[138]

Karl Thieme's new vision was drawn from many sources, yet it was only beginning to attract adherents. He had staked new territory by the early 1950s, and now came the time to defend it. For the decade that remained to him, he attracted numerous opponents, primarily theologians who knew that his ideas broke with what the church had taught for centuries. Surprisingly, one of the fiercest opponents was the man who had tried to convince him that Jews were not enemies: John Oesterreicher, whose resistance grew so determined that Thieme began suspecting him of building an "anti-Freiburg" conspiracy among Western European theologians. Just a few years earlier, Oesterreicher had been chiding Thieme for not going far enough; now he suspected Thieme of going too far. In July 1960, the tension between them became unbearable, for Thieme at least, and a correspondence going back to 1934 suddenly came to a halt. It was not resumed before Thieme died of cancer three years later.

7

Who Are the Jews?

In October 1951, the German Jew Kurt Kaiser-Bluth wrote to the *Freiburger Rundbrief* informing the editors that "most Germans meet your idealistic efforts with indifference and hostility while the Jews look upon your Coordinating Council for Christian-Jewish cooperation with distrust. The basis of your work is too narrow, your goals too abstract."[1] The editors hardly quarreled. Who could deny they were idealists? Yet their idealism was tightly enveloped in a sense of reality.[2] Karl Thieme and his collaborators knew that the theological underpinnings of contempt had hardly been touched six years after the war. In the shadow of Auschwitz, old ideas of Jewish deficiency and guilt sounded obscene (who could say that God destined Jews to suffer against the background of the extermination camps?), but the religious arguments supporting these views were completely intact.

The Freiburg Circle felt the best way to replace old ideas was to engage those holding them in print. In 1953, Karl Thieme wrote one friend that the *Rundbrief* "very consciously permits an enormous number of more or less eminent theologians to print their absurdities in order to have occasion for patient refutation."[3] They made their refutations, Thieme proudly reported, with the explicit approval of the church's local censors in Freiburg and the teaching office in Rome. This was an extraordinary feat on the background of international Catholicism in those years, in which the Vatican curtailed the work of leading theologians, including proponents of religious freedom such as Henri de Lubac, Karl Rahner, and John Courtney Murray. Yet in the case of the *Freiburger Rundbrief,* one prominent official, Monsignor Augustin Bea, S.J., rector of the Papal Biblical Institute and confessor to Pius XII, came to act as a quiet protector. In 1959, John XXIII made the charismatic Bea a cardinal and charged him with crafting a statement on the Jews, which became chapter four of *Nostra Aetate,* the 1965 declaration through which the church expressed an about-face in its teaching. Bea appointed veterans of the struggle against anti-semitism as his consultants at the council, and in effect made theses on the Jews drafted in the 1950s by Catholics at Freiburg, Paris, Apeldoorn (the Netherlands), and elsewhere the basis for new church teaching. Cardinal Bea was the engineer, and Karl Thieme and his friends in Freiburg had been architects.

Because of the shame many Christians felt after the Holocaust, the Freiburg Circle had difficulty luring opponents of the emerging vision into print. In the case of one esteemed authority on the New Testament, Rev. Professor Max Meinertz of Münster, they lifted views he printed elsewhere and practically provoked him to self-defense. Otherwise, theologians hesitated to state in public the anti-Judaic ideas they held in private. Thus, revealing controversies of these years often took place behind the scenes in private correspondence. The most ferocious involved Thieme's old allies from the 1930s: the anti-national former mayor of Vienna Ernst Karl Winter, and John Oesterreicher, both in American exile, both resisting the idea that the church could recognize any national group as holding divine promises. In their view, grace resided in the church, which was the new people of God and New Israel. Winter and Oesterreicher represented ideas held by the theological establishment throughout Europe and North America. Yet in the shadow of the Holocaust these ideas—according to which the Jewish people were not Israel—indeed sounded absurd and shameful, and Winter refused to have his objections printed. Thieme printed Oesterreicher's ideas only in part. Thieme's unpublished letters merit attention because they permitted him—arguably the main architect of the church's new vision of the Jews—fullest elaboration of his ideas. The letters are lost blueprints of the intellectual structure in which the church has lived since *Nostra Aetate*.

Just as architects' work occurs within rules of physics, so Karl Thieme's work took place within the strictures of Catholic theology. Martin Buber had sensitized him to the perils of spirituality divorced from ethics, but there was also the opposite danger: emotional and ethical identification that pretended to be theology. Scripture scholars waited at every turn toward a new vision to decry excessive "irenicism."[4] New Testament scholar Meinertz, for example, was sympathetic to the need to speak in a new way about the Jews, but felt that unsound theology served no one. The Freiburg group agreed. "What good would it do the Jews," they asked, "to be lavished with the affection of a few well-meaning enthusiasts, if their views were not recognized by the Church as resting firmly in the ground of Catholic Christian belief?"[5] In December 1949, Thieme explained to one of his supporters at the Vatican, papal personal secretary Robert Leiber, that the *Rundbrief* was operating on a "dogmatically clear basis" on which "principles could be developed that enable dialogue." The dialogue with Jews, he implied, took place within signs revealed by a new time, representing "what one must expect from Catholic circles after the events of 1933."[6]

The fact that signs of the time seemed relevant when reading scripture made the 1950s an exciting decade, a rare moment when assumptions governing Christian thought for centuries were suddenly open to question. Yet the challenges were daunting. One could not simply throw away the Epistle to the Hebrews with its claim that the Old Covenant was "obsolete," nor could one ignore the fact that even the liberating passages of Romans 9–11 called the Jews "unbelieving," "disobedient," and "enemies." The problem was not limited to what one said about Jews, but also concerned what a new vision of the Jews implied about the church itself. The entire Christian tradition said: those who believed in Christ were Abraham's children, whether or not they were circumcised (Romans 4:11). That is, Israel had been transformed to include Christians, and the Old Testament was fulfilled in the New. From its early days, Christian thinkers had called the church the true "spiritual" Israel, and had denigrated the Jews as "Israel of the flesh," broken as a nation, condemned to wandering the earth, kept alive as evidence of the church's message.[7] Judaism had acted out its role in delivering truths to the Christians as well as their sacraments and liturgy. Why should it continue in the old form?

And there was the vexing charge of deicide, according to which Jews wandered aimlessly through history as punishment for rejecting and killing Christ. Given the well-known diaspora of Jews in the time of Christ, it was easy to say that the overwhelming majority of Jews knew nothing about Christ's crucifixion. But what about Jewish leaders, did they not represent the Jewish people? And if Christ was fully man and fully God, was not the act of killing him the killing of God?

Vatican Censure and Support

Karl Thieme drew the attention of church censors in 1950 when he called these charges of deicide absurd, something only "poorly educated Christians" might believe. The church authorities instructed Thieme not to dispute the correctness of the word "deicide" when referring to the crucifixion. No one could "kill God," they agreed; yet to the extent that God took flesh in Jesus, his "human nature" could be "murdered," and thus "the condemnation and crucifixion of Christ were objectively deicide." Catholics could not deny the "subjective guilt" of the Jewish leaders, but they were *not* required to assign this guilt to the entire Jewish people.[8]

We learn two lessons from the turnaround of the censors at this point. First, that the crimes of the Nazi regime caused Catholic officials to think carefully about the resonance of what they said about the Jews. Clearly, the men in Freiburg—but also Robert Leiber or Augustin Bea in Rome—felt implicated in some deep way as Germans for what the German state had done to Europe's Jews. But their ethnic sensitivity also came with a strange twist. Though as Germans they felt shame for the Holocaust, as Germans they also came to detest ideas of collective guilt. That in turn made them more open to reappraisals of deicide. All Germans could not be held responsible for acts of their leaders during the war, and similarly, all Jews could not be held responsible for the acts of Jewish leaders at the time of Christ.[9]

Of more general importance was a second fact: the censors could easily justify this about-face in terms of older Christian teaching. The fact that some Jewish leaders had wanted Christ dead did not "justify antisemitism or the criminal acts of violence against the children of Israel," they wrote, "especially since they had a unique religious mission to humanity and thereby 'became a blessing' to all humans."

After this clarification every issue of the *Rundbrief* went out with the explicit approval of the Freiburg Episcopate. Yet the challenges from the Catholic hierarchy were not exhausted. About this time, the Holy Office in Rome issued a *monitum* (warning) against "indifferentism" of Catholics who participated in meetings of the International Council of Christians and Jews. Church officials appreciated the council's struggle against antisemitism but feared that it fostered "religious tolerance, indeed the complete equality of various religions." At a congress "in Freiburg," the officials went on, "one speaker argued that youth should be raised in a spirit of absolute indifference in regard to nationality, race, and religion."[10] Three Jesuit priests stationed in Rome were dispatched to investigate the work of the *Freiburger Rundbrief:* Augustin Bea, Robert Leiber, and Father Charles Boyer, who was, like Leiber, of the Gregorian University and a specialist in ecumenism.[11]

The choice of papal secretary Leiber proved fortuitous. Karl Thieme had known Leiber from the late 1930s, when he, Joseph Wirth, and other émigrés interceded with him hoping to make the pope speak out in favor of German Jews. After the war, Thieme renewed the contact, sending Leiber copies of the *Rundbrief* along with clever personal notes demonstrating the journal's faithfulness to Catholic teaching. Thieme knew the other investigators from a visit to the Vatican about half a year before the *monitum*'s release, during which he saw Leiber and Bea as well as Thomas Grendel, S.V.D. (Consultor of the Sacred Office), Father Felix Morlion, O.P. (Rector of the International Ecumenical Institute Pro Deo), and Father Ernst Vogt, S.J. (Bea's replacement as rector of the Biblical Institute). Thieme reported that Grendel "strongly" approved of the "general tendencies of conciliation among all people of good will," and that Leiber was "strongly affected by the ravages which Hitlerian propaganda has caused above all in the spirit of young people." As an example, Leiber cited a Bavarian woman, thirty years old, who said that "Jews have a different God from the one we Christians have."[12] Leiber agreed that the problems facing Germany called for special redress, and expressed "great sympathy for the activities of the societies for Christian-Jewish friendship." The Roman contacts insisted on strict confidence. The "smallest public mention of this could only have unfortunate consequences, because Vatican figures could not to be cited publicly in favor of any cause, no matter how good it may be, without their [i.e., ecclesiastical authorities'] express authorization." For the moment, it was enough to know that they "approve of our conciliatory work."

Still, the Holy Office issued its *monitum* mentioning Freiburg just months later and sent the priests whom Thieme had just met to carry out the investigation. It seems that Vatican authorities had been misinformed, however, confusing the German Freiburg im Breisgau with the Swiss Fribourg (which in German is "Freiburg in der Schweiz"). In the latter town, a meeting of the International Council of Christians and Jews had indeed occurred where a speaker had indeed endorsed "indifferentism" toward nationality, race, and religion.[13] "Indifferentism" stood high on the list of errors the Vatican was sworn to combat, and as a consequence church authorities forced Catholics to withdraw from Jewish-Christian cooperation in other countries such as Great Britain. Yet the *monitum* had no further effects in Germany.[14]

Thieme actually welcomed the initial targeting of the *Freiburger Rundbrief* by Rome because it gave him a "massive tool for stopping the rather strong tendency toward indifferentism in the Societies [for Christian-Jewish Cooperation]" in Germany.[15] It also gave a patina of orthodoxy to everything done after this point. By December 1950, with clear authorization not only of church authorities in Freiburg but also in Rome, the Freiburg circle was sending instructional materials to priests in all but three German Catholic dioceses as well as the Protestant *Landeskirchen* of Bavaria, Berlin, Bremen, Hessen, Lübeck, Northwest Germany (Reformed), Rhineland, and Württemberg. The bishop of Baden volunteered to send the material to pastors through his office.[16] Evidently, he and other Protestants were not concerned with "indifferentism," especially since so much of the *Rundbrief* was inspired by Protestant sources.

Still, Thieme acted to clarify the implications of the Vatican's warning for their work. In April 1951, he again visited Rome, this time meeting fathers Bea, Leiber, and Boyer as well as Monsignor Bruno Wüstenberg, Father R. W. von Moos, S.J., and other officials interested in Christian-Jewish relations. He was told that the main points guiding the German Societies for Christian-Jewish Cooperation that he represented were "fully approved," and that the Societies' work would not be affected by the *monitum* issued in October 1950.[17]

Signaling a quiet crossing of a threshold in Catholic teaching, Father Bea now approved a set of instructions for Catholic teaching about Jews drafted by Thieme and his Protestant colleague Adolf Freudenberg at a meeting of the Coordinating Council of the German Societies for Christian-Jewish Cooperation at Bad Schwalbach (near Wiesbaden) in May 1950.[18] Freudenberg had been a member of the Confessing Church who took shelter from Nazi Germany in Switzerland, where he in turn gave shelter to persecuted Germans and Jews during the war. Among his guests was Dietrich Bonhoeffer. The stimulus for the meeting at Bad Schwalbach was concern over the continuing desecration of Jewish cemeteries. The attendees worked out a set of theses meant to be better grounded biblically than the Seelisberg theses of 1947 so that they could be used in Christian religion classes at German public schools. After approval, the "Schwalbach theses" went out to 25,000 religion teachers and pastors of both confessions in West Germany and West Berlin. Two years later, Father Paul Démann of the Notre Dame de Sion fathers in Paris achieved a similar effect with ten theses approved by the Archbishop of Aix that were distributed throughout French-speaking Europe.[19]

The Schwalbach theses were revolutionary in several regards. They spoke directly about German guilt for the mass murder of Jews, making clear that Jews had been victims while Christians had mostly stood by, failing to offer assistance; they spoke bluntly of "Christian sins against Jewish persons." Contrary to what Thieme had forcefully maintained just a few years previously, Schwalbach (in thesis six) specified that Jews could not be called enemies of Jesus. The murder of Jews had been carried out not by God but against God. If any people was under God's judgment, it was the German people, and they were failing to heed the signs of their time. Using a metaphor developed by Karl Thieme, Schwalbach portrayed the relation between church and Israel as the fraternal bond of *"old and new peoples of God,"* thus anticipating the language of the Second

Vatican Council. As younger brothers, the Christians had to oppose all slander of the older brother. Thesis four reminded Christians of a fact little known to them: that Christ's first command, to love God and neighbor, had already been "pronounced in the Old Testament."

Many consider the deicide charge to have been the most difficult issue facing the Second Vatican Council, yet the authors of the Schwalbach theses undermined this age-old idea in simple language, proclaiming that it was "unbiblical and unchristian to think of Christ's passion in the light of certain historical individuals or a particular people." The consequence of Christ's death was not that a curse had fallen upon anyone, but rather that God had effected a blessing upon "his people"—that is, the Jews—and all other peoples. The sins of all humankind had brought Christ to the cross, and not the sins of any one people. The call of an "agitated crowd" in Matthew 27:25 that "his blood be upon us and our children" could never be used to justify the spilling of Jewish blood. After all, the early Christians had venerated Jews who had shed their blood for the faith as martyrs. The crowd in Matthew was therefore in no way representative. As Jules Isaac reminded Christians, Christ's first followers were Jews.

If the Schwalbach theses offered the first explicit development of themes taken up in *Nostra Aetate* fifteen years later—deploring deicide, confirming the Jewishness of Jesus, condemning antisemitism—they also reveal a continued shortcoming of Christian thought at this point, even among the most committed advocates of reconciliation. According to the final thesis, Jews would speak their "Yes" to Jesus as the "last word of their history." Schwalbach had succeeded in converting the old Christian narrative from negative to positive: Christians should love Jews in order to lead them to Christ. According to Romans 11, Jews were not to be seen as living under a curse; they were loved by God. Yet with these words the Christian authors still presumed to tell the Jews what they would do in the future.

From 1933, Karl Thieme had worked to undo Christian antisemitism stage by stage, and stage by stage he had unearthed deeper levels of anti-Judaism. In the interwar years, he refuted stereotypes about Jews and showed how racist assumptions contradicted biblical teaching. Yet in doing so he also revealed a deeper assumption in Christian thinking about a curse resting upon the Jews. Now he had undermined the idea of a curse only to arrive at a still deeper level of contempt: assumptions about how Jews must act in the future. They would turn to Christ not as free human beings but as unthinking automatons, in the tight embrace of a Christian narrative. This was not a view of the Jewish other that could serve as a basis for deeper understanding between Christians and Jews.[20]

Thieme and his allies rejected the idea that they were continuing a mission to the Jews. Thieme eschewed proselytization and spoke of the need to engage the world by evangelization of deed rather than word. He recognized that if Jews found Christianity unacceptable that was a Christian and not a Jewish fault.[21] Yet Christian eschatology remained key to his vision of the Jewish other, and it kept the mission question alive even if it was postponed to a moment before eternity. Four years later, in his theses on the ecumenical council at Evanston in 1954, Karl Thieme finally put this last obstacle behind him, arriving at "biblically grounded" visions of the end of time that both Christians and Jews could accept. For the time being, the Schwalbach theses represented a high-water mark among German Christians interested in reconciliation with the Jews.

In general, the younger generation and many in the older were receptive to the ideas from Schwalbach, yet the Freiburg Circle encountered resistance at the top levels of the German Catholic hierarchy. Cologne's Cardinal Frings, head of the German bishops conference, held the Freiburg group in suspicion; perhaps he generated the denunciation that led to the October 1950 *monitum* from the Vatican. Frings warned German bishops of "indifferentism" and attempted to harass Christian-Jewish dialogue from behind the scenes until sometime in 1954.[22] The Freiburg group adjusted tactics by establishing contact with other German bishops independently of the German bishops conference, going through Caritas, the German Catholic Relief Services, which acted as their formal sponsor. Yet even here there were difficulties. In May 1952, Gertrud Luckner confessed her "consternation" to Thieme that the President of Caritas, Alois Eckert, refused to sign letters to the bishops. "He was bothered by the title 'Old and New People of God'"[23] Eckert was not acting capriciously. The 1965 declaration *Nostra Aetate* indeed called the church the "new people of God." But applying the term "old people of God" to the Jews at this point was a problem for Central European Catholics because of the still untouched idea that Jews were "Israel according to the flesh," while the church represented the "spiritual Israel."

Jews as Spiritual Israel?

The Seelisberg and Schwalbach theses had fast-forwarded beyond this old understanding, yet it was well rooted in Christian discourse, and soon theologians were registering dissent, plunging Thieme into debates on key issues of Jewish identity that would consume his energies for several years. First was the issue of whether the Jewish people of the present were indeed the "same" as the biblical Jewish people, or whether there was a break at the time of Christ. Second, if there was continuity, were the Jewish people still embraced by a covenant that Christians could recognize without questioning the New Covenant established by Christ? Finally, if the Old Covenant was still in force, how should one imagine the relation between Old Israel and the New Israel? Thieme called the Jews "older Brothers," and argued that the approach to Israel should be ecumenical. Before 1949, no one had uttered such things in the Christian world, and the words proved difficult to digest for many Catholics of good will, like Alois Eckert.[24] Indeed, even in our day, many Christians call relations to Jews not ecumenical but "interfaith."

We feel Thieme's sensitivity on the question of continuity in a dispute he brought to the pages of the *Rundbrief* with Father Paul Démann of Paris, originally a Hungarian Jew, who, along with Thieme and John Oesterreicher, was an eminent Catholic pioneer of Jewish-Christian dialogue in these years.[25] In his pathbreaking instructions for French Catholics of 1952, Démann hinted with a citation from Paul's letter to the Galatians (3:27) that Jewish identity had ceased to be real.[26] The passage reads: "For as many of you as were baptized into Christ have put on Christ. There is neither Jew nor Greek, there is neither slave nor free, there is neither male nor female, for you are all one in Christ Jesus." Thieme disagreed with Démann's interpretation. Since Paul was not claiming that gender or status differences had disappeared, Thieme argued, he was also not claiming that ethnic distinctions had disappeared; there had been no "leveling of the difference made by God himself through the irrevocable election [Romans 11:29] of Israel of two groups: Israel and the rest of humanity."[27]

Paul Démann ceded the point without further argument, yet German and Dutch theologians pressed related objections.[28] In April 1951, the Jesuit Rudolf Leder of Berlin questioned the use of the term "old people of God" to refer to the Jews of the present because "only a very small part of today's Jewry professes faith in the divine revelation of the Old Covenant, while the great majority has succumbed to modern liberalism, relativism, materialism, etc."[29] Leder shared a belief of many Christians that the church could consider as Jews only those Jews who practiced Judaism. Otherwise, one risked propagating a fiction, perhaps even forcing Jewish identity upon persons of Jewish descent who did not consider themselves Jewish. Furthermore, Leder wrote, to speak of the old people of God was theologically incorrect because it suggested a coexistence of old and new, when in fact "the new people of God stepped into the place of the old one."[30]

As he had in the 1930s, Karl Thieme turned to Paul's letter to the Romans for guidance. There he found that Paul did not make distinctions among various kinds of Jews (more and less religious), but instead referred to the Jewish people, which would exist to the end of time, and continued to "possess promises" even though "hardened" to the Gospel.[31] In a private letter to Gertrud Luckner, Thieme signaled the emergence of a larger vision. "Differences about what to make of a [shared] tradition, such as we have with Protestants, don't mean that we deny these differences any right to life and declare a discussion about them pointless. Just as Judah— despite the rejection of Jeroboam—still recognized prophets from the Northern Kingdom of Israel in its canon, so a Christian can recognize the validity of Jewish teachers!"[32] Echoing a statement made by the Dutch Reformed church in 1949, and before them by Karl Barth, Thieme was projecting the divisions between Christians and Jews as similar to earlier divisions among Jews themselves as well as later divisions (or "schisms") among Christians.[33] The people of God was one but had divided many times.

Thieme conducted his most sustained and serious defense of the continuity and coherence of the Jewish people in private correspondence with Ernst Karl Winter, former vice-mayor of Vienna, who like Thieme was a highly educated, richly argumentative, principled Christian. Similar to Thieme, he also lived on borders, standing solidly in the camp of Austrian

Catholicism (he knew Engelbert Dollfuss from the same unit of the Austrian army) yet at the same time bridging gaps to the Austrian working class. Like Thieme, he wanted to reconcile socialism and Christianity—a rare sentiment indeed among prewar Catholics. The one constant in Winter's personality—as was true of Dietrich von Hildebrand, John Oesterreicher, or Karl Thieme—was opposition to all nationalism. For Winter, the essence of being Austrian was to be politically independent, not simply a German tribe but rather a political nation like the Swiss. Winter sensed the dangers of nationalism so keenly that he introduced an unusual word into the local discourse, namely, the word "ethnos." Even to begin thinking of Austrians as "ethnically" German was to launch their absorption into Germany.[34]

This anti-nationalism caused him not only to seek overtures to socialists but also to treat all anti-Nazis as dear allies. During the 1930s, his Gsur publishing house in Vienna printed an exposé of the Jewish plight in Germany (Peter Drucker, *The Jewish Question in Germany*, 1936); a searching critique of racism (Walter Berger, *What is Race?* 1936); a play inspired by the plight of a Jewish family in Germany (Awrum Halbert, *The Border: The Fate of Six Hundred Thousand*, 1936); satires on Nazism (Hermynia Zur Mühlen, *Our Daughters the Nazis;* Walter Mehring, *Chronicle of a German Clan from Tacitus to Hitler*), and perhaps the earliest full-scale Catholic critique of Nazism (Zyrill Fischer, O.F.M., *Men of the Swastika*, 1932).

Though not all of them were Catholic or even Christian, Winter's writers give a sense of the border-crossing milieu from which he sought to oppose Nazi racism, and bring new dimensions about race and the Jews into Catholic thought. In the 1930s, Father Zyrill Fischer investigated Nazism by traveling to Germany incognito. When he figured on an assassination list of the Munich Gestapo, Fischer fled to Budapest before making his way to Santa Barbara and assisting Franz Werfel (whom he tried to convert) with the theology for his best-selling novel *The Song of Bernadette.* While in Austria, Fischer was a surprise guest at meetings of Marxists and Zionists.[35] Drucker grew up in a Viennese Protestant family of Jewish background, yet became an enthusiast of the right-wing radical Othmar Spann, even befriending Carl Schmitt before becoming sobered by Nazism after the purging of 1933. He emigrated to the United States and became the founder of management science, by common consent one of the most influential and original thinkers of the twentieth century.[36]

Of Winter's satirists, Walter Mehring, whose mother was an opera singer from Prague, had cofounded the Berlin Dada movement before becoming a correspondent for the left-wing press in Paris and writing historical fiction about the seventeenth-century Catholic Flemish mystic Antoinette Bourignon de la Porte. Nazi Storm Troopers heaved Mehring's works into the flames during the bonfire orchestrated at the University of Berlin in 1933. The book published by Winter poked fun at the pretensions of a racially pure German family.[37] Hermynia Zur Mühlen was born into the Austrian nobility and spent her youth with her diplomat father in Constantinople, Lisbon, Algiers, and Milan. Upon reaching maturity, she disappointed her parents by marrying a Baltic count; after divorcing him, she joined the Communist Party and married the journalist Stefan Isidor Klein.

Drucker, Fischer, Mehring, Zur Mühlen, and Ernst Karl Winter escaped Europe before Hitler's attack on Poland. Though he desperately wanted to return home from the moment hostilities ceased in May 1945, Austria's professors kept the gadfly Ernst Karl Winter out of a teaching position from which he might remind them of the attraction they had felt for racism and antisemitism during the 1930s. Winter therefore languished in unremunerative semiretirement in a house large enough for his large family just off the George Washington Bridge in Teaneck, New Jersey, whence he corresponded with displaced Central Europeans such as Irene Harand, the von Trapp family singers, political theorist Aurel Kolnai, and the Franciscan Abbot Georg Moenius, who joined Father Zyrill Fischer as pastor to Hollywood. With limited success, Winter participated in debates on politics and theology in German and Austrian journals, and he had plenty of time for five- and six-page single-spaced letters illuminating political and theological truths for his friend Karl Thieme at the *Freiburger Rundbrief*.

Thieme and Winter had both opposed Nazi racism when it mattered, and their dispute from the 1950s is interesting because it represented choices open to the Catholic mind as it pondered how to oppose antisemitism after Auschwitz: one recognizing continuing blessing resting upon Jews as a *Volk*; the other questioning ethnicity or nationhood as basis for any judgment, positive or negative. Each alternative drew upon deep readings of Christian tradition and scripture. Like Thieme, Winter was a serious amateur theologian who dated letters by days of saints, and relaxed while rereading the Bible in the original languages. He believed that the New Testament repudiated the idea of grace still resting in the Jewish *Volk*. Christ had brought into being a new people of God, which Jews could enter but only by ceasing to be Jewish. As a religion based in law, Judaism was the "absolute antithesis" of Christianity. Winter's view was based in commentary dating back to the early church fathers, and he defended it against all comers, including Jewish friends who had urged him to consider the "anti-Judaistic spirit of the Gospels and the life of Christ an error of the time . . . not essential to Christianity." Winter refused. To argue such a thing would be "to deny Christ and the Gospels." Without the anti-Judaism of the Gospel and Christ's uncompromising struggle against the religion of the law that "killed the spirit of religion," Christianity was "superfluous."[38]

Ernst Karl Winter imagined a hierarchy of texts in the New Testament that made Paul's epistles secondary. In the Gospels, there was a progression from Matthew to John. "John's Gospel draws out the anti-Judaistic consequences of Matthew's in uncompromising purity," he wrote to Karl Thieme in August 1949: "whereas Paul still thought of himself as belonging to the Jewish people and expected that a full conversion of Israel would happen in the immediate future, John already faced 'the Jews' as a foreigner, who had gotten over his own Judaism."[39] John, who wrote later than Paul (around A.D. 70) had a clearer vision of the rupture between Jews and Christians. The Temple had fallen, Jews had not converted, and John was no longer a Jew: he had made the necessary break.

Within a perspective centering on Paul's letter to the Romans, Thieme pondered Winter's claim that the church had become the new Israel, and that "all objectification of a Jewish folkdom as a category of salvation economy after Christ is at best unconscious Jewish nationalism in a theological dressing." "I can find no trace," Thieme commented dryly, "of a condition in Romans 9–11 that the Temple must continue to exist, whereas I can find in John's Gospel as well as in his Revelation unequivocal typological references to the conversion of 'all of Israel' at the end of time."[40] If this was true, then the Jewish people must exist to the end of time. The following year, Thieme put Winter on the spot: what to do with Paul? Either one recognized his words as divinely inspired, or one thought of them as one person's private opinion. Paul's letter to Romans, Thieme argued, had to be central for Christians seeking orientation about Jews, because it was his "only pastoral letter instructing believers about his people."[41] He claimed to be reading Romans in terms of scripture and tradition and challenged Winter to a public debate.[42]

Winter did not accept this challenge but instead issued several of his own based on biblical passages that Thieme had neglected. What did Thieme suggest doing with the Letter to the Hebrews, whose author referred to elections of other peoples before Israel? What did Thieme make of the puzzling figure of Melchizedek, who blessed Abram and is called a Priest of God most high (Genesis 14:18; Hebrews 7)? For Winter, this held a message about the Jews: their election and their priesthood were neither first nor last. Thieme responded by pointing to the controversies about the authorship of Hebrews (it was not written by Paul, and had to be understood "in the context of the fullness of his teaching"), and to the obvious fact that Winter was straining interpretation. Hebrews did not speak as directly about the Jews as Romans 9–11. Nothing in the Melchizedek story questioned the validity of the promises made to Abraham "and his progeny." Winter then asked about the "Woes discourse" (Matthew 23), in which "Christ was what the philosemites would call an antisemite," tracing the "negative character" of his people back to Isaiah. In his rejoinder, Thieme stressed the "dialectic" of Christ's words, of which only the negative side had been registered among Christians. Now it was time to draw out the other side in full clarity.[43] More important was that no words in the Gospels abolished the Jews' election.

Perhaps sensing that he could not prevail using arguments from scripture, Winter moved outside the Bible and pressed an argument from historical philosophy, maintaining that the Israel of today could not be the Israel of earlier times. "There can be no lasting election of a people," he explained, "because all peoples, Jews as well as Germans are destined to cease to be, and because there is no people which after one thousand years remains the same: racially, intellectually, or culturally. No theology of election can get around this truth of historical sociology."[44] In response, Thieme went back to his own book, *God and History.* If there was history, then only peoples were its subjects, and only subjects that changed could possess historical identity, that is, remain themselves through time. An unchanging people of the sort Winter imagined would not be historical.[45] In the end as in the beginning, the Habsburg Legitimist Winter worried about nationalism, and how holy texts could be abused to support its demands. Any nation could imagine itself as "preferred" by God, when actually its fate was to be absorbed into Christianity.[46] Meanwhile, Thieme boasted that the *Rundbrief*'s view of the continued spiritual vitality resting in the Jewish people (as the "old people of God") went out in every issue "with the approval of the [Freiburg] Episcopate to 20,000 priests and religion teachers."[47]

The Question of Covenant

The Jewish people continued from the deep past into the present. But what about the Covenant God made with Israel at Mount Sinai? Citing Hebrews 8:13, Ernst Karl Winter maintained that the "first" Covenant was "becoming obsolete and growing old and ready to vanish away." Thieme retorted that Winter should recognize Paul's letter to the Romans as divinely inspired. Could not Winter demand the same from Thieme as regards the letter to the Hebrews? Monsignor Professor Max Meinertz of Münster posed this and related questions in correspondence printed in the *Rundbrief* in 1952 and 1953.[48] Christians of the present had no "right to tone down" the message of Hebrews that the Old Covenant "has been replaced by the New Covenant once and for all," Meinertz wrote, with all the authority of a top Catholic New Testament scholar. In his view, Israel's salvation at the end of time, foretold in Romans, did not fulfill the old covenant, but rather signaled Israel's assumption into the new covenant. The only mediator of grace, as even the liberal Protestant theologian Krister Stendahl was writing in 1961, was Jesus Christ.[49]

Three points underlie Karl Thieme's response to Meinertz stretching across several issues of the *Rundbrief.* First, the Epistle to the Hebrews was written with a special purpose. Its point was not to ask about the relation between law and Gospel, but rather to probe the relation between the Old Testament priesthood and the priesthood of Jesus. It called certain liturgical practices of the Old Covenant temporary. Second, though not authored by Paul, that letter needs to be understood in the context of Paul's entire message, and indeed of scripture as a whole. And most importantly third, neither Paul, nor the author of Hebrews, nor of course Christ himself, claimed that Christ was replacing the law. In fact, Hebrews made its arguments with implicit reference to a still vital Torah. The old Covenant was therefore not made obsolete, but was somehow contained within the New, vital and valid, similar to how the people of God was one but divided, old and new until end of time, awaiting final reconciliation, expanding God's offer of salvation but not excluding those living within law. Striking here, as in the brief quarrel over deicide with the Freiburg censors, was how the new vision could easily be derived from existing Catholic interpretations, indeed those open to lay Catholics. In his response, Thieme had simply quoted from passages in the *Theological Dictionary of the New Testament*.[50]

Unlike E. K. Winter, Meinertz repudiated anti-Judaism and had no doubt that Jews continued as Israel, even using the expression "character indelibilus" to insist on the familylike coherence of the Jewish people. Yet Thieme revealed that Meinertz's defense of tradition had left him in an untenable position after the Holocaust, and accused Meinertz of imagining that Israel inhabited a historical "waiting room," living a limbolike existence without any protection from God, subject to retribution as well as whim, in a place where intellectual resistance to anti-Judaism had no valence. What after all was the point of Jews continuing as a people in an uncovenanted existence?

Yet having asserted the continuation of that covenant, the Freiburg Circle confronted new questions; most immediately, what should the Christian relation be to the Jewish people? How did one initiate fraternal dialogue after centuries of strife? Once the vision of Israel living in a kind of theological no-man's land had been repudiated, a major question remained, perhaps unanswerable, but nevertheless pressing: how to fit Auschwitz into the new vision? Even if one rejected the idea that Jews lived under a curse, one could not deny that they had suffered unlike any other people.

In the summer of 1954, Karl Thieme formulated theses by which Christians might refer to Jews in language appropriate to the time after Auschwitz. For the first time, he found formulations that accorded with

Christian scripture but also recognized the freedom of Jews to accept their Messiah as they saw fit. He read them at the German Catholic Congress in August, but also submitted them to an international ecumenical council meeting at Evanston, Illinois. Christians hoped "in common with our separated 'elder brethren' of the *stem of Abraham*, for the day of the Lord, which will surely come. But, in still irreconcilable contrast with them, we hope for that day to be the glorious enthronement of Him who began His kingship in the obscurity of His Cross and resurrection: the returning Jesus of Nazareth."[51] Making no secret of continuing differences between Christians and Jews on the question of salvation, he encouraged tactful exchange until the day came when there would be "one flock and one shepherd" (John 10:16) and when "all peoples would serve God shoulder to shoulder" (Zephaniah 3:9).

Ten years later, John Oesterreicher would lift some of this language for the Vatican II statement *Nostra Aetate*. But at this point Oesterreicher registered severe disagreement, dwelling at length on the inappropriateness of considering Jews the "older brothers" of Christians. He could understand that "biblically" the "people" of Israel was "the older brother" and the "world of Gentiles" was the younger, but he rejected applying this logic to the relation between Jews and the Catholic Church. "The people of the patriarchs and prophets is the older brother," he admitted, "but only in relation to the peoples of the world," that is, to other nations. Yet "the Jew is never the older brother of the Christian. For the new and general covenant not only reaches beyond and above the old one . . . the new one was in a certain sense before the old one . . . that which comes last in execution is the first in intention and in the plan."[52]

Oesterreicher was bothered by the evident influence on Thieme of Franz Rosenzweig, a German Jew who had tasted but rejected Christianity and wrote that Jesus would be subordinated to the father in the end, and then "God will be all in all." (1 Corinthians 15:28).[53] Rather than redefine the relation between Jew and Christian, Rosenzweig's understanding reprised the old heresy of subordinationism.[54] Thieme the pioneer had ventured too far. In a book written just before the Vatican council, Gregory Baum, a theologian esteemed for tolerance and careful argumentation, and with Oesterreicher a drafter of *Nostra Aetate*, likewise rejected Thieme's choice of language. "The Jew who rejects Jesus Christ," wrote the young

Augustinian monk, "falls into a religion devoid of promise. He is not the elder brother of the Christian, except potentially . . . In our age the path of the Synagogue no longer lies in the sun . . ."[55] In 1948, Oesterreicher had written a book on the "apostolate" of the church to the Jews, and in the decade that followed he eagerly sought signs that Jews were turning to Christ—even though he had succeeded in converting at best a handful of Jews while working in New York City. He interpreted Rosenzweig's letters "together with the statements of many others" as "the dawning of our hope, a sign that Jesus is again living in the consciousness of many Jews and leaving them no peace in their hearts."[56]

Ironically, it had been Oesterreicher who encouraged Karl Thieme to call Jews "brothers" after the war—and not enemies. Yet now that he did so, Thieme wondered what kind of brother the Jew was. During the struggle with Nazism, he reminded Oesterreicher, Catholics had called Protestants "separated brothers." How much more, he now asked, did this word fit the Jews, whom Paul had called his "brethren" (Romans 9:3, Acts 23:5)? "If they are brothers," he continued, "then what other than the factually older: in relation to those 'who have received faith from among the Gentiles?' . . . The Gentiles cannot cease being the younger ones in time and in history."[57]

Augustine had also considered the relation of Christians and Jews as resembling that between brothers. "This people has never transgressed against God's law," he preached, "this [older] son is not personified in all Israelites, but in those who never fell from worship of the one true God to worshiping idols. This is confirmed in the witness of the father himself: you are always with me."[58] These words of the bishop of Hippo helped Thieme reverse the tendency of some Christians (such as Dietrich von Hildebrand) to see the Jew as prodigal. No, said Augustine, the Christian was prodigal.[59] This reading, perhaps gained from Franz Rosenzweig, complemented the message of Romans 11, according to which the attention of the Church should be toward Gentiles and Gentile Christians.[60] After all, the Jewish people were "always with God." But the insight was also a challenge. It had caused Franz Rosenzweig to conclude that the Jewish people did not need Jesus. Oesterreicher saw no sense in Jewish existence separate from Christ, and still maintained a better-known Augustinian view according to which Christians should not harm Jews because, like Cain, they bore a stigma "that they might be witnesses everywhere to him whom they denied and persecuted and killed."[61]

John Oesterreicher continued to defend an elaboration of this Augustinian view that was developed by the Jewish thinker Maurice Samuel: in his book *The Great Hatred* (1940) Samuel wrote that Nazi violence against Jews in fact targeted Christ. Nothing else could explain its implacable fury.[62] By contrast, Karl Thieme worked out a Catholic understanding of modern antisemitism that criticized its Christian sources while not making Jews at Auschwitz unwitting witnesses to Christ, thus steering a middle course among thinkers who had tried to make sense of antisemitism with reference to Christianity. On the one hand, he rejected the view of Hannah Arendt or Charles Journet, who, with Oesterreicher, argued that modern antisemitism was entirely separate from ancient anti-Judaism. Yet on the other he took exception to Jules Isaac, Franz Rosenzweig, James Parkes, and Michel Müller-Claudius, who thought that Christianity had imprinted on the Western mind the idea that Jews must answer for the death of Christ, meaning that antisemitism "in its origin and inner being" was religiously conditioned. Thieme did not deny the explosive new energies of modern antisemitism, but he argued that the underlying will to destroy was the same whether a person was motivated by the older anti-Judaism ("they killed our savior") or the recent view that Jews were *Untermenschen*, racial enemies. The instruments of the modern state had permitted a magnification of the desire to kill: but this desire remained the same. The question was, why did this hatred focus on Jews?

It did because of the Jewish religion—whether the Jews being persecuted were religious or not.[63] Deep down, antisemitism was not about stereotypes. Here, Thieme fully endorsed the views of Maurice Samuel. In the eyes of non-Jews, Jews were always different because of the laws handed down from the Patriarchs, and therefore, whatever form antisemitism took, its origin remained religious and had to be opposed as one would oppose hatred of religion. It was racism only superficially, less like the tension between whites and blacks than like the conflict between religious majority and minority groups.[64] "The simple refutation of superficial accusations made against Jews is in no way sufficient for combating antisemitism," Thieme argued. Christians hoping to combat the hatred of

Jews that had reached full poisonous bloom at Auschwitz had to under-stand Jews as a priestly people, enjoying a communal, sacramental exis-tence, a participation in grace which transcended the will, knowledge, and character of the individual. Jews lived and died for a purpose that was independent of Christ and Christianity.

Thieme's earlier belief that Jews were destined to suffer was rooted in the words from Amos that he cited in 1937: "For you alone have I cared among all the nations of the world; therefore will I punish you for all your iniquities."[65] However, in the emerging postwar vision suggested by Karl Barth, his emphasis shifted: beneath the threat of punishment lay the reality of responsibility. "No one who knows Scripture," Thieme wrote, "particularly of the Old Covenant . . . will fail to take seriously the special responsibility of those to whom the prophet Amos said: 'I have chosen you alone from all peoples of the earth, and therefore I punish all your trans-gressions' (3:2) . . . [this is] a responsibility that goes beyond mere human strength . . ." Amos had given no warrant to think that all suffering en-dured by Jews was God's punishment. Thieme now contended that Israel suffered for its *faithfulness to God*, for acting as light to the nations, true to responsibilities growing out of a living Covenant.[66] Under encouragement from Martin Buber and others, Karl Thieme had put aside not only the idea that Jews lived under a curse, but also that he, the Christian, could read history as a story of crime and punishment, by now the last remaining pillar of the once-popular theology of history.

Still, a person obsessed with history could not help wondering about Auschwitz. Perhaps the death of six million Jews had no purpose humans could identify, but Thieme was not willing to say it was an event without meaning. There were two options. "If Jews were not condemned to thou-sands of years torture as deicides," Thieme wrote to Oesterreicher, "which no serious theologian would dare to claim any more, then they died as God's martyrs. A third possibility does not exist."[67] Relying on a thesis provided by Paul Démann, he continued, "According to scripture, deep suffering for which the individual person does not bear blame has a func-tion of witness, or of being born for the sake of others. If this is true, then we must recognize that the persecutions which were imposed on the Jews by Hitler, and before that by Christians, are to be seen, in [Hans Urs] von Balthasar's words, as additional chapters in the mystery of suffering of the one who founded the Church with his cross." As such, the Jews who died in World War II were not simply victims but Martyrs, now in the presence of God. The point was not to accord some higher sacredness to Jews but to recognize that when people with a divinely ordained responsibility suffer for reasons that are not their fault, then we must assume that they are doing so for a purpose that is salvific, similar to the way that Christ had suffered for all humans.[68]

Thieme's insistence that antisemitism be read as originally religious permitted him to speak of *Christian roots* of this age-old hatred without causing Jews to become servants of a Christian narrative of history. Unlike Oesterreicher, he did not contend that Auschwitz was about destroying Christ. Yet he could also argue that Christianity did not necessitate anti-Judaism. In his view, the originally religious impulse within antisemitism produced different manifestations at different times. In the early church, a teaching of hatred had grown out of competition between church and synagogue: in order to subdue the challenge coming from vibrant and attractive and Jewish teachers, Christian counterparts like John Chrysostom portrayed Judaism as lost and illegitimate. In doing so, they began to bury the teaching of Romans 9–11, according to which "all Israel will be saved." Following Léon Bloy, Thieme hoped to restore the prophetic meaning of Paul's final epistle to its rightful place, yet unlike Bloy he did not dwell on the revolutionary character of this move but rather matter-of-factly dismissed centuries of teaching as though it had been an unfortunate, temporary digression from the true message.

Perhaps Thieme understated the degree to which the deicide motif had indeed imprinted itself on the Western mind, making something as absurd as the blood libel charge appear a logical outcome of the Jews' "wickedness" to generations of Christians. Like Oesterreicher, he portrayed Christianity as essentially resistant to antisemitism. The two remained what they had been in the 1930s: missionaries to Christians as well as analysts of a problem whose roots they uncovered in stages. In the meantime, neither man spoke of the shifts taking place in his own thought, which each portrayed as consistent, deriving from steady opposition to the supposedly unchanging quantum of antisemitism.

Oesterreicher refused to publish Thieme's reflections on the religious roots of antisemitism in his yearbook *The Bridge*, and he refused to

acknowledge that Christianity had anything to do with modern antisemitism. He, of course, knew that many Catholics had been "brown Catholics," and he admitted that millions of Christians did not see Nazi crimes
for what they were because their consciences had been "maimed" by the
"horrifying charge that all Jews are deicides." Yet he thought that such a
belief was theologically insubstantial and not Christian.[69] In retrospect, it
appears that Oesterreicher might have known better.[70] After all, as a Catholic theologian he had subscribed to the notion that Nazism was a trial sent
to the Jews. To some extent, he still did. What was the reason for the Jews'
suffering without end? With what purpose did they live after rejecting
Christ? He had no answer to these questions before the council. Though
he rejected the "poor theology" of deicide, his vision of the Jewish people
was mostly dark.

Still, from other Christian sources glimmers of light were entering his
thinking, opening him to the idea that Jews had access to grace independently of Christianity. In fact, the church had never denied that Jews
could be saved, because from its earliest days it had taught that people
who lived good lives lived in God's presence. In the 1950s, like Karl Thieme
and the censors in Freiburg, John Oesterreicher was unearthing Christian
ideas which though little known had long been orthodox, building upon
work he had commenced two decades earlier when he informed readers in
Vienna of Augustine's idea of "hidden Christians."[71] Shortly after Oesterreicher fled Austria in 1938, the eminent Jesuit theologian Karl Rahner
took refuge in Vienna, having been expelled from Tirol with all other Jesuits. Working in the diocese pastoral counseling office, he began to transform this ancient insight into one of the best-known theological metaphors
to animate theologians at the Second Vatican Council, the "anonymous
Christian." This counseling office was under the leadership of the priest
Dr. Karl Rudolf, who had been a frequent guest at afternoon meetings
at Dietrich von Hildebrand's and belonged to the advisory council of
Oesterreicher's *Pauluswerk*.[72]

    After the war these ideas of tolerance took on new urgency for Oester-
reicher. "Yes I have had news about my parents," he wrote the eminent
Austrian writer Felix Braun in February 1946. "My dear father died in
Theresienstadt—thank God, of pneumonia. It is some consolation to

think that he, who although not Christian in belief was one at heart, to whom the Beatitude of the Peacemakers applied, died a relatively peaceful death. My poor mother, however, was taken to Poland; I need not tell you what that implies."[73] Reflection on the good lives led by his Jewish parents opened Oesterreicher to neglected Catholic teachings on salvation outside the church. In the encyclical *Quanto conficiamur moerore* (1863), Pius IX had reminded Catholics of a teaching going back to the Council of Trent and earlier whereby those who obeyed the "natural law and its precepts inscribed by God on all hearts" were "able to attain eternal life by the efficacious virtue of divine light and grace." He was connecting to a tradition running back to the scholastics of "baptism by desire" and the "implicit faith" of people living good lives. Like the teachings from Trent on the guilt of all for Christ's death, those ancient insights were rarely taught, and in the face of widespread ignorance, the Vatican had been forced in the late 1940s to reconfirm this teaching against Father Leonard Feeney, Catholic preacher at Harvard, who was telling students that those outside the Catholic Church were destined for hell.[74]

Oesterreicher's embrace of this teaching strengthened within the more tolerant atmosphere of the U.S. Catholic Church, and he bristled at suggestions that unbaptized Jews were consigned to hell, reacting with characteristic indignation when this view was attributed to him in a review of a piece he had written on Simone Weil.[75] Oesterreicher briefly met Weil in Marseilles while fleeing the Gestapo in 1940, and for the sake of accuracy he emphasized to Karl Thieme that he "never considered her a Christian."[76] He did not doubt that God loved Weil, and believed that an unbaptized Jew like her could indeed be regarded as saved. In their thinking about Simone Weil, the paths of Thieme and Oesterreicher coincided, a fact each failed to appreciate. But Oesterreicher did not believe that Simone Weil was loved by God because she was a Jew. His view was rather: she was loved no less than other non-Christians because she was a Jew.

Oesterreicher's source of hope was Christian scripture. Christ had not excluded faithful Jews from salvation, but had said: no one comes to the father except through me. Oesterreicher continued to foster this questioning of Catholic exclusivism in writings of the 1950s, publishing, for example, this important statement of Monsignor (later Cardinal) Charles Journet in *The Bridge* in 1955:

The Church of Christ, entrusted to Peter, is at once purer and vaster
than we know. Purer, because though not without sinners she is without sin, and because the faults of her members do not soil her. Vaster,
because she gathers around her everyone in the world who is saved.
She is aware that from the depths of space and time there are tied to
her by desire, in an incipient and hidden way, millions who, by an in-
vincible ignorance [Pius IX] are prevented from knowing her, but
who have not, in the midst of the errors in which they live, refused the
grace of living faith which God offers them in the secrecy of their
hearts.[77]

Journet's words appeared within a lengthy discussion of the "Finaly affair" penned by Oesterreicher's collaborator Father Edward Flannery. The
affair involved the Austrian Jewish couple Dr. Fritz and Annie Finaly, who
had taken refuge near Grenoble after 1938 and lived there until their arrest
by the Gestapo and deportation to Auschwitz in February 1944. Months
earlier, they had entrusted their boys, ages two and three, to a convent,
which, lacking facilities to care for small children, had placed them in the
care of the devout Catholic Antoinette Brun. After the war, members of
the Finaly family tried without success to gain custody of the boys. In
1948, after Brun had them baptized, the family sued in French courts and
finally gained an order for the boys' repatriation in January 1953. With
collusion by the clergy, Brun then spirited the boys across the border to
Spain, and the affair blew up into an embarrassing scandal for the Catholic Church. The Archbishop of Lyon entered discussions with the Finaly
family as well as with France's Chief Rabbi Jacob Kaplan, and agreed that
the children must join their relatives as soon as possible. In June 1953, two
Basque priests took the boys back across the border, and soon they journeyed to Israel, where one became a doctor and the other a military
officer.

The case forced French Catholic theologians to ask about the church's
paramount interest in salvation of the soul. In the past, church authorities
had taught that it was immoral to baptize a child against the will of the
parents; still, they held that Jewish children validly baptized must be removed from their families and brought up as Christians. In the French
Republic, the church could no longer assert its authority in this way, but

still theologians raised the question of whether Catholics must despair at the salvation of the children. The answer was a clear no. God willed that all humans, Catholic or not, be saved and brought to the knowledge of the truth.[78] Furthermore, there was no need to lament the church's loss of temporal power with which to enforce ecclesiastical laws. "In these new circumstances," Flannery concluded, "and as her methods become more spiritual, the Church can act more as a 'leaven' among souls."[79] In these words we sense the spirit of the Vatican Council before anyone imagined it would be convened.

In a letter written in July 1960, Karl Thieme expressed confidence that "thanks to John XXIII among other things," John Oesterreicher would "keep coming closer" to the Freiburg point of view."[80] Thieme prayed that his old collaborator might receive the grace of converting to a new way of looking at the Jews, as he himself had a decade earlier. Thieme expected the new Oesterreicher would journey to his original self, representing a Jewish point of view in the church just as Thieme represented a Protestant viewpoint. By healing divisions within themselves, they might help unite the divided people of God. Oesterreicher forcefully rebuffed the idea:

> You wish for me a conversion that would make it possible for me 'to represent the Jewish point of view in the church.' Let God come first! In the spirit of Mary, that is, in the sense of her Magnificat, I grate-fully acknowledge my Jewish heritage, and the God-given legacy of Israel in the Church. But me a representative of the Jewish point of view in the Church? No and a thousand times no! I do what I can to act against false beliefs about the Jews among Catholics from the past and from the present, in order to put an end to inherited clichés, etc. But I see in this a real Christian point of view—and not simply a Jew-ish one. As imperfect as my work may be, I want nothing other than to serve the one Lord and with that, the whole and complete truth."[81]

Thieme thought the Freiburg group's ecumenism stood in opposition to Oesterreicher's mission to the Jews, when in fact Oesterreicher no longer preached or even practiced mission to the Jews. Unbeknownst to Thieme, Oesterreicher was describing the approach of his Institute for

Judeo-Christian Studies at Seton Hall as "ecumenical."[82] But rumors had reached Freiburg that Oesterreicher doubted the orthodoxy of the *Rundbrief*'s work, and Oesterreicher did not help matters by hinting to Thieme that *unnamed* theologians in Europe had accused him of simplifying the "tension of Pauline theology."[83] Thieme haughtily rejoined that Oesterreicher should denounce him to Rome. There he would discover that the Freiburg group's work was approved at every step and was finding the applause of "ever more bishops."[84] In letters to other friends, Thieme began calling Oesterreicher a "grand inquisitor," not because he had any real power but because Thieme suspected he might be partly right. In July 1960, upon learning that Oesterreicher was granted the role of advisor at the council called by John XXIII, Karl Thieme confided deep misgivings to Gertrud Luckner.[85]

At that point, all correspondence between the two men ceased and was never to be resumed. Their estrangement had to do more with perception than substance, not so much with denial of the other's viewpoint but with fear of what the other thought. Oesterreicher the born Jew hated being suspected of antisemitism (as a supposed missionary); Thieme the former Protestant hated being thought of as a less than fully orthodox Catholic (and excessively ecumenistic). As converts, they had been drawn to each other in the struggles against racism of the 1930s—they shared perception, insight, and trust—but the underlying insecurity of the convert now made each wary of the other.

Ultimately, Thieme's hopes were fulfilled. Oesterreicher never underwent the sudden conversion that Thieme prayed for, but his vision did change between the early 1950s and late 1960s. Mission became ministry: not to the Jews but to other Christians, often supported by arguments of Jewish friends.[86] The process of change accelerated in the early 1960s, when Oesterreicher and theologians of a Vatican II subcommittee faced blank sheets of paper on which to inscribe a new teaching of the Christian's closest other. They read ancient texts in radically new ways and revolutionized the church's understanding of that other and of itself. By 1970, Oesterreicher was speaking of Christianity and Judaism as "two ways of righteousness that have complementary functions."[87]

Yet before the Vatican Council Oesterreicher feared taking what Thieme called the "Jewish position" in the church, and for good reason.

He never stopped seeing himself as a Jew. Late in life, he objected when rabbis introduced him to their congregations as a "former" Jew.[88] His involvement in Christian-Jewish understanding hinged upon his sense of self as Jewish-Christian, and that Jews were his "blood brothers." Still, if his influence derived from the passion of the former Jew, it would vanish the moment he presumed that his Jewish heritage made him more relevant. That would be the moment when other Christians directed his attention to the third chapter of Paul's letter to the Galatians: in the church there was "neither Jew nor Greek . . . for you are all one in Christ Jesus."

Oesterreicher heard nothing of Thieme's cancer diagnosed early in 1963, and was shocked and saddened to hear that Thieme had died that July.[89] He never learned that Thieme was acknowledging the positive role played by Oesterreicher at the council.[90] Afterward, Oesterreicher recognized Thieme's contributions in numerous statements, and dedicated his history of the "New Encounter" between Christians and Jews to Thieme and a few other pioneers. Their views, the explicitly pro-Jewish (Thieme) and the explicitly anti-racist (Oesterreicher), though in tension, in fact complemented each other, and we see both reflected in the final draft of *Nostra Aetate*, which recognized the continuing vocation of "Abraham's stock" while condemning all racism. The question was not one option or the other, but, like two magnetically charged substances, how to configure them so that they bonded rather than repelled one another. That was the achievement of chapter four of *Nostra Aetate*, which Oesterreicher drafted with much inspiration from Karl Thieme.

During the decisive deliberations of the Vatican Council, Oesterreicher was the sole figure from the interwar struggle against antisemitism still active. Karl Thieme and Waldemar Gurian, his two collaborators in the Memorandum of 1937, had died. Dietrich von Hildebrand, Annie Kraus, and Jacques Maritain were alive but had ceased writing on Jewish-Christian relations. Hildebrand, a philosopher at Fordham University, suspected Oesterreicher of being too ecumenical. In Paris, Paul Démann and Geza Vermes had left the Notre Dame de Sion order. Renée Bloch died tragically in 1955. Of all the pioneers in Catholic Jewish dialogue, this left Oesterreicher to incorporate the continuity of Catholicism's reaction to racist antisemitism, carrying forward the lessons positive and negative from three decades, of what worked and did not, of what was possible and what was necessary. The word *race* to describe Jews may have become passé after World War II, but the sensitivity that grew out of the struggle against racist antisemitism was not.[91] Yet Oesterreicher had no idea of where events would go, especially since the church as a whole, though reverent when speaking of the Jews after the Holocaust, cared little about its relations to them.

8

The Second Vatican Council

The Second Vatican Council helped reconcile Catholics to the modern world. For the first time, they celebrated mass in their own languages, and for the first time they were entreated to think of other religions as sources of truth and grace. The most authoritative voice of the church—an ecumenical council—surrendered the idea that the state or any other institution should force people to become Catholic. It spoke of the church as "people of God," strengthened the position of the laity, and suggested a more collegial—and democratic—ordering of relations between bishops and the pope. Most importantly, the Council recognized that the church could change.[1] Histories of the event center upon the bishops, almost 2,500 in number, who deliberated for three years before voting on sixteen statements and making them binding church teaching in the fall of 1965. Yet the Council would not have occurred but for Angelo Roncalli, the Italian Archbishop who succeeded Pius XII as John XXIII in 1958. Many of the Council's reforms and ideas became popular, but it was not a response to a groundswell of popular pressure. In suddenly calling for a meeting of the bishops to bring the church "up to date" [*aggiornamento*], Roncalli had acted with an impulsiveness virtually unique in the upper reaches of the Church hierarchy.[2]

The statement on the Jews, chapter four of the Declaration on non-Christian religions (*Nostra Aetate*), which Pope Paul VI promulgated on October 28, 1965, was approved by the Council fathers by a vote of 2,312 to 88.[3] Despite the near unanimity, this statement was the most contested matter the bishops faced over four years of deliberations. Yet it would not have been considered at all without the direct intervention of John XXIII. Six years earlier, when he was fielding ideas for the Council, almost none of the bishops and theologians canvassed suggested that the church speak out on the Jews, and without the pontiff's directive to German Cardinal Augustin Bea in the fall of 1960, the Council might well have been silent on this issue. Even theologians from the land of the Holocaust seemed disinterested. In 1961, the Catholic journal *Wort und Wahrheit* surveyed readers on what they expected of the Council. Only three of eighty-one responses mentioned the question of relations between the church and the Jewish people. One of these came from the Dominican friars of Walberberg; the other two came from Karl Thieme and John Oesterreicher.[4]

In turn, Pope John might not have requested a statement on the Jews without the intervention in 1960 of the Holocaust survivor Jules Isaac. That is not to say that the pope was uninterested. His concern for Jewish-Christian relations dated to his wartime service as Papal Nuncio in Turkey, where he witnessed the plight of Holocaust survivors and helped some 25,000 of them with clothes, identity papers, and money so that they could continue their journeys to safety. Shortly after becoming Pope, he altered one of the most egregious affronts to Jews in Catholic liturgy, namely, the Good Friday prayers in which Catholics asked God's illumination for "perfidious Jews." Yet despite his evident comprehension of the need to revise church teaching on the Jews, John probably would not have requested a statement from the Council had Jules Isaac not made an impassioned plea during an audience of June 1960. Isaac had lost his wife, daughter, and son-in-law during the Holocaust, and according to knowledgeable sources, Isaac's appeal made the difference.

Once he had commissioned the statement, John XXIII backed off and left matters in the hands of Cardinal Bea, friend of the *Freiburger Rundbrief,* and director of the Council's "Secretariat for Promoting Christian Unity," which produced statements on ecumenism, religious freedom, and relations to other religions.[5] Bea formed a subcommission for studying the Jewish question to which he summoned two pioneers who had cooperated with the Freiburg Circle: Monsignor John M. Oesterreicher of Seton Hall University and Abbot Leo Rudloff, originally of a German-Jewish family, who had founded Benedictine abbeys in Jerusalem and New England. Joining them was the brilliant Augustinian Monk Gregory Baum, an expert in ecumenism who had been in touch with Oesterreicher and Karl Thieme in the late 1950s. Baum, from a Berlin Protestant family of Jewish origin, escaped Germany with a *Kindertransport* in 1939 and converted to Catholicism after the war in Canada, where he lives to this day. By late 1964, the subcommission had expanded to include seven more priests, one of whom, Monsignor Antonius C. Ramselaar, had founded the Dutch "Catholic Council for Israel" (Katholieke Raad voor Israël).[6]

The Apeldoorn Initiative

In August 1960, shortly before Bea formed his Secretariat, Ramselaar had invited Oesterreicher, Rudloff, and a dozen other pioneers in Christian-Jewish dialogue—from the Dutch and Freiburg groups, but also *Cahier de Sioniens* (France), the *Freiburger Rundbrief* (Germany), and the *Oeuvre de St. Jacques* (Israel)—to a retreat house in Apeldoorn Holland to draft a set of theses that might guide Catholic-Jewish dialogue. Although the attendees knew nothing about the pope's plan to commission a statement on the Jews, they understood the Council as an opening to the world that must impact Catholic-Jewish relations. The theses they worked out reflect a high point of pre-Vatican II deliberation, forming, as Oesterreicher later wrote, "the prophetic element that over the years prepared a place in the church, intellectually and spiritually, emotionally and theologically, for the Council declaration of which they as yet knew nothing."[7] Anticipating the Vatican II statements, the Apeldoorn group shifted the weight of Christian understanding of the Jews to Paul's letter to the Romans, according to which all Israel would be saved but only after the full number of Gentiles had entered the Messianic kingdom. Therefore, any mission by Christians should focus on non-Jews. Upon the basis of Romans,

Paul's only prophetic statement about his people, they corrected the idea that Jews were irrevocably lost, a frequent misinterpretation of Matthew 27:25 and the first letter of Paul to the Thessalonians 2:16. Judaism was understood as an ancient but also living tradition, upon which Christianity depended for core beliefs, for example, the command to love one's neighbor.[8]

In 1964, Cardinal Bea deconstructed the most controversial aspect of anti-Judaism—the charge of deicide—in reliance upon the Apeldoorn theses, yet the drafters of these theses were relying upon Jules Isaac, who had recalled that Christ had many followers among his people. Therefore, one could therefore not say that "the Jews" had rejected him. Furthermore, Jews lived throughout the Mediterranean world in Christ's time, and far from rejecting Christ most had never heard of him. The Apeldoorn authors reminded Catholics of the teaching of the Council of Trent according to which all humans were to be reckoned as Christ's crucifiers. The Apeldoorn group rejected the central anti-Judaic idea that a curse rested upon the Jewish people. Any claim that the Jews' "sufferings and humiliations over the centuries" reflected punishment from God contradicted the church's "teaching on the meaning of suffering."[9]

This was a deeply a-historical reading of the church's past. In fact, for centuries the church never hesitated to imagine the Jews as carrying a special burden, "suffering" for rejecting Christ. In order to avoid the impression that the Apeldoorn theses completely rejected Catholic tradition, Oesterreicher portrayed them as part of a supposed turn initiated by modern popes against "patristic and medieval conceptions of the Jews," returning to deeper, truer foundations of belief.[10] He was invoking a controversial process known among practitioners of "la nouvelle theologie" as *ressourcement*, a return to sources, in which the past was taken as a lens to understand the present.[11] This indeed would become the strategy guiding the drafters of what became the statement on the Jews of *Nostra Aetate*. By 1965, they were reaching backward many centuries and formulating new teaching with texts written just decades after Christ's death, texts without which the church would have no language to talk about the Jews in the time after Auschwitz.

Early Drafts

The Apeldoorn theses were too long and theologically complicated to become a statement of the Vatican Council, yet they were in Oesterreicher's mind as he prepared an early study for Bea's Secretariat in April 1961 at an isolated retreat house at Ariccia on Lago de Nemi.[12] There, far enough from Rome that the bishops could not skip out of meetings to visit friends in the city, Bea's Secretariat bonded into a community of intense work, shared prayer, and recreation of shared walks and chats.[13] Oesterreicher's study was the first of numerous drafts ultimately leading to the statement on the Jews voted on by the bishops in October 1965. In it, he anticipated the shift in Catholic thought on the Jews toward Romans 9–11 ("which certain exegetes have awakened from its long slumber") and projected the church as rooted in the life of ancient Israel. Yet he was more explicit than the Apeldoorn group about the Jews' identity in the present, asserting that they remained spiritually vital because they were "God's favorites: 'for the sake of their forefathers, they are forever dear to Him'" (Romans 11:28). This interpretation had implications for the relations between individual Jews and Christians: "A Christian who bears in mind God's constant fidelity to His people will experience his or her own kinship to them, even though faith in Christ separates one from the other."[14]

Oesterreicher strayed further from the Apeldoorn script by instructing Catholics that when Paul spoke of "all Israel" being saved, he indeed meant the Jewish people, or as theologians wrote, "Israel according to the flesh." Spiritual and carnal Israel were one and inseparable. This view was not immediately accepted among the theologians at Ariccia or elsewhere because it broke with virtually all exegetes going back to the early days of the church. Oesterreicher asked his colleagues to be mindful that Paul had been free in drafting Romans, and if he had wanted to he could have found in the prophetic tradition a series of "violent expressions with which to castigate the leaders and the masses." Instead, with "tender restraint" Paul termed the Jews' failure to recognize Jesus a "misstep" and a "blunder." No one could claim that "the Jews" had rejected Christ because the earliest Christians were Jews. Echoing the analysis of Jules Isaac, Oesterreicher recalled that in the Gospels the "multitudes listened to Him eagerly and heard him with delight."[15]

Oesterreicher's draft next connected the particular to the general. The church had to condemn antisemitism as one manifestation of the evil of racism. Yet, he continued, "hatred of Jews has a special quality of evil. It violates truth, justice, and love; over and above that, it deals a blow to faith. Considered from without, Jew-hatred, like any other form of hatred, contradicts the article of faith that every human is created in the image of God. At its core, however, Jew-hatred wishes to deny, even do away with the fact that at the Incarnation the eternal Son of God became a Jew, son of David and son of Abraham (Matthew 1:1)." The ultimate evil of antisemitism for the Christian was that it went against Christ—against his teaching as well as his person.[16]

With these formulations, Oesterreicher was reprising his analysis from 1943, when he relied upon Maurice Samuel's belief that the German National Socialists wanted to destroy Christ. Yet by tying together the critiques of racism and antisemitism, Oesterreicher was also meeting expectations of a prominent Jewish observer of the Council, the European director of the Jewish Service Organization B'nai B'rith, theologian Ernst Ludwig Ehrlich, who stood in close contact with him as well as Karl Thieme in the early 1960s. Yes, Ehrlich wrote, it was good and necessary that the Catholic Church condemn racism. But that was not enough. To undo the evil of antisemitism, the church also had to remind believers of the positive relation it had to Judaism through the person of Jesus Christ and his family and disciples, as well as the inheritance of Jewish scripture.

Oesterreicher's participation in the early drafts worried Karl Thieme, who called his old associate "Monsignor Grand Inquistor," supposedly an intemperate defendant of a waning orthodoxy. There had been resistance to Oesterreicher's appointment to Bea's commission.[17] Some Jewish observers, like Gerhard Riegner, Secretary General of the World Jewish Congress, also held Oesterreicher in suspicion, remembering his work to convert Jews.[18] Indeed, Oesterreicher was less radical than Karl Thieme—although both had collaborated at Apeldoorn—and had yet to take the final step of imagining Jews outside a narrative dictated by Christianity. Like mainstream Christian theologians, he continued to doubt that Jews living as Jews could enjoy the fullness of God's grace.[19] He thought Karl Thieme and Paul Démann went too far in sacrificing Catholic positions and called them "pseudo-ecumenists."[20] Yet at the same time Oester-reicher found St. Paul's eschatological vision vague, admitting of two interpretations. Either history would reach its completion through the Jews' mass conversion so that "Paul's phrase 'life from the dead' (Romans 11:15) would mean none other than the resurrection of all flesh." Or, in the interpretation Oesterreicher had favored in disputes with Karl Thieme, the words "life from the dead," not found elsewhere in scripture, had a spiritual but not historical meaning. Thus, Israel's "turning" would be the "signal for a new outpouring of grace, a reawakening of love over the whole earth." As Oesterreicher wrote, it *"cannot be the task of a Council to choose between these two exegeses."*[21] The bishops could say nothing about the circumstances of Israel's final "ingathering." All that was certain was the "essence of hope" (see Romans 11:12, 15, 25–26). What may seem a theological quibble—the relation between Christians and Jews at the end of time—in fact touched upon the most controversial question the drafters of the Decree of the Jews (*Decretum de Judaeis*) would encounter, almost frustrating the statement completely in the fall of 1964.

Before that point was reached, the subcommittee on the church's relation to the Jews within Cardinal Bea's Secretariat produced a series of drafts building upon Oesterreicher's early study. They did so in a largely favorable atmosphere because, on the one hand, most bishops agreed that the church could not be silent on the Jews after the Holocaust, and on the other, the bishops favored the church's opening to the world, and supported statements on religious freedom and human dignity. The agendas overlapped and reinforced each other. Still, Council theologians as well as bishops in Bea's Secretariat posed penetrating questions about the ideas in Oesterreicher's draft. Some of his conclusions were taken for granted among the handful of converts at Apeldoorn, but they sounded strange to those operating within mainstream theology. After the Council, Oester-reicher remarked upon the divergence in views: for Jews, *Nostra Aetate* came late, too late.[22] But for Catholic theology it came too soon, and to this day has not been fully digested.

In 1961, Cardinal Bea's Secretariat for Christian Unity met for three plenary sessions (April, August, November) and discussed the issues raised in Oesterreicher's initial study.[23] The Secretariat's theologians and bishops were united in good intentions, but the questions they posed remind one that good intentions were not enough to carry a document claiming to represent Catholic thought. Knotty questions emerged that had absorbed the argumentative energies of Thieme and Oesterreicher for decades, but were new to most of Bea's group. Could a national group continue through time, from the Old Testament to the present, to the end of time? And if so, could the universal church, blind to barriers of nationality or ethnicity, recognize holiness as residing in such a group? And what was the appropriate word to describe the relation between the church—which called itself the New Israel—and that group? For Catholic theologians these questions were potentially self-destructive. Why have a New Covenant if salvation could be had through the covenant God had established with the Jews? Humanity could simply become Jewish.

According to German theologian Hermann Volk—addressing the Secretariat in November, just months before becoming bishop of the important See at Mainz—two factors seemed relevant when thinking of the Jews from the standpoint of New Testament theology. The first was the salvation of people through direct relation to Christ by faith, "people as individuals and not as members of a people." The second was the framework for imagining the origins of a people. "Does accession to the Christian faith signify a separation from the line of origin of this people?" Volk asked. Why should the fact that one happened to be born into a particular people matter for the destiny of one's eternal soul? Volk felt that it would be easy for the church to condemn antisemitism; Christianity opposed all hatred. But it would be more difficult to develop a theology of the Jewish people, specifying a relation of the Jews of the present to the people of the Old Testament.[24]

Joining the discussion was Karl Thieme's old sparring partner on the subject of Jewish spiritual identity, the theologian Frans Thijssen of Utrecht, a consultant to the Secretariat at this point, and expert on ecumenism. In Thijssen's view, Oesterreicher's work fell far short of the mark. For him, Catholic theology must insist upon the "discontinuity" between the "old people" of Israel and the "new people" of Israel, or the church.[25] Professor Gustave Thils, dogmatic theologian from Louvain and expert in ecumenism but relatively unversed in Christian-Jewish dialogue, shared the skepticism, and he returned to the supposed foundation for Christian thought contained in the idea of two Israels: "Israel according to the flesh, and Israel according to the spirit." Wisdom such as this was precisely the problem, however, something Karl Thieme had learned in 1949 after alleging that Martin Buber was spiritually dead. Abbot Leo Rudloff—like Oesterreicher, an Apeldoorn veteran—hastily redirected the discussion to a view that would become conciliar understanding. There was Israel that had become the church, Rudloff said, but there was also Israel which had not accepted its completion in Christ, but whom God had not rejected because of his faithfulness to his promises.[26]

One can almost feel veterans of the Jewish-Christian dialogue such as Oesterreicher and Rudloff squirming as the newcomers fell into anti-Judaic tropes despite their goodwill. This was true even of Cardinal Bea, whom we now recognize as heroically pushing forward Pope John's desire for a statement on the Jews all the way to the fall of 1965. At the Secretariat's August 1961 meeting at Ariccia, Bea insisted that the Jews of that day were "just like any other people." "With the greatest possible reverence," Oesterreicher dissented from the cardinal's viewpoint. Was it not instead the case that "by a special promise the Jews constitute a special people, not because of their own merits, but because of the faithfulness of God"?[27] Oesterreicher managed to carry this argument, and within months Bea was speaking a different language.[28]

More unsettling was Bea's continued adherence to basic elements of the deicide paradigm. The cardinal maintained that the crowd in Matthew 27, 25 in calling the blood of Christ upon themselves had brought destruction upon Jerusalem. Evidence of the fate Jews had willed upon themselves were the tears Christ wept for the women of Jerusalem.[29] Dutch Theologian Thijssen claimed that the crowd's calling of blood upon the Jews had a "prophetic character." Again, Oesterreicher objected. "The 'crowd' of which the Gospel speaks did not represent all the people," he argued. The point of the study he presented to the Secretariat was to signal the Jews' "corporate personality." As such, it was true that for the most part Israel rejected the Messiah. But if nowadays preachers talked of Jews rejecting Christ, they thought not of the people as such (en corps), but rather of all the individuals. In short, they converted belief into prejudice.

The Belgian Dominican theologian (later cardinal) Jean Hamer concurred with Bea and Thijssen on the idea that Jews had brought destruction upon themselves. "We always talk about the responsibility of the

Jews for the death of Christ," he asserted. "We ought to talk of the unbelief of the Jews and the connection between this unbelief and the death of
Christ." The bishop of Bruges, Emiel-Jozef De Smedt, a man with enthusiasm for ecumenism but also a newcomer to Christian-Jewish relations,
posed basic questions about the consequences of the Jews' rejection of
Christ. "What happened to the Jewish race who did not accept Christ?" he
asked. "This people remains the people from which our salvation was
born." But what is this people today? What is the attitude of our church on
this subject? Like Bea, some of the theologians thought the church could
speak of the Jews as it did about other peoples, meaning that antisemitism
was a variant of racism which the church could refute with arguments for
human unity. Dr. Thijssen called racism "a sin against the humanity of
Christ" which "does not apply only to the Jews, but to all peoples." A second
theologian wondered about Oesterreicher's tendency to cite Romans 9–11
at the expense of Ephesians 2, according to which the "wall has fallen between Jews and Greeks." Abbott Leo Rudloff again attempted to mediate.
The church must condemn racism, he agreed, but where the Jews were
concerned, that was not enough. They were not a people like other peoples. The church also had to speak out on the "special relations between
Christians and Jews."[30]

By early December 1961, the subcommittee on relations to the Jewish
people worked out a draft decree featuring six points: (1) the church had
roots in the Israel of the Patriarchs and Prophets; (2) even though most of
Jewish people were "separated from Christ," it would be a mistake to portray them as "accursed"; (3) Jews were beloved by God for the sake of their
forefathers; (4) Christ, his apostles, and mother sprang from this people;
(5) the church believed "in the union of the Jewish people with herself as
integral part of Christian hope"; and (6) the church condemned wrongs
done to the Jews. At this stage, the drafters had yet to find language to
refer to the Jews of the present in a way that captured their spiritual and
historical identity, and called them at one point "the children of Abraham
according to the flesh." The authors still insisted upon seeing Jews as
locked in a Christian narrative.[31] But this draft had begun deconstructing
the idea of deicide, insisting that the Jewish people in the time after
Christ were loved by God. That signaled the revolution in church teaching that was to follow.[32]

Yet before this draft could be presented to the bishops, the Council's Coordinating Commission dropped *Decretum de Judaeis* from the agenda in the wake of a political controversy stirred by Nahum Goldmann, President of the World Jewish Congress. In the summer of 1962, Goldmann tried to nominate Dr. Chaim Wardi an observer to the Council without first clearing this move with the other Jewish organizations or the Vatican. Because Wardi was also an official in the Ministry of Education of the State of Israel, allegations emerged from Arab states—which sheltered vulnerable Christian minorities—that the Vatican was taking the side of Israel.[33] Cardinal Bea would not let *De Judaeis* disappear and die, however, and intervened with John XXIII to ensure that the item be returned to conciliar business.[34] In December 1962, Bea wrote the pope that a statement on the Jews was "demanded by the bond of kinship between Christians and Jews which is far deeper than the bond which unites all humans." The "appalling crimes of National Socialism against six million Jews" required a "purification of spirit and conscience." He lamented that all too often Catholic preachers had accused the Jewish people of deicide.[35]

In this note to the pope, the cardinal was reversing two ideas he had defended in the Secretariat just a year earlier: that the Jews were just one people among others, and that they had suffered a curse for rejecting Christ. What changed his point of view? The favor he showed the *Freiburger Rundbrief* through the 1950s had done nothing to alter his belief in the deicide myth, a belief he had expressed in academic prose as early as 1920. Perhaps, as was the case with Karl Thieme, Cardinal Bea found a new language to talk about Jews only after he began talking to Jews. Among the people with whom the cardinal entered a sustained conversation in late 1961—just as the Secretariat was discussing *De Judaeis*—was the American rabbi of Polish origin Abraham J. Heschel, who like Bea was a German-trained theologian. The two met for the first time on Sunday, November 26, 1961, in the company of the German-Jewish philosopher Max Horkheimer, Zachariah Shuster of the American Jewish Committee, and Karl Thieme's old Vatican supporter Father Felix Morlion (also the American Jewish Committee's most highly placed Catholic advocate). At this meeting, Heschel presented the cardinal with two volumes of rabbinic commentary on the Torah with place markings indicating

commentaries on the Song of Songs, on which Bea had written an introduction to a critical edition in Hebrew. During their conversation,
Heschel emphasized that "Jews want to be known, and understood, and
respected as Jews [*als Juden*]."[36] When Bea and Heschel next met in New
York City in March 1963, they quickly disappeared from public view for
an intimate exchange of ideas "like old friends."[37]

After the first meeting Heschel had gotten busy compiling a memorandum for Bea's Secretariat on what he hoped a Vatican declaration on the
Jews might say. Among other things, he hoped it would reject the deicide
charge and recognize "Jews as Jews." Indeed, after this point, drafts of
De Judaeis did precisely these things, explicitly condemning deicide and
dropping all reference to the Jews' joining the church.

Yet the fate of the decree was far from secure as *De Judaies* began a migration from text to text. Initially presented to the Central Coordinating
Commission of the Council in June 1962 (then dropped), drafts of the
decree reappeared in November 1963 as chapter IV of the schema on ecumenism, then, in the spring of 1964, as the appendix of this schema. At
this point, opponents of the resolution, mostly conservative bishops from
southern Europe supported by the Vatican administration (the "Roman
Curia"), had it shortened behind Cardinal Bea's back and then made it part
of the schema on the church, where it was to function as part of an appendix.[38] John XXIII had been dead since June 1963, and this handful of
opponents, led by the reactionary Cardinal Ernesto Ruffini of Palermo,
appear to have enjoyed the tacit support of the new pope, Paul VI. Supporting their skepticism were bishops of eastern Catholic Churches in Arab states
who worried that their small flocks would suffer if the Catholic Church
appeared to favor the Jews. Representatives of these states made their displeasure known from the moment rumors of a planned statement on the
Jews emerged in 1961, at times threatening punitive measures, at times
involving themselves in theological argumentation. The government of
Syria, for example, protested plans to free Jews from the charge of deicide
and the Premier of Jordan promised to "blacklist" the bishops who signed
the "declaration absolving Jews from guilt in Christ's crucifixion."[39]

The shortened draft produced in the Roman Curia in the spring of
1964 indeed dropped a condemnation of deicide and revived Catholicism's
efforts to convert Jews by expressing hope that one day Jews would join

the church.[40] The substance of the changes was leaked to the press from within Bea's Secretariat, and in May 1964 John Oesterreicher contacted powerful Cardinal Franz König of Vienna for intervention. "Unfortunately the news about the scheme on the Jews are not favorable," Oesterreicher wrote. "The original draft has been weakened more than once, so that in the end probably no more than a few noncommittal phrases will be left. If the current should continue, then we will face, I fear, a new Hochhuth affair."[41] He was referring to the play *The Deputy* (1963) by the German playwright Rolf Hochhuth, which portrayed Pius XII as unconcerned about the Holocaust, unleashing a controversy about the pope that lasts to this day. Though Oesterreicher himself had strongly criticized Pius in 1939, he stood in the first rows of the pope's defenders in the early 1960s, even appearing on the U.S. news program *The Huntley-Brinkley Report* to refute Hochhuth's allegations.

Oesterreicher addressed a second letter to König in June, informing him that some "higher office" had further shortened the statement. He also wrote Boston's Richard Cardinal Cushing, the most prominent American Catholic foe of antisemitism, to tell him that members of the Curia had stricken "reference to the Jewishness of Jesus, Mary and the Apostles." "If the draft should be presented to the Fathers of the Council and passed by them," Oesterreicher lamented, "a cloud of distrust, even despair will settle on many hearts. They will see in it a disavowal of the work of reconciliation begun by good Pope John." Opponents of reconciliation had suppressed references made in earlier drafts to the Epistle to the Romans, thus reversing the gradual shift to St. Paul in Catholic thought about Jews going back to Léon Bloy.[42] Oesterreicher asked both cardinals to intervene with Paul VI.[43]

Yet perhaps the opponents had waited too long to make their move. By early 1964, the international press knew of early drafts condemning deicide; to remove them now would suggest that the church stood by the belief that the Jews had killed God. In their private meetings, the bishops attached to Bea's Secretariat worried about public opinion, fearing that the church might be made a "laughing stock," or worse, might seem to confirm allegations that it was not concerned about the destruction of Europe's Jews. Hochhuth's name appears repeatedly on the transcripts of the bishops' deliberations. Because a "monk living in Rome" kept leaking draft documents, the newspapers knew precisely what was being added and subtracted at any moment.[44]

Whether König and Cushing contacted the pope is unclear, but like other bishops from North America and transalpine Europe the two cardinals returned to Rome in September 1964 deeply concerned about the weakened statement, and made their views known in the 88th congregation of the Council, later known as the "Great Debate," which saw the most passionate oral presentations made to this point.[45] Bea, who introduced the new text for discussion, practically invited the more than 2,500 church dignitaries to amend it, especially where the crucial issue of deicide was concerned.[46] Though disputing the idea that deicide could be seen as the "principal basis of antisemitism," Bea himself took the ancient accusation apart point by point: the leaders of the people did not "fully understand the divinity of Christ" and therefore can not "be formally called deicides;" Christ had forgiven his tormentors on the cross; some 4.5 million Jews lived in diaspora outside Palestine in biblical times ("are all these to be accused of the deeds done by the members of the Sanhedrin on that sad Friday?"); and, most importantly, guilt could not be transferred from the guilty to an entire people.[47]

Conservative Archbishop John Heenan of Westminster, vice-president of Bea's Secretariat, recognized the problem the Curia had created: if deicide was condemned in the first version and now dropped, "the interpretation will be made that the Fathers of the Council, having had a year to think it over, now solemnly judge that the whole Jewish people . . . are in fact guilty of the crime of deicide."[48] In a private letter to Bea, Heenan called the revised text "doctored," and ridiculed the idea that one had to assure modern Jews that they had not killed Christ. "It seems to ignore the fact the Jesus and the Apostles were all Jews and therefore it is meaningless to say that the 'Jews' killed Jesus," He wrote. "It is like saying the Italians killed Mussolini."[49] During the course of the debate, lasting from 26 to 28 September 1964, twenty bishops, mostly from Northern Europe and North America, joined Bea and Heenan in demanding that a refutation of deicide be reinstated.[50] Archbishop O'Boyle of Washington DC wondered why the text limited its acquittal of Jews to the Jews of that day. Only a full vindication of the Jewish people would "free them from the insult laid upon them for centuries."[51] Boston's Cardinal Cushing exhorted colleagues to recall that according to St. Paul the rejection of Jesus by most Jews must remain a mystery. Christ had died freely for all humans, and therefore "we must deny that the Jews are guilty of the death of our savior." He concluded asking "whether we ought not to confess humbly before the world that Christians, too frequently, have not shown themselves as true Christians, as faithful to Christ, in their relations with their Jewish brothers?"[52] Cushing's passion was clear to everyone, but many had trouble understanding Latin spoken in a Boston accent, and had to wait for a translation.[53]

A consensus rapidly formed holding that Jews were not responsible for the death of Christ. The more vexing question of whether Jews must become Christians did not figure in the debate, yet it was this feature of the "doctored" declaration that troubled Jewish observers most, and stood at the heart of the international publicity in the summer of 1964. The unidentified figures in the Roman Curia had inserted the following lines into the draft: "It is also worth remembering that the union of the Jewish people with the Church is part of the Christian hope. Therefore, following the teaching of the Apostle (cf: Romans 25) the Church waits with unshaken faith and deep longing for the entry of that people into the fullness of the people of God established by Christ."[54] Knowledge of this section stirred Rabbi Abraham Heschel to make his famous declaration that he was "ready to go to Auschwitz any time, if faced with the alternative of conversion or death."[55] Other Jewish observers such as Joseph Lichten (B'nai B'rith, U.S.), Ernst Ludwig Ehrlich (B'nai B'rith, Europe), Marc Tanenbaum, Zachariah Schuster, and John Slawson (all American Jewish Committee) likewise made their dissatisfaction known. The situation appeared so critical that the American Jewish Committee arranged an audience for Heschel with Pope Paul VI, after which the rabbi left a lengthy theological memorandum for Bea's Secretariat.

The End of Catholic Mission to the Jews

On September 29, 1964, as a result of the protests, Cardinal Heenan of Westminster announced that the offending text would simply be dropped.[56] Yet neither he nor the other bishops suggested an alternative formulation, and it fell to Bea's advisors to find new language when they reassembled in

October after the bishops' debate. At the suggestion of John Oesterreicher, they replaced the text that spoke of Jews joining the church with the following lines, inspired by the minor prophet Zephaniah: "The Church awaits that day, known to God alone, on which all peoples will address the Lord in a single voice and 'serve Him shoulder to shoulder.' "[57] This formulation survived alterations made in the following months and belongs to the statement approved by the bishops in October 1965.

Yet Oesterreicher's choice was not original. He never admitted as much after the Council, but he was borrowing language from theses drafted by Karl Thieme for the Evanston Ecumenical Congress of 1954, and reprinted in Oesterreicher's *The Bridge* the following year. Thieme, in turn, drew from biblical sources on the concept of "nation" as well as postbiblical Jewish commentary—probably from Maimonides—on the roles of Christianity and Islam in the world.[58] Thus, Thieme, by that point dead over a year, helped settle the most troubling issue to confront Bea's Secretariat and perhaps the Vatican Council as a whole. And Oesterreicher, the man Thieme feared seeing at ecumenical meetings in Europe, widely suspected of wanting to convert the Jews, helped close the chapter on mission in Catholic-Jewish relations. For once, his estrangement from Christians and Jews made Oesterreicher the ideal mediator because both sides recognized his unique comprehension of the other.

The effect of this alteration was historical. "The Schema on the Jews is the first statement of the Church in history," Rabbi Heschel later wrote, "which is devoid of any expression of hope for conversion . . . And let me remind you that there were two versions."[59] Oesterreicher took his inspiration from a prophet of the Old Testament, but he also could turn to interpretations of the New Testament supplied to Cardinal Bea's Secretariat by Jewish activists and intellectuals. In the summer and fall of 1964, Oesterreicher was receiving a stream of letters from Ernst Ludwig Ehrlich of B'nai B'rith. A week before Bea addressed the bishops, Ehrlich sent Oesterreicher two letters to his residence in Rome. In the first, he attempted to be conciliatory, writing that the revised text was "fine for a Catholic document." It did not speak of "conversion but rather of the eschatological addition of the Jews to the communion with Christ, thus a legitimate Christian hope."[60]

Yet by the time he wrote the second letter five days later he had changed his mind. "I have had time to concern myself with the text and unfortunately have reached the same conclusion as [Rabbi] Heschel," he wrote. "Please do yourself and me a favor," Ehrlich insisted, "Hurry to the Secretariat and show the people there that the text is simply wrong, and that a well-grounded New Testament reading must be found . . . otherwise they will be making themselves laughing stocks before the entire world, that is, in front of everyone who can read the New Testament." The new declaration "distorted" Paul's letter to the Romans. In Romans 11 there was no mention of "entry" of the Jewish people into "the fullness of the people of God established by Christ"—as claimed in the doctored text— rather, Paul had written "a hardening has come upon part of Israel until the full number of Gentiles has come in, and so all Israel will be saved . . ." It was the Gentiles and not the Jews who would "come in." "Paul is speaking in a clearly eschatological sense," wrote Ehrlich, "because 'plenitudo gentium' is clearly the apocalyptic full number of the Gentiles . . . any notion of conversion is excluded entirely . . . I really cannot understand how they could claim to be making reference to Paul." He seemed sure of Oesterreicher's support because the two of them had already agreed in Zurich that Paul's vision was an "eschatological hope and not proselytism."[61] Similar views of Paul can be found in communications that Bea's Secretariat received from American Rabbi Marc Tanenbaum.

Ehrlich's and Tanenbaum's interpretations conformed to ideas expressed by Karl Thieme in the *Freiburger Rundbrief* in the 1950s as well as the Apeldoorn group's theses. By this point, the question of mission to the Jews transcended divisions between Christian and Jewish theologians involved in interfaith dialogue because these theologians supported a reading of Paul that provided the church language it needed after Auschwitz.[62] After years of collaboration with the Freiburg Circle, Ehrlich was accustomed to suggesting alternative readings of the New Testament, and now he encouraged Oesterreicher to see what his brothers in faith (in the Curia) had been blind to. "The Council is not a Jewish world Congress," he conceded, "but one can only say about the Jews what the New Testament itself says, and which Christians believe is divine revelation. *Paul knew exactly why he treated Romans 11,25 as mystery.*" In their last letters of 1960, the former Protestant Karl Thieme had asked Oesterreicher to represent the Jewish point of view, but now the Jew Ehrlich insisted simply that Oesterreicher be Catholic. Oesterreicher must "fight with all his energy to make sure that this really becomes a 'Catholic' document, and not some silly unbiblical nonsense." Ehrlich, trained in theology under Leo Baeck, and consulted by Cardinal Bea, wrote that over the years he had "learned that the New Testament itself is the only means of promoting understanding between Christians and Jews."[63]

In retrospect, one might wonder at the focus on three chapters of Paul's letter to the Romans. Why privilege them over all other scripture? Sections of the Gospels, other epistles and the Acts of the Apostles suggested the opposite of the conclusions Ernst Ludwig Ehrlich or Thieme and Oesterreicher had drawn from Romans. In other parts of the New Testament one could read that Jews were killers of Christ, that Jews should be baptized, that Jews were spiritually dead and children of the devil. Yet the bishops of Vatican II judged those other sources—"almost all the teachings about Jews and Judaism in Christian thought prior to Vatican II"—as inappropriate to the post-Holocaust age. In "affirming the continued inclusion of the Jews in the covenant after the coming of Christ," the bishops were picking up where St. Paul left off in the first century."[64] Without Romans and its confirmation of God's promises to the Jews as well as the eschatological hope for unity in an unspecified future, the church would not have had a language to talk about the Jews after the Holocaust.

According to Karl Thieme, the choice for Romans also made sense in light of the career of St. Paul. This was Paul's final Epistle (A.D. 55–58), and it represented a culmination of learning, beginning with Thessalonians (A.D. 51) when "a few weeks in Europe, he had naively provoked hostility to Jews." In the course of his journeys, Paul had learned that Christians would feel tempted to exalt themselves above Jews, and he warned them: "Do not boast . . . remember it is not you that support the root, but the root that supports you" (Romans 11:18).[65] Chapters 9–11 of this Epistle also represented Paul's *only* pastoral letter directly instructing believers about his people.[66]

We do not know for certain the influence of Ernst Ludwig Ehrlich upon Oesterreicher's reasoning, but we do know that after the Council Oesterreicher rejected allegations that a "Jewish lobby" had somehow manufactured the text, claiming that Cardinal Bea never referred to the memoranda of the American Jewish Committee during the sessions of the Secretariat.[67] Furthermore, there were many interest groups in Rome, why should Jews not have attempted to represent their interests?[68] Indeed, papers of the Subcommission on Jewish Affairs contain numerous letters from representatives of Jewish organizations making recommendations about theology, but also about the structures within which the Council might think about Jews.[69] Jewish observers did not dictate chapter four of *Nostra Aetate*, but through correspondence, public addresses, position papers, academic memoranda sent to bishops, as well as lunches and dinners taken in Rome, New York, and elsewhere, they assured that the drafters knew of Jewish sensitivities. In his history of *Nostra Aetate*, Oesterreicher admitted that his compromise formulation on the question of mission had succeeded in part because it found the acceptance of "Jewish officials in Rome."[70]

Probably the most memorable statement made by anyone about *De Judaeis* was Rabbi Abraham Heschel's pledge to prefer Auschwitz over conversion, words that resounded through the international press and could not be ignored by those redrafting the statement.[71] Yet Heschel also had an excellent personal rapport with leaders in the Secretariat, especially Cardinal Bea and his successor, Johannes Willebrands of Utrecht. Willebrands later recalled that Heschel had learned of the Secretariat's plan to express "the hope for the conversion of the Jewish people to Christ at the end of time and had told the pope that any inclusion of the theme of conversion would produce exceedingly negative reactions in the Jewish communities, and would nullify the many good things that the document contained. Indeed, all such thoughts were subsequently abandoned."[72]

On this point Willebrands may have been optimistic, however. There is little doubt that he, Cardinal Bea, Archbishop Heenan as well as the theological advisors of the Secretariat had the sentiments of Heschel and other Jewish observers in mind in the fall of 1964. Recall that Heenan withdrew the offending sentence on mission as soon as the bishops returned to Rome to discuss *De Judaeis*. Yet the pope himself, distant from the Jewish-Christian dialogue, lent an ear to conservative bishops who argued that the Jews must be converted and that any statement issued by the church must state this explicitly. In the summer of 1964, Mario Luigi Ciappi, the pope's personal theologian ("Master of the Sacred Palace"), still demanded language urging the Jews to accept Christ. In a memorandum for the pope, he wrote that "the *infidelity* of the Jews is not simple, inculpable ignorance of Christ, but is a *positive* infidelity, even if judgment on individuals is reserved to God alone. Therefore the Church cannot be uninterested in their conversion or leave them 'in good faith,' and simply pray for them. In the text of the declaration the drafters have not had the courage to mention explicitly either the *duty* of Catholics to work for the 'conversion' of the Jews or the *serious duty* of the Jews to acquire a better knowledge of the Christian religion."[73]

Paul VI never lost his desire to appease competing factions in the church. A little over a week after the bishops had signaled their will for a strongly positive statement on the Jews in their "Great Debate," the Secretary of the Council, Bishop Pericle Felici, informed Bea's Secretariat that the pope wished a revision of the document it had drafted on religious liberty, and that this would be achieved by a commission of theologians known to be opposed to the text. *De Judaeis* would also be revised by a "mixed commission," also consisting partly of skeptics, and stood to be radically shortened. Word leaked to the media and once again the church tripped into a full-blown crisis. Only around-the-clock lobbying by Cardinal Bea, combined with intense pressure of the Council's most powerful cardinals, frustrated this renewed attempt to undermine the work of three years.

Who Are the Jews?

The statement on the Jews had thus been rescued once more, but again it migrated, becoming in November 1964 the core of a new Conciliar Declaration on the Relation of the Church to Nonchristian Religions, which the bishops voted on a year later as *Nostra Aetate*.[74] In the meantime, Bea's Secretariat for Christian Unity took on new advisors while formulating the other chapters in *Nostra Aetate* dealing with Hinduism, Islam, and Buddhism, and human unity. An additional change of substance took place as Bea's theologians gathered after the bishop's Great Debate to redraft *De Judaeis*, and that concerned how precisely the church would refer to the Jews. Clearly after the Wardi affair of 1962 the wording could not have political resonance. Any expression containing the word "Israel" was therefore excluded. The "Jewish people" appeared a logical choice, but these words did not seem to capture the Jews' religious identity, a minimal expectation of a Catholic document produced after the Holocaust. At the same time, the Jews (unlike the other subjects of *Nostra Aetate*) were not simply religious. And so the authors struggled for an expression that would make absolutely clear what Judaism meant to the church: as people and religion.

Drafts of *De Judaeis* made from 1961 to 1964 reflected theological uncertainty. When the language was hopeful, according Jews a role in salvation history, it referred either to the Jewish people of the past ("Israel of the Patriarchs," "people of the Old Covenant") or beyond the end of history ("the Church believes in the union of the Jewish people with herself as an integral part of Christian hope . . ."). Words relating to the Jews of the present were entirely religious ("Synagogue"), ostensibly nonreligious ("the Jews," the "Jewish people"), or intentionally a-religious ("children of Abraham according to the flesh"). Making clear the religious vocation of the Jewish people as an ethnic or national group seemed impossible. In these drafts, the church referred to itself as "a continuation of the people with whom God, in His inexpressible mercy, was once pleased to enter into the Old Covenant." It was as though after Christ the Jewish people had been erased from history.

The solution found in the first weeks of October 1964 was to refer to the Jews as the "Stock of Abraham" (*stirps Abrahae*). This formula replaced the expression "*Judaeis*" (the Jews) of the previous draft, and it entered the final statement the bishops voted for a year later. The drafters claimed to make the revision in response to Cardinal Giacomo Lercaro's insistence during the Great Debate that the Council proclaim "a peculiar defense of the Jewish people, considered purely as a religious community."[75] If this was true we see a great irony at the end point of the church's struggle against racist antisemitism: that the effort to find an unequivocally religious formulation produced words that sound racialist.[76] Yet ethnicity was not race. For the German translation, the church chose the words "*Stamm Abrahams*"—tribe of Abraham—precisely the expression Jewish thinker Erich Kahler insisted upon to describe the Jews in an age when "race" and "nation" were either inadequate or inappropriate.[77] In French, the words chosen were "*lignée d'Abraham*," which suggest progeny. The Italian was "*stirpe*," or offspring, stock, heritage.

The origins of the new expression are not entirely clear. "Stock of Abraham" does appear in the Douay-Rheims ("men, brethren, children of the Stock of Abraham") as well as King James versions of the Bible (Acts

13:26) and has been used by Jews to refer to themselves in discussions with Christians. For example, the Jewish Community of Newport, Rhode Island, called themselves "Children of the stock of Abraham" in a congratulatory address to George Washington upon his visit to that city in August 1790.[78] Also, church fathers Jerome, Augustine, and Aquinas used the words "*stirps Abrahae*" to refer to the Jews at various points of their voluminous writings. But it is also true that Calvin referred to Jews as *lignée d'Abraham*, and Martin Luther called them *Stamm Abrahams*.

The drafters of *Nostra Aetate* did not claim to be inspired by the citation from Acts, or the *Summa Theologica*, let alone Luther and Calvin. Instead, personal recollections and marginal notations by Secretariat members point to Cardinal Lercaro's contribution from the Great Debate as the source of inspiration. But the link is not straightforward. The cardinal did use both of these words at various points in his remarks, but they were not connected. He never said "*stirps Abrahae*." However, if one consults the mimeograph of his words made by the Vatican printshop for the Secretariat's deliberations, one sees that the words "*stirpis*" and "Abraham" fortuitously appear *on top of* one another.[79] On a cursory glance, they seemed to belong together. Perhaps a cursory glance of Father Baum, or Father Stransky, or Father Oesterreicher of this accidental alignment of words indeed helped produce one of the most important formulations of a Vatican II document. In any case, the phrase quickly found assent: it fit well with references made by Oesterreicher and others in previous years to the Jews as the "sons and daughters of Abraham."[80] It satisfied Cardinal Lercaro's expectation that the reference to the Jews have an evident religious quality. The German equivalent was precisely the phrase used by Karl Thieme in his Evanston theses (theses that were also the source for the words of Zephaniah that put an end to the controversy over mission to the Jews).[81] Thieme in turn was probably drawing upon the work of Karl Barth, his neighbor in Basel, who referred to the Jews as *Stamm Abrahams* in an exegesis of Romans 9–11 from 1942.[82]

Besides their charge to devise unpolitical language to refer to the Jews, the drafters faced the challenge that Paul's letter to the Romans was at the root of the anti-Judaic belief that spiritual and carnal Israel lived as separate entities, the first representing the church, the latter the "unbelieving" Jews.[83] The formula selected, "*stirps Abrahae*," was not contained in

Romans (or indeed in the entire Vulgate New Testament), however, and it fortuitously balanced an understanding of the Jews as a familylike group still enjoying promises made by God, with the church's understanding of itself as the new people of God, which is linked *spiritually* to the Jews.[84] One sentence after calling the Jews "stock of Abraham," *Nostra Aetate* refers to the church as "Abraham's children according to faith."[85] This was a first step in healing a rift in vision that dated back to Paul's ambiguous use of the words "Jews" and "Israel," at times suggesting overlap, at times distinction.[86]

This new formulation was embedded in a draft relying more heavily upon Paul's letter to the Romans than previous versions, making clear that the promises made to the "stock of Abraham" remained in force in postbiblical times ("theirs is the sonship and the glory and the covenants and the law and the worship and the promises"), and that God continued to love this people in the present ("God holds the Jews most dear for the sake of their Fathers"). For the first time, the church unequivocally recognized that the Covenant made with the Jews remained valid: the use of the present tense to refer to the Jews' "sonship" was itself revolutionary.[87]

Yet doubts remained among Catholic theologians as to whether this wording captured the identity of the Jewish people. Gregory Baum reminded Oesterreicher that the new wording contradicted interpretations going back to the church's earliest days. There was no basis at all in Catholic tradition for the assertion that St. Paul was referring to the Jewish people ("empirical Israel") when he wrote that "all Israel will be saved" in Romans 11:26.[88] The Bible scholar, later cardinal, and pioneer in the French Jewish-Christian dialogue, Jean Daniélou, likewise made his severe doubts known in private ("in the corridors of the council") to the Dominican Exegete Jacques Dupont. "They want to say that the Jewish people is not a people like the others," Daniélou complained. "This reflects Jewish ideology but not Christian theology. As we see it, the fleshly Israel lost all its privileges, and we have inherited them. Israel is now a people like all the others, exactly like all the others."[89]

Daniélou's qualms were understandable. The church had never recognized a national group. The pressure to be "exclusively religious" only grew further in 1965 as Eastern bishops and members of Orthodox churches coordinated pressures upon the Vatican not to seem to favor

Israel or the Jewish people. Joining them were conservative bishops and members of the Vatican Curia who feared that by turning its back on centuries of teaching, the church was conceding error. In the spring and summer of 1965, memoranda arrived in the Secretariat recalling in excruciating detail the unwavering adherence to anti-Judaic ideas by popes as well as Catholic thinkers over the ages. The authors of these memoranda hinted that by tugging at one element of anti-Judaism—the sense of a curse resting upon the Jews, or of the Jews as "Israel of the flesh," or of the need to conduct an active mission to the Jews—the bishops risked bringing down a theological edifice constructed over many generations.

The objections extended even to members of Cardinal Bea's subcommittee on relations to the Jews. In August 1965, just weeks before the final vote, the French Dominican and archeologist Pierre Benoit of Jerusalem, who had joined the group in the fall of 1964, submitted a memorandum alleging bias in favor of Jews in the planned decree. The Apostle Paul had not had such a one-sided bias. If one cited Paul's claim in Romans that God loved the Jews, Benoit insisted, then one also had to mention that Paul considered Jews enemies of the Gospel. A citation used in the draft from Romans 9:4–5 gave the impression that the "unfaithful" Israel of the present retained all the privileges promised to Abraham and Moses, while in fact, according to Benoit, Paul thought Israel's election belonged to the past. The Jews may not have been forsaken for all time, but they were lost while they remained outside the body of the church, "cut off branches" in Paul's formulation. Benoit exploited the ambiguity of Paul's language to make a basic challenge: if we are going to cast aside tradition of many centuries and return to original scripture, then we must be accurate.

Indeed Paul did not celebrate Judaism in his letter to the Romans. The letter was a remorseful meditation on how his "kin" had failed to accept Christ, a fact that caused Paul "continual sorrow in my heart."[90] But John Oesterreicher had anticipated Benoit's objections in his study of April 1961, saying that Paul could have been truly harsh. If he had wanted to say the Jews were damned or accursed, for example, he would have said so.[91] Yet he did not. Paul indeed called the Jews "broken off" branches, and alluded to their joining the church at an unspecified moment in the future. But he spoke of these branches in the present tense, and made clear that they remained blessed even if separated from the church. Most important,

Paul told the early Christians of Rome "do not boast, do not make yourself superior to the branches" (Romans 11:18). This core message of Romans chapter 11 became the core of *Nostra Aetate* chapter four: Christians should not presume to raise themselves above Jews. These were resonant words for bishops of transalpine Europe and North America in the fall of 1965 because by attempting to raise themselves above Jews, Christians had generated centuries of antisemitism. Beyond all debates surrounding scripture or tradition, for the bishops *De Judaeis* was about removing the bases for hatred, and it aligned well with Romans, even if that letter set God's love for the Jews off against the Jews' hostility for the Gospel.

Going beyond what John XXIII anticipated when commissioning it in 1960, *Decretum de Judaeis* was now featured among statements on other religions. That seemed reasonable. Bishops from Japan and the Middle East had asked whether the church could remain silent about Buddhism, Hinduism, or Islam if it spoke about the Jews. But the statement on the Jews was not placed among statements about *other peoples*. Karekin Sarkissian, a representative of the Armenian Apostolic church and later its supreme patriarch, afforded the conciliar fathers an opportunity to clarify this matter. At a meeting of Bea's Secretariat in May 1965, Sarkissian wondered why the church was making no statement about the Armenians, an ancient people who, like the Jews, had seen persecution throughout their history. Bishop Willebrands gave two reasons. First, the Armenians had not been persecuted by the Catholic Church, and second, Christian theology had had an "antisemitic tendency" but not an anti-Armenian tendency.[92] In a protocol drawn up several days later, the bishops added a third reason: "The historical context: six million Jewish dead. If the Council, taking place twenty years after these facts, remains silent about them, then it would inevitably evoke the reaction expressed by Hochhuth in the 'Deputy.'"

Karekin Sarkissian had given the bishops a chance to remind themselves that chapter four of *Nostra Aetate* was about Auschwitz. In his play *The Deputy*, Rolf Hochhuth portrayed a church unable to speak out against antisemitism, and the bishops no longer wished to inhabit such a church. Alluding to Pius XII, who had risen through the ranks of the Vatican Secretariat of State on his way to the papacy, Bishop Josef Stangl of Würzburg wondered whether the church's business was diplomacy or truth. "Can we really justify Pius XII?" Stangl asked. "If we speak in the name of God, in the name of Jesus Christ, as his representatives, our speech must be Yes—No, that is truth not tactics, for 'anything more than this comes from evil' (Matthew 5:37)." Eastern bishops like Sarkissian who wanted to attenuate the document were not concerned about truth. "Has not the Church been walking the way of the children of this world, who calculate and follow earthly considerations?" Stangl wondered.[93] He demanded immediate promulgation, and an end to all delays in the name of Near East diplomacy. Other members of Bea's Secretariat likewise used the specter of Hochhuth's silent pope in arguments for a strong statement; though detested by Oesterreicher, the German playwright in fact performed a service for advocates of reconciliation.[94] The bishops could have no illusions about the response of world opinion if the Council was silent on the Jews.

The arguments made by representatives of Eastern churches like the Armenian Sarkissian or Maximos IV, Patriarch of the Melkite Greek Catholic Church, were backed by warnings of what would happen if the Council seemed to favor the Jews. A high ecclesiastic in Beirut advised Cardinal Heenan not to visit Lebanon because of all his "Jew-talk" at the Council. Another told him not to go to Bombay because his life would be at risk. During a stay in Rome in May 1965, Lebanese President Charles Helou promised Cardinal Bea there would be "perturbations" throughout the Near East if a statement on the Jews was promulgated. Yet ultimately the threats angered the bishops and proved counterproductive. "The sight of Maximos IV walking out of the Council does not daunt me in the slightest," Heenan told his colleagues in May 1965. Calling fear a "bad counselor," he refused to cancel his trips.[95] Bishop De Smedt added that a statement on the Jews was for the good of the whole church, and that was something the Eastern bishops would have to explain to the their congregations.

Attempts to alter the text continued to the end, even after the subcommittee submitted final drafts. Just days before the vote in October 1965, opponents tried to change the title of chapter four of *Nostra Aetate* from "on the Jews" to "on the Jewish religion." John Oesterreicher later reflected on the damage the new title would have caused. "The Jewish religion without the Jewish people is a fiction," he wrote, "it exists only in a 'History of Religions,' that is to say, in books. Those who chose the heading were simply unaware of the fact that the Jewish religion cannot be separated from the Jewish people. For it is undoubtedly a people *sui generis,* that is, a community of experience and destiny which can hardly be called anything but 'people' whether or not it has a state of its own and lives in its own country. It is a question of Jewish existence which is not the existence of individuals but of a community, of an incarnate vocation." Oesterreicher was perhaps more sensitive on this question than other members of Cardinal Bea's Secretariat. He wrote the journalist Lisa Palmieri-Billig that his colleagues had not "given much thought to the inseparability of peoplehood and religion." Oesterreicher did believe that the pope understood the singularity of Jewish identity: before promulgation the Pontiff had taken Oesterreicher's "right hand into his hands and said with great warmth that even made members of his entourage glow: 'tomorrow will be a great day for you, I will pray for you and your people—for its peace.'"[96] Fortuitously, the subheadings reducing Judaism to a "religion" were dropped in the final versions of the decree produced at the Vatican print shop.[97]

Promulgation

When the bishops finally approved *Nostra Aetate* on October 28, 1965, Oesterreicher called it a "miracle."[98] The breakthroughs in language, toward recognition of the continued holiness of the Jewish people, were not appreciated at the time. Instead, many observers lamented changes made to the text after the spring of 1964, when the word "deicide" disappeared, and the church was said to "deplore" rather than "deplore and condemn" antisemitism. The former change was made in an attempt to mollify opponents, and in direct response to concerns of Paul VI for the fate of Christians living in the Middle East. Cardinal Heenan may not have minded Maximos IV leaving the council, but the pope did. Paul VI wanted as much support for each measure of the Council as possible, and declared even a two-thirds majority insufficient.[99] The word "condemn" was dropped for the sake of brevity.[100]

But these changes were cosmetic. After that point, it was impossible to portray hostility toward Jews as compatible with Catholic doctrine. Jews were not enemies of God or of Christians. The revised draft featured several improvements, above all in the eschatological vision that took conversion off the table. But there was more. Signaling an epochal break with teaching on the Jews dating back to the early church, *Nostra Aetate* called the Jews "beloved by God"—using the emotive Latin verb *carissimi*. The drafters expanded upon these words taken from St. Paul (in the vulgate), adding the word "*adhuc*" (until now), to make absolutely clear that God's love for the Jews continues.[101] *Nostra Aetate* said that Christ's "passion cannot be charged against all the Jews, without distinction, then alive, nor against the Jews of today" thus defusing the deicide charge—even if that word was not used. Therefore, a correspondent of the *New York Times* in our day "remembers" *Nostra Aetate* as "absolving the Jews of the deicide charge."[102] This was the intent: in a meeting of Bea's Secretariat on May 12, 1965, Cardinal Joseph-Marie Martin of Rouen concurred that "deicide" should be removed if that word irritated some of the bishops from the East, but the Secretariat would "keep the idea in the text without the word."[103]

In many ways, the irrational nature of anti-Judaism was set against formulating reasonable statements. The idea of absolving the Jews of deicide seemed so absurd that the theologian John Courtney Murray, a guiding light behind the Vatican II theology, felt even to mention it was to accord it some dignity, legitimating its assumption that such guilt was possible. As an American Catholic, he had never heard of this strange idea until he was forty years old. American Rabbi Arthur Gilbert of the U.S. National Council of Christians and Jews, with whom Murray shared the podium at the annual meeting of the World Congress of the Catholic Press in May 1965, had mixed feelings. On the one hand, he agreed that absolving the Jews of this "crime" was absurd. "Jews felt no guilt and no need of absolution," he wrote.[104] Yet on the other, Gilbert recalled the many centuries of Christian contempt based in this allegation. He therefore believed the Council could not be silent on deicide. He was right in thinking the problem had not gone away: in August 1964, Joseph Lichten of B'nai B'rith circulated a University of California study to the bishops showing that a substantial minority of American Catholics—perhaps over five million—held the Jews collectively responsible for Christ's death. "How could Father Murray not realize," Gilbert asked, "that the issue was a live one for Christian theology? Had he not read in history how Jews had suffered at the hands of Christian princes and prelates?"[105] Gilbert also seems to have had a keener sense than Murray of the Central European context. Just a few years earlier, even people of goodwill like Karl Thieme or Jacques Maritain were speaking of Jewish guilt in a way Murray claimed not to have heard of. As late as March 1965, the progressive theologian Gregory Baum said that "Reprobation of the Synagogue is not because of crucifixion but because of refusal of the Evangelium Christi." In other words, the idea that the Jews lived under a curse was not tied simply to the "deicidal act" but to a deeply rooted idea about the path taken by Jews in history.[106]

Whether or not the idea of deicide seemed relevant to believers in the United States in the middle years of the twentieth century, the Declaration on the Jews shattered centuries of harmful teaching. The effect went beyond simple words and extended to symbolism; referring to the atmosphere of Christian-Jewish encounters in the United States just before the decree was promulgated, Arthur Gilbert wrote that that "Vatican II seemed already to have worked its magic."[107] Rabbi A. James Rudin compared *Nostra Aetate* to the Magna Carta because it "broke new ground and provided the mandate for constructive change."[108] His colleague Gilbert S. Rosenthal wrote that the "main points of the statement represent a Copernican revolution in Catholic thinking about the Jewish religion and people."[109] The broadcaster and scholar Geoffrey Wigoder credited John XXIII with initiating a "revolution in the attitude of the Church as a whole," indeed "inaugurating a new era in the history of the church."[110] The "long-term impact of the Declaration was not so much perhaps in what it actually said as in the new attitudes in initiated."[111] Its "very tone constitutes a breakthrough. For example, its stress on the spiritual bond between the Church and the Jewish people and the statement that the Church 'received the Old Testament through the people with whom God concluded the Ancient Covenant' were unprecedented. The acknowledgment of the Judaic roots of Christianity, starting with the Judaic roots of Jesus himself, opened up vistas not previously possible."[112] The message was no longer a whisper uttered in subterranean passages among a few converts but a banner flown from the highest towers of the church.

Because chapter four of *Nostra Aetate* was brief—fifteen sentences in Latin—much was left unsaid. There was no reference to the Holocaust or the church's own historical responsibility. The Declaration might have done more to satisfy Abraham Heschel's request for reference to "the permanent preciousness" of Jews as Jews—something a number of Council fathers came close to expressing in other formulations.[113] Yet there was something providential to keeping the statement focused. It took away impediments to deeper understanding, and given the mentality of the time, saying more harbored risks. In October 1965, many bishops raised their hand in ethical assent while unthinkingly keeping to their anti-Judaic views. Even Cardinal Bea, who tirelessly defended the statement in the darkest moments, had not fully absorbed its implications. In November 1965 Bea wrote that Jerusalem had once been destroyed because of the "guilt" of its inhabitants "since they directly witnessed the preaching, the miracles, the solemn entrance of Jesus." Furthermore, he wrote, the Jewish people was "no longer the people of God in the sense of being the instrument of salvation for humanity."[114]

Yet why did Israel continue to exist if it had no role in humanity's salvation? Bea's words stood in direct contradiction to the spirit of De Judaeis: that the promises to the Jews were irrevocable. If Bea had expressed his own views more fully in the Declaration, he would have continued to nourish what Jules Isaac called the roots of contempt. It was fortunate that the Council text cited Paul's view on the irrevocability of the Jewish calling without further elaboration. Bea was an instrument of change and not a source of ideas. A further advocate for a strong declaration, Bishop Léon-Arthur Elchinger of Strasbourg, admitted that "crimes have been committed against the Jews by the children of the Church, and not infrequently, in the name of the Church." Elchinger opposed "any kind of call for the conversion of the whole Jewish people," and argued that the "second Covenant does not annul the first." Yet he insisted that the "Gospel of Christ" remained the Jews' "true fulfillment."[115] It is true that the Catholic church cannot deny Christ's universal offer of salvation, but the presence of such words in the final declaration would have retarded Catholic-Jewish dialogue.

Similar points can be made about Cardinal Giacomo Lercaro of Bologna, a charismatic Franciscan known for his personal generosity and by far the most theologically sophisticated of the bishops who spoke during the Great Debate.[116] "In the eyes of the Church," he declared, "the Jewish people has a dignity that has supernatural roots and a corresponding value, not only in the past . . . [but] in the present order of salvation they are able to give a certain biblical, paschal witness."[117] He spoke of "Paul's certainty that the children of Israel remain utterly loved and set apart by the love of God."[118] Cardinal Lercaro probably inspired the phrase "stock of Abraham." Nevertheless, Lercaro continued to believe that the Jews' witness was "covered by a veil (2 Corinthians 3:15)," thus disregarding Jules Isaac's call to no longer to represent Jews as a "blind and refractory people."[119] Lercaro went on to project the Jewish people "solely as a religious community."[120] Lercaro (or his ghost-writer Giuseppe Dossetti) was perhaps reflecting anti-racist high sentiment, but also revealing that he had failed to plumb the theological depths traveled by Jacques Maritain, Dietrich von Hildebrand, and Karl Thieme, who called the Jews the "people of peoples," "*Menschheitsvolk*," and "priestly people." To reduce Jews to a "religious community" meant in fact to deny them the possibility of religious existence, asking them to be priests without a church.

By contrast, *De Judaeis* made clear the close, kinlike bonds of the Jewish people. If it recognized an intimacy of the Jewish people once described as "racial," the church also condemned racism in the final words of *Nostra Aetate*. The human race had one origin and one goal: God. Nations should live "in good fellowship," and the promises made to "the stock of Abraham" remained in force. Thus did the church condemn racism and antisemitism while affirming what many call the ethnic character of the Jewish people.

We are reminded of the tenuousness of the new approach by the pope's failure to accept the implications of the text he later promulgated. During Lent 1965, Paul VI preached on the Crucifixion. "It is a grave and sad page," he told the congregation. "It describes in fact the clash between Jesus and the Jewish people. That people predestined to receive the Messiah, who awaited him for thousands of years and was completely absorbed in the hope . . . at the right moment when Christ came, spoke, and presented himself not only did not recognize him, but fought him, slandered him, and injured him; and in the end they killed him." Cardinal Bea downplayed the matter, writing that the "Jews cannot expect that their leaders of that time be absolved from all blame in the death of the Savior!"[121] Yet one Anglo-Jewish newspaper caught the general mood among those who had followed the evolution of *De Judaeis*, writing: "The Pope's Revival of the Deicide Charge Shows the Need of the Council Schema."[122]

Nostra Aetate was needed as instruction for the pope himself, who had less sympathy and sense for Christian-Jewish dialogue than his predecessor.[123]

The cases of Paul VI and Cardinal Bea alert us to a fact noted by the Jewish thinker Ernst Ludwig Ehrlich: besides Ernesto Cardinal Ruffini of Palermo, no bishop had dared speak out against a strong statement on the Jews. The sense of guilt was too strong.[124] But this was deceptive. One of the most respected theologians of the century, the American John Courtney Murray, may have never heard the charge of deicide, but it was so deeply rooted in the European mind that Paul VI could not think of the crucifixion without conjuring up this idea. Recall the case of Jean Daniélou, willing to whisper his doubts but not to proclaim them openly. Ehrlich explains: the near unanimity "probably happened above all because no Council father wanted to be suspected of being an enemy of the Jews. An anti-Jewish statement would not only have damaged his own reputation, but stained the image of the Church in the eyes of Catholics and non-Catholics." Nevertheless, Ehrlich had no doubt that many "tenacious anti-Jewish prejudices continued among a minority within the Church."[125]

The issue was not just prejudice but also ignorance, and failure to appreciate subtlety. Pope Benedict XVI, once a theologian enthusiastic for the changes of Vatican II, made headlines in 2008 with an amendment of the 1962 Good Friday prayer for the Jews in the Roman missal containing the words: "Let us also pray for the Jews, that God our Lord should illuminate their hearts, so that they will recognize Jesus Christ, the savior of men." This revised prayer seemed out of touch with the sentiments of the Council, reflected, for example, in the 1970 edition of the Roman missal, which had stated: "Let us pray for the Jewish people, the first to hear the word of God, that they may continue to grow in the love of his name and in faithfulness to his covenant . . . Almighty and eternal God, long ago you gave your promise to Abraham and his posterity. Listen to your Church as we pray that the people you first made your own may arrive at the fullness of redemption."

What had happened? We may never know for sure, but it seems the pope acted on his own authority: for all his brilliance, he was arguably out of touch with the complex dialogue between Christians and Jews. Karl Thieme was right that more was required to advance this dialogue than good intentions. Cardinal Walter Kasper, president of the Pontifical Council for Promoting Christian Unity (and thus a successor to Cardinal Bea) attempted damage control within a day of the release of the new prayer: "If the Pope speaks of the conversion of the Jews, then one must understand him correctly," he told the German Catholic Press agency (February 7, 2008). Benedict quoted "literally from the eleventh chapter of Paul's letter to the Romans. There the Apostle says that we Christians hope that when the full number of the Gentiles have entered the Church, then all of Israel will be converted. That is an eschatological hope for the end of times and does not mean that we have the intention of conducting a mission to the Jews, in the way that we have a mission to the Gentiles."[126] A week later, Kasper wrote the chairman of the International Jewish Committee on Interreligious Consultations (IJCIC), Rabbi David Rosen, as follows: "The text is a prayer inspired by Saint Paul's letter to the Romans, Chapter 11, which is the very text that speaks also of the unbroken covenant. It takes up Paul's eschatological hope that in the end of time all Israel will be saved. As a prayer the text lays all in the hands of God and not in ours. It says nothing about the how and the when. Therefore there is nothing about missionary activities by which we may take Israel's salvation in our hands."[127]

The cardinal's words are remarkable for three reasons: first, they make no reference to the actual wording of the new prayer. That is, Kasper made no defense of a prayer of illumination for Jews. Second, the new prayer has no connection to Romans 11. Rather, it is a modification of a pre-Vatican II prayer inspired by 2 Corinthians 3:14 (Let us pray for the Jew that almighty God remove the veil from their hearts). But third, Kasper clearly reaffirmed that Romans, Chapter 11 is the source of the church's understanding of its relation to the Jewish people after the Holocaust.[128] Yet in Romans 11, contrary to the words of Cardinal Kasper, one finds no talk of Israel being "converted," of illumination, of church, or even of Christ. Instead one finds the images that inspired Léon Bloy and Karl Thieme: "Has God rejected his people, by no means!" "Have they stumbled . . . by no means!" "if you do boast, remember it is not you that supports the root, but the root that supports you!," and "the gifts and the call of God are irrevocable." But it was revealing that Cardinal Kasper made reference to part of Romans 11 implied but not included in *Nostra*

Aetate, Paul's inscrutable theological vision about the end of time. The full passage reads: "Lest you be wise in your own conceits I want you to understand this mystery brethren: a hardening has come upon part of Israel, until the full number of Gentiles come in, and *all Israel will be saved* . . ."

9

A Particular Mission
for the Jews

Did the Apostle Paul limit Christians to "eschatological hope" for the final reconciliation of Jews with Gentiles? Or must Christians follow the call in Matthew 28 to "baptize all nations," including Jews? These questions keep flaring up, most recently after a 2009 statement of the American bishops criticizing theologians who restricted their evangelical efforts to "individual Jews." No, the bishops declared, Catholics must look forward to the "inclusion of the whole people of Israel." And the previous year, Pope Benedict released a new version of a Good Friday Prayer for the Jews: "that God our Lord should illuminate their hearts, so that they will recognize Jesus Christ, the Savior of all men."

Karl Thieme and John Oesterreicher knew something about eschatological hope as well as mission to the Jews, and their experience may be instructive. The troubles of their age—the age of Hitler and Stalin—had grown to such a scale that the only possible remedy seemed apocalyptic, and the Bible told them that the Jews had a crucial role to play at the end of time. God would not resolve the issue through a "trick," Thieme wrote in 1944, but required Christians' active work: "no one else is called to convert them than we ourselves."[1] The war's conclusion did nothing to weaken Thieme's fervor. On New Year's Day 1948, he confided to Oesterreicher that the last days were approaching "with huge steps." Would Jesus find them sleeping when he came?[2] The following year he wrote Theodor Adorno that "not very much time is left."[3] He was desperate to convert Jews, but then he began speaking to them, and found he needed a new language.

In a short essay written ten years later, Thieme was pleading for a new relation to Jews, no longer missionary but "ecumenical."[4] He did not deny that all humans were destined to turn to Christ, but insisted that Jews were meant to remain Jews. With scripture, he called Jews a priestly people (Exodus 19:6) and specified their vocation: "non-conformists willed by God," "persons charged by God to do away with false idols," and finally, "participants in the messianic mystery of suffering, the humiliation suffered by Christ for the salvation of all the world." He read Romans 11:25 to imply that Jews would remain a historical people not simply until a "certain number" of pagans had entered the kingdom of God but up until the time of "full ripening," the promised hour when the fullness (*plērōma*) of the Gentiles arrived and all Israel would be saved. This would coincide with the "final judgment." Until that time, it was "evident" that Jews have a "particular mission. "The Jew who fulfills the purpose of his existence in the economy of salvation makes a contribution to fulfilling the will of God. Has not Israel been made an escort to the nations (like Socrates to the Athenians)," he asked, "braking them constantly, never letting them sleep, warning us any time our belief threatens to become superstition? Does not Israel always wake us up when we think we have found the perfect societal order but it is not the Kingdom of God?"[5]

St. Paul had not implied that Jews do not need Christ, but rather: don't worry, God will take care of them. Christians could be certain of the end, but not the how. "All Israel would be saved" (Romans 11:26) in a way that no one could imagine. The Jesuit scripture scholar Joseph Fitzmyer has admitted to two interpretations: the theological and the Christological. The former is passive, a "merciful act independent of any acceptance of Jesus as the messiah"; the latter involves all Israel accepting Christ their Deliverer at the second coming.[6] In his history of the Vatican II declaration on the Jews, John Oesterreicher wrote that it could not be "the task of a Council to choose between these two exegeses." *Nostra Aetate* had said nothing about the circumstances of Israel's final "ingathering." All that was certain was the "essence of hope": Israel's "turning" would be the signal for a new outpouring of grace, a reawakening of love over the whole earth."[7]

But what about the idea that Christians were called upon to baptize Jews? Thieme renounced his own conversion agenda in the early 1950s, but Oesterreicher did not, at least not openly. He broke with his friend in 1960 by continuing to insist that Jews needed to turn to Christ, something he felt called to help effect. In May 1938, even before he could speak English, Oesterreicher was determined to construct a mission to the Jews in the United States. "It pains me to have to leave the part of the world that is culturally German," he confessed to Thieme in a letter written from Rome. "But a missionary cannot ask what is convenient for him personally. In this sense I am thinking strongly of the USA." Europe was too small for him to "build the type of work I intend to build."[8]

Yet by 1970 Oesterreicher was discussing the vocation of the Jewish people in exactly the language of Karl Thieme. Christianity and Judaism should coexist, both serving the cause of God's justice, their "polarity" meant to "be an agent that makes both communities, and the world with them, run toward the final consummation of which the prophets dreamed. Do not both communities," Oesterreicher asked, "each in its own way, serve the will of God, and though seemingly apart, push together toward the ultimate goal: God's perfect reign and man's delivery from all and every evil?" Were not Christianity and Judaism "two ways of righteousness that have complementary functions?" The belief in mission was subsumed in a new eschatological vision: two covenant theology.[9] He described his work with Jews as a "ministry of reconciliation," and his "mission" shifted to Catholic lay people, legal scholars, and theologians, whom he hoped to make more aware of the "life-giving knowledge" of "our Jewish roots."[10] Thieme was no longer alive to hear Oesterreicher adopt the very words from scripture about Jews that had animated the Freiburg group in the 1950s: "You are not far from the kingdom of God" (Mark 12:34).

Oesterreicher knew every angle of the basic message American bishops want to impress upon their flocks today: the church must preach the gospel

to all humans, Jews included. Yet he insisted that the Jewish people would
exist to the end of time and play a salutary role in what theologians call
the "economy of salvation." Unlike Karl Thieme, or later Gregory Baum,
Oesterreicher did not dwell upon the distance he had traveled in his own
vision of Jews.[11] At some point in the 1960s, he reinterpreted his original
intent in leaving Europe as "seeking a new encounter between Christians
and Jews."[12] He never discussed his abandoning of a mission to the Jews in
print, and indeed Oesterreicher the actor intrudes only episodically in his
own historical reflections, while great men like Pope John and August Bea
control the scene. He appears more hinge than mover. Perhaps his conversion to a new understanding of the Jews grew so gradually that he could
identify no point of crystallization.

We get glimpses of the process in Oesterreicher's unpublished letters.
In April 1961, the seminarian David W. Connor approached Oesterreicher because he was "intensely interested in the work of converting our
Jewish brethren." He had just written a paper on the church's "organized
efforts" in this regard, and "didn't dream that our efforts were so limited,"
especially compared with those of the Protestants. Connor wondered
whether Oesterreicher had realized his ambition to carry out missionary
work in an "Institute of St. Peter" as envisioned in his 1948 brochure
Apostolate to the Jews.[13] Oesterreicher responded that he had not founded
such an institute nor did any diocese in the United States train priests "for
the work of reconciliation between Church and Synagogue."[14] Instead, he
had founded an Institute for Judeo-Christian Studies at Seton Hall University in 1953. It differed "from the proposed Institute of St. Peter mainly
in these respects: It is an academic institution, its emphasis is on study and
literary output, and its spirit is ecumenical rather than missionary." There
was a parallel evolution in the work of the sisters and fathers of Notre
Dame de Sion in France—the only true international mission to the Jews
ever attempted in the Catholic Church. By 1960, they too were at the forefront of Catholics seeking to improve relations between Christians and
Jews.

Here, in a private letter, Oesterreicher was using precisely the language
of Karl Thieme and the Freiburg group from whom he was estranged. But
he did not explain to Connor why he had abandoned mission for ecumenism. Perhaps that had to do in part with sobering experience. Though he

and the Notre Dame de Sion priests had racked their brains after World War II for ways to convert Jews, the results were meager. Oesterreicher believed that Jews were opening to Christ's message—the argument of his 1954 book *The Walls Are Crumbling*—yet at most small handfuls were actually converting. One reason he turned away from mission was that mission was an obvious dead end. But there was more to the story.

Christopher Clark has identified a process among nineteenth-century Protestant missionaries in Germany that we see replicated in the work of other missionaries: before they could convert Jews, they first had to speak to them. That left missionaries open to absorbing the other's viewpoint.[15] After World War II we see a similar dynamic at work in Karl Thieme's conversations with Martin Buber. The difference in Oesterreicher's case was that the other's viewpoint had once been his own. As a schoolboy, he had been active in Zionist youth of Moravia, and the elected representative of the Jewish boys of his school, who supported him even after he began reading Christian texts. Perhaps he never described his turn to a new way of thinking as conversion because it was a return.

The point of conversion work, he told his audience in October 1970, months after his first visit to Israel, had changed after Vatican II. "No matter how firmly we reject any 'conversionist tactics,'" Oesterreicher said, "we must, at the same time, love the concept of, and call to, conversion. In the pre-ecumenical age, Christians sought to convert others. Today, Catholics realize much more their own need to be converted. 'Conversion' stands at the threshold of Judaism as well as of Christianity; both ways of righteousness are unthinkable without it. In saying this I am not thinking of conversion as a change from one religious group or spiritual family to another, or even a turning from a life of sin to one of goodness. *I take conversion in its deepest sense as a reorientation of one's total existence in the sight of God.*"[16]

The audience for this talk, held at Seton Hall University, consisted of Christians and Jews. After Vatican II, Jews came to Seton Hall to teach and lecture, and Oesterreicher was a frequent guest at Jewish community functions of all sorts. These encounters helped further the profound self-reflection that Oesterreicher called "conversion."[17] One close friendship grew out of an initially harsh exchange. In February 1957, Rabbi Jacob Petuchowski of Hebrew Union College in Cincinnati rebuked

Oesterreicher for selectively using a review he had published in *Commentary* of Oesterreicher's *The Bridge* (volume 1).[18] Contrary to Oesterreicher's suggestion that Petuchowski had found *The Bridge* a valuable resource, the rabbi had in fact disputed the journal's scholarly character, pointing to its assumption that all Jews must become Christians. Yet in the end, Petuchowski wrote, one could hardly expect Christians to have any other belief. The point of dialogue was to learn from the other, but also to strengthen each side in his faith. Upon this small foundation the two built, and from 1964 until Petuchowski's death in 1991 we witness the growth of a warm friendship, with priest and rabbi trading visits to each other's homes, and advising each other on all manner of issues, Oesterreicher eager for Petuchowski's thoughts on his writings and Petuchowski regarding Oesterreicher's interpretations of Christian teachings about the Jews as refreshingly enlightened.[19]

More centrally involved in meetings of Jews and Catholics was another intimate of Oesterreicher, Dr. Joseph Lichten, a pioneer in interfaith relations, director of the intercultural affairs department at the Anti-Defamation League (ADL) of B'nai B'rith in Rome, and a refugee from Central Europe like Petuchowski and Oesterreicher. At the Second Vatican Council, Lichten provided the bishops with data on how the deicide charge fomented antisemitism among American Catholics, and Oesterreicher came to value Lichten's "excellent grasp of Catholic doctrine as well as the delicacy of our problem."[20] Lichten's relations with Oesterreicher dated from 1961 and lasted until the former's death in 1987, in the course of which the monsignor spent happy hours socializing with Lichten and his wife Carol on two continents, occasionally learning from the ADL representative what was going on in the Vatican.

In the 1950s, Oesterreicher rekindled friendships from his boyhood in Olmütz, especially with Hans Spitzer (whom Oesterreicher addressed with the Czech "Janku") and Moshe Tavor (originally Tauber), both of whom studied Hebrew with him in Zionist youth organizations.[21] Tavor, who was close to Max Brod and Heinrich Böll, served as cultural attaché at the Israeli mission in Cologne in the 1960s, and kept up a vigorous correspondence with Oesterreicher and the *Freiburger Rundbrief*. On the first evening of his first visit to Israel in the spring of 1970, Oesterreicher managed to see their old Hebrew teacher from Olmütz (Händel) just weeks before he died. In condolences to his widow for this "wise man and good teacher," Oesterreicher wrote, "if I did not go the way he wished for me, the influence he had upon me was not in vain."[22] In a letter to Tavor, Oesterreicher recalled a common friend from Moravia who had emigrated to Palestine and made a career helping the developmentally disabled, and commented that "Israel brings out the best in a man."[23]

In his last decades, Oesterreicher acted as a Christian Zionist, insisting that the success of Israel was a sign of divine favor, due not simply "to the cunning of her statesmen, the superior strategy of her generals, the bravery of her soldiers, and the steadfastness of her citizens," but to the "'outstretched arm' (Exodus 6:6) of the Lord which once more rescued His people . . . Today's Israel is new proof that God stands by His covenant; that the last word lies, not with the inventor of the 'final solution', but with Him."[24] In 1976, he appeared at the American Zionist Federation in New York and expressed his "love" for Zion, comparing the mystery of Zionism to the mystery of Christianity.[25] To the charge of one Lutheran theologian that those calling Israelis God's chosen people were making "race the basis for God's covenant action," Oesterreicher countered fiercely that "to consider the Jewish people, not just Israelis, God's 'special possession' is in keeping with Deuteronomy, St. Paul's letter to the Romans, and the Declaration of Vatican II."[26]

He did not add that he had helped author the last text. When looking at Oesterreicher's public life, from representative of Jewish students at Olmütz's high school in 1920, to Catholic defender of Israel at an all-day meeting of the America Israel Friendship House on the Upper East Side of New York in 1976, one is reminded of Czesław Miłosz's notion of *ketman*, a figure possessed of higher knowledge who uses skills of persuasion from behind the scenes to unleash an evolution within a system of belief.[27] As a high school student, Oesterreicher may have unwittingly picked up the book *Words of Christ* in one of Olmütz's bookstores, but when he entered the church half a dozen years later it was as a critical thinker, eyes wide open. From an early point he was faithful to the idea of Christ as Messiah, but it had taken the persuading of Cardinal Newman to dispel deep skepticism about Catholicism's claims to represent the Gospel. Once a Catholic, he jettisoned medical studies for theology and finished seminary a year ahead of everyone else. A little over a decade later, Oesterreicher had become a "great friend" of Vienna's Cardinal Innitzer, and soon he was in touch with Vatican state secretary Cardinal Eugenio Pacelli, and presumed to tell the pope what language to employ when talking about the Jews.[28]

Oesterreicher, whom Miłosz might have called ketman of Judeo-Christianity, was humbly obedient when that venture failed. Never deterred by Catholic indifference, he persisted through years of uncertainty: from first exile in Paris in the late 1930s and a hair-raising trek through Spain, Portugal, and over the high seas in 1940; to unending soap-boxing for converts from Catholic parishes in Manhattan during the war and early postwar years, then (in the 1950s) ceaseless petitioning of American bishops, fundraising for Seton Hall, hundreds of public presentations, and then (in the 1960s) three years of intense collaboration with friendly, hostile, and indifferent theologians at Cardinal Bea's Secretariat, whom he enlightened gently and firmly but above all tirelessly. Where Oesterreicher's case may differ from that of Miłosz's Polish intellectuals pursuing hidden agendas under Stalinism (for example, "national" ketman or "aesthetic" ketman) is that he was not as conscious a manipulator. In a train of events he called miraculous, by the early 1960s he helped unleash a revolution in the Catholic Church while himself evolving into the staunchest defender of Pius XII on the planet—a pope he had once compared to the Duke of Windsor, a reputed Nazi sympathizer.[29] But in a sense Oesterreicher was returning a favor; without knowing it, the quiet pope had once saved his life. In May 1940, a French policeman was sent to arrest the troublesome intellectual Oesterreicher, but left him in peace upon spying letters on Oesterreicher's desk bearing the insignia of Cardinal State Secretary Pacelli. The policeman happened to be a pious Catholic.

The interaction between Oesterreicher and Catholicism was dialectical, triggering as much change in the institution of the church as in the Judeo-Christian missionary to that institution. It took *Nostra Aetate*, partly Oesterreicher's own creation, to convince him to adopt a more ecumenical attitude toward Jews.

Before, during, and after the Council, Johannes/Jan/John Maria Oesterreicher proceeded with caution, drawing strength from a position in two worlds, but weakness from standing between them: he was Jew and Christian, and Jews and Christians saw him as both and neither. He knew that many Jews would have preferred dialogue with "an Irish or Italian or even German Catholic" rather than a "Jew qualified by 'having gone over to the other side.'"[30] He also knew that for many Christians he seemed too defensive of Jews, too interested in Judaism, and too zealous in his support for Jews and for Israel.[31] In 1969, Oesterreicher wanted to come out in favor of the Armenian patriarchate of Jerusalem because "it might help me with some of my detractors here if I proved in this way my sympathy for true Christian concerns."[32] But if taken too far, such "advocacy" would cause him to lose any influence he possessed on either side. His dilemma was this: he had to become other to be his new self; yet only as his old self did he understand the new other.

Oesterreicher knew that Jews disputed his claims to be a Jew. In 1963, he conceded to Rabbi Theodore Friedman, editor of *Judaism*, that he was the argumentative sort. Oesterreicher asked Friedman to remember that "despite the Israeli Supreme Court decision, I am a son of the prophets who has the future of his people (in this country and elsewhere) very much at heart.[33] To this Friedman replied, "I would insist, of course, that such a son has disowned his paternity and would therefore be disowned by his forebears."[34] The German-Jewish thinker Ernst Ludwig Ehrlich was gentler, but still insisted that a "missionary" disqualified himself as a Jew. Oesterreicher had written Ehrlich about a Sephardic rabbi who had offered to inscribe him in the "*Sefer ha chajjim*." What did Ehrlich think of this? "You know from the affair of Father Daniel Rufeisen that we Jews have a very unclear position toward Jewish Christians," Ehrlich responded. "Emotions and Halakah constantly get caught up in one another, and I would say that there can be no theology on this question, even if the Jewish Christians often claim there is one. My own inclination is to view Jewish Christians as parts of the Jewish people (*as long as they do not engage in Mission to the Jews*), and my personal solidarity with the Jewish Christians is no less than with the Jews. It seems to me that there can be no general decisions in this question—fortunately Jews don't have the authority that could make them. Otherwise we would have the same concerns as the Catholics."[35]

Oesterreicher had the additional problem of being an alien to his new domicile, where he spoke eloquent English in the heavy accent of the Habsburg lands. Monsignor John Gilchrist, pastor of Holy Cross Parish in Harrison, New Jersey, and chair of the Newark Archdiocesan Commission for Inter-Religious Affairs, was a young priest at Seton Hall in the 1950s:

> I remember Father Oesterreicher very well in those days. I can say for certain that he was not the most popular priest on campus. And it was for two reasons.
>
> The first was personal. Father Oesterreicher was not a benign personality. He had a brilliant mind. He had strong opinions. And if a person were to carelessly make a general statement he would be quick to point out a particular weakness in the statement. His European training demanded precision of thought. I personally learned to be careful with him. In a debate he took no prisoners. He was a man to be respected but not one that American priests would love.
>
> Secondly, while there was not an overt antisemitism among priests, there was not much enthusiasm for intellectual intercourse with Jews. Catholics were Catholics. Jews were Jews. Period. That was it, even though individually almost every Catholic priest had Jewish friends.[36]

If he seemed unmistakably Central European, Oesterreicher felt permanently alienated by the hostility of the Austrian Catholic hierarchy to his efforts of the 1930s, recalling how he had begged to get a few lines about his work in the major Catholic daily *Reichspost*. He could not forget the "feeble way in which Austrian Catholics like Dr. [Michael] Pfliegler tried to explain and excuse their early Nazi sympathies."[37] He refused repeated entreaties to return to Vienna by cardinals Innitzer and König. In 1974, Oesterreicher wrote, "I do not consider myself an exile. I feel thoroughly at home here but do not whenever I return to Austria."[38] Still, the first thing he did upon getting U.S. citizenship in 1948 was go back to Europe. Having seemingly broken all bridges to his native land, he remained a priest of the diocese of Vienna to the end and took European-style summer vacations in Western Austria.

This unusual Moravian American called himself Jew and Christian. He spoke in 1986 about a rabbi who asked him to speak about Jesus at a Passover celebration. "He introduced me as someone who knows both camps saying, 'He *was* a Jew and now is a Catholic.'" But Oesterreicher told them: "I *am* a Jew and a Catholic." "If you want to tell me that to be a Jew is something negative," he continued, "that I don't believe in Christ, then I am not. To be a Jew is to be called to that people, to be part of its heritage, destiny and suffering. I was persecuted by Hitler because I gave sermons like that. I was subject to the Nuremberg laws—according to (Rabbinical) law I am a Jew. But I believe in Jesus Christ with all my heart and with the fullest consent. They couldn't figure that out," Oesterreicher remembered.[39]

In the years before his death in 1993, Oesterreicher gained inspiration from another Central European, the Archbishop of Paris, Jean-Marie Cardinal Lustiger, who was baptized at age fourteen in Vichy France but considered himself Jewish to the end of his life.[40] The former chief rabbi of Paris Meyer Jays dissented, proclaiming that "a Jew becoming a Christian does not take up authentic Judaism, but turns his back to it."[41] Yet Lustiger did not know how else to describe himself:

> I never claimed to be at the same time a good Jew according to the requirements of the rabbis and a good Christian according to the requirements of the church. But I am sure you understand that I cannot repudiate my Jewish condition without losing my own dignity and the respect I owe to my parents and to all those to whom I belong; that is true both in times of persecution and in times of peace. I claim to be a Jew not to hurt anyone, but because I respect the truth and what is due the truth . . . what I can say is that in becoming a Christian I did not intend to cease being the Jew I was then. I was not running away from the Jewish condition. I have that from my parents and can never lose it. I have it from God and He will never let me lose it.[42]

Still, there had been a struggle. In the 1970s, Lustiger began learning Hebrew from cassettes, and preparing for his return to Israel, his *aliyah*. He told the Jewish Telegraphic Agency in 1981: "I thought then that I had finished what I had to do here, that I was at a crossroads."[43] Yet he stayed in the church and was soon appointed bishop of Orleans by fellow Pole John Paul II, causing him to put plans for a return to the Holy Land on the shelf. What interested the old Oesterreicher even more than Lustiger's thoughts on personal identity were his reflections upon the Jewish people—which read much like Karl Thieme's of 1958:

> The "totality" of humanity according to God's plan is made up of Israel and the nations, who are to be finally united in the one and only Covenant. If you put things that way, it is clear that the last days have not yet been fulfilled . . . the figure of the messiah is a hidden one. Christians tend to forget sometimes that they are still waiting for the coming in glory of their Messiah . . . Israel on the other hand must remain faithful as long as the times are not accomplished; it is still loved by God because of his election and because of the Patriarchs. God's gifts and his call cannot be abolished.[44]

In the margin of the section on Israel remaining "faithful" Oesterreicher had impressed a thick exclamation mark. The one-time apocalyptic missionary also underlined sections where Lustiger chided Christians who tried to hurry history. They lacked faith in "God's decisions," the Archbishop wrote.[45]

Lustiger's Judeo-Christian identity survived the tensions the conciliar statement posed for Jewish Christians, the knowledge that their church viewed Judaism as a faith—and a people—that would persist to the end of time. One person dear to Oesterreicher who did not survive this challenge as a Christian was the French convert Suzy Allemand (b. 1919), baptized by Oesterreicher in Marseilles in 1939. She was among those who helped save his life. After the war, Allemand worked for the Agence Juive pour la Palestine in Marseilles, living among converts but spending her days helping Jewish refugees embark upon a new life.[46] She felt "entirely Jewish as though my conversion was but a strong spiritual enlightening without anything restrictive in it."[47] She enjoyed her work:

> it is most interesting because here in Marseilles we have some contacts with all sorts of people, both delegates and leaders of the Jewish Agency such as Moshe Shertock whom you may happen to meet because he is now staying in the States . . . and many others, and emigrants coming from the whole world. These days we even saw

some Jews coming from Shanghai. And I am happy because, on the whole I always feel so much at home among my people, and although my religious and national position usually astounds them to begin with, they usually admit it as soon as they know me a little better.[48]

But a sobering was setting in. "I may be mistaken," Allemand wrote Oesterreicher in 1947, "but I have the impression that not so many of our people do nowadays refuse the light coming from Christianism but most of them never had an opportunity of seeing it *because so few Christians, excepting a few converts, do try to incarnate Jesus's love towards them.* This is what my experience has taught me about 'our problem' and I do not think I am partial, at least I hope I am not."[49]

In the late 1970s, Allemand wrote Oesterreicher while working on an essay on Simone Weil—whom Oesterreicher had met while he was hiding in Marseille.[50] Perhaps Weil had hoped he could provide clarity for her own dilemmas with Christianity. Oesterreicher could not answer questions Allemand now posed about the Zohar, but he did reflect upon his time of need decades earlier. "Unlike many other people," Oesterreicher wrote, "I do not live in or dwell in the past. Still, whenever I recall my flight from France I think of you. Frankly you were a gift of God, a little miracle . . ."[51] Allemand wrote back to inform Oesterreicher that she no longer considered herself a Christian:

After more than thirty years of trying to include in my Christian faith my ancestor's faith: the Torah, mainly the 10 commandments and the messianic hope . . . I came to the conclusion that God chose me to belong to His chosen people and that I must not and cannot betray such a choice.

When I became a Christian in February 1939 I knew practically nothing of the Jewish faith, our world wide and tragical history, of our values, culture, heroes, etc.

Moreover, I thought that at least in Europe the time of racial persecutions was ended. Then I was shocked by the silence of the Pope and his passivity concerning the Nazi crimes although Nazism had been condemned by Pius XI.

When finally the people of Israel (that is some of those who had survived) were able to go back to their homeland, a fact which had been foreseen by several prophets and which is for us one of the signs of the fulfillment of our messianic hope, again the Christian churches, except for a few individuals, were on the wrong side.

So I believe my people are nearer to Jesus Christ and to his teaching even without mentioning him than those who on a large scale failed in teaching the world the faith, love and peace for which he lived and died united to his people and for the sake of all mankind (and not only Christians).[52]

Cardinal Lustiger would not have argued. Nor did Oesterreicher, though he seemed happy to argue about all matters large and small to the end of his days. In the 1980s, Suzy Allemand wrote once more, asking for evidence that she had been active in the underground so that she could receive a pension from the French state. Oesterreicher produced a letter, confirming that she helped hide him and Dietrich von Hildebrand and then took them across the border to Spain (at Perpignan), thus keeping them "out of the clutches of the Gestapo."[53]

Christians had also tested Oesterreicher's faith in Christianity. From the start of his life in the church, he witnessed high-level Catholic officials saying things for which there was no warrant in Christian teaching. A poisonous challenge came from one of the few Catholic intellectuals with whom he shared the intimate *"Du,"* Father Georg Bichlmair, who thought that Jews carried a special sinfulness, present in their physical bodies. Oesterreicher and his émigré friends desperately tried to move two popes to speak against antisemitism, and sought in vain inspiration from the supposed shepherds of Central Europe's Catholics, the German Episcopate. In his writings, Oesterreicher dwelt upon the positive: having worked with Augustin Bea, having received blessings from John XXIII, and having contributed to *Nostra Aetate*. Was he tempted to leave the church? Perhaps Cardinal Lustiger helped establish a sense of harmony. In his final years, Oesterreicher could be seen wearing a simple gold pin on his black lapel: it read *"Shalom."*[54]

Toward a Reborn Church

The hyperintellectual theologian John Oesterreicher, who spent decades poring over obscure arguments in languages comprehensible to handfuls of scholars, was as unrepresentative of the Catholic communion as one can imagine. It would seem absurd to claim that he could tell us anything about the church in general. Yet perhaps better than anyone he incorporates the church's journey from past to present in the Jewish question: from a time when mission was the only Catholic relation to the Jews, to a time when mission is repudiated and Jews are understood as older brothers. "Older brothers," a phrase used by John Paul II to describe the Christian relation to the Jews, was unthinkable in the 1930s. But if the church accepts these words, then proselytization becomes an attempt to do away with one's brother.[55]

Like virtually every figure leading the church on this journey of conciliation, from the 1840s to the 1960s, Oesterreicher had come into the Catholic Church from the outside. The two men he collaborated with (Karl Thieme and Waldemar Gurian) on the Catholic statement about the "Church and the Jews" of 1937 were converts; the other editors of journals promoting Catholic-Jewish understanding after the war (Gertrud Luckner and Paul Démann) were converts; the priests who worked with Oesterreicher in October 1964 (Gregory Baum and Bruno Hussar) to produce a new draft of the statement on the Jews were converts.[56] A partial list of these border transgressors going back four generations would consist of: the Lémann brothers, Léon Bloy, Jacques and Raïssa Maritain, Sophie van Leer, Dietrich von Hildebrand, Erik Peterson, Annie Kraus, Alfred Fuchs, Rudolf Lämmel, Walter Berger, Waldemar Gurian, Paul Démann, Renée Bloch, Gregory Baum, Geza Vermes, Theodor Haecker, Gertrud Luckner, Bruno Hussar, Miriam Rookmaaker van Leer, Ottilie Schwarz, Leo Rudloff, Jean-Roger Hené, Charlotte Klein, Kurt Hruby, Irene Marinoff, Karl Thieme, and Johannes Oesterreicher. There are hardly even exceptions to prove the rule, at least not on the European continent. Without converts to Catholicism, the Catholic Church would never have "thought its way" out of the challenges of racist anti-Judaism. And so if Providence remains visibly active for the Catholic Church in history, it can be seen in how the Church has absorbed light from beyond its visible membership.

The high percentage of Jewish converts like Oesterreicher makes sense: they hoped to resolve a tension within themselves between present and past. As a result, they helped heal a rift between past and present in the church, returning Catholicism to the Jewish sources of its heritage which, as St. Paul foresaw, Christians have always been tempted to disown. Chapter four of *Nostra Aetate* emphasized obvious facts buried for centuries: the Jewishness of Jesus, of the early saints, and of holy scripture. The broader function of converts, whether from Jewish or Protestant families, in promoting tolerance also makes sense. These were people who learned to thrive amidst complex intermixings of ethnic and religious groups before they became Catholic. Hildebrand was raised speaking French, Italian, and German in Florence and Munich; Oesterreicher spoke German and rudimentary Czech in multiethnic Moravia before learning Hebrew; Karl Thieme hailed from Saxony but was entirely at home in the Swiss/German/French borderlands of his mother's side of the family; Gertrud Luckner was born of German parents in Liverpool as Jane Hartmann, became a Quaker (and then Catholic) and maintained British citizenship to the end of her life. In the 1930s she organized an English Club in Freiburg.[57] In his teenage years, Oesterreicher was active in leftist Zionist scouting, and Jacques Maritain and Karl Thieme belonged to socialist groups before moving on to left-wing variants of "third way" movements.[58] Though now considered by many an arch-conservative Catholic, the young Dietrich von Hildebrand moved easily among non-Christian phenomenologists in Göttingen as well as the Catholic left-wing in France.

Just as the Apostle Paul always considered himself a Jew, none of these Catholics left their former selves behind. Oesterreicher cherished the company of Jewish friends from Moravia, and he always honored the memory of his "dear parents." And just as he vigorously refuted all claims that he was no longer Jewish, so his friend Karl Thieme proclaimed himself a Protestant influence upon Catholicism. Nothing predestined their becoming Catholic, but once they crossed the boundaries of the new faith, the converts represented a "church" that was less bounded, exploiting freedoms afforded within this community to make it a place more hospitable to their original selves. These converts knew about fluid boundaries from their Central Europe homelands, a region of notoriously incomplete nation states, either mixing ethnicities into combustible mixtures, leaving huge numbers of ostensible national groups outside national boundaries, or failing to produce anything like a nation, as was the case in Austria of the 1930s, where Catholic émigrés debated the reality of racial boundaries.

We will never fully understand why this motley group converted to Catholicism. The decisions were individual. Oesterreicher said he fell in love with Christ; Thieme that he was repelled by German Protestants' rejection of Jewish converts; Erik Peterson that he came to understand Catholicism—for all its problems—as embodying the "church" in terms of apostolic succession. But what gave them their predispositions? A series of lightning strikes would serve as well as any other explanation. What we do know is that they expected the church to live up to its catholicity.

Yet there is more to their role in the church than sensitivity to hypocrisy. Like other converts, they felt specially touched by grace: conversion involved embracing a mission from God, and one's life had to be visibly new. We see in John Oesterreicher, but also Dietrich von Hildebrand and Karl Thieme, not only passion but obsessive fervor; not only involvement but extraordinary commitment based not simply in belief but unwavering conviction; not only disinterest in popularity but insistence upon influence. Conversion had involved not just willingness to accept but courage to refuse, and therefore a readiness to defend unpopular positions. Many people are tempted to leave secure communities of origin—religious or otherwise—but converts are those who have summoned the conviction to do so, and it was belief rather than doubt that characterized them.

They were perhaps the least cynical of Catholics, and idealism led them to hone a sense of the practical. Karl Thieme ridiculed Oesterreicher for his attempt to find Catholic voices against racism, yet he cultivated the highest figures in the Catholic hierarchy, including Freiburg's Archbishop Conrad Gröber—a man who had once espoused racist antisemitism, but during the war gave Gertrud Luckner funds to assist German Jews.[59] Oesterreicher agonized with Thieme about the compromises of the "timorous" Pius XII and was haunted by visions from Christian mystics of men in "red capes" standing passively at the foot of the cross, but we see him and Thieme in the company of men in red capes from the 1930s to the end of their lives.

The converts teach us something about solidarity. This book began as an open-ended study of Catholics who opposed racism and antisemitism in the interwar years. I wanted to find out about those who swam against the racist currents of their time. It turned out that virtually all of the Catholics concerned about protecting the "other" were people Catholics in Central Europe considered "others." The solidarity of these new Catholics with the other was in a sense self-interest: Oesterreicher recalled with bitterness that some Catholics refused to take Communion from the fingers of a "Jew."

Catholics fighting antisemitism were so unusual that Europeans of the time assumed they must be Jewish converts. The Gestapo took for granted that the "British" Gertrud Luckner came from a Jewish family, and his opponents in Vienna called Dietrich von Hildebrand "the Jew."[60] In her weekly newspaper against racism Irene Harand routinely assured her readers that she was a true "Aryan," the wife of an Austrian Captain. Occasionally, the activists did not deny the rumors. In the 1930s, French fascists accused Jacques Maritain of "violating the race" because of his marriage to Raïssa. He had "judafied his life," they said.[61] On this point, Maritain did not argue. As early as 1906 Jacques Maritain was praising his wife for her origins. "Everywhere she carries about with her the nobility and the privilege of the race from which she comes," he wrote.[62] He later claimed that association with Raïssa had made him Jewish—not merely "spiritually Jewish" (all Christians were that) but "ethnically Jewish—connected in my flesh and my sensibility to the tribes of Israel and their destiny."[63] In a sense the non-Jew Jacques Maritain, but also Karl Thieme or the Anglican James Parkes, went "native," much like Jesuit missionaries to China or Latin America, who imagined themselves parts of the cultures they were supposed to transform.[64]

Maritain felt solidarity with the Jewish other so strongly that the other seemed to become the self. Yet there was more. He liked the idea that as a "Jew" he was part of a special community, one that began with his wife, in whom he admired the "Jewish" vocation to "stimulate the human conscience" and demands for "absolute justice."[65] As a "Jew" Maritain was at the forefront of the struggle against racism in the United States and in

Europe.[66] Perhaps he also liked to think that Jews had the vocation of alerting Catholics to aspects of Christianity they had missed: in effect, Jewish neighbors reminded Catholics of Christ's command to love their neighbor as themselves—an originally Jewish idea.[67]

The presupposition of those bringing Christianity into the church was that the church was more than Catholicism or even Christianity. Maritain's meetings at Meudon in the 1930s included people of all backgrounds: Protestants, Jews, Hindus, Confucians, Marxists. Dietrich von Hildebrand liked the idea of making Austria a Catholic state, yet he likewise invited people of many backgrounds to write in his journal: Jews, Protestants, atheists. The entry fee as far as he was concerned was opposition to *Rassenwahn*: racial insanity. John Oesterreicher's failings as missionary gave him a new respect for the boundary separating Christians from Jews, yet he continued going back across that boundary all his life, seeking ideas that would make Catholicism less alienating to those outside. In a similar way, Karl Thieme felt at ease drawing upon the ideas of his Protestant home. He and Oesterreicher knew very well what constituted Catholic orthodoxy, but when it came to racism they happily published non-Catholics such as Eric Voegelin, Hans Kosmala (at whose institute in Vienna Oesterreicher perfected his Hebrew), Erwin Reisner (a convert from Catholicism), or Karl Barth, and like them, each read the Bible for himself. Cradle Catholics like Joseph Eberle or Father Bichlmair tended to defer to the scholastics. If "pure Catholic" sources had been available—from natural law or papal encyclicals—the Catholic converts would eagerly have exploited them. They were also guided by a simple logic. The susceptibility of the Christian churches to racism predated the split between Protestants and Catholics and pointed to earlier sources: a vision of the Jew rooted in basic Christian teachings.[68]

The trend continued after the war: to protect the church from paganism, these subversively orthodox converts persisted in ignoring Vatican warnings about the indifferentism of ecumenism. While keeping one ear open to Cardinal Bea and the local Catholic censors, Karl Thieme was listening with the other to Theodor Adorno, who told him that many Christians were in fact "poorly baptized heathens, who had not accepted Christianity, but took out their anger over the command to love on the Jews."[69] Thieme informed John Oesterreicher that the rabbis he knew were right in refusing "to call nations 'Christian peoples' or 'Christian West.'" In fact, he wrote, "these nations have at most fragments of Christians of evangelical, not to speak of Catholic confession."[70]

Among the most vital inspirations for John Oesterreicher, Jacques Maritain, and Karl Thieme came from the Jewish critic Maurice Samuel, who had taken for granted that antisemitism was "anti-Christian in the sense that it is repugnant to the spirit of Christianity." Yet "in connection with antisemitism the observation is actually pointless," Samuel wrote. "For antisemitism is not anti-Christian in the sense that it is un-Christian. It is the expression of the movement to put an end to the Christian episode in human history. While all other forms of hatred are lapses from Christian practice, antisemitism is the conspiratorial, implacable campaign against Christ the Jew ... it is precisely because Christ hatred is afraid to name itself and afraid to make the direct attack that it must find vent in the folk pathology which is antisemitism."[71] In other words, modern antisemitism pitted de-Christianized pagans against Jews. The Jewish intellectual Ernst Ludwig Ehrlich believed that Christianity failed as Christianity precisely when it became anti-Judaic. "Only when it is possible," he wrote, "to surmount completely the pseudo-theological hatred of Jews, will Christianity begin to heal inside, and be able to take real joy in its own gifts of salvation."[72]

Such thinking assumed that Christianity was something from Judaism for the sake of the non-Jewish nations. That view was not unchristian. To return to the question posed at this chapter's beginning about the call to baptize all nations in Matthew 28, that passage uses "*ethnos*" for nation, a word understood not to include the Jews. The "nations" to be baptized were the Gentiles. This was an interpretation Viennese Rabbi Armand Kaminka impressed upon Oesterreicher in their dispute of the 1930s. Kaminka, a scholar who had once collaborated with Theodor Herzl, was outraged at the expansion of Oesterreicher's Jewish mission *Pauluswerk* in 1936. "Along come the adherents of a faith in whose religious ethics there is not a single sentence not derived from our Hebrew scripture," he wrote, "and they do us the favor of offering us the salvation we ourselves have drawn forth."[73] Kaminka assumed that he and the Christians could argue from a common starting point: the self-evident validity of faith in God.

"Those who promote our conversion must know," he wrote, "that according to our firm belief, when they bury and fill in the pure wellsprings of ageless religious tradition in a Jewish soul, this soul will never strengthen in faith in God, nor will it become more robust in moral sensitivity. In our view shaking the faith of a Jew cannot be a pious work pleasing to God." Kaminka demanded that Catholics send "apostate Jews" to the nearest synagogue regardless of whether the person in question felt himself to be Jewish or wanted to be Christian. Catholics should say, "You do not need our help, son of the people whom God chose and to whom he proclaimed his teaching more than a thousand years before our faith emerged. Go back into your Jewish community and be a faithful Jew."[74] Oesterreicher's response to Kaminka revealed the schizophrenia of the Christian position at that point. In the course of a single essay, he wrote that the Israel of today was not the Israel of old, but that the Israel of today continued to be God's people. God demanded that Christians love his people Israel; but God "above all demanded the love of Israel to the Messiah which it failed to recognize."[75]

Though he never turned away a candidate for baptism, Oesterreicher appeared to reach Kaminka's viewpoint in old age, when he embraced Parisian Cardinal Lustiger's idea that the "'totality' of humanity according to God's plan is made up of Israel and the nations, who are to be finally united in the one and only Covenant."[76] The idea here is not one of Jews becoming Christians, or anything but Jews. It was Pauline, absorbed into Lustiger's thought as a result, indirectly, of the efforts of people like John Oesterreicher and Karl Thieme.

John Oesterreicher's life journey started from the tranquil environment of Habsburg Moravia, a once religiously dynamic region that Jesuit missions and forced expulsions had made ninety-eight percent Catholic centuries before his birth in 1904. Some years earlier, his father had left the security of a German-speaking island of Iglau in eastern Bohemia to take up a veterinary practice in another German region several counties to the east, Stadt Liebau. Thus began a life experience of liminality for Johannes ("Hans" as a child) Oesterreicher, of supporting one threatened identity against the burgeoning presence of another. From high school in Olmütz he made his way to multiethnic Vienna, and there he happened upon the stirring preacher Max Josef Metzger, missionary of ecumenism and peace, who would be executed by the Nazi Regime in 1944 for his inability to suppress his deep conviction that Nazism must fail. One man of unswerving conviction baptized another man of unswerving conviction. In the years immediately following ordination Oesterreicher organized Catholic scouting in the mountains west of Vienna, drawing upon the knowledge and sensitivity of his years in Zionist youth. In 1929, he returned to the Austrian capital, and Father Metzger made him editor of the ecumenical journal *Missionsruf*. Four years after that, at the tender age of thirty, Oesterreicher founded his own journal, *Die Erfüllung*, where he combined personal experience of discrimination with newly acquired editorial skills to combat Nazi antisemitism.

He did so from a place that would seem as unsuited for such work as any place Europe. Michael Mann has called the Austrofascist regime of Englbert Dollfuss one of five cases of a successful *fascist* movement in power. But far from unsuited, Vienna was predestined. In addition to Oesterreicher, there was the intrepid Irene Harand, who built the World League Against Racial Hatred and Human Need in Vienna and in 1934 alone distributed a million copies of her anti-Nazi weekly *Gerechtigkeit*. Austrofascist Vienna had as vice-mayor Ernst Karl Winter, one of Europe's staunchest opponents of nationalism, it produced a diverse and vibrant Jewish press, and it permitted anti-Nazi émigrés to function freely. Dietrich von Hildebrand and Irene Harand made clear that the Christian corporatist world afforded them ideal working conditions; for them, Engelbert Dollfuss was not a fascist but a martyr for human rights— rights that Weimar democracy had failed to protect by permitting the rise of Nazism.[77]

Because it harbored both racism and anti-racism, Oesterreicher's Austrofascist Vienna produced the fiercest clash in these two "Catholic" options in Europe, helping propel the process leading to Vatican II. Catholics in Austria felt the temptation but also revulsion of Nazism more keenly than Christians to the west or east; the revulsion in turn generated a return to Paul's letter to the Romans, which led to the new vision of the Jews expressed in *Nostra Aetate*.

But the Austrian specificity was also a matter of demography. Further east, Catholics interpreted the size of Jewish communities—in some urban settings, one-third the population—as ruling out compromise. The

"Jewish problem" was thought to require a radical solution, and the consensus on this matter was so overwhelming that one can count alternative views among Polish Catholics on the fingers of one hand.[78] Further west and north—including Oesterreicher's Moravian hometown of Stadt Liebau—Jewish communities were smaller, and the Jewish question was not as prominent in the consciousness of Catholics. If antisemitism has social bases, then it was bound to be more a factor in areas where Jews were more socially relevant. So too with its critics. In that sense, Vienna was a city of the center: where Jews were relevant enough to fuel the fears of nationally minded Catholics, but not so numerous that there was practically no willingness to think of them as co-citizens.

For all the books written on interwar Europe, conceptual confusion persists on how to describe the politics of that unsettled time. Political expectations of the decades before 1914 or after 1945 give little guidance as to how to locate people religiously in the years between the wars. Christian progressives fomented racism while conservatives opposed it. Religion and politics had an ambivalent relationship, reminding one of the philosopher Ernst Bloch's idea of "non-simultaneous" historical development. Many German Catholic thinkers of the 1920s embraced theological modernity, rejecting the neo-scholastic belief that the natural and supernatural were separate worlds; they were determined to tear down the walls of the Catholic ghetto, becoming socially relevant after the persecution and isolation of the *Kulturkampf.* Young Catholics organized in youth movements and became active in politics, a politics that validated the irrational and praised the "vital" and "organic." They eagerly accepted the arguments of brown Catholics who were building bridges between Christianity and Nazism.[79]

Those who keep his thought alive describe Dietrich von Hildebrand's anti-Nazi opposition as a direct result of his "personalist" philosophy.[80] No doubt there is truth to this, though personalists in other contexts did not reject antisemitism; in fact, some seemed drawn toward fascistic "third ways."[81] But more important is the question of what drew Hildebrand to personalism to begin with. If one looks at him and the group around him, the explanation for their engagement is not personalist philosophy, but personal history: the unpredictable legacy of converts.

Converts to Catholicism

It was above all as Catholic Christians that Oesterreicher, Hildebrand, Thieme, and Waldemar Gurian fought antisemitism. Irene Harand said that antisemitism "dishonored" Christianity, but for them the problem went deeper: antisemitism undid Christianity's claims to recognizing the supremacy of God over creation; it made Christian churches places of pagan cultism, worshiping not the Lord but the idol of race. This was what Karl Thieme meant when he wrote Pius XI in October 1933 that Protestant churches discriminating against Jewish converts had become a "new church," no longer abiding by the will of Him who had commanded His followers to give unto God what was God's, and unto Caesar what was Caesar's.

Until that point in his busy life, Thieme had no special interest in antisemitism—other than that he opposed it as a Marxian socialist—but the shock of witnessing Christianity reduced to paganism had quickly opened his mind to a powerful countertruth to Nazi racism: that Jesus had loved his people, "baptized or not." A few months later, he and John Oesterreicher inaugurated their lifelong work against antisemitism because they wanted to protect Christianity from blasphemy; thirty years later, we see the same passion and conviction still alive in both men: Thieme, stricken with cancer, lecturing students at Swiss Einsiedeln to his last breath; and Oesterreicher at the Council in Rome, pulling aside any bishop who would listen to his message: the decree on the Jews was about the "inner life of the Church," its very capacity to act as an instrument of salvation for humankind.[82]

For converts, anti-racist conviction often built upon familial solidarity, but the process of creation involved intense dispute; especially after the war, struggles over the theology necessary to refute antisemitism became so heated that they divided comrades of a quarter century such as John Oesterreicher and Karl Thieme. Thieme was a Socialist in the tradition of Karl Marx, and one can compare his efforts to stem anti-Judaism in Christianity to those of Marxist revisionists trying to reform Soviet-style socialism. In both cases, revisionism involved a return to original sources and their "true" interpretations. But there is also a limit to this comparison: Catholics felt they were advancing not simply knowledge but inspired, esoteric understanding, something they not only argued over but prayed for and hoped to attain through the workings of the Holy Spirit. The issue was not only reasoned dispute, but finding a new language to give truer access to mysteries of faith. Given the degree of change the converts ultimately effected, the process could only be understood as invested with special blessing.

New ideas gained through debate and interpretation were therefore essential but not sufficient. In the 1930s, the converts had embarked on a journey whose end they could not see. The young priest Johannes Oesterreicher possessed no orientation in Christian thought besides seminary education spiced with readings of Protestants and former Protestants like Kierkegaard and Cardinal Newman. His goal at the beginning was the opposite of what became the end point: it was to convert the Jews and not the church. To retrace his journey is to suggest a reorientation for historians working on Christian-Jewish relations, who often look through moments in the past as one might browse through a box of old postcards, pulling out the exotic ones that appeal to or repel the sensitivity of one's own day. Histories of Christian thought on the Jews survey the past for people who seem ahead of their time or behind our own, people who used today's language in spite of the language of their time. Perhaps they do so because re-creating the context in which antisemitic ideas were spoken is a perilous exercise. In 2008, Adam Gopnik wrote that those who claim we must understand the antisemitism of a Christian like G. K. Chesterton in the "context of his time" may in fact serve to make easy excuses that foreclose deeper understanding of Chesterton and of his time.[83] Thus, we have biographies praising Irene Harand or finding fault with Pius XII as if these long-dead Catholics were our contemporaries. This kind of procedure, focusing on the supposed "static essence of Christianity rather than its changing history," tells us little about the Catholic Church's journey to *Nostra Aetate* or indeed the new appreciation expressed at the Vatican Council in other statements: on religious freedom, human dignity, or the church in the world.[84]

Not only the end point of this journey but also its intellectual starting point defy what we have been led to think about the church. For one thing, its history is indeed not of static essence but of change, change produced by struggle. For another thing, the new church teaching of *Nostra*

Aetate grew out of a dispute about racism that had entered Christianity. According to current understanding, race should not have been an issue for Catholics, especially where the Jews were concerned. Even anthropologists agreed the Jews were not a race, and in its openness to converts, the Catholic Church could claim to be race-blind—not perfectly, but more so than any other institution in the early twentieth century. Yet it was precisely racial discrimination that drew Johannes Oesterreicher and his friends into conflict with the Nazis and with many co-believers, whom he called "brown Catholics."

With the turn to Paul's letter to the Romans, Oesterreicher and other Catholic converts also turned inward to gaze upon their own anti-Judaism, however. The achievement of the prewar period—to remind Catholics that Jews could *become* Christians—seemed to make impossible an answer to the urgent question of the postwar period: should there be a mission to the Jews after Auschwitz? Except for the Anglican James W. Parkes, before World War II no Christian theologian of note interpreted St. Paul to imply that Jews could be saved without turning to Christ.

Paul had indeed supplied a refutation to the Catholic racism that emerged in the 1930s; but with his idea of Israel of the spirit existing separately from Israel of the flesh (Romans 9), Paul also figured as a progenitor of Catholic anti-Judaism. Over the centuries, other Christians had built upon this idea, claiming that Israel of the flesh was bound to suffer torment until the day it realized its true calling. Before the war, Johannes Oesterreicher was a foremost apostle of this view, writing that whoever tears the heart out of his body must die.[85] After the war, he and other Christians faced a second urgent question, inseparably bound to the question of mission: was the murder of six million Jews, including over a million children, a further sign to Jews that they must turn to Jesus?

Because of his own Jewish parents, Oesterreicher was quick to grasp the idea that the Holocaust was not punishment from God. He had greater difficulty than Karl Thieme in abandoning his mission to the Jews because he insisted that Jews were no less in need of grace mediated by the church than anyone else. Not to hold out the fruits of baptism to Jews was a negative discrimination. Yet, as we see in his letters to the seminarian David Connor, by 1960 he thought the church's relation to the Jews must be ecumenical. In meetings of the Secretariat for Christian Unity in 1961,

Oesterreicher revealed his unwillingness to live with the anti-Judaic assumptions of fellow Catholics—still very alive among theologians in the Secretariat, including Cardinal Augustin Bea, who said that Jews brought destruction upon themselves by rejecting Christ. To undo this idea, the church returned to scripture, and emphasized three messages inspired by Paul's letter to the Romans, Chapter 11: first, that the Jews are very dear to God; second, that the promises of God to the Jewish people remain in place to the end of time; third, that the church looks forward to a day when "all peoples will address the Lord in a single voice." No mention is made of conversion. *Without this turn to Paul's letter to the Romans, the church would have had no language to speak to the Jews after the Holocaust.* The new reading was not preordained by the Holocaust, however: ultimately it was the personal solidarity of the converts that was needed to take the church into the postconciliar understandings.

In recognizing that special blessings rested upon the Jews, the universal church spoke in terms of one people's particular identity, but five decades later we see that recognizing the particular also led to a new appreciation for the universal. Without its need to speak about the Jews after the Holocaust, the church may not have spoken about other non-Christian faiths. But having spoken about the Jews, it could not remain silent on the others. In *Nostra Aetate* the church celebrated the truth in Hinduism, Buddhism, and Islam before speaking of the Jews.[86] Then, after chapter four on the Jews, it logically condemned all discrimination by race or nationality. By answering the question "Who are the Jews?" the Catholic Church had found its way across previously insurmountable boundaries to tolerance, to recognizing that God extends grace to all humans.

That was the church that John Oesterreicher inhabited after the Council, when he quarreled with a new generation of scholars for whom he seemed insufficiently progressive. He also became a fierce proponent of Israel's mission in the Holy Land, and in his last decade pondered his own journey next to that of his fellow convert Cardinal Jean Lustiger of Paris. We see in John Oesterreicher's long life, stretching from the relative peace of Habsburg Moravia in 1904 to the turbulence of an American metropolis at the height of the Cold War eighty years later, how each chapter built upon the other, creating sense visible only in retrospect. His life and the life of the church were not snapshots but a moving picture where each answer emerged out of the solutions to the previous stage's problems, all connected; only after turning his mind to the problem of racism could he see the problem of anti-Judaism; only after embracing the tasks of missionary to the Jews could he become missionary to the Christians; and, only after losing both parents in the Holocaust could he come to appreciate the enduring presence of their world in his new home.

Notes

Introduction

1. Witold Bereś and Krzysztof Burnetko, *Duchowny niepokorny: Rozmowy z księdzem Stanisławem Musiałem* (Warsaw, 2006), 137. On the origins and degree of change, see also the fundamental study of Michael Phayer, *The Catholic Church and the Holocaust, 1930–1965* (Bloomington, Ind., 2000), 208–215 and passim.

2. Edward Flannery, *The Anguish of the Jews: Twenty-Three Centuries of Antisemitism*, rev. ed. (New York, 1985).

3. US Conference of Catholic Bishops, "A Note on Ambiguities Contained in Reflections on Covenant and Mission," 18 June 2009, at http://www.usccb.org/doctrine/covenant09.pdf (accessed 25 July 2011).

4. John Cornwell maintains a strict separation between "racist antisemitism and religious antisemitism." John Cornwell, *Hitler's Pope: The Secret History of Pius XII* (New York, 1999), 28. Susan Zuccotti argues that while Pius XI failed to speak out on anti-Judaism, he did condemn racism. Susan Zuccotti, *Under His Very Windows: The Vatican and the Holocaust in Italy* (New Haven and London, 2001), 21–23, 30, 33–35. References to Catholic racism are sprinkled throughout a vast literature on Christianity and antisemitism. Alan Davies notes the widespread currency of "racist terminology" among French Catholics of the late nineteenth century. The one case of a priest claiming that Jews could not be converted because of their racial traits was the cleric Ernest Jouin. Alan Davies, *Infected Christianity: A Study of Modern Racism* (Montreal, 1988), 142. David Kertzer works his way through additional cases scattered through time and space. "Given the level of hostility against Jews inculcated by the Church," Kertzer asserts that it "strained credulity to imagine that a people so demonic could be so easily changed, that the person who until yesterday was Jewish could today be one of us." David Kertzer, *The Popes against the Jews* (New York, 2001), 211. Some historians depict Catholicism of the 1930s as steadfast against racism and therefore

also against racist antisemitism. See Hubert Wolf "'Pro perfidis Judaeis,' Die 'Amici Israel' und ihr Antrag auf eine Reform der Karfreitagsfürbitte für die Juden (1928)." *Historische Zeitschrift* 279, no. 3 (December 2004), 655; Thomas Brechenmacher, *Der Vatikan und die Juden: Geschichte einer unheiligen Beziehung vom 16. Jahrhundert bis zur Gegenwart* (Munich, 2005), 161. The official view has been that Catholicism was unaffected by racism. See, for example, the report "Text of Vatican Document on the Holocaust," *New York Times*, 17 March 1998. For a lucid general discussion of the place of racism in Catholic antisemitism, see Urs Altermatt, *Katholizismus und Antisemitismus: Mentalitäten, Kontinuitäten, Ambilenzen* (Frauenfeld, 1999), 120–124.

5. Olaf Blaschke is one of the few scholars to express well-grounded skepticism about Catholicism's resistance to racism. See his *Katholizismus und Antisemitismus im Deutschen Kaiserreich* (Göttingen, 1999).

6. For a perceptive discussion of this relationship, see Christhard Hoffmann, "Christlicher Antijudaismus und moderner Antisemitismus," in *Christlicher Antijudaismus und Antisemitismus: Theologische und kirchliche Programme deutscher Christen*, ed. Leonore Siegele-Wenschkewitz (Frankfurt am Main, 1994), 293–317.

7. From 1958, he published the journal *Christus en Israël*. Hedwig Wahle, "Some Known and Unknown Pioneers of Continental Europe," *SIDIC* 30 (1997/2), 2–9. He benefited from contacts with Jewish converts. Geert van Klinken, *Christelijke stemmen over het Jodendom: Zestig jaar Interkerkelijk Contact Israël (ICI), 1946–2006* (Delft, 2009), 36.

8. Anton Ramselaar, "Events and Persons," *SIDIC* 1 (1968/3), 11–15.

9. Christhard Hoffmann has written that the "religious tradition of Judeophobia has no specific relevance for political and social historical interpretations of modern Antisemitism. It is usually not even referred to as an explanatory factor." Rather, historians like Hans Rosenberg or Peter J. Pulzer focused on economic slump, impeded social mobility of the lower middle classes, and manipulation by new political movements. The new quality of antisemitism could not be explained by Christianity in a period where Christianity rapidly appeared to be losing its social relevance. Jews were targeted because they were considered "'undoubted representatives of the liberal-capitalist economic system and of bourgeois modernity.'" "Christlicher Antijudaismus," 300–301.

10. On the debunking of old paradigms, see Margaret Lavinia Anderson, "The Limits of Secularization: On the Problem of the Catholic Revival in 19th Century Germany," *Historical Journal*, 38, no. 3 (1995), 647–670; Christopher Clark and Wolfram Kaiser, eds., *Culture Wars: Secular-Catholic Conflict in Nineteenth-Century Europe* (Cambridge, United Kingdom, 2003). Olaf Blaschke describes religious antisemitism as "a complete system" within Catholicism of the Kaiserreich, reflecting a "deep underlying structure," including talk of Jews as anti-Christ, the syndrome of Judas, the Jewish mockery of Jesus, deicide, divine condemnation, "substitution thesis," belief in Jewish "legal fanaticism," and instrumentalizing of Jews for salvation understood in Christian terms. *Katholizismus und Antisemitismus*, 89.

11. For the conflicting messages, see Adolf Kardinal Bertram, *Hirtenbriefe und Hirtenworte* (Cologne, 2000), 437, 510.

12. Bernard Lazare, *Antisemitism, Its History and Causes* (New York, 1903); Anatole Leroy-Beaulieu, *Israel among the Nations: A Study of the Jews and Antisemitism*, trans. Frances Hellman (New York, 1895); Abram Leon Sachar, *Sufferance Is the Badge* (New York and London, 1940); Solomon Andhil Fineberg, *Overcoming Antisemitism* (New York and London, 1943). See also Abraham S. Schomer, *The Primary Cause of Antisemitism: An Answer to the Jewish Question* (New York, 1909); William W. Simpson, *Jews and Christians Today: A Study in Jewish and Christian Relationships* (London, 1940); Hugo Valentin, *Antisemitism: Historically and Critically Examined* (New York, 1936).

1. The Problem of Catholic Racism

1. Instead, Catholicism preached the inviolability of the "human person," and made a decisive contribution to our current understanding of human rights. Samuel Moyn, "Personalism, Community, and the Origins of Human Rights," *Human Rights in the Twentieth Century*, ed. Stefan-Ludwig Hoffmann (Cambridge, 2011), 91. The description of the church as ostensible "bulwark against the disorders afflicting the age" comes from Andrew J. Bacevich, "Selling our Souls: Of Idolatry and iPhones," *Commonweal*, 12 August 2011, 11.

2. Stephen Ochs, *Desegregating the Altar: The Josephites and the Struggle for Black Priests, 1871–1960* (Baton Rouge, La., 1990), 283.

3. Ibid., 283–284.

4. *New York Times*, 30 October 1939, 1.

5. David W. Southern, *John LaFarge and the Limits of Catholic Interracialism, 1911–1963* (Baton Rouge, La., 1996), 191; Ochs, *Desegregating*, 202–203.

6. The New Testament contains calls to bring Christ to Jews. Matthew 10:5–7 calls upon the disciples to preach to the "lost sheep" of the house of Israel. Luke 24:47 commands that "repentance and forgiveness of sins should be preached in his name to all nations, beginning from Jerusalem." Acts 1:8 calls the disciples to be "witnesses in all Judea and Samaria and to the end of the earth." Acts 2:36–38 reads: "Let all the house of Israel therefore know assuredly that God has made him both Lord and Christ, this Jesus whom you crucified . . . 'Repent and be baptized every one of you in the name of Jesus Christ . . .'" Thanks to David Hollinger for these citations.

7. In 1934, the Holy Office considered consulting Wilhelm Schmidt to draft a Vatican condemnation of "race and blood as bases of religion." Dominik Burkard, *Häresie und Mythus des 20. Jahrhunderts: Rosenbergs nationalsozialistische Weltanschauung vor dem Tribunal der Römischen Inquisition* (Paderborn, 2005), 357.

8. Faulhaber concurred with Hitler on the need to combat racial degeneration, though he said that Catholic methods differed from those of the Nazis. Peter Pfister, Susanne Kornacker, Volker Laube, eds., *Kardinal Michael von Faulhaber 1869–1952: Eine Ausstellung des Archivs des Erzbistums München und Freising, des*

Bayerischen Hauptstaatarchivs und des Stadtarchivs München zum 50. Todestag (Munich, 2002), 541–547.

9. Ludwig Volk, ed., *Akten deutscher Bischöfe über die Lage der Kirche 1933–1945*, vol. 6: 1943–1945 (Mainz, 1985), 144.

10. John V. H. Dippel, *Two against Hitler: Stealing the Nazis' Best-Kept Secrets* (Westport, Conn., 1992), 7–8, 102–03.

11. Hermann Muckermann, *Rassenforschung und Volk der Zukunft* (Berlin, 1928), 18–19.

12. Ibid., 17.; "Ewiges Gesetz" (1957), cited in Dagmar Grosch-Obenauer, "Hermann Muckermann und die Eugenik" (Ph.D. diss., University of Mainz, 1986), 30.

13. Muckermann, *Rassenforschung*, 36

14. He also objected to Jewish immigration into Germany. Muckermann, *Rassenforschung*, 19–20; and *Grundriss der Rassenkunde*, 121–123 cited in Grosch-Obenauer, "Hermann Muckermann," 32.

15. Hermann Muckermann, *Volkstum, Staat und Nation eugenisch gesehen* (Essen, 1933), 69, 73–75; cited in Hermann Greive, *Theologie und Ideologie: Katholizismus und Judentum in Deutschland und Österreich 1918–1935* (Heidelberg, 1969), 134.

16. Muckermann, *Rassenforschung*, 16.

17. Muckermann, *Grundriss der Rassenkunde*, 2nd ed. (Paderborn, 1935), 122. See also Dagmar Herzog, *Sex after Fascism: Memory and Morality in Twentieth Century Germany* (Princeton, N.J., 2005), 44–45.

18. He exerted considerable influence on elites active in welfare policy, social work, and education. Michael Schwartz, "Konfessionelle Milieus und Weimarer Eugenik," *Historische Zeitschrift* 261, no. 2 (October 1995), 420, 422. On Pacelli's esteem for Muckermann, see Houten, *Two against Hitler*, 8.

19. Nothing came of Muckermann's request to found an institute for family studies at the Vatican. Pius did, however, present him with a rosary for his mother. Friedrich Muckermann, *Im Kampf zwischen zwei Epochen. Lebenserinnerungen*, ed. Nikolaus Junk (Mainz, 1973), 242–243.

20. Muckermann, *Im Kampf*, 242–243; Grosch-Obenauer, "Hermann Muckermann," 1–13.

21. Houten, *Two against Hitler*, 102.

22. Ibid., 15.

23. Muckermann also gained Respondek's wife access to Pius XII via his old friend Robert Leiber, the pope's secretary and also a German Jesuit. Ibid., 102–104; John H. Waller, *The Unseen War in Europe: Espionage and Conspiracy in the Second World War* (London, 1996), 197.

24. Houten, *Two against Hitler*, 7.

25. Ibid., 145.

26. Suzanne Marchand, "Priests among the Pygmies: Wilhelm Schmidt and the Counter-Reformation in Austrian Ethnology," in *Worldly Provincialism: German Anthropology in the Age of Empire*, Social History, Popular Culture, and Politics in Germany Series, ed. H. Glenn Penny and Matti Bunzl (Ann Arbor, Mich., 2003).

27. John LaFarge, *Interracial Justice: A Study of the Catholic Doctrine of Race Relations* (New York, 1937), 12–13.

28. Antonio Messineo, "Gli elementi costitutivi della nazione e la razza," *La Civiltà Cattolica*, 6 August 1938.

29. It is the leading journal to this day because of its competitor's closer association with Nazi racial science. Thomas Hauschild, "Christians, Jews, and the Other in German Anthropology," *American Anthropologist* 4 (1997), 747.

30. See Wilhelm Schmidt, *Der Ursprung der Gottesidee: eine historisch-kritische und positive Studie*, 12 vols. (Münster, 1926–1955).

31. Wilhelm Schmidt, *Rasse und Volk: Eine Untersuchung zur Bestimmung ihrer Grenzen und zur Erfassung ihrer Beziehungen* (Munich, 1927), 13.

32. Cited in Edouard Conte, "Völkerkunde und Faschismus? Fragen an ein vernachlässigtes Kapitel deutsch-österreichischer Wissenschaftsgeschichte," in *Kontinuität und Bruch 1938—1945—1955. Beiträge zur österreichischen Kultur- und Wissenschaftsgeschichte*, ed. Friedrich Stadler (Vienna, Munich, 1988), 240.

33. Cited in Conte, "Völkerkunde," 239.

34. The second edition of his major work *Rasse und Volk* could not appear in Germany in 1935 and was published in Austria as *Rasse und Volk: Ihre allgemeine Bedeutung, ihre Geltung im Deutschen Raum* (Salzburg, 1935). Ilsemarie Walter, "Missionsarbeit, Rassentheorie und Geschlechterbeziehungen; eine Annährung an das Thema" (Seminararbeit, Department of History, University of Vienna, 2003), 8.

35. Karl Josef Rivinius, *Biographisch-Bibliographisches Kirchenlexikon* 17 (2000), 1231–1246.

36. From Wilhelm Schmidt, *Die Stellung der Religion zu Rasse und Volk* (Augsburg, 1932), 8, 24–25, cited in Walter, "Missionsarbeit," 9.

37. Schmidt, *Die Stellung der Religion*, 27, cited in Walter, "Missionsarbeit," 10.

38. Hedwig Köb has argued that Schmidt never resolved the tension between his loyalty to the church and his desire to produce first-class science. He stood between the "fronts of the [Catholic Church's] struggle with modernity." Hedwig Köb, "Die Wiener Schule der Völkerkunde als Antithese zum Evolutionismus. Pater Wilhelm Schmidt und der Streit um Evolutionismus und Naturwissenschaft in der Ethnologie" (Diplomarbeit, Department of History, University of Vienna, 1996), 58.

39. Walter, "Missionsarbeit," 12.

40. Cited in Conte, "Völkerkunde," 239.

41. Hans Kreidler, *Eine Theologie des Lebens: Grundzüge im theologischen Denken Karl Adams* (Mainz, 1988), cited in Andrea Tafferner, *Gottes- und Nächstenliebe in der deutschsprachigen Theologie des 20. Jahrhunderts* (Innsbruck, 1992), 53.

42. Robert Anthony Krieg, *Karl Adam: Catholicism in German Culture* (Notre Dame, Ind., 1992), 52.

43. Karl Adam, *The Spirit of Catholicism*, trans. Justin McCann (New York, 1960), 176–178.

44. Karl Adam, "Deutsches Volkstum und katholisches Christentum," *Theologische Quartalschrift* 114 (1933), 40–63, cited in Georg Denzler, "Antijudaismus

und Antisemitismus in der Theologie unserer Jahrhunderts: Karl Adam, Michael Schmaus, und Anton Stonner," *Facta Universitatis, Series Law and Politics* 1, no. 1 (1997), 12. On Adam, see also Kevin Spicer, *Hitler's Priests: Catholic Clergy and National Socialism* (DeKalb, Ill., 2008).

45. The lecture's title was "Jesus Christ and the Spirit of our Time." Cited in Krieg, *Karl Adam*, 131.

46. Denzler, "Antijudaismus," 13.

47. Adam, *Spirit of Catholicism*, 39, 41.

48. Ibid., 37; Adam, "Deutsches Volkstum," 40ff., cited in Greive, *Theologie*, 178.

49. Adam, "Deutsches Volkstum," 40ff., cited in Greive, *Theologie*, 180.

50. Denzler, "Antijudaismus," 14.

51. Pope Benedict XVI, *Jesus of Nazareth* (New York, 2007), xi.

52. Lucia Scherzberg, *Kirchenreform mit Hilfe des Nationalsozialismus: Karl Adam als kontextueller Theologe* (Darmstadt, 2001) 115.

53. For Vidler, Merton, and Orwell see Robert A. Krieg, "Karl Adam, National Socialism, and Christian Tradition," *Theological Studies* 60 (1999), 439; Hans Küng, *My Struggle for Freedom: Memoirs*, trans. John Bowden (Grand Rapids, Mich., 2003), 222; James Carroll, *Constantine's Sword: The Church and the Jews: A History* (Boston, 2002), 518.

54. Küng, *My Struggle*, 222.

55. Krieg, "Karl Adam, National Socialism," 446.

56. Küng, *My Struggle*, 222.

57. Yves Congar, "Ecclesia ab Abel"; Karl Rahner, "Zur Theologie der Busse bei Tertullian," *Abhandlungen über Theologie und Kirche*, Festschrift für Karl Adam, ed. Marcel Reding (Düsseldorf, 1952). 79–108, 139–168.

58. Guenter Lewy, *The Catholic Church and Nazi Germany* (Cambridge, Mass., 2000), 276.

59. See Dorothy Thompson's introduction to Kurt von Schuschnigg, *My Austria* (New York, 1938), xxii–xxiii.

60. Aurel Kolnai, *Political Memoirs*, ed. Francesca Murphy (Lanham, Md., 1999), 117–188.

61. Gudula Walterskirchen, *Engelbert Dollfuss, Arbeitermörder oder Heldenkanzler* (Vienna, 2004).

62. Jana Leichsenring, "Die katholische Gemeinde in Theresienstadt und die Berliner Katholiken," *Theresienstädter Studien und Dokumente* 11 (2004), 188–189.

63. Clemens Holzmeister, ed., *Kirche im Kampf* (Vienna, 1936).

64. Georg Bichlmair, "Der Christ und der Jude," in Holzmeister, ed., *Kirche im Kampf*, 169–170.

65. Michael Kater, *Doctors under Hitler* (Chapel Hill, N.C., 1989), 83.

66. Albert Niedermeyer, *Wahn, Wissenschaft und Wahrheit: Lebensbekenntnisse eines Arztes*, 3rd ed. (Salzburg, 1934), 191.

67. Ibid., 194.

68. Ibid., 188, 191.

69. Ingrid Richter, *Katholizismus und Eugenik in der Weimarer Republik und im Dritten Reich: Zwischen Sittlichkeitsreform und Rassenhygiene* (Paderborn, 2001), 320.

70. Niedermeyer, *Wahn*, 197.

71. Ibid., 201.

72. Ibid., 201–202.

73. Alois Hudal, *Grundlagen des Nationalsozialismus: Eine ideengeschichtliche Untersuchung von katholischer Warte* (Leipzig and Vienna, 1937). The book's impact is hard to gauge. In Austria, the book went through five printings and found many adherents. Most of the two thousand copies of the book's first edition sent into Germany were confiscated, however. Peter Eppel, *Zwischen Kreuz und Hakenkreuz: Die Haltung der Zeitschrift "Schönere Zukunft" zum Nationalsozialismus in Deutschland 1934–1938* (Vienna, 1980), 332.

74. St. Thomas Aquinas, *Summa Theologica*, II/II q, 172, a. 6c. Cited in Hudal, *Grundlagen*, 17.

75. Hudal, *Grundlagen*, 15–17.

76. "'Race' is more than an imaginary abstraction" (ibid., 76–77).

77. Ibid., 87.

78. Ibid.

79. Ibid., 89.

80. Among the war criminals he helped escape via the Vatican were Franz Stangl and perhaps also Gestapo chief Heinrich Müller and Adolf Eichmann. Rena Giefer and Thomas Giefer, *Die Rattenlinie: Fluchtwege der Nazis* (Frankfurt am Main, 1991), 99–100.

81. Eppel, *Zwischen Kreuz*, 250, 297.

82. Cited in Joop Wekking, *Untersuchungen zur Rezeption der nationalsozialistischen Weltanschauung in den konfessionellen Periodika der Niederlande 1933–1940* (Amsterdam, 1990), 249.

83. Jacob Nötges, *Nationalsozialismus und Katholizismus* (Cologne, 1931), 159. On the condemnation, see Hubert Wolf, *Pope and Devil* (Cambridge, Mass., 2010), 141ff.

84. Kevin Spicer, *Resisting the Third Reich: The Catholic Clergy in Hitler's Berlin* (De Kalb, Ill., 2004), 136.

85. Reinhard Göllner, "Zeit der Bewährung: Die Katechetischen Blätter während der Nazi-Zeit," *Katechetische Blätter* 125, no. 4 (2000), 228–380.

86. Ibid.

87. *Katholisches Kirchenblatt* (Berlin), 7 November 1937, cited in *Schönere Zukunft*, 28 November 1937, 232.

88. "Innuendo by Nazis Arouses Catholics," *New York Times*, 17 December 1936, 14.

89. See, for example, the pastoral letter of Cologne's Archbishop Frings of 27 May 1945 in Volk, *Akten deutscher Bischöfe*, vol. 6, 501.

90. National unity could not be realized *exclusively* through the criteria of race and blood. In 1932, the Berlin diocesan newspaper criticized heathen nationalism that elevated "commonality of blood to its *highest* principle" (emphasis added). Spicer, *Resisting*, 124–125.

91. Werner Pütz, *Krieg und Nationalsozialismus im Bergischen Land* (Overath, 2005), 16.

92. Hirtenwort des deutschen Episkopats, 19 August 1943, in Volk, *Akten deutscher Bischöfe*, vol. 6, 201. For a similar statement by Bishop Konrad von Preysing of Berlin, see Spicer, *Resisting*, 130–131.

93. "If all the bishops on one particular day had taken a stand openly from the pulpit against the Nazis, then they could have prevented a lot of things from happening. But that did not occur and there is no excuse for that. If the bishops had been put in jail or in concentration camps because of this act, then that would not have hurt—to the contrary." Letter to Pastor Bernhard Custodis (Bonn), 23 February 1946. *Konrad Adenauer: Briefe 1945–1947*, ed. Hans Peter Mensing (Berlin, 1983), 172–173.

94. "Injustice remains injustice, even in the war, even toward the enemy, especially one who cannot defend himself." Pastoral letter of German bishops of 19 August 1943 in Volk, *Akten deutscher Bischöfe*, vol. 6, 179–183. For many other examples: Heinz Hürten, *Deutsche Katholiken 1918 bis 1945* (Paderborn, 1992).

95. Christianity "alienated people from the spirit of Nazism." See the argument of Richard Löwenthal, "Widerstand im totalitären Staat," in *Widerstand und Verweigerung in Deutschland 1933 bis 1945*, ed. Richard Löwenthal and Patrik von zur Mühlen, (Bonn, Berlin, 1982), 19–20.

96. Volk, *Akten deutscher Bischöfe*, 144.

97. Jeanne Benay, *L'Autriche 1918–1938* (Rouen, France, 1998), 192. The letter went through eight editions and was translated into foreign languages. Friedrich Heer, *God's First Love: Christians and Jews over Two Thousand Years*, trans. Geoffrey Skelton (London, 1970), 273.

98. Heer, *God's First Love*, 271–272.

99. Sylvia Maderegger, *Die Juden im österreichischen Ständestaat 1934–1938* (Vienna and Salzburg, 1973), 130.

100. From the pastoral letter of 21 January 1933, cited in Anton Pelinka, *Stand oder Klasse? Die christliche Arbeiterbewegung Österreichs, 1933–38* (Vienna, 1972), 216.

101. Rudolf Zinnhobler, "Studien zur Kirchengeschichte des Mittelalters und Neuzeit," in *Neues Archiv zur Geschichte der Diözese Linz* 10, eds. Johannes Ebner and Monika Würthinger (Virtuelles Museum Oberösterreich, 1996), 126; Stefan Moritz, *Grüß Gott und Heil Hitler: Katholische Kirche und Nationalsozialismus in Österreich* (Vienna, 2002), 38.

102. Moritz, *Grüß Gott*, 38.

103. For the Innitzer speech, see Maximillian Liebmann, "Die österreichischen Katholikentage," in *Geistiges Leben im Österreich der Ersten Republik*, ed. Isabella Ackerl (Munich, 1986), 161.

104. Christian Klösch, Kurt Scharr, and Erika Weinzierl, "Gegen Rassenhass und Menschennot," Irene Harand, *Leben und Werk einer ungewöhnlichen Widerstandskämpferin* (Innsbruck, Austria, 2004), 156.

105. This from Cardinal Theodor Innitzer's 1936 speech at the Pauluswerk. *Reichspost*, 14 February 1936, 4.

106. "Pfui Innitzer," *Time*, 24 October 1938.

107. "Classic Tragedy," *Time*, 17 July 1939.

108. Moritz, *Grüß Gott*, 136.

109. Viktor Reimann, *Innitzer Kardinal zwischen Hitler und Rom* (Vienna, 1988), 257.

110. Heer, *God's First Love*, 273.

111. Evelyn Adunka in "Antisemitismus in der Zweiten Republik. Ein Überblick anhand einiger ausgewählter Beispiele," in *Antisemitismus in Österreich nach 1945*, ed. Heinz P. Wassermann (Vienna, 2002), 14.

112. Alfred Diamant, *Austrian Catholics and the First Republic* (Princeton, N.J., 1960), 248–249.

113. Orel was arrested in 1943. Emmerich Talos, *NS-Herrschaft in Österreich* (Vienna, 2001), 200.

114. Anton Orel, *Der weltgeschichtliche Gegensatz zum Christentum*, 3rd ed. (Graz, Austria, 1934), 70.

115. Heinrich Busshoff, *Das Dollfuss-Regime in Österreich: In geistesgeschichtlicher Perspektive unter besonderer Berücksichtigung der "Schöneren Zukunft" und "Reichspost"* (Berlin, 1968), 257.

116. Cited in ibid., 259–60. On Czermak's leading role in writing about the "Jewish question" see Eppel, *Zwischen Kreuz*, 149.

117. Cited in Busshoff, *Dollfuss-Regime*, 252.

118. He was able to cite a former Austrian chancellor in support of these ideas. In 1916, Father Ignaz Seipel wrote that baptism admitted one to the community of the church but not the people: a baptized Chinese always remained Chinese. Stephan Neuhäuser, ed., *"Wir werden ganze Arbeit leisten . . ." Der austrofaschistische Staatsstreich 1934, Neue kritische Texte* (Norderstedt, 2004), 103.

119. The comparison to "the world of nature" was made by Emmerich Czermak. Busshoff, *Dollfuss-Regime*, 263.

120. Andreas Amsee, *Die Judenfrage* (Lucerne, Switzerland, 1939).

121. Urs Altermatt, *Katholizismus und Antisemitismus: Mentalitäten, Kontinuitäten, Ambivalenzen* (Frauenfeld, Switzerland, 1999), 238–241.

122. Emphasis added. Volk, *Akten deutscher Bischöfe*, vol. 6, 480; Alexander Gross, *Gehorsame Kirche: Ungehorsame Christen im Nationalsozialismus* (Mainz, 2000), 79.

123. See the extensive discussion of the high walls placed in Vienna, in Nina Scholz and Heiko Heinisch, *"Alles werden sich die Christen nicht gefallen lassen." Wiener Pfarrer und die Juden in der Zwischenkriegszeit* (Vienna, 2001), 84–85.

2. The Race Question

1. Mark 12:30–31; Matthew 22:37–39.

2. "One of the greatest dangers for a believer is marriage with a person not professing the Catholic faith." *L'Osservatore Romano*, November [14?] 1938, cited in "Two Papal Notes Opposed Race Law," *New York Times*, 15 November 1938, 1.

3. Hubert Wolf, *Pope and Devil: The Vatican's Archives and the Third Reich* (Cambridge, Mass., 2010), 26.

4. Jean Pierre Gury, S.J. (1801–1866), was a moral theologian in Mailleroncourt. Rudolf Reinhardt, ed., *Franz Xaver Linsenmann: Sein Leben, Vol. 1, Lebenserinnerungen* (Sigmaringen, 1987), 241n.83. First published in 1853, by 1939 Gury's moral theology had gone through thirty-four editions in Latin alone, and had also been translated into German, French, and English. See Jean Pierre Gury; Antonio Ballerini; Aloysius Sabetti; Timothy Barrett; Daniel F Creeden; *Compendium theologiæ moralis*, ed. 34 (Cincinnati, Ohio, 1939).

5. John A. Gallagher, *Time Past, Time Future: An Historical Study of Catholic Moral Theology* (New York, 1990), 51. Noldin's manual had gone through thirty printings by 1956 and was the most important work in U.S. seminaries next to that of Heribert Jone. James M. O'Toole, "In the Court of Conscience: American Catholics and Confession," in *Habits of Devotion: Catholic Religious Practice in Twentieth Century America*, ed. James M. O'Toole (Ithaca, NY, 2004), 273n.51

6. J. P. Gury, S.J., *Moraltheologie* (Regensburg and Mainz, 1869), 102.

7. Ibid., 102–103.

8. The order was: "spouse, children, parents, siblings, other relatives, friends, etc. In extreme need our parents should be preferred to all others, because we have existence from them." Heribert Jone, *Katholische Moraltheologie* (Paderborn, 1941), 108. This section was unchanged (including the preference for persons of one's own race) in the edition of 1961. See *Katholische Moraltheologie*, 17th ed. (Paderborn, 1961), 110. Jone was so popular among mid-century priests that he makes repeated appearances simply as "Jone" (e.g., "You can't think how Jone has simplified life for me . . .") in Graham Greene, *Monsignor Quixote* (Penguin Books, 2008), 59–61 and passim. On the widespread use of Jone in U.S. seminaries, see O'Toole, "In the Court," 273n.51.

9. Ronald E. Modras, "The Interwar Polish Catholic Press on the Jewish Question," *Annals of the American Academy of Political and Social Science*, 548 (November 1996), 179; Eugene Fisher, "The Catholic Church and Antisemitism: Poland, 1933–39," *Commonweal*, 5 April 1996.

10. Paul Hanebrink, *In Defense of Christian Hungary: Religion, Nationalism, and Antisemitism, 1890–1944* (Ithaca, N.Y., 2006), 162.

11. His source: St. Thomas Aquinas, *Summa Theologica*, 2,2 qu. 101 a.c. Cited in Joop Wekking, *Untersuchungen zur Rezeption der nationalsozialistischen Weltanschauung in den konfessionellen Periodika der Niederlande 1933–1940* (Amsterdam, 1990), 249.

12. Speech of 1939 cited in Lucia Scherzberger, "Katholische Dogmatik und Nationalsozialismus," in *Die katholische Schuld? Katholizismus im Dritten Reich zwischen Arrangement und Widerstand*, ed. Reiner Bendel (Münster, 2004), 181.

13. Matthew 12:50 (RSV). For a discussion of kinship language in Paul, see Reidar Assgaard, ed. *"My Beloved Brothers and Sisters!": Christian Siblingship in Paul* (London, 2004).

14. Matthew 25:40 (RSV).

15. John Mahoney, *The Making of Moral Theology: A Study of the Roman Catholic Tradition* (Oxford, United Kingdom, 1987), 305.

16. St. Augustine, Sermon 90, 10; PL 38, 566 (trans. Joseph Komonchak), available at www.commonwealmagazine.org/blog/?p=12840 (accessed 18 April 2011).

17. Jone, *Katholische Moraltheologie* (1941), 110.

18. See the critique of Adam Michnik in Adam Michnik, Józef Tischner, and Jacek Żakowski, *Między Panem a Plebanem* (Krakow, 1995), 548.

19. Paul Hanly Furfey, *The Respectable Murderers; Social Evil and Christian Conscience* (New York, 1966), 147–148. The major text of Antony Koch does precisely this: it divides sins against the "honor" of "fellow men" into internal and external acts. See his *Handbook of Moral Theology*, vol. 5, ed. Arthur Preuss (St. Louis, Mo., 1933), 96ff.

20. Irena Sławińska, *Szlakami moich wód* (Lublin, Poland, 1998), 61–62.

21. Heer, *God's First Love*, 30–31.

22. *Katholische Kirchenzeitung* (Salzburg), 30 July 1936, 244ff, cited in Günter Fellner, *Antisemitismus in Salzburg 1918–1938* (Vienna and Salzburg, 1979), 216–217.

23. The Berlin diocesan catechism of this period defined "neighbor" in the similar kind of theological balance: Every person was worthy of love, but one did not have to love all people to the same extent. Kevin Spicer, *Resisting the Third Reich: The Catholic Clergy in Hitler's Berlin* (DeKalb, Ill., 2004), 128–29. After this work, Weber was forbidden to publish in Germany and was frequently interrogated by the Gestapo. What strikes us as racialist was insufficiently racist for the regime. Manfred Hermanns, "Caritas in Deutschland während der Zeit des Nationalsozialismus," in *Wohlfahrtspflege, Volkspflege, Fürsorge*, ed. Barbara Dünkel and Verena Fesel (Münster, 2001), 150.

24. Also outside Germany, women took leading roles in Catholic efforts to aid Jews—for example, Germaine Robiere and Marie-Rose Gineste in France; Matylda Getter, Irena Sendler, and Zofia Kossak-Szczucka in Poland; and Margit Szlachta in Hungary. Richard Rubenstein and John K. Roth, *Approaches to Auschwitz: the Holocaust and Its Legacy* (Louisville, KY, 2003), 278; Michael Phayer and Eva Fleischner, *Cries in the Night: Women who Challenged the Holocaust* (Kansas City, 1997).

25. Christine Alix, *Le Saint-Siège et les nationalismes en Europe, 1870–1960* (Paris, 1962), 65.

26. In the encyclical *Mit brennender Sorge* (1937), the pope stressed that the church is "one, the same for all races and all nations," but noted that "there is room for the development of every quality, advantage, task and vocation which God the Creator and Savior has allotted to individuals as well as to *ethnical communities. The church's maternal heart is big enough to see in the God-appointed development of individual characteristics and gifts, more than a mere danger of divergence. She rejoices at the spiritual superiorities among individuals and nations*" (emphasis added). See www.vatican.va/holy_father/pius_xi/encyclicals/documents/hf_p-xi_enc_14031937_mit-brennender-sorge_en.html (accessed 19 April 2011).

27. In 1915, Benedict XV warned of the dangers of anti-nationalism. "Let us take it deeply to heart: nations do not die. If they are humiliated and oppressed,

they writhe under the yoke that has been laid upon them. They prepare their revenge and they pass from generation to generation a melancholy heirloom of hatred and vengeance." This from *Apostolic Exhortation Allorche Fummo*, 28 July 1915. AAS, 1915, t.7. Cited in an unpublished essay of John LaFarge, "The Jews and Anti-Semitism." LaFarge collection, box 56, folder 41, Georgetown University Library, Special Collections Division, Washington, D.C.

28. Point 72 of *Summi Pontificatus*, also cited in Alix, *Le Saint-Siège*, 32.

29. Alix, *Le Saint-Siège*, 74.

30. One section of Pius XI's encyclical directed to Germany, *Mit brennender Sorge* (1937) was emphatic on this point: "None but superficial minds could stumble into concepts of a national God, of a national religion; or attempt to lock [God] within the frontiers of a single people, within the narrow limits of a single race." These words were read once more from the pulpits of German churches in a pastoral letter of the German bishops of August 1943. See Ludwig Volk, ed., *Akten deutscher Bischöfe über die Lage der Kirche 1933–1945*, vol. 6: 1943–1945 (Mainz, 1985), 178–179.

31. The U.S. press of the period emphasized Vatican condemnations of (unnamed) totalitarian states. See *New York Times*, 30 October 1939, 1; see also *Chicago Daily Tribune*, 28 October 1939, 7.

32. The American Jesuit John LaFarge "labored in vain, however, to find a quotable passage in the document that hit directly on racism." David Southern, *John LaFarge and the Limits of Catholic Interracialism* (Baton Rouge, La., 1996), 237.

33. Frank J. Coppa, *The Papacy, the Jews, and the Holocaust* (Washington, D.C., 2006).

34. *New York Times*, 30 October 1939, 8. Hitler Youth attacked churchgoers in the Rhineland and in Austria in retaliation for the unread papal message. *New York Times*, 4 November 1939, 3.

35. *Los Angeles Times*, 25 December 1939, 4.

36. Cited in Alix, *Le Saint-Siège*, 65.

37. Ernstpeter Heiniger, *Ideologie des Rassismus: Problemsicht und ethische Verurteilung in der kirchlichen Sozialverkündigung* (Immensee, Switzerland, 1980), 259.

38. Lewis Hanke, *All Mankind Is One: A Study of the Disputation Between Bartolomé de Las Casas and Juan Ginés de Sepúlveda in 1550 on the Intellectual and Religious Capacity of the American Indians* (Dekalb, Ill., 1974), 21.

39. These laws were revoked, and later racial antisemites did not cite them as precedent. James Carroll, *Constantine's Sword: The Church and the Jews: A History* (Boston, 2002), 381.

40. María Elena Martínez, "The Black Blood of New Spain: Limpieza de Sangre, Racial Violence, and Gendered Power in Early Colonial Mexico," *William and Mary Quarterly* 61, no. 3 (2004), 8.

41. The Spanish idea of *limpieza de sangre* "referred to the status or condition of having unsullied 'Old Christian' ancestry, free of Jewish, Muslim, and heretical antecedents" (ibid., 7).

42. Ibid., 11.

43. Robert Michael, *A Concise History of American Antisemitism*, (Lanham, Md., 2005), 39.

44. Heiniger, *Ideologie des Rassismus*, 216.

45. Séverine (Caroline Rémy), "Le Pape et l'antisémitisme. Interview de Léon XIII," *Le Figaro*, 4 August 1892, cited in Thomas Brechenmacher, *Der Vatikan und die Juden: Geschichte einer unheiligen Beziehung vom 16. Jahrhundert bis zur Gegenwart* (Munich, 2005), 133–136.

46. Michael F. Feldkamp, *Pius XII. und Deutschland* (Göttingen, 2000), 113.

47. "Nazis Warned at Lourdes," *New York Times*, 29 April 1935, 8.

48. *Die Erfüllung* 3 (September 1937), 3.

49. Sigrid Schultz, "Nazis Sentence Priest Who Wed Jew and Aryan," *Chicago Daily Tribune*, 13 July 1937, 8.

50. "Innuendo by Nazis Arouses Catholics," *New York Times*, 17 December 1936, 14.

51. Racism was a minor point in the encyclical. See Klaus Wiegrefe, "Der Pakt zwischen Himmel und Hölle," *Der Spiegel*, 29 January 2008, 84–87. See also Martin Rhonheimer, "Katholischer Antirassismus, kirchliche Selbstverteidigung und das Schicksal der Juden im nationalsozialistischen Deutschland," in Andreas Laun, ed., *Unterwegs nach Jerusalem: Die Kirche auf der Suche nach ihren jüdischen Wurzeln* (Eichstätt, 2004), 30.

52. Some accounts exaggerate the directness of the pope's criticism of Hitler. Contrary to what Anthony Rhodes in *The Vatican in the Age of the Dictators* (New York: Holt, Rinehart, Winston, 1973, 205) writes, there were oblique references to Hitler. It was not the case that Pius failed to "spare the Führer," or called him a "mad prophet possessed of repulsive arrogance." The text limits it its critique of arrogance to unnamed Nazi "reformers."

53. The "Instruction on the Errors of Racism" of April 1938 counts as the "sole, precise document we have from the Holy See referring specifically to racism . . ." Bonaventure Hinwood, *Race: Reflections of a Theologian* (Rome, 1964), 61.

54. The total number of errors was eight. They are reproduced in ibid., 55–56.

55. Ibid., 62.

56. Ibid., 62, 69.

57. Heiniger, *Ideologie des Rassismus*, 259n.6.

58. Appeared in *L'Osservatore Romano*, 30 July 1938, cited in Susan Zuccotti, *Under His Very Windows: The Vatican and the Holocaust in Italy* (New Haven and London, 2001), 34–35. See also "Pope Warns Italy Not to Hit Church in Race Campaign," *New York Times*, 30 July 1938, 1.

59. Francis E. McMahon, *A Catholic Looks at the World* (New York, 1945), 84.

60. "Pope Asserts Right to His Racist View," *New York Times*, 8 September 1938, 4.

61. "Pope Warns Italy," 1.

62. *New York Times*, 8 September 1938, 4; "Pope-Duce Feud Ends in Compromise," *Washington Post*, 21 August 1938, M1.

63. Emphasis added. "Two Papal Notes Opposed Race Law," *New York Times*, 15 November 1938, 1.

64. Ibid.

65. John LaFarge, *Interracial Justice: A Study of the Catholic Doctrine of Race Relations* (New York, 1937), 144.

66. Hans-Walter Schmuhl, *Grenzüberschreitungen: Das Kaiser-Wilhelm-Institut für Anthropologie, menschliche Erblehre und Eugenik 1927–1945* (Göttingen, 2005), 290ff.

67. The two "sides" have been described eloquently by Elazar Barkan, *The Retreat of Scientific Racism: Changing Concepts of Race in Britain and the United States between the World Wars* (Cambridge, 1992).

68. See St. Augustine's "The Literal Meaning of Genesis" in *Ancient Christian Writers*, no. 41, J. H. Taylor, ed. (New York, 1982).

69. From an address to the Pontifical Academy of Sciences, 30 November 1941. Don O'Leary, *Roman Catholicism and Modern Science* (New York, 2006), 142.

70. In 1931, the *Catholic Encyclopedic Dictionary* called the kind of evolution Catholics could accept "moderate evolution," which permitted belief in "natural development of all the species of the animal and vegetable world from a few primitive types created by God." R. Scott Appleby, "Exposing Darwin's 'Hidden Agenda': Roman Catholic Responses to Evolution, 1875–1925," in *Disseminating Darwinism: The Role of Place, Race, Religion and Gender*, ed. Ronald L. Numbers and John Stenhouse (Cambridge, 1999), 173, 185–193.

71. Antonio Messineo, "Gli elementi costitutivi della nazione e la razza," *La Civiltà Cattolica*, 6 August 1938.

72. "Religion: The Right to Tolerance," *Time*, 4 December 1950.

73. See Antonio Messineo's *Giustizia ed espansione coloniale* (Rome, 1937).

74. The nation by contrast was "distinguished above all by spiritual characteristics," and elements of civilization that amount to "culture." Antonio Messineo, "Nation et race," *La Documentation Catholique* 39 (1938), 1080.

75. Messineo, "Nation et race," 1079; he cites Christel Schroeder, *Rasse und Religion* (Munich, 1937), 165.

76. This is the impression from the literature that Messineo had consulted, above all Napoleone Colajanni, *Latini e Anglo-Sassoni* (Rome, 1906), which in turn depends upon work of William Dalton Babington.

77. Messineo, "Nation et race," 1081.

78. Even the Catholic newspaper *L'Avvenire d'Italia* was permitted to report only in vague terms the pope's statements on race from 1938, "in such polysyllabic and apologetic phraseology as to take all the punch that the Pope had put into it." James M. Gillis, "This 'Aryan' Madness," *Catholic World* 147 (September 1938), 647.

79. Susan Zuccotti, *Under His Very Windows: The Vatican and the Holocaust in Italy* (New Haven and London, 2001), 28.

80. Zuccotti writes that *L'Osservatore Romano* contained another courageous piece against racism on 20 April 1938 (ibid., 30).

81. Angelo Brucculeri wrote that "from a philosophic position, there is nothing to object [to]" (ibid., 34).

82. Ibid., 30.

83. Among his major works is a refutation of the "Protocols of the Elders of Zion." An English version appeared in Oesterreicher's journal: Pierre Charles, S.J., "The Learned Elders of Zion," *The Bridge* 1 (1955), 159–190.

84. "Les antécédents de l'idéologie raciste," in *Racisme et Catholicisme* (Paris, 1939), 13–15.

85. Susan D. Pennybacker, "The Universal Races Congress, London Political Culture, and Imperial Dissent, 1900–1939," *Radical History Review* 92 (Spring 2005), 103–117.

86. Lorson escaped German units in World War I and finished the war in France. He was medic then chaplain in the French army in World War II. His father was a miner in the Saar (Differten). Lorson studied theology in Belgium (Thieu) and entered the Society of Jesus in 1915. Hugues Beylard, "Pierre Lorson," in *Catholicisme: Hier, Aujourd'hui, Demain*, vol. 7 (Paris, 1975), 1089–1090. Thanks to Prof. Peter Burg for this reference. See also Peter Burg, *Saar-Franzose: Peter/Pierre Lorson SJ* (Trier, 2011).

87. Lucien Valdor [Pierre Lorson], *Le Chrétien devant le racisme* (Paris, 1938), 6.

88. Ibid., 16.

89. There was no method for measuring the "mental capacities of two races" (ibid., 19). On Garth, see Graham Richards, "Reconceptualizing the History of Race Psychology: Thomas Russell Garth (1872–1939) and How He Changed His Mind," *Journal of the History of the Behavioural Sciences* 34, no. 1 (1998), 15–32.

90. Valdor [Lorson], *Le Chrétien*, 20–21.

91. Lorson cited *Mit brennender Sorge* (ibid., 22, 24).

92. Ibid., 22.

93. Ibid., 22–23.

94. Dr. Alfred Fuchs, "Rasa a náboženství," *Katolík* 1, no. 10 (June 1936), 76; second installment in ibid., "Duch času," 1, no. 11 (September 1936), 84–85. For his publications, see Jiří Hanuš, *Tradice českého Katolicismu ve 20. století* (Brno: Centrum pro studium demokracie a kultury, 2005), 61.

95. Fuchs, "Duch času."

96. Czech directly translates *Erbsünde* as *"dědičný hřích."*

97. Rudolf Lämmel, *Die menschlichen Rassen: Eine populärwissenschaftliche Einführung in die Grundprobleme der Rassentheorie* (Zurich, 1936), 117.

98. See the discussion of Lämmel's work in *Jüdische Wochenschrift Die Wahrheit* 50 (13 November 1936), 6.

99. Rudolf Lämmel opposed keeping a race pure, but supported eugenic measures to keep defective people from reproducing: see *Die menschlichen Rassen*.

100. Ibid., 26 (plate).

101. "La theoria moderna delle razze: impugnata da un acattolico," *La Civiltà Cattolica*, 2 July 1938, 62–71.

102. See his letters to Ernst Karl Winter, Dokumentationsarchiv des österreichischen Widerstandes, Vienna (DÖW), 15060/5.

103. Alois Hudal, *Grundlagen des Nationalsozialismus: Eine ideengeschichtliche Untersuchung von katholischer Warte* (Leipzig and Vienna, 1937), 76–77.

104. *Der Christliche Ständestaat*, 12 April 1936, 363.

105. *Die Erfüllung*, 27 September 1936, 939.

106. Hugo Iltis thus helped forge links between leftist politics and Lamarckism in the 1920s. Loren Graham, "Science and Values: The Eugenics Movement in Germany and Russia in the 1920s, *American Historical Review* 82, no. 5 (December 1977), 1142.

107. Hugo Iltis, *Mythus von Blut und Rasse* (Vienna, 1936). The recommendation of Berger is found at the end of the work. Iltis remained on friendly terms with the Nazi scientist Fritz Lenz through the 1920s.

108. Matthew Hoehn, ed., *Catholic Authors: Contemporary Biographical Sketches* (Concord, N.H., 1952), 630–632.

109. See Hans Conrad Ernst Zacharias, "Einheit und Mannigfaltigkeit des Menschengeschlechtes," *Der Christliche Ständestaat*, 8 December 1935, 1180–1181.

110. Cited in Barkan, *Retreat of Scientific Racism*, 299.

111. Veronika Lipphardt, *Biologie der Juden: jüdische Wissenschaftler über Rasse und Vererbung* (Göttingen, 2008), 252.

112. "Wissenschaftliche Rassenkunde oder Nicht?" *Der Christliche Ständestaat*, 1 November 1936 1051–1052.

113. Paul Weindling, "Central Europe Confronts German Racial Hygiene," in Marius Turda and Paul Weindling, eds., *"Blood and Homeland": Eugenics and Racial Nationalism in Central and Eastern Europe* (Budapest, 2007), 273–274.

114. "Rasse und Kultur," *Der Christliche Ständestaat*, 10 January 1937, 5–6.

115. Barkan, *Retreat of Scientific Racism*, 326; Carole Reynaud Paligot, *Races, Racisme et Antiracisme dans les années 1930* (Paris, 2007), 44–45.

116. Barkan, *Retreat of Scientific Racism*, 299.

117. Graham, "Science and Values," 1134.

118. Paligot, *Races, Racisme*, 44–45.

119. Ursula Ferdinand, "Bevölkerungswissenschaft und Rassismus," in *Bevölkerungslehre und Bevölkerungspolitik im "Dritten Reich,"* ed. Rainer Mackensen (Opladen, 2004), 90.

120. Jacques Millot and Jean de Pange, also active in the *Races et Racisme* group, also believed in a hierarchy of races. Paligot, *Races, Racisme*, 45.

121. J. Zollschan, "Die Bedeutung des Rassenfaktors für die Kulturgenese," *Problèmes qualitatifs de la population*, Congrès International de la Population, Paris 1937, vol. 8 (Paris, 1938), 103.

122. Beylard, "Pierre Lorson," 1089–1090; Norbert Leser, *Grenzgänger. Österreichische Geistesgeschichte in Totenbeschwörungen*, vol. 1 (Vienna, 1981).

123. See the excellent biography by Peter Burg, *Saar-Franzose*.

3. German *Volk* and Christian *Reich*

1. Urs Altermatt has spoken of the "syndrome of Catholic antisemitism." See his "Der Antijudaismus und seine Weiterungen. Das Syndrom des katholischen Antisemitismus," *Neue Zürcher Zeitung* 20/21 (November 1999), 93.

2. "Vom öffentlichen Gebrauch der Historie," *Die Zeit*, Nr. 46, 7 November 1986, 12–13.

3. On Maria Laach see Marcel Albert, *Die Benediktinerabtei Maria Laach und der Nationalsozialismus* (Paderborn, 2004), 37–43.

4. Cornelia Rauh-Kühne, *Katholisches Milieu und Kleinstadtgesellschaft: Ettlingen 1918–1939* (Sigmaringen, 1991), 359.

5. Uriel Tal, *Religion, Politics, and Ideology in the Third Reich* (London and New York, 2004), 107. According to Sigrid Frind, Nazi language consisted of a merging of concepts and symbols from the religious realm, speech areas of *völkisch* circles, and biology (cited in ibid).

6. See Peter Fritzsche, *Germans into Nazis* (Cambridge and London, 1998); Jeffrey Verhey, *The Spirit of 1914: Militarism, Myth, and Mobilization in Germany* (Cambridge, 2000).

7. Heinrich Lutz, *Demokratie im Zwielicht: Der Weg der deutschen Katholiken aus dem Kaiserreich in die Republik 1914–1925* (Munich, 1963), 102–103.

8. Klaus Schatz, *Zwischen Säkularisation und Zweitem Vatikanum. Der Weg des deutschen Katholizismus im 19. und 20. Jahrhundert* (Frankfurt am Main, 1986), 214; Jeffrey Herf, *Reactionary Modernism: Technology, Culture, and Politics in Weimar and the Third Reich* (Cambridge, 1984).

9. Dagmar Pöpping, *Abendland: Christliche Akademiker und die Utopie der Antimoderne 1900–1945* (Berlin, 2002), 95.

10. Hermann Platz, "Anmerkungen zur Burgtagung," *Schildgenossen* 1 (1920/21), 30ff, cited in Lutz, *Demokratie im Zwielicht*, 111.

11. Thomas Ruster, "Zwischen Erwählung und Abgrenzung. Überlegungen zum ekklesiologischen Prozeß im 19. und 20. Jahrhundert," *Lebendiges Zeugnis* 50 (1995), 107.

12. Gregory Baum, "Catholics in the Weimar Republic and the Third Reich through the Eyes of Walter Dirks," in *Why Weimar? Questioning the Legacy of Weimar from Goethe to 1999*, ed. Peter M. Daly, Hans Walter Frischkopf, Trudis E. Goldsmith-Reber, and Horst Richter (New York, Bern, 2003), 259–270.

13. Schatz, *Zwischen Säkularisation*, 216.

14. Cited in Lutz, *Demokratie im Zwielicht*, 112.

15. Ruster, "Zwischen Erwählung," 105–106.

16. Franz M. Kapfhammer, *Neuland: Erlebnis einer Jugendbewegung* (Graz, 1987), 80–81.

17. Andrea Tafferner, *Gottes- und Nächstenliebe in der deutschsprachigen Theologie des 20. Jahrhunderts* (Innsbruck, 1992), 59. Karl Adam's work also features numerous examples of his facility of mixing spiritual and biological metaphors. For a sampling, see Hermann Greive, *Theologie und Ideologie: Katholizismus und Judentum in Deutschland und Österreich 1918–1935* (Heidelberg, 1969), 158.

18. Victor Conzemius, "Églises chrétiennes et totalitarisme national-socialiste," *Revue d'histoire ecclésiastique* 63 (1968), 874.

19. Alois Baumgartner, "Die Auswirkungen der Liturgischen Bewegung auf Kirche und Katholizismus," in *Religiös-kulturelle Bewegungen im deutschen Katholizismus seit 1800*, ed. Anton Rauscher (Paderborn, 1986), 129–130.

20. Dawn Gibeau, "Fr. Virgil, St. John's Monks Spread Idea That Liturgy Creates Community," *National Catholic Reporter* 10 (December 1993).

21. Franz Kapfhammer, *Neuland* 9 (1932), 218; cited in Gerhard Seewann, *Österreichische Jugendbewegung 1900 bis 1938* (Frankfurt am Main, 1971), 700–701.

22. Kapfhammer, *Neuland*, 107ff.

23. Spann's influence was huge among Catholics in Germany and Austria, but extended to the Germans of Czechoslovakia and to Mussolini's Italy. Klaus Breuning, *Die Vision des Reiches: Deutscher Katholizismus zwischen Demokratie und Diktatur (1929–1934)* (Munich, 1969), 37.

24. Thus summarized by Dagmar Pöpping, *Abendland*, 169.

25. Othmar Spann, from his book *Der wahre Staat* (Leipzig, 1921) cited in Breuning, *Die Vision*, 36.

26. Excepted in German Catholicism from these leanings toward authoritarian rule were the circles around the *Rhein-Mainische Volkszeitung:* Henrich Scharp, Ernst Michel, and Walter Dirks. See Lutz, *Demokratie im Zwielicht*, 122–123.

27. Ibid., 113–114.

28. Ibid., 121–122.

29. Greive, *Theologie*, 157.

30. Ibid., 44.

31. Karl Adam, *The Spirit of Catholicism*, trans. Justin McCann (New York, 1960), 39, 41.

32. Greive, *Theologie*, 179.

33. Georg Denzler, "Antijudaismus und Antisemitismus in der Theologie unserer Jahrhunderts: Karl Adam, Michael Schmaus, und Anton Stonner," *Facta Universitatis, Series Law and Politics*, 1, no. 1 (1997), 12.

34. The belief that the old Reich could be resurrected to reestablish political legitimacy and historical greatness is called *Reichstheologie*. Breuning, *Die Vision*, 17.

35. Oded Heilbronner, "The Place of Catholic Historians and Catholic Historiography in Nazi Germany," *History* 88, no. 290 (2003), 284.

36. Ibid., 284, 290. According to Heilbronner (though he does not give specific cases), following the meeting at Maria Laach, *Reichstheologie* as a bridge between Catholicism and Nazism "won many new supporters" (ibid., 286).

37. Ibid., 287ff.

38. For Heilbronner, it is not difficult in retrospect to understand the enthusiasm for the idea of *Reich;* the word promised a Germany "rooted in past traditions, drawing strength from kinship, region and religious community" (ibid., 291–292).

39. In 1933, the priest of the Cologne diocese Robert Grosche said that "*Reich* was a concept not only of creation but of Salvation, it is the political life form of Christian peoples, the realization of Christianity in politics." Breuning, *Die Vision*, 238.

40. Robert Grosche was a chaplain for students in Cologne in 1933. Thomas Ruster, "Roman Catholic Theologians and National Socialism: Adaptations to

Nazi Ideology," in *Christian Responses to the Holocaust: Moral and Ethical Issues*, ed. Donald Dietrich (Syracuse, N.Y., 2003), 20.

41. Klaus-Dietmar Henke, *Die amerikanische Besetzung Deutschlands* (Munich, 1996), 370.

42. Breuning, *Die Vision*, 7–8.

43. Heilbronner finds that Protestants were more drawn to racist ideas ("Place of Catholic Historians," 289).

44. That the Holy Roman Empire had a role in salvation history was taken for granted. For historian Albert Mirgeler, Central Europe was a staging area of God's influence on earth, a *"Gotteszentrum"* as Pöpping calls it (*Abendland*, 170–171).

45. "Gegen die Feinde Oesterreichs," *Jüdische Wochenzeitung Die Wahrheit*, 1 May 1936, 1.

46. Mager also believed that there was some truth to the "Protocols of the Elders of Zion." Günter Fellner, *Antisemitismus in Salzburg 1918–1938* (Vienna and Salzburg, 1979), 218–220.

47. Pöpping, *Abendland*, 189–190.

48. In 1927, Nuncio Eugenio Pacelli secretly described Una Sancta as "in complete opposition to Catholic belief." Hubert Wolf, *Pope and Devil* (Cambridge, Mass., 2010), 239–241.

49. Hinting at his complexity Pöpping calls him a "universalist," however (*Abendland*, 187).

50. Some 150 of the members and friends of the Catholic Academic Union (including Nazis) met at Maria Laach for the third sociological meeting of the Union from 21 to 23 July 1933. Breuning, *Die Vision*, 207.

51. Letter of 2 February 1944, Ludwig Volk, ed., *Akten deutscher Bischöfe über die Lage der Kirche 1933–1945*, vol. 6: *1943–1945* (Mainz, 1985), 307.

52. On Adam's attraction to Nazism, see also Kevin Spicer, *Hitler's Priests: Catholic Clergy and National Socialism* (DeKalb, Ill., 2008), 187. For the dedication see Jerome-Michael Vereb, *"Because He Was a German!" Cardinal Bea and the Origins of Roman Catholic Engagement in the Ecumenical Movement* (Grand Rapids, Mich., 2006), 97.

53. There is no entry under *"Royaume de Dieu"* in the French theological encyclopedia of this period. See A. Vacant, E. Mangenot, and É. Amann, eds., *Dictionnaire de Théologie Catholique* (Paris, 1937). *The New Catholic Dictionary* (New York, 1929, 530) writes as follows on the "Kingdom of God": "Not only a place to be attained, but an influence under which our minds come when we are one with Christ and acting under His ideals; the sway of Grace in our hearts; the rule of God in the world, Thy kingdom come; the place where God reigns; the goal at which we have to aim; the Church . . ."

54. That was not true of sixteenth-century Spain, which viewed itself as "Kingdom of Christ," and therefore understood its political and religious missions as overlapping. Just as "every Indian in the New World had to become a subject of his majesty, the Catholic king, so too every Indian *had* to become a subject of the Vicar of Christ." Ronan Hoffman, "Some Missiological Reflections on

Current Theology," *Revolution in Missionary Thinking*, ed. William Richarson (Maryknoll, N.Y., 1966), 100–101.

55. Brian F. Connaughton, "Conjuring the Body Politic from the Corpus Mysticum: The Post-Independent Pursuit of Public Opinion in Mexico, 1821–1854," *The Americas* 55, no. 3 (January 1999), 459–479; Douglass Sullivan-González, "'A Chosen People': Religious Discourse and the Making of the Republic of Guatemala, 1821–1871," *The Americas* 54, no. 1 (July 1997), 17–38. Thanks to Mark Healey for these references.

56. Instead, they turned to the cult of St. Laszlo, who had forbidden marriages of Christians and Jews in his kingdom. Paul Hanebrink, *In Defense of Christian Hungary: Religion, Nationalism, and Antisemitism, 1890–1944* (Ithaca, N.Y., 2006), 142.

57. We have *il peccato originale* (Italian), *grzech pierworodny* (Polish), *le péché original* (French), *pecado original* (Spanish). The Croatian, Hungarian, and Lithuanian express the idea of origin through "seed" (*iskonski grijeh*), "root" (*eredendő bűn*), and "home" (*gimtosios nuodėmės*). Czech and Slovak use the equivalent of "original sin" (*prvotního hřichu* and *prvotného hriechu*) though Czechs also have the option of *dědičný hřích* (inherited sin), which is a translation from the German, a language imposed upon Czechs (along with Catholicism) after the Battle of White Mountain in 1620. The Czech case shows the importance of overall context: the secularism of the culture, the anti-Catholicism of the national movement, and the need to set oneself off against Germany gave the similar expression a very different valence.

58. Joanna B. Michlic, *Poland's Threatening Other: The Image of the Jew from 1880 to the Present* (Lincoln, Neb., 2006), 99–100.

59. Paul Airiau, *L'antisémitisme catholique aux XIXe et XXe siècles* (Paris, 2002), 63.

60. See the condemnations of the "Aryan paragraph" throughout the U.S. Christian Press in Fredrick Ira Murphy, "The American Christian Press and Pre-War Hitler's Germany, 1933–1939" (Ph.D. diss., University of Florida, 1970), 179–183. This did not mean that the U.S. Christian press was free of propagating antisemitic ideas about Jews. Ibid., 151–161. Thanks to Gene Zubovich for this reference.

61. "Racial Ideas and the Church," *The Month* 173 (June 1939), 562–563. The original was *Das Heil der Völker* (Paderborn, 1937). Ulrike Ehret also notes that British Catholic publications did not dwell upon the racial otherness of Jews, though she attributes the German distinctiveness to the conditions of dictatorship, not local culture. See her "Catholicism and Judaism in the Catholic Defence against Alfred Rosenberg," *European History Quarterly* 40, no. 1 (2010), 35–56.

62. Michael Banton, *Racial Theories*, 2nd ed. (Cambridge, United Kingdom, 1998), 160–161; Michel Wieworka, "Racism in Europe, Unity and Diversity," in *Racism, Modernity and Identity on the Western Front*, ed. Ali Rattansi and Sallie Westwood (Oxford, 1994), 173–188; Pierre-André Taguieff, *The Force of Prejudice: On Racism and Its Doubles* (Minneapolis, 2001).

63. Peter Walkenhorst, *Nation, Volk, Rasse: Radikaler Nationalismus im Deutschen Kaiserreich 1890–1914* (Göttingen, 2007), 329–330.

64. "Daily plebiscite" was the classic "French" definition of nation of Ernest Renan. Debunking Rogers Brubaker [*Citizenship and Nationhood in France and Germany* (Cambridge, Mass., 1992)] has become a cottage industry among historians of Germany and France, yet the (limited) comparative work they have produced has focused on legal discourses of citizenship rather than on popular discourses of nation, thus not touching Brubaker's central contention about distinction between civic and ethnic nationhood, which though imperfect, still explains much about the penetration of racist thought in the German and French contexts. For critical perspectives on Brubaker, as well as copious references, see Geoff Eley and Jan Palmowski, eds., *Citizenship and National Identity in Twentieth Century Germany* (Stanford, 2008).

65. Historians interested in the French/German divide on citizenship have been attracted to Patrick Weil's evidence that in the nineteenth century certain German states: 1) copied their citizenship laws from France, 2) had provisions for naturalization like those of France. More important for the French/German divide as far as debates about race are concerned is that Weil shows how French opponents of racism after World War I could portray ethnic nationhood as a Germanic tradition. See Patrick Weil, *How to Be French: Nationality in the Making Since 1789*, trans. Catherine Porter (Durham, N.C., and London, 2005), 177–179.

66. Cited in Pierre-André Taguieff, "Des thèmes récurrents qui structurent l'imaginaire antijuif modern: Sur le Mur de Menargues: quelques sources antisémites 'classiques' autour du 'racisme juif'," *L'Arche* 560 (November–December 2004), 77.

67. Pierre Pierrard, *Juifs et catholiques français: De Drumont à Jules Isaac (1886–1945)* (Paris, 1970), 65–66; Airiau, *L'antisémitisme catholique*, 81

68. Airiau, *L'antisémitisme catholique*, 81.

69. Ibid.

70. Michael Curtis, *Verdict on Vichy* (New York, 2003), 49.

71. Ralph Schor, *L'Antisémitisme en France dans l'entre-deux-guerres: Prélude à Vichy* (Brussels, 1992), 45.

72. Ibid., 224.

73. The other person cited by Schor (ibid., 116) as denying the power of baptism was Henri-Robert Petit, who was a neo-pagan and propagated astrology and Druidism after the war.

74. Ibid., 111.

75. Herman de Vries de Heekelingen, *Israël: Son passé, son avenir* (Paris, 1937), 54, 55, 69, cited in Pierre-André Taguieff, *La judéophobie des Modernes: Des Lumières au jihad mondial* (Paris, 2008), 344.

76. Herman de Vries de Heekelingen, *Juifs et catholiques* (Paris, 1939), 19–20, cited in Taguieff, *La judéophobie*, 344.

77. Schor, *L'antisémitisme*, 68.

78. Laurent Joly, "Darquier de Pellepoix, 'champion' des antisémites français (1936–1939)," *Revue d'histoire de la Shoah* 173 (September–December 2001), 59.

79. Ibid., 59.

80. Schor, *L'Antisémitisme*, 224.

81. Ibid., 223.

82. Ibid., 240, 243.

83. Ibid., 75–76. Maurras wrote that "Antisemitism does not need racism." Maurras was criticized on the right for his failure to support Germany by the anti-Catholic (former Catholic) Lucien Rebatet, a fascist writer who shows that French intellectuals who wanted to openly embrace racism tended to gravitate toward German culture and away from Catholicism. Alan Riding, *And the Show Went On: Cultural Life in Nazi-Occupied Paris* (New York, 2011), 234. For Rebatet's anti-Catholicism see Pascal A. Ifri, "Anatomy of an Exclusion: Les Deux Etendards by Lucien Rebatet," *Symposium* 45, no. 1 (1991), 343–344.

84. Schor, *L'Antisémitisme*, 81–82.

85. The issue is dealt with in chapter four.

86. See the encyclical *Casti Connubii*, 31 December 1930.

87. Michael F. Feldkamp, *Pius XII und Deutschland* (Göttingen, 2000), 113.

88. Ingrid Richter, *Katholizismus und Eugenik in der Weimarer Republik und im Dritten Reich: Zwischen Sittlichkeitsreform und Rassenhygiene* (Paderborn, 2001), 207, 213–214, 217. Ruland was one of the rare Catholic priests to join the NSDAP. Spicer, *Hitler's Priests*, 285.

89. For a lucid description of the process whereby the Nazi regime made clear to Catholics where Catholicism and Nazism differed, see Kevin Spicer, *Resisting the Third Reich: The Catholic Clergy in Hitler's Berlin* (De Kalb, Ill., 2004). For a differing interpretation of Muckermann, see Donald J. Dietrich, "Catholic Eugenics in Germany, 1920–1945: Hermann Muckermann, S.J. and Joseph Mayer," *Journal of Church and State*, 34 (1992), 575–600.

90. This was also a view of two major texts of the time: Henry Davis, S.J. (a major moral theologian), in *Eugenics: Aims and Methods* (London, 1930), as well as Tihamer Toth, *Die Eugenik vom katholischen Standpunkt* (Vienna, 1937).

91. Anne Carol, *Histoire de l'eugénisme en France: Les médecins et la procréation* (Paris, 1995), 267–268.

92. Catholic medical societies referred to the killing of the "unfit" as a "monstrosity" and said of the eugenics project that "great thinkers have run it off the rails" (ibid., 265–266).

93. Ibid., 265–267.

94. Even "positive" methods of eugenics such as marital counseling, though in keeping with Catholic teaching, therefore never caught fire in French Catholic milieus. Ibid., 266. A Catholic perspective on neo-Malthusianism is lucidly stated by H. S. Spalding, S.J., of Loyola University in "Ethics and neo-Malthusianism," *The American Journal of Sociology*, 22, no. 5 (March 1917), 612.

95. So it was possible for the philo-Semitic Catholic journal *La Juste parole* to lament the "invasion" of France of racist ideas from "beyond the Rhine" (Schor, *L'Antisémitisme*, 289–290). In Poland, Catholic writers opposed eugenics by associating it with liberal opponents. See Magdalena Gawin, *Rasa i nowoczesność: Historia polskiego ruchu eugenicznego* (Warsaw, 2003), 240–244.

96. Józef Pastuszka, *Rasizm jako światopogląd* (Poznan, 1939), 50–51; *Filozoficzne i społeczne idee A. Hitlera (Rasizm)* (Lublin, 1938), 89.

97. Toth, *Die Eugenik*, 70–75.

98. Jiří Hanuš, *Tradice českého katolicismu ve 20. století* (Brno, 2005), 127.

99. Josef Florian Babor, "Bludy rasizmu v dnešnom Nemecku," *Františkánsky obzor* 1, no. 4 (1938), 99.

100. Alfred Fuchs, "Duch času," *Katolík* 11 (1939).

101. Sharon Leon, "Hopelessly Entangled in Nordic Pre-suppositions: Catholic Participation in the American Eugenics Society in the 1920s," *Journal of the History of Medicine and Allied Sciences* 59, no. 1 (2004), 8.

102. Ibid., 15.

103. Ibid., 14.

104. Ibid., 25. Cooper was of English Quaker background, and as a child had spent summers with Quaker relatives in Pennsylvania. Regina Flannery, "John Montgomery Cooper, 1881–1949," *American Anthropologist* 52, no. 1 (January–March 1950), 64–65.

105. Leon, "Hopelessly Entangled," 21.

106. Joseph Mayer, "Eugenics in Roman Catholic Literature," *Eugenics* 8 (February 1930), 43–51. Mayer's article had been translated from the German by the American eugenicist Paul Popenoe. It is of great value for historians because it serves as an attempt to find any Catholic of even moderate standing who spoke out in favor of negative eugenics before the Vatican shut down any such discussion.

107. John A. Ryan, *Human Sterilization* (Washington, D.C., 1929).

108. For example, Stephen M. Donovan, Franz Hürth, Alfred Vermeersch, Franz Walter, Hubert Schorn, and Augustino Gemelli. Mayer, "Eugenics," 43–51.

109. For a list of opponents, see Josef Grosam, "Sterilisation aufgrund privater Autorität und gesetzlicher Ermächtigung," *Theologisch-praktische Quartalschrift* 83 (1930), 296.

110. Richter, *Katholizismus und Eugenik*, 221–222.

111. Leon, "Hopelessly Entangled," 39–40.

112. John T. McGreevy, *Catholicism and American Freedom: A History* (New York, 2003), chapter four.

113. Councils of Christians and Jews emerged to combat religious and racial bigotry in the United States in 1928, earlier than anywhere else. Josef Foschepoth, "Vor 50 Jahren: Die Gründung der Gesellschaften für Christlich-Jüdische Zusammenarbeit," in *Der Dialog zwischen Juden und Christen: Versuche des Gesprächs nach Auschwitz*, ed. Hans Erler and Ansgar Koschel (Frankfurt am Main, 1999), 173–176.

114. This while composing his book *Racisme*. See below, chapter five. The process of integration of Catholics in the United States extends backward several generations, and was by no means smooth, involving suspicions in the United States that Catholics were authoritarian and undemocratic, and in Rome that they were excessively democratic and tolerant. The success of social and cultural integration, perhaps achieving a highpoint in the 1960s, preceded an extraordinary erosion of the Catholic milieu. For general guidance: McGreevy, *Catholicism*; Philip Gleason, *Contending with Modernity: Catholic Higher Education in the*

Twentieth Century (Oxford, 1995); Claude S. Fischer and Michael Hout, *Century of Difference: How America Changed in the Last One Hundred Years* (New York, 2006).

115. Sebastian Conrad, for instance, shows how the radical nationalism in Germany was related to German colonialism, but colonialism was not specific to Germany. Both Conrad and Peter Walkenhorst alert us to the promise of comparative studies of German nationalism, but for whatever reason, historians have yet to take up this call. Sebastian Conrad, *Globalisation and the Nation in Imperial Germany* (Cambridge, 2006), 384–385; Walkenhorst, *Nation*, 332.

116. Susannah Heschel, *The Aryan Jesus: Christian Theologians and the Bible in Nazi Germany* (Princeton, N.J., 2008).

117. Daniel J. Goldhagen, *Hitler's Willing Executioners: Ordinary Germans and the Holocaust* (New York, 1996). The influence of this book is seen, among other things, in the massive interest in motivations of perpetrators in the last fifteen years.

4. Catholics against Racism and Antisemitism

1. Dietrich von Hildebrand, *Memoiren und Aufsätze gegen den Nationalsozialismus, 1933–1938*, ed. Ernst Wenisch (Mainz, 1994), 121.

2. Hubert Wolf, *Pope and Devil* (Cambridge, Mass., 2010), 263.

3. Until recently, scholars have tended to assume the irrelevance of religious beliefs for the emergence and growth of antisemitism in Germany. Christhard Hoffmann, "Christlicher Antijudaismus und moderner Antisemitismus," in *Christlicher Antijudaismus und Antisemitismus: Theologische und kirchliche Programme deutscher Christen*, ed. Leonore Siegele-Wenschkewitz (Frankfurt am Main, 1994), 293–317.

4. The priests were Crutched Friar Anton Van Asseldonk and the Franciscan Laetus Himmelreich. Menahem Macina, "Essai d'élucidation des causes et circonstances de l'abolition, par le Saint-Office, de l'Opus sacerdotale Amici Israel (1926–1928)," in *Juifs et chrétiens, entre ignorance, hostilité et rapprochement (1898–1998)*, ed. Annette Becker (Lille, 2003), 87–110.

5. Hubert Wolf, " 'Pro perfidis Judaeis,' Die 'Amici Israel' und ihr Antrag auf eine Reform der Karfreitagsfürbitte für die Juden (1928)," *Historische Zeitschrift* 279, no. 3 (December 2004), 618.

6. The association was suppressed because of sympathy with Zionism and abandonment of substitution theology. Marcel Poorthuis and Theo Salemink, "Chiliasme, anti-judaïsme en antisemitisme. Laetus Himmelreich OFM," *Trajecta* 9 (2000), 45–76.

7. This concern was admitted in a surviving drafts (of 14 March 1928): "La motivazione del Decreto e basata sulla necessita di prevenire nei riguardi della S. Sede l'assusa di 'antisemitismo.' " Wolf, "Pro perfidis," 641.

8. Georges Passelecq and Bernard Suchecky, *The Hidden Encyclical of Pius XI*, trans. Steven Rendall (New York, 1997), 98.

9. Thomas Brechenmacher, *Der Vatikan und die Juden: Geschichte einer unheiligen Beziehung vom 16. Jahrhundert bis zur Gegenwart* (Munich, 2005), 164.

10. Ibid., 196. Georg Denzler cites similar calls of other German Catholics of the period for the Church to break its silence: Waldemar Gurian, Ingbaart Naab, Johannes Kraus, and Josef Lechner. *Widerstand oder Anpassung? Katholische Kirche und Drittes Reich* (Munich, 1984), 228–230.

11. J. M. Oesterreicher to K. Thieme, 6 January 1939, Thieme Papers, Institut für Zeitgeschichte [IfZG], Munich, Germany, ED 163/60.

12. Brechenmacher, *Der Vatikan*, 186.

13. Gustav Gundlach, "Antisemitismus," *Lexikon für Theologie und Kirche I* (Freiburg im Breisgau, 1930), columns 504–505.

14. Anton Rauscher, ed., *Wider den Rassismus: Entwurf einer nicht erschienenen Enzyklika (1938). Texte aus dem Nachlass von Gustav Gundlach SJ* (Paderborn, 2001), 161–162.

15. Ibid., 166.

16. Ibid., 164.

17. Ibid., 165–166.

18. Passelecq and Suchecky, *The Hidden Encyclical*, 249.

19. Ibid., 250.

20. Ibid., 251.

21. Ibid., 252.

22. Ibid., 253.

23. Ibid., 254.

24. Ibid., 254–256.

25. Drafts of the encyclical reached Pius XI after he had lost the strength to study them seriously. Gundlach believed that his successor Pius XII did not want to make his first public statement openly political, and that he therefore consigned the drafts to the Vatican archives. Michael F. Feldkamp, *Pius XII und Deutschland* (Göttingen, 2000), 119; Brechenmacher, *Der Vatikan*, 187.

26. Wolf, *Pope and Devil*, 239–241.

27. Stanley Payne, *A History of Fascism, 1914–1945* (Madison, Wisc., 1995), 251.

28. This is one of Michael Mann's criteria for fascism, in *Fascists* (Cambridge, 2004).

29. George Eric Rowe Gedye, *Fallen Bastions: The Central European Tragedy* (London, 1939), 59.

30. Ibid.

31. Alexander Waugh, *House of Wittgenstein: A Family at War* (London, 2008), 211.

32. Gudula Walterskirchen, *Starhemberg oder die Spuren der 30er Jahre* (Vienna, 2002), 105–106, 113, 313–314.

33. Bertrand Perz, *Faschismus in Österreich und International* (Vienna, 1982), 203.

34. Tim Kirk, "Fascism and Austrofascism," in *The Dollfuss/Schuschnigg Era in Austria: A Reassessment*, ed. Günter Bischof, Anton Pelinka, and Alexander Lassner (New Brunswick, N.J., 2003), 26–27.

35. Alexander Pinwinkler, "Wilhelm Winkler und der Nationalsozialismus," in *Bevölkerungslehre und Bevölkerungspolitik im "Dritten Reich,"* ed. Rainer Mackensen (Opladen, 2004), 167.

36. Martin Luksan, "'Fremde Typen' und 'gesunde Gefühle.' Über die Geschichte des Rassensaals," in *Rasse Mensch: Jeder Mensch ein Mischling*, ed. Petrus van der Let and Christian Schüller (Aschaffenburg, 1999), 46–47.

37. Klaus Taschwer, "'Anthropologie ins Volk' Zur Ausstellungspolitik einer anwendbaren Wissenschaft bis 1945," in *Politik der Präsentation: Museum und Ausstellung in Österreich 1918–1945*, ed. Herbert Posch and Gottfried Fliedl (Vienna, 1996), 246–248.

38. This occurred in 1935. Gudrun Exner, "Eugenik in Österreich bis 1938," in Mackensen, ed., *Bevölkerungslehre*, 353.

39. Taschwer, "Anthropologie ins Volk," 250.

40. Robert Kriechbaumer, *Die großen Erzählungen der Politik. Politische Kultur und Parteien in Österreich von der Jahrhundertwende bis 1945* (Vienna, 2001), 170–171.

41. Bruce F. Pauley, *From Prejudice to Persecution: A History of Austrian Antisemitism* (Chapel Hill, N.C., 1992), 263.

42. G. E. R. Gedye, "Dollfuss Spurned Socialists' Aid, Fugitive Party Leader Declares," *New York Times*, 18 February 1934, 1.

43. See Dorothy Thompson's introduction to Kurt von Schuschnigg, *My Austria* (New York, 1938), xxii–xxiii.

44. Robert Pyrah, "Enacting Encyclicals? Cultural Politics and 'Clerical Fascism' in Austria, 1933–1938," in *Totalitarian Movements and Political Religions* 8, no. 2 (2007), 369–382.

45. Rudolf Ebneth, *Die österreichische Wochenschrift "Der Christliche Ständestaat": Emigration in Österreich 1933–1938* (Mainz, 1976), 253.

46. John T. Noonan Jr., *Contraception: A History of Its Treatment by the Catholic Theologians and Canonists* (Cambridge, Mass., 1966), 495.

47. Hildebrand admired Sangnier for his religiosity, but also because he was a "heroic fighter against nationalism and all prejudices." Hildebrand, *Memoiren und Aufsätze*, 2–3.

48. In 1933, Hildebrand returned to Paris in order to hold a talk "on political themes" by invitation of Cardinal Baudrillart at the Institut Catholique, and met with the Goethe expert (and anti-Nazi publicist) Count Robert d'Harcourt, the peace activist Friedrich Wilhelm Foerster (a friend of Albert Einstein), as well as Maritain, who took Hildebrand out to his house Meudon. Hildebrand, *Memoiren und Aufsätze*, 76. On the roles of Bloy and Peterson in the emerging Catholic vision of the Jews, see below, chapter six. Hildebrand and Peterson knew each other from Göttingen, and traveled in the same circles in the 1920s. Barbara Nichtweiss, "Wanderungen am Ufer von Welt und Zeit," in *Vom Ende der Zeit: Geschichtstheologie und Eschatologie bei Erik Peterson*, ed. Barbara Nichtweiss (Hamburg, 2000), 20.

49. Hildebrand, *Memoiren und Aufsätze*, 2–3

50. Ibid., 5.

51. Dietrich von Hildebrand, *Zeitliches im Lichte des Ewigen: Gesammelte Abhandlungen und Vorträge* (Regensburg, 1932), 193–198.

52. Ibid., 192–194.

53. Ebneth, *Die österreichische Wochenschrift*, 36.

54. Ibid., 35–36.

55. From the preface by Joseph Ratzinger of Alice von Hildebrand, *Soul of a Lion: Dietrich von Hildebrand, a Biography* (San Francisco, 2000), 10.

56. Walter Romig, *The Book of Catholic Authors*, Sixth Series (Gross Pointe, Mich., 1962), 209–215.

57. Hildebrand, *Memoiren und Aufsätze*, 59.

58. *Der Christliche Ständestaat*, 15 February 1934; 4 February 1934.

59. *Der Christliche Ständestaat*, 18 March 1934. Klaus Dohrn (1909–1979), a journalist, was related to Wilhelm Furtwängler and also to Hildebrand. Klaus Dohrn, *Von Bürgern und Weltbürgern* (Stuttgart, 1999); Hildebrand, *Memoiren und Aufsätze*, 50.

60. Zyrill Fischer, "Die Deutsche Volkskirche," *Der Christliche Ständestaat*, 8 April 1934, 3–5.

61. Hildebrandt, *Memoiren und Aufsätze*, 72.

62. Ibid., 58.

63. Ferdinand Frodl, "Nazibazillus im Taufbecken?" *Der Christliche Ständestaat*, 17 December 1933, 23. Frodl was professor of moral theology in Klagenfurt, and after 1936 Director of Typography at the papal university Gregoriana. Hildebrandt, *Memoiren und Aufsätze*, 58, 72.

64. Frodl, "Nazibazillus im Taufbecken?," 23.

65. Ibid.

66. The specific charge against Frodl was complicity in smuggling information to a foreign country. See "Fotos aus der Erkennungsdienstlichen Kartei der Gestapo Wien: Römisch-katholische Kirche," www.doew.at/php/gestapo/index.php?c=detail&l=de&id=505 (accessed 22 April 2011).

67. A. G. Kraus, "Der religiöse Antisemitismus," *Der Christliche Ständestaat*, 8 April 1934.

68. Andreas Mix, "Hilfe im katholischen Milieu: Das Überleben der Konvertitin Annie Kraus," in *Überleben im Dritten Reich: Juden im Untergrund und ihre Helfer*, ed. Wolfgang Benz (Munich, 2003), 141.

69. Hugo Rahner, "Verjudung der Kirche?" *Der Christliche Ständestaat* (17 February 1935), 174–175.

70. *Der Christliche Ständestaat*, 17 March 1935, 269.

71. Hans Scholl and Sophie Scholl, *Briefe und Aufzeichnungen* (Frankfurt am Main, 1984), 235.

72. A. G. Kraus, "Der religiöse Antisemitismus," *Der Christliche Ständestaat*, 8 April 1934.

73. Hildebrandt, *Memoiren und Aufsätze*, 43.

74. Mix, "Hilfe im katholischen Milieu," 131–142.

75. Gerhard Rexin, "Annie Kraus," *Bautz Kirchlexikon* 30 (2009), 810–814.

76. See John Henry Crosby, "Commentary on the Text of the Jews and the Christian West," *Logos: A Journal of Catholic Thought and Culture* 9, no. 4 (2006), 139.

77. Hildebrandt, *Memoiren und Aufsätze*, 79–80, 106–107.

78. Houston Stewart Chamberlain, *Worte Christi* (Munich, 1903).

79. "Msgr. Oesterreicher," *The Advocate* (Newark, N.J.), 7 October 1965, 4.

80. John O'Brien, "Jew, Noted Scholar, Is Convert, Priest," *Catholic Sentinel* (Portland, Ore.), 11 June 1959.

81. *Reminiscences,* 12, NXCP94-A3, Columbia University Oral History Research Project, Columbia University Center for Oral History, New York.

82. Letter to Thieme, 21 April 1936, ED 163/59, IfZG.

83. Papen wrote that "Father S. H. [sic] Bichlmair, one of the most important and prominent representatives of the Jesuit Order in Austria, spoke here of the Jewish question." This lecture "caused a sensation" and was "vividly discussed in the press." Report of Papen to Hitler, 20 May 1936, German Foreign Ministry Archives, E 454630, National Archives Microform Publication T-120, R-2889. U.S. National Archives, College Park, Md.

84. See Anton Pelinka, *Stand oder Klasse? Die christliche Arbeiterbewegung Österreichs, 1933–38* (Vienna, 1972), 226.

85. Leo Seifert, "Grundsätzliches zur Judenfrage," in *Neue Ordnung* (1934), 37, cited in Ibid., 217.

86. Klemens Honek, "P. Georg Bichlmair: Leben und Wirken für die Kirche in Wien," Wiener Katholische Akademie, Arbeitskreis für Kirchliche Zeit- und Wiener Diözesangeschichte, *Miscellanea* 53 (Vienna, 1979), 16.

87. Aurel Kolnai, *Political Memoirs,* ed. Francesca Murphy (Lanham, Md., 1999), 117–188.

88. Gudula Walterskirchen, *Engelbert Dollfuss, Arbeitermörder oder Heldenkanzler?* (Vienna, 2004).

89. As reported in *Reichspost,* 19 March 1936, 7.

90. Clemens Holzmeister, ed., *Kirche im Kampf* (Vienna, 1936).

91. Georg Bichlmair, "Der Christ und der Jude," in *Kirche im Kampf,* ed. Clemens Holzmeister (Vienna, 1936), 157.

92. Ibid., 158.

93. Ibid., 159–160.

94. Oesterreicher to Thieme, 21 April 1936, IfZG, ED 163/59.

95. Letter to Thieme, 16 April 1936, IfZG, ED 163/59.

96. He also wrote to Karl Barth, Otto Bauer, Karl Jaspers, Otto Suhr, and Eugen Kogon. Benjamin called Thieme the "Godfather" [*Pate*] of his book *Deutsche Menschen.* The two met in Paris in 1936, and Thieme succeeded in having the book published in Switzerland. Erdmut Wizisla, "Plaquette für Freunde," in *Walter Benjamins Deutsche Menschen,* ed. Erdmut Wizisla and Barbara Hahn (Göttingen, 2008), 60.

97. At Thieme's death in 1963, the Dutch Catholic organization Katholieke Raad voor Israel commented that "no one else can fill the empty space he leaves in Germany as well as the international arena." *Freiburger Rundbrief* 57/60 (January 1964), 73.

98. More predictably, two years later he made his way to the Association of Religious Socialists, of which he became the Prussian managing director in 1930. Karl Thieme "Mein Leben in Deutschland vor und nach dem 1.1.1933," 1940, IfZG, ED 163/133.

99. Thieme, "Mein Leben," 33–38.

100. Ibid., 80; Wolfgang Benz and Barbara Distel, eds., *Der Ort des Terrors: die Geschichte der nationalsozialistischen Konzentrationslager*, vol. 2 (Munich, 2005), 43–48.

101. Karl Barth wrote in 1938 that "antisemitism is a sin against the Holy Spirit, because antisemitism means rejecting the grace of God." See Andreas Pangritz, "Politischer Gottesdienst Zur theologischen Begründung des Widerstands bei Karl Barth, *Communio Viatorum* 39 (1997), 215–247.

102. Text of letter to Pius of 31 October 1933 in Jörg Ernesti, *Ökumene im Dritten Reich* (Paderborn, 2007), 28–31.

103. Josef Höfer, "Karl Thieme in Rom," *Freiburger Rundbrief* 73/76 (1968), 15.

104. Ernesti, *Ökumene*, 28.

105. On Schauff see Dieter Marc Schneider, *Johannes Schauff (1902–1990): Migration und "Stabilitas" im Zeitalter der Totalitarismen* (Oldenbourg and Munich, 2001).

106. Höfer, "Karl Thieme in Rom," 15.

107. Some fifty Catholic youth functionaries were arrested when *Junge Front* was closed, but Maassen continued Catholic youth work in the underground. Ger van Roon, *Widerstand im Dritten Reich*, 7th ed. (Munich, 1998), 44; Werner K. Blessing, "Kirche und Kirchenvolk in einer katholischen Region," in *Von Stalingrad zur Währungsreform: Zur Sozialgeschichte des Umbruchs in Deutschland*, ed. Martin Broszat et al. (Munich, 1990), 26

108. A number were executed in 1944: Nikolaus Gross, Bernhard Letterhaus, Alfred Depp. See Schneider, *Johannes Schauff*, 68–69.

109. Edmund Forschbach, *Edgar J. Jung: Ein konservativer Revolutionär* (Tübingen, 1984), 136.

110. The resistance circles also stood in contact with members of the Wehrmacht. Schneider, *Johannes Schauff*, 68–69.

111. Thieme, "Mein Leben," 75.

112. Letter to Oesterreicher, 12 July 1935, IfZG, ED 163/59.

113. *Freiburger Rundbrief* 57/60 (1964), 72.

114. "Grundpositionen Karl Thiemes," *Freiburger Rundbrief* 73/76 (December 1968), 11

115. Schneider, *Johannes Schauff*, 39, 90.

116. See John M. Oesterreicher, *Anatomy of Contempt: A Critique of R. R. Ruether's Faith and Fratricide* (South Orange, N.J., 1975).

117. *Freiburger Rundbrief* 57/60 (January 1964), 161.

118. Letter to Thieme, 21 April 1936, IfZG, ED 163/59.

119. *Schönere Zukunft*, 19 July 1936, 1109.

120. "Die Juden in unserer Mitte," *Die Erfüllung* 2, no. 2 (June 1936), 49.

121. Joseph Eberle, "Katholizismus und Judenfrage," *Schönere Zukunft*, 19 July 1936, 1109.

122. *Schönere Zukunft*, 26 July 1936, 1144.

123. Oesterreicher to Thieme, 21 April 1936, IfZG, ED 163/59.

124. 1 Timothy 3:6 for the statement of Paul.

125. Joseph Eberle, "Katholizismus und Judenfrage," *Schönere Zukunft*, 19 July 1936, 1107.

126. Hildebrand, *Memoiren und Aufsätze*, 115.

127. *Reichspost*, 28 June 1936.

128. Letter of 11 November 1936 to Pacelli, in Dominik Burkard, *Häresie und Mythus des 20. Jahrhunderts: Rosenbergs nationalsozialistische Weltanschauung vor dem Tribunal der Römischen Inquisition* (Paderborn, 2005), 369.

129. Letter to Thieme of 2 July 1936, IfZG, ED 163/59.

130. Andrew Chandler, ed., *Brethren in Adversity: Bishop George Bell, the Church of England and the Crisis of German Protestantism, 1933–1939* (New York, 1997), 127, 174.

131. Johannes M. Oesterreicher, "Dr. Eberle zur Judenfrage," *Die Erfüllung* 3 (September 1936), 139.

132. Joseph Eberle, "Katholizismus und Judenfrage," *Schönere Zukunft* 2 August 1936, 1172.

133. Oesterreicher, "Dr. Eberle zur Judenfrage," 134–135.

134. Dietrich von Hildebrandt, "Falsche Antithesen," in *Memoiren und Aufsätze*, 327; originally published in *Der Christliche Ständestaat* 17, no. 26 (April 1936), 391–394.

135. Dietrich von Hildebrandt, "Die Juden und das christliche Abendland," in *Memoiren und Aufsätze*, 357; originally published in *Die Erfüllung* 3, no. 1/2 (1937), 9–32.

136. Ibid., 354–355.

137. *Der Christliche Ständestaat* 9 May 1937.

138. Hildebrandt, "Falsche Antithesen," in *Memoiren und Aufsätze*, 326. This is from Mark 3:35: "Whoever does the will of God is my brother, and sister, and mother" (RSV).

139. Joseph Eberle, "Katholizismus und Judenfrage," *Schönere Zukunft*, 19 July 1936, 1107.

140. Hildebrandt, "Falsche Antithesen," in *Memoiren und Aufsätze*, 326.

141. Hildebrandt, "Die Juden und das christliche Abendland," in *Memoiren und Aufsätze*, 356–357.

142. Ibid., 356.

143. Ibid., 351.

144. Ibid., 352.

145. Jean-Louis Clément, *Monseigneur Saliège: Archevêque de Toulouse 1929–1956* (Paris, 1994), 200.

146. Rauscher, *Wider den Rassismus*, 161–162.

147. Karl Borromäus Heinrich (Maria-Einsiedeln), "Zur Psychologie des Antisemitismus," *Die Erfüllung* 2, no. 4 (November 1936), 173.

148. From Karl Borromäus Heinrich, *Was ist der Mensch*, 67, in "Die Singularität der Juden," *Die Erfüllung* 3 no. 1/2 (June 1937), 90.

149. "The entire time since the ascension of Jesus has been the end of time in a broader sense of the word." Thieme, "Der Apokalyptiker Karl Kraus," *Die Erfüllung* 2, no. 3 (September 1936), 115.

150. Ibid., 116.

151. Ibid., 117.

152. Johannes M. Oesterreicher, "Israel und das Werden der abendländischen Kultur," *Die Erfüllung* 2, no. 2 (June 1936), 78–82.

153. *Die Erfüllung* 2, no. 4 (November 1936), 184–85. The Buber statement is reprinted in Martin Buber, *Der Jude und sein Judentum: Gesammelte Aufsätze und Reden* (Gerlingen, 1993), 572–574.

154. Buber, *Der Jude*, 574.

155. Letter to Thieme, 17 March 1937, IfZG, ED 163/59.

156. Sylvia Maderegger, *Die Juden im österreichischen Ständestaat 1934–1938* (Vienna and Salzburg, 1973), 145.

157. Hildebrandt, "Die Juden und das christliche Abendland," in *Memoiren und Aufsätze*, 345–346.

158. *Der Christliche Ständestaat*, 10 May 1936, 441–442.

159. Hildebrandt, "Falsche Antithesen," in *Memoiren und Aufsätze*, 324.

160. Thieme to Oesterreicher, 22 February 1937, IfZG, ED 163/59.

161. Maurice Friedman, *Martin Buber's Life and Work* (Detroit, Mich., 1988), 165.

162. Pastoral Constitution of the Church in the Modern World, *Gaudium et Spes* (1965), chapter four.

163. Jacques Maritain, *Redeeming the Time* (London, 1946), 125, 133–134. On Maritain's evolving thought on this matter, see Richard Francis Crane, "Jacques Maritain, the Mystery of Israel, and the Holocaust," *The Catholic Historical Review* 95 (2009), 35–37, 44–45.

164. "The mystical body of Israel is an unfaithful and a repudiated Church (and that is why Moses had figuratively given forth the *libellum repudii*)— repudiated as a Church, not as a people." Maritain, *Redeeming*, 134.

165. Hildebrandt, "Die Juden und das christliche Abendland," in *Memoiren und Aufsätze*, 355–356.

166. Armand Kaminka, "Die missionärische Beeinflussung der Judenschaft," in *Jüdische Wochenschrift Die Wahrheit* 21 (February 1936), 2–3. Kaminka (1866–1950), rabbi and scholar, was born in Berdichev and studied in Berlin and Paris and at the Orthodox seminary in Berlin. In 1924, he founded Maimonides College in Vienna for spreading Jewish knowledge among Viennese Jewry. From 1926, he lectured at University of Vienna on Talmud and Jewish philosophy. Kaminka went to Palestine in 1938. *Encyclopedia Judaica*, 2nd ed., vol. 11 (New York, 2006), 756–757.

167. Ibid.

168. Esther Benbassa, *The Jews of France: A History from Antiquity to the Present* (Princeton, N.J., 1999), 155–156.

169. Ralph Schor, *L'Antisémitisme en France dans l'entre-deux-guerres: prélude à Vichy* (Brussels, 1992), 240; "Comment by Vicki Caron," in Michael Brenner, Vicki Caron, and Uri R. Kaufmann, *Jewish Emancipation Reconsidered: The French and German Models* (Tübingen, 2003), 153.

170. Oscar de Férenzy, *Les Juifs, et nous Chrétiens* (Paris, 1935), 49.

171. Bonsirven testified to the high standards of Jewish morality (ibid., 53).

172. Schor, *L'Antisémitisme*, 240.

173. Catherine Poujol, "Oscar de Férenzy: ou Les limites du philosémitisme dans l'entre-deux guerres," *Archive Juives. Revue d'histoire des Juifs de France* 40:1 (2007), 17.

174. Irene Harand, *So oder So: Die Wahrheit über den Antisemitismus* (Vienna, 1933), 5–12.

175. *Gerechtigkeit*, 25 March 1937, 1.

176. Harand, *So oder So*, 13; Férenzy, *Les Juifs, et nous Chrétiens*, 38.

177. Emphasis added.

178. *Gerechtigkeit*, 2 April 1937, 1.

179. Catherine Nicault, "Le procès des protocoles des sages de sion, une tentative de riposte juive à l'antisémitisme dans les années 1930," *Vingtième Siècle: Revue d'histoire* 53 (January/March 1997), 74.

180. This was true even of Abbot Leo Rudloff, one of the drafters of the Vatican II statement on the Jews. See his Letter of 12 August 1964 to Willebrands, Paulist Office for History and Archives, North American Paulist Center, Washington, D.C. Thomas Stransky papers, box 10, folder 4. [Hereafter: POHA, NAPC, Stransky Papers.]

181. *Gerechtigkeit*, 4 March 1937, 1–2.

182. Kalasantiner = Kongregation der christlichen Arbeiter vom heiligen Josef Calasanz (Congregation of Christian Workers of Saint Joseph Calasanz). Bruno Meusburger, "'Jesus, vertilge sie, wenn sie lau wird!' Ein Beitrag zur Geschichte der von P. Schwartz gegründeten Kongregation (von seinem Tod bis zur Machtübernahme der Nationalsozialisten" (Diplomarbeit, University of Vienna, 1989), 100.

183. Samuel Goodfellow, "From Germany to France? Interwar Alsatian National Identity," *French History* 7, no. 4 (1993), 450–471; Poujol, "Oscar de Férenzy," 15.

184. Autobiographical manuscript, Dokumentationszentrum des österreichischen Widerstandes, Akte Nr. 11059/1, 2–3. [Hereafter: DÖW.]

185. Autobiographical manuscript, DÖW, Akte Nr. 11059/1, 7–9.

186. Chaim Chertok, *He Also Spoke as a Jew: The Life of the Reverend James Parkes* (London, 2006), 203.

187. *Freiburger Rundbrief* 2/3 (1949), 45–46; 17/18 (1952), 20.

188. Chertok, *He Also Spoke*, 309.

5. Conspiring to Make the Vatican Speak

1. Johannes M. Oesterreicher, "Credidi, propter quod locutus sum," *Die Erfüllung* 3, no. 1/2 (June 1937), 3–8.

2. Karl Thieme to Johannes Oesterreicher, 2 December 1938, Thieme Papers, Institut für Zeitgeschichte [IfZG], Munich, Germany, ED 163/59.

3. Letters of 26, 29 August 1939. *Journet-Maritain: Correspondence*, vol. 2 (1930–1939), ed. Pierre Mamie and Georges Cottier (Fribourg and Paris, 1997), 876–877. On Maritain's apocalyptic view, see Richard Francis Crane, *Passion of Israel: Jacques Maritain, Catholic Conscience and the Holocaust* (Scranton, Pa. and London, 2010), 35–68.

4. *An Essay in Aid of a Grammar of Assent* (London, 1870), 423. Oesterreicher to Thieme, 17 June 1939, IfZG, ED 163/59.

5. Oesterreicher to Thieme, 17 June 1939, IfZG, ED 163/59.

6. Karl Thieme, "Die Juden in unserer Mitte," *Die Erfüllung*, 2, no. 2 (June 1936), 49.

7. Johannes M. Oesterreicher, "Die Juden und Das Reich Gottes," *Die Erfüllung* 3, no. 1/2 (June 1937), 99.

8. Ibid., 98–99.

9. Johannes M. Oesterreicher, "Die Entleerung der Religion," *Die Erfüllung*, 2, no. 2 (June 1936), 92.

10. Ibid., 91–92.

11. Elias H. Füllenbach, "Shock, Renewal, Crisis: Catholic Reflections on the Shoah," in *Antisemitism, Christian Ambivalence, and the Holocaust*, ed. Kevin Spicer (Bloomington, Ind., 2007), 202.

12. Ulrich Schlie, "Altreichskanzler Joseph Wirth im Luzerner Exil (1939–1948)," *Exilforschung* 15 (1997), 195.

13. Thieme to Oesterreicher, 2 December 1938, IfZG, ED 163/59.

14. Heinz Hürten, *Waldemar Gurian; ein Zeuge der Krise unserer Welt in der ersten Hälfte des 20. Jahrhunderts* (Mainz, 1972), 129.

15. On its purpose: Oesterreicher to Thieme, 20 February 1937, IfZG, ED 163/59. *The Church and the Jews: A Memorial Issued by Catholic European Scholars*, trans. Gregory Feige (Washington, D.C., 1937). This was no. 26 in the publications of the "Catholic Association for International Peace," part of an informational series on the Catholic Church. The French edition was entitled *L'Église catholique et la question juive*, trans. Arnold Mendel (Paris, 1938).

16. *Journet-Maritain: Correspondence*, vol. 2, 969–970.

17. This from a letter of Bonsirven to the Jesuit provincial in Toulouse, 19 January 1937, cited in Laurence Deffayet, "Le Père Joseph Bonsirven: Un parcours fait d'ombres et de lumières," *Archives Juives* 40/41 (2007), 39.

18. Deffayet, "Le Père," 39–41.

19. Letter to Thieme, 16 February 1937, IfZG, ED 163/59.

20. *Church and the Jews: A Memorial*, 15n.53.

21. Ibid., 19.

22. Ibid.

23. Ibid., 29.

24. Ibid., 30–31.

25. Ibid., 26.

26. Ibid., 15.

27. Ibid., 13. He cites Gerhard Esser and Joseph Mausbach, *Religion, Christentum, Kirche*, vol. 2 (Munich, 1913), 55.

28. *Church and the Jews: A Memorial*, 14.

29. Cited here: Isaiah 49:3, 49:15.

30. Friedrich Maier, *Israel in der Heilsgeschichte* (Münster, 1929), 134, cited by Thieme in *Church and the Jews: A Memorial*, 13.

31. *Church and the Jews: A Memorial*, 33–34.

32. Oesterreicher to Thieme, 13 March 1939, IfZG, ED 163/59.

33. Thieme to Oesterreicher, 2 December 1938 (ibid.).

34. Thieme to Oesterreicher, 10 December 1938 (ibid.). On the name "Rabbi" for Barth, see Peter André Bloch, "Karl Thieme im Briefwechsel mit Jacques Maritain und Karl Barth über den Plan eines Gebetsfeldzugs in Europa gegen die Gefahren des Nationalsozialismus," in *Christen im Widerstand gegen das Dritte Reich*, ed. Joël Pottier and Peter André Bloch (Stuttgart, Bonn, 1988), 29.

35. Thieme to Oesterreicher, 10 December 1938, IfZG, ED 163/59 (This statement was attached).

36. Thieme to Oesterreicher, 10 December 1938; Oesterreicher to Thieme, 13 December 1938, IfZG, ED 163/59.

37. Oesterreicher to Herbert A. Strauss, 13 July 1981; to Franz Cardinal König, 5 August 1966, John M. Oesterreicher Collection, Seton Hall University Archives & Special Collections Center, South Orange, N.J. [SHU—SCC, JMO Collection], RG 26.4.1, boxes 5, 9.

38. Oesterreicher to Thieme, 6 January 1939, IfZG, ED 163/59.

39. Oesterreicher to Thieme, 25 April 1939 (ibid.).

40. Thieme to Oesterreicher, 20 April 1939; 24 April 1939 (ibid.).

41. Thieme to Oesterreicher 24 April 1939; 27 April 1939; Oesterreicher to Thieme, 25 April 1939 (ibid.).

42. Oesterreicher to Thieme, 25 April 1939 (ibid.).

43. Oesterreicher to Thieme, 1 May 1939 (ibid.).

44. The original: "Wer nicht den Mut zur Anklage hat sollte sich und uns sittliche Appelle schenken." Oesterreicher to Thieme, 12 May 1939 (ibid., emphasis added).

45. "Pope Sees Rescue of Christian Ideal by Franco Troops," *New York Times*, 12 June 1939, 1.

46. Heer, *God's First Love*, 491–492.

47. Letter of June 1940. Peter Godman, *Hitler and the Vatican: Inside the Secret Archives* (New York, 2004), 163.

48. Oesterreicher to Thieme, IfZG, ED 163/59, 2 January 1940.

49. Oesterreicher to Thieme, 30 March 1939 (ibid.).

50. See the afterward by Robert A. Graham, who discovered the transcripts in Koblenz, in John M. Oesterreicher, *Wider die Tyrannei des Rassenwahns: Rundfunkansprachen aus dem ersten Jahr von Hitlers Krieg* (Salzburg, 1986), 110.

51. Ibid., 41.

52. Ibid., 63.

53. Ibid., 20–21, 63.

54. Ibid., 35.

55. Ibid., 67.

56. Samuel Moyn, "Personalism, Community, and the Origins of Human Rights," in *Human Rights in the Twentieth Century: A Critical History*, ed. Stefan-Ludwig Hoffman (Cambridge, United Kingdom, 2011), 91.

57. See the afterword of Robert Graham, in Oesterreicher, *Wider die Tyrannei*, 112.

58. Oesterreicher, *Wider die Tyrannei*, 14–15, 112. See also the report from Wiener Neustadt of a Nazi factory floor operative on the treasonous broadcasts by a "dirty priest" named Oesterreicher. Alfred Potyka to Oesterreicher, 24 April 1961, SHU—SCC, JMO Collection, RG 26.3.1.14.

59. Oesterreicher, *Wider die Tyrannei*, 41.

60. Roger-Henri-Marie Beaussart was auxiliary bishop of Paris.

61. John M. Oesterreicher, *Racisme, antisémitisme, antichristianisme: Documents et critique* (Paris, 1940; New York, 1943); German translation: *Rassenhass ist Christushass* (Klagenfurt, Austria, 1993).

62. This was a copy (for Thieme) of Rauschning's letter to Oesterreicher of 20 March 1939, IfZG, ED 163/60.

63. Oesterreicher, *Racisme*, 46.

64. Ibid., 33.

65. Ibid., 40.

66. Ibid., 41–42.

67. Ibid., 59–61, 149–151.

68. Ibid., 23.

69. Ibid., 123.

70. Ibid., 144.

71. Ibid., 104–106.

72. Oesterreicher seems to have gotten them from *Documentation Catholique*.

73. Thieme to Oesterreicher, 2 December 1938, IfZG, ED 163/59.

74. *Catholic Herald*, 18 November 1938, cited in *Racisme*, 99.

75. Oesterreicher, *Racisme*, 109–110, 119–120, 131.

76. Ibid., 110–112.

77. Ibid., 114–115.

78. Ibid., 109.

79. See the analysis and correspondence in Bloch, "Karl Thieme," 19–35. Maritain allowed that it was completely reasonable for bishops of the various countries at war to call their peoples to be loyal to their respective states. Thieme responded that it was a scandal that German bishops would call Germans to be loyal to Hitler. Ibid., 36.

80. Michael F. Feldkamp, *Pius XII. und Deutschland* (Göttingen, 2000), 128. Pius proposed that children of all countries pray to the Virgin to intercede for peace. If children "down to the most distant village" came to church for prayer, he wrote to his state secretary Cardinal Maglione in May 1939, he was certain that "under the protection of the Virgin Mother of God the mutual quarrels of the peoples would dissolve." Bloch, "Karl Thieme," 47–48.

81. Oesterreicher, *Racisme*, 125.

82. Ibid., 126–127, 197.

83. Ibid., 131–139.

84. Maurice Samuel, *The Great Hatred* (New York, 1940), cited in Jacques Maritain, *Redeeming the Time* (London, 1946), 126. Maritain also claims that "representative Jewish writers like Scholem Asch and Waldo Frank . . . agree with Maurice Samuel that 'Christophobia' is the spiritual essence of the demoniacal racism of our pagan world" (154).

85. Hubert Wolf, *Pope and Devil* (Cambridge, Mass., 2010), 105–106.

86. Review of Jean Dujardin, *L'Église catholique et le peuple juif: Un autre regard* in *Esprit et Vie* 103 (April 2004), 26–29.

87. Oesterreicher, *Racisme*, 130.

88. Johannes M. Oesterreicher, "Opportune—importune!" *Die Erfüllung* 2, no. 4 (November 1936), 145.

89. Johannes M. Oesterreicher, "Gericht und Erneuerung," *Die Erfüllung* 2, no. 4 (November 1936), 185.

90. Oesterreicher, *Racisme*, 192–193.

91. John Paul II wrote in his apostolic letter "*Salvifici Doloris*" (1984), "In bringing about the Redemption through suffering, Christ *has* also *raised human suffering to the level of the Redemption.* Thus each man, in his suffering, can also become a sharer in the redemptive suffering of Christ." On Jacques Maritain's ideas of Jews suffering redemptively, see the discussion in Crane, *Passion*, 69–99.

92. St. Teresa of Avila related the following words told her by the Lord: "Believe me my daughter, his trials are the heaviest whom my Father loves the most; trials are the measure of his love." *The Relations of St. Teresa*, III, 21 in *The Life of St. Teresa of Avila* (New York, 2006), 380.

93. Stephen Schloesser, *Jazz Age Catholicism: Mystic Modernism in Postwar Paris, 1919–1933* (Buffalo, N.Y., 2005), 67.

94. Oesterreicher, *Racisme*, 192–193.

95. Oesterreicher, *Rassenhass*, 162–163.

96. Oesterreicher, *Rassenhass*, 167–168; Oesterreicher, *Racisme*, 191–192.

97. Günter Fellner, *Antisemitismus in Salzburg 1918–1938* (Vienna and Salzburg, 1979), 216–217.

98. On Hitler's view that he was "performing a great service to the Church," see Hubert Wolf, *Pope and Devil*, 200.

99. For a brilliant interrelating of the various parts of Vatican II teaching, see Stephen Schloesser, "Against Forgetting: Memory, History, and Vatican II," in *Vatican II: Did Anything Happen?* ed. David Schultenover (New York, 2008), 92–152.

6. Conversion in the Shadow of Auschwitz

1. Deborah E. Lipstadt, *Beyond Belief: The American Press and the Coming of the Holocaust, 1933–1945* (New York, 1986), 166–169. The reports in American papers mix descriptions of atrocities committed against Jews with those committed against other groups, for example, Poles. The *New York Times* paid more attention to non-Jewish victims (ibid, 169).

2. Raul Hilberg, *The Destruction of the European Jews* (Chicago, 1961); Peter Novick, *The Holocaust in American Life* (New York, 1999).

3. 1 Thessalonians 1:16 (NEB).

4. Karl Thieme, "Der Weg zur christlich-jüdischen Wiederbegegnung in der Mitte des 20. Jahrhunderts," *Freiburger Rundbrief* 29/32 (1955), 8.

5. Karl Thieme "Das Ringen um die rechte Verkündigung der Passion Jesu Christi," *Freiburger Rundbrief* 8/9 (1950), 6–10.

6. Josef Foschepoth, *Im Schatten der Vergangenheit: die Anfänge der Gesellschaften für Christlich-Jüdische Zusammenarbeit* (Göttingen, 1993), 21ff.

7. This was the view of Karl Thieme, "In katholischer Sicht," *Freiburger Rundbrief* 49 (September 1960), 24.

8. John S. Conway, "Protestant Missions to the Jews 1810–1980: Ecclesiastical Imperialism or Theological Aberration?" *Holocaust and Genocide Studies* 1, no. 1 (1986), 140; Elias H. Füllenbach, "Shock, Renewal, Crisis: Catholic Reflections on the Shoah," in *Antisemitism, Christian Ambivalence, and the Holocaust*, ed. Kevin Spicer (Bloomington, Ind., 2007).

9. Rosemary Ruether, *Faith and Fratricide: The Theological Roots of Antisemitism* (New York, 1974).

10. Josef Foschepoth, "Vor 50 Jahren: Die Gründung der Gesellschaften für Christlich-Jüdische Zusammenarbeit," in *Der Dialog zwischen Juden und Christen: Versuche des Gesprächs nach Auschwitz*, ed. Hans Erler and Ansgar Koschel (Frankfurt am Main, 1999), 173–176.

11. Foschepoth, *Im Schatten der Vergangenheit*, 130.

12. "Verscharrt, exhumiert und auf dem Scheiterhaufen verbrannt," *Main-Post*, 25 January 2010.

13. All three cases, from September/October 1949, described in *Freiburger Rundbrief* 5/6 (December 1949), 17.

14. Foschepoth, "Vor 50 Jahren," 177.

15. For the text, see International Council of Christians and Jews, "The 10 Points of Seelisburg, 1947," Jewish-Christian Relations, http://www.jcrelations .net/en/?id=983 (accessed 15 July 2011).

16. Norman C. Tobias, "The Influence of Jules Isaac on Roman Catholic Teaching about Jews and Judaism (MA thesis, St. Michael's College, Toronto, 2008), 25–26.

17. Pierre Pierrard, *Juifs et catholiques français : D'Édouard Drumont à Jacob Kaplan 1886–1994* (Paris, 1997), iv–v.

18. Hedwig Wahle, "Some Known and Unknown Pioneers of Continental Europe," *SIDIC* 30 (1997/2), 2–9.

19. Anton Ramselaar, "Events and Persons," *SIDIC* 1 (1968/3), 11–15.

20. Giovanni Miccoli, "Two Sensitive Issues: Religious Freedom and the Jews," in *History of Vatican II*, vol. 4, ed. Giuseppe Alberigo and Joseph A. Komonchak (Leuven, Belgium, 2002), 136–137. Walter Dirks's remarks are found in *Freiburger Rundbrief* 57/60 (1964), 72. See also: Walter Lipgens, "Christen und Juden heute," *Hochland* 51, no. 6 (August 1959), 285–289.

21. John Cogley, "A Program for Tolerance," *Commonweal*, 10 June 1949, 217.

22. Letter to the editor, *Commonweal*, 24 June 1949, 270.

23. "Catholics and Jews," 6 January 1950, 365–366; "Pope Pius XII and the Jews," 7 November 1958, 153–154.

24. James O'Gara, "The Eichmann Case," *Commonweal*, 12 May 1961, 166.

25. Judith Hershcopf, "The Church and the Jews: The Struggle at Vatican II," *American Jewish Yearbook* 66 (1965), 108.

26. Examples include Jerome Taylor, "Church and Synagogue," 29 December 1961, 355–358; "Jews and Christians," 19 January 1962, 425; "After Eichmann, What?" 19 January 1962, 437–439; "Eichmann and Buber," 374–376; and articles by David Danzig, Arthur Hertzberg, Arthur A. Cohen, Menachem Schneerson, and James O'Gara in the special issue of 28 September 1962.

27. The editors of *Commonweal* chastised colleagues at *America* for warning the U.S. Jewish community about the increase in antisemitism that might be provoked by support for an end to school prayer. No, they argued, any warning about antisemitism should go to Christians, because antisemitism was a sin. "On Warning Jews," *Commonweal*, 7 September 1962, 483.

28. *Documentation Catholique* 49/1137 (1952), 1626–1628; 49/1137 (1952), 1628–1636. Finally in 1960 there is a pastoral letter of Cardinal Liénart of Lille condemning antisemitic violence manifested in Germany. "La question juive et la conscience chrétienne," 57/1323 (1960), 298–302.

29. Incongruously or symptomatically, the author was a leader in Catholic-Jewish dialogue in France, Jean Daniélou. Daniélou rejected any link between Christianity and the fate of the Jews in Hitler's Europe. "Jésus et Israël," *Études* 258 (1948), 68–74. Other pieces of note in *Études* during this period include a review of Charles Journet's *Destinies of Israel* [253 (1947), 264–265]; a reflection by Jean Daniélou on the resurgence of thought about "Israel," caused in part by resistance to Nazi antisemitism ["Penseurs et mystiques d'Israël," 268 (1951), 362–371], a discussion of baptizing Jewish children [277 (1953), 99–110], reviews of works on antisemitism of Léon Poliakov and Jules Isaac [291 (1956), 446–447], and a brief consideration of a "liberal" argument that Jesus was no more than prophet of Israel [297 (1958), 254–255].

30. Friedrich Oppler, "Kollektivschuld des jüdischen Volkes am Kreuzigungstode Jesu," *Stimmen der Zeit* 153 (1953/54), 384–386. At the end of the decade, the editors printed Franz Werfel's letter to Egbert Munzer explaining why he had not become Catholic. *Stimmen der Zeit* 165 (1959/60), 52–55.

31. O. Simmel, review of G. Metzler, *Heimführen werde ich euch von überallher* (Vienna, 1959) in *Stimmen der Zeit* 164 (1959), 237.

32. *Hochland* played a courageous role of intellectual resistance until closed by the Nazis in 1941. The first postwar piece dealing with the roots of antisemitism appeared in 1958, but then left out a consideration of Christianity, tying the phenomenon to "emotions" and resignation from reason. Hermann Graml, "Die Wurzeln des Antisemitismus," *Hochland* 50, no. 4 (April 1958), 371–375.

33. See, for example, the following prewar contributions in *The Month:* "Christianity, Judaism and the New Paganism," 165 (April 1935), 355–357; "The Jews and Ritual Murder," 165 (June 1935), 561–562; "Antisemitism," 168 (August 1936), 176–177; "The Problems of Church and Race," 168 (December 1936), 528–536; "The Crime of Jew-baiting," 171 (June 1938), 490–491; "Race Doctrines Spread,"

172 (September 1938), 198–199; and "The Credulity of Antisemitism," 172 (December 1938), 491–492.

34. Thomas Stransky, "The Genesis of *Nostra Aetate*," public lecture at Georgetown University, 4 October 2006.

35. Miccoli, "Two Sensitive Issues," 136–137.

36. Wahle, "Some Known and Unknown Pioneers," 2–9; Jean Dujardin "Les relations entre chrétiens et Juifs depuis 50 ans: Aperçu historique," *Théologiques* 11, no. 1–2 (2003), 19.

37. *The Church and the Jews: A Memorial Issued by Catholic European Scholars*, Catholic Association for International Peace series no. 26, trans. Gregory Feige (Washington, D.C., 1937), 17; Karl Thieme, "Katholiken und Juden: Die Stellungnahmen in der modernen katholischen Christenheit gegenüber der Judenfrage," *Judaica* 1–4 (1947), 37.

38. John M. Oesterreicher, "Kirche und Judentum," in *Kirche in Österreich: 1918–1965*, vol. 1, ed. Ferdinand Klostermann, Hans Kriegl, Otto Mauer, and Erika Weinzierl (Vienna/Munich, 1966), 173–174.

39. Albert Béguin, *Léon Bloy: A Study in Impatience* (New York, 1947), 112.

40. Richard Francis Crane, *Passion of Israel: Jacques Maritain, Catholic Conscience and the Holocaust* (Scranton, Pa. and London, 2010), 15.

41. Pierre Birnbaum, *Antisemitism in France: A Political History from Leon Blum to the Present* (Oxford, 1992), 200. Ruth Harris has called Bloy's *Le Salut* "judeophobic," [*Dreyfus: Politics, Emotion and the Scandal of the Century* (New York, 2010), 229] and John Hellman writes of the "unadulterated, racialist loathing" in Bloy's writing on the Jews ["The Jews in the New Middle Ages: Jacques Maritain's Antisemitism in Its Times," in *Jacques Maritain and the Jews*, ed. Robert Royal (Notre Dame, Ind., 1994), 92].

42. Pierrard, *Juifs*, 219; Schor, *L'Antisémitisme*, 273–274. Of Bloy's attacks on the opponents of Dreyfus, James Carroll writes: "Bloy's repugnance at the mindless antisemitism of the time has a ringing eloquence to it." *Constantine's Sword: The Church and the Jews: A History* (Boston, 2002), 456.

43. Gustav Janouch, *Conversations with Kafka* (New York, 1953), 48.

44. This English translation of Hildebrand's essay is provided by John Henry Crosby in *Logos: A Journal of Catholic Thought and Culture* 9, no. 4 (2006), 145–172.

45. Béguin, *Léon Bloy*, 112.

46. Jean-Luc Barré, *Jacques and Raïssa Maritain: Beggars for Heaven* (Notre Dame, Ind., 2005), 69.

47. Béguin, *Léon Bloy*, 116–117.

48. Jacques Maritain, *Redeeming the Time* (London, 1944), 160–161. On the inspiration of Bloy for the Maritains, see Crane, *Passion*, 14–16.

49. Jacques Petit, Introduction, *Oeuvres de Léon Bloy*, vol. 9 (Paris, 1969), 8–9.

50. Cited in Bernard Doering, *Jacques Maritain and the French Catholic Intellectuals* (Notre Dame, Ind., 1983), 136. See also Crane, *Passion*, 15.

51. See Maritain, *Redeeming the Time*, 126–127.

52. Karl Thieme, "Rationabile Obsequium," in *Menschen, die zur Kirche kamen,* ed. Severin Lamping (Munich, 1935), 33.

53. Barbara Nichtweiss, *Erik Peterson: Neue Sicht auf Leben und Werk* (Freiburg im Breisgau, 1992), 458–459, 465–466.

54. Thomas Michels, "Geliebte um der Väter willen," *Die Erfüllung* 2, no. 4 (1936), 155.

55. Jacques Maritain, "Answer to One Unnamed," in *Ransoming the Time* (New York, 1941), 161; Barré, *Jacques and Raïssa,* 69.

56. Rayner Heppenstall, *Léon Bloy* (New Haven, Conn., 1954), 12.

57. Innitzer to Oesterreicher, 4 September 1946, John M. Oesterreicher Collection, Seton Hall University Archives & Special Collections Center, South Orange, N.J. [SHU—SCC, JMO Collection], RG 26.4.1, box 12.

58. Oesterreicher to Msgr. Joseph Moore, undated (late 1952, early 1953), SHU—SCC, JMO Collection, RG 26.4.1, Box 7.

59. Oesterreicher to Msgr. Joseph Moore, 2 February 1951 (ibid.).

60. As in: John M. Oesterreicher, *The Walls Are Crumbling: Seven Jewish Philosophers Discover Christ* (New York, 1952), with chapters on Marc Chagall, Edith Stein, Simone Weil, and Edmund Husserl.

61. Ramselaar, "Events and Persons," 11–15.

62. Thieme to Oesterreicher, 27 September 1954, SHU—SCC, JMO Collection, RG 26.4.1, box 10.

63. He is not mentioned at all in Franz Mussner, *Traktat über die Juden* (Munich, 1979), one of the most important Catholic works promoting Christian-Jewish understanding.

64. *Freiburger Rundbrief* 57/60 (January 1964), 73.

65. Willehad Paul Eckert and Ernst Ludwig Ehrlich, eds., *Judenhass: Schuld der Christen?!* (Essen, 1964), 11.

66. Gerhart M. Riegner, *Never Despair: Sixty Years in the Service of the Jewish People and the Cause of Human Rights* (Chicago, 2006), 235–236, 246.

67. Thieme to Oesterreicher, 27 September 1954, SHU—SCC, JMO Collection, RG 26.4.1, box 10; Thieme to Luckner, 30 October 1954, Thieme Papers, Institut für Zeitgeschichte [IfZG], Munich, Germany, ED 163/50.

68. Füllenbach, "Shock, Renewal, Crisis," 218, cites his skeptical piece which appeared in *Stimmen der Zeit* 76 (1950), 34–42.

69. Michael Phayer, *The Catholic Church and the Holocaust, 1930–1965* (Bloomington, Ind., 2000), 199.

70. To Thieme, 16 July 1963, IfZG, ED 163/64.

71. Füllenbach, "Shock, Renewal, Crisis," 218.

72. Phayer, *Catholic Church and the Holocaust,* 115–116.

73. Thieme to Oesterreicher, 10 May 1946, SHU—SCC, JMO Collection, RG 26.4.1, box 10.

74. Oesterreicher to Thieme, 14 September 1946 (ibid.).

75. Thieme to Balthasar, 13 April 1944, IfZG, ED 163/4.

76. Thieme to Oesterreicher, 10 May 1946, SHU—SCC, JMO Collection, RG 26.4.1, box 10.

77. Karl Thieme, *Kirche und Synagoge: Die ersten biblischen Zeugnisse ihres Gegensatzes im Offenbarungsverständnis* (Olten, 1945), 213.

78. Oesterreicher to Thieme, undated (September 1945), SHU—SCC, JMO Collection, RG 26.4.1, box 10.

79. This understanding, shared by Erik Peterson [*Die Kirche aus Juden und Heiden* (Salzburg, 1934), 64], is also reflected in some up-to-date translations. See, for example, the *New English Bible* (1972), the *Gute Nachricht Bible* (1997), *La Bible du Semeur* (1999), and *Slovo na cestu* (1988).

80. Oesterreicher followed the argumentation of the Protestant scripture scholar Theodor Zahn.

81. Letter to Thieme, undated (September 1945), SHU—SCC, JMO Collection, RG 26.4.1, box 10.

82. Oesterreicher to Thieme, 1 May 1946 (ibid.).

83. Thieme to Oesterreicher of 17 October 1945, (ibid.).

84. Thieme, *Kirche und Synagoge*, 212–213.

85. Letter to Thieme, undated (September 1945), SHU—SCC, JMO Collection, RG 26.4.1, box 10.

86. Johannes M. Oesterreicher, "Dr. Eberle zur Judenfrage," *Die Erfüllung* 2:3 (1936), 132–141.

87. Thieme, *Kirche und Synagoge*, 267.

88. Füllenbach, "Shock, Renewal, Crisis," 213.

89. Letter to Thieme, undated (September 1945), SHU—SCC, JMO Collection, RG 26.4.1, box 10.

90. Hans Urs von Balthasar, "Mysterium Judaicum," *Schweizer Rundschau* 43 (1943/44), 211–221

91. Balthasar to Thieme, 15 October 1943, IfZG, ED 163/4.

92. On the fading of the tendency to call Jews a "race" after World War II, see Heide Fehrenbach, *Race after Hitler: Black Occupation Children in Postwar Germany and America* (Princeton, N.J., 2005), 10.

93. Robert Brunner, "Judenmission nach dem Zweiten Weltkrieg?" *Judaica* 1–4 (1945), 298, 301.

94. Conway, "Protestant Missions," 138–139.

95. Lothar Rothschild, "Die 'Judenfrage' in jüdischer Sicht," *Judaica* 1–4 (1945), 333.

96. Ibid., 336.

97. Thieme to Winter, 2 February 1951, IfZG, ED 163/98.

98. Letter to Oesterreicher 10 February 1954. He cites Hebrews 6:6. SHU—SCC, JMO Collection, RG 26.4.1, box 10.

99. Karl Thieme, "Die Christen, Die Juden und das Heil," *Frankfurter Hefte* 4, no. 2 (February 1949), 123.

100. Thieme to Buber, 5 April 1954, IfZG, ED 163/10.

101. Karl Thieme, "'Antisemitismus—Antiklerikalismus,' Ein Vortrag im Bayerischen Rundfunk," *Freiburger Rundbrief* 8/9 (August 1950), 12–14.

102. This people consisted of "fallible human beings, as we all are," yet just as an anticleric had no right to despise the clergy, so the antisemite was wrong in

demonizing the Jews. Karl Thieme, "Briefwechsel mit einem jungen Christen," *Freiburger Rundbrief* 17/18 (August 1952), 11.

103. Matthew Hockenos, "The German Protestant Church," in Spicer, ed., *Antisemitism*, 186.

104. John Conway, "Changes in Christian-Jewish Relations since the Holocaust," in *Contemporary Responses to the Holocaust*, ed. Konrad Kwiet and Jürgen Matthäus (Westport, Conn., 2004), 62–64.

105. Letter to Kurt Kaiser-Bluth, *Freiburger Rundbrief* 12/15 (December 1951), 40.

106. Thieme to Adorno, 9 June 1949, IfZG, ED 163/10.

107. *Freiburger Rundbrief*, 1/1 (August 1948), 6; Mark 5:42.

108. Buber to Thieme, 12 June 1949, IfZG, ED 163/10.

109. Radio Broadcast of Tribune de Paris, 10 June 1948, reprinted in *L'Amitié judéo-chrétienne* 1 (September 1948). I thank Norman Tobias for this reference.

110. Karl Thieme, "Brief an einen Kritiker," *Freiburger Rundbrief* 2/3 (1949), 50–51.

111. Dietrich von Hildebrand, *Memoiren und Aufsätze gegen den Nationalsozialismus, 1933–1938*, ed. Ernst Wenisch (Mainz, 1994), 346.

112. Buber to Thieme, 25 June 1949, IfZG, ED 163/10.

113. Buber to Thieme, 10 October 1949 (ibid.).

114. Thieme to Buber, 15 October 1949 (ibid.).

115. See the work of the Jesuit and later cardinal Jean Daniélou, *Le mystère du salut des nations* (Paris, 1946), 107–108.

116. Thieme to Buber, 18 June 1949, IfZG, ED 163/10.

117. Thieme, "Die Christen, Die Juden und das Heil," 115.

118. Ibid., 117.

119. Karl Thieme, "Briefwechsel mit einem Zweifler," *Freiburger Rundbrief* 8/9 (August 1950), 21.

120. Thieme, "Briefwechsel mit einem jungen Christen," 10.

121. Thieme to Conrad Hoffmann, 19 December 1950, IfZG, ED 163/39.

122. Thieme, "Die Christen, Die Juden und das Heil," 118–119.

123. Ibid., 119.

124. Ibid.

125. John M. Oesterreicher, *The Rediscovery of Judaism: A Re-examination of the Conciliar Statement on the Jews* (South Orange, N.J., 1971), 40–41.

126. Emphasis added. He had admitted that his 1944 work *Kirche and Synagoge* was marked by "dialectical exaggeration." *Freiburger Rundbrief* 8/9 (August 1950), 21.

127. Thieme, "Die Christen, Die Juden und das Heil," 119.

128. Karl Thieme, "Neue christliche Sicht des 'Israel nach dem Fleisch'," *Catholica: Vierteljahresschrift für Kontroverstheologie* 16, no. 4 (1962), 284–286.

129. Conway, "Protestant Missions," 141.

130. Hockenos, "German Protestant Church," 191.

131. Matthew Hockenos, *Church Divided: German Protestants Confront the Nazi Past* (Bloomington, Ind., 2004), 165.

132. Norman Tobias, "The Influence of Jules Isaac," 15–16.

133. Karl Thieme, "Paulinismus und Judentum: Ein Literaturbericht," *Freiburger Rundbrief* 17/18 (1952), 25.

134. Karl Thieme, "Der Weg zur christlich-jüdischen," 5–6.

135. Peter Browe, *Die Judenmission im Mittelalter und die Päpste* (Rome, 1942), cited in Karl Thieme, "Der Weg zur christlich-jüdischen," 6.

136. "Israel in Evanston. Ein Bericht von Paul Démann NDS., Paris," *Freiburger Rundbrief* 29/32 (1955), 25–29.

137. Foschepoth, *Im Schatten der Vergangenheit*, 133.

138. Ibid.

7. Who Are the Jews?

1. *Freiburger Rundbrief* 12/15 (December 1951), 40.

2. "Verscharrt, exhumiert und auf dem Scheiterhaufen verbrannt," *Main-Post*, 25 January 2010.

3. Thieme to Winter, 25 February 1953, Thieme Papers, Institut für Zeitge-schichte [IfZG], Munich, Germany, ED 163/98.

4. See, for example, *Freiburger Rundbrief* 12/15 (December 1951), 41; 17/18 (August 1952), 34.

5. Their response to Meinertz of 8 August 1952 in *Freiburger Rundbrief* 17/18 (August 1952), 35.

6. Thieme to Robert Leiber, S.J. (Rome), undated (December 1949), IfZG, ED 163/46.

7. Edward Flannery, *The Anguish of the Jews: Twenty-Three Centuries of Anti-semitism*, rev. ed. (New York, 1985), 62–63.

8. Erzbischöfliches Ordinariat to Thieme, 30 November 1950, IfZG, ED 163/49.

9. Friedrich Oppler, "Kollektivschuld des jüdischen Volkes am Kreuzigung-stode Jesu," *Stimmen der Zeit* 153 (1953/54), 384–386.

10. The *monitum* was issued in October 1950. Thomas Brechenmacher, *Der Vatikan und die Juden: Geschichte einer unheiligen Beziehung vom 16. Jahrhundert bis zur Gegenwart* (Munich, 2005), 229–230.

11. Giancarlo Caronello, "Zur Rezeption Erik Petersons in Italien," in *Vom Ende der Zeit: Geschichtstheologie und Eschatologie bei Erik Peterson*, ed. Barbara Nichtweiss (Hamburg, 2000), 301.

12. This is from a confidential *aide-memoire* for the "Congressistes de Stras-bourg," 12 to 16 June 1950, IfZG, ED 143/46.

13. Füllenbach notes that here the Holy Office was confusing Swiss and Ger-man Freiburg; thus, Phayer's belief (189) that the *monitum* was "intended for the Freiburg activists" is probably mistaken. See Michael Phayer, *The Catholic Church and the Holocaust, 1930–1965* (Bloomington, Ind., 2000), 189; Elias H. Füllenbach, "Shock, Renewal, Crisis: Catholic Reflections on the Shoah," in *Antisemitism, Christian Ambivalence, and the Holocaust*, ed. Kevin Spicer (Bloomington, Ind., 2007), 214, 217.

14. Füllenbach, "Shock, Renewal, Crisis," 217.

15. Ibid., 215.

16. Thieme to Brunner, 13 December 1950, IfZG, ED 163/10.

17. Brechenmacher, *Der Vatikan*, 230.

18. Draft of 20 April 1951, IfZG, ED 163/49. On the Schwalbach theses, see Martin Stöhr, "Christlich-Jüdische Zusammenarbeit: Rückblicke," in *Wenn nicht ich, wer*, ed. Christoph Münz and Rudolf Sirsch (Münster, 2004), 63ff.

19. Karl Thieme, "Neue christliche Sicht des 'Israel nach dem Fleisch'," *Catholica: Vierteljahresschrift für Kontroverstheologie* 16, no. 4 (1962), 280.

20. For a critical assessment, see Rolf Rendtorff, *Hat denn Gott sein Volk verstossen? Die evangelische Kirche und das Judentum seit 1945. Ein Kommentar* (Munich, 1945), 29.

21. For example, Karl Thieme, "Das Ringen um die rechte Verkündigung der Passion Jesu Christi," *Freiburger Rundbrief* 8/9 (1950), 9.

22. Brechenmacher, *Der Vatikan*, 230; Füllenbach, "Shock, Renewal, Crisis," 218.

23. Luckner to Thieme, 7 May 1952, IfZG, ED 163/49.

24. According to Karl Thieme, the first official use of the word "ecumenical" to describe the relation of church to synagogue took place in 1948 at a meeting of the Dutch Reformed Church. It was implicitly approved in Rome in 1960, when the Council for Christian Unity was charged with considering relations to the Jews, and not a conciliar commission dealing with missions. Thieme, "Neue christliche Sicht," 282.

25. He acted as editor of the *Cahiers Sioniens* in Paris, where he carried out his own campaign against Christian antisemitism.

26. Paul Démann and Renée Bloch, "La catéchèse chrétienne et le peuple de la Bible: Constatations et perspectives." *Cahiers sioniens*, Special Number 3/4 (1952).

27. "Ergänzende Gesichtspunkte zur Demannschen Schrift," *Freiburger Rundbrief* 17/18 (August 1952), 16.

28. See the exchange between Thieme and the Dutch theologian Frans Thijssen, *Freiburger Rundbrief* 25/28 (September 1954), 37–38.

29. IfZG, ED 163/49. He in turn was responding to the letter of 7 May 1951 of Luckner and Joerger that had responded to his own doubts about Jews as People of God, which appeared in *Stimmen der Zeit*, April 1951, 36, 38, 39.

30. Leder to Luckner, 11 June 1951, IfZG, ED 163/49.

31. Gertrud Luckner and Kuno Joerger (Direktor) to *Stimmen der Zeit*, 7 May 1951, IfZG, ED 163/49.

32. From Thieme's advice to Luckner on Leder, 18 January 1954, IfZG, ED 163/49.

33. Alan Davies attributed the original insight to Karl Thieme on this matter. *Antisemitism and the Christian Mind: The Crisis of Conscience after Auschwitz* (New York, 1969), 98.

34. Anton Pelinka, *Stand oder Klasse? Die christliche Arbeiterbewegung Österreichs, 1933–38* (Vienna, 1972), 210–211. For an appreciation of Winter, see Norbert Leser, *Grenzgänger. Österreichische Geistesgeschichte in Totenbeschwörungen*, vol. 1 (Vienna, 1981).

35. Karl Lugmayer, "Pater Zyrill Fischer, OFM," in *"Meine ganze Seele hängt an dieser Gegend. Wenn ich irgendwo völlig genese, so ist es dort"—Schwarzenberg und*

das Dreiländergebiet im Leben und Werk Adalbert Stifters, ed. Franz Haudum (Schwarzenberg am Böhmerwald, Austria, 2005), 45–49.

36. In May 1939, Winston Churchill praised Drucker's criticism of totalitarianism while rejecting Drucker's prediction that Stalin would ally with Hitler. *Times Literary Supplement*, 27 May 1939.

37. This book provoked a full-page attack in Joseph Goebbels's *Der Angriff* under the title "To the Gallows!" Walter Mehring, *Müller: Chronik einer deutschen Sippe. Roman.* (Vienna, 1935).

38. Winter to Thieme, 28 August 1949, IfZG, ED 163/98.

39. Ibid.

40. Thieme to Winter, 14 September 1949. IfZG, ED 163/98.

41. Thieme to Winter, 19 December 1950, IfZG, ED 163/98.

42. Thieme to Winter, 5 January 1950, IfZG, ED 163/98.

43. The dialectic consisted in expressing the negative in order to achieve the positive, to heal and save, not destroy and abolish. Gregory Baum, *The Jews and the Gospel: A Re-examination of the New Testament* (Westminster, United Kingdom, 1961), 45.

44. Winter to Thieme, 10 January 1951, IfZG, ED 163/98.

45. Thieme pointed out that geography might shape history, but it was not a subject of history. See his letter of 12 March 1951 [ED 163/98] and his book *Gott und die Geschichte, Aufsätze zu den Grundfragen der Theologie und der Historik* (Munich, 1948), 258–259, 263, 270.

46. Winter to Thieme, 15 March 1951, IfZG, ED 163/98.

47. Thieme to Winter, 25 February 1953 (ibid.).

48. The first series appeared in *Freiburger Rundbrief* 17/18 (August 1952), 34–36; the second in *Freiburger Rundbrief* 19/20 (January 1953), 23–27.

49. Krister Stendahl, *Paul among Jews and Gentiles and Other Essays* (Philadelphia, 1976), 81.

50. "If one reads what a neutral expert had to say on the matter [in the *Theological Dictionary of the New Testament* (IV, 1071)], one finds that 'that Hebrews does not ask about the relation between law and Gospel, but rather thematically probes the relation between the Old Testament [*atlich*] priesthood and the priesthood of Jesus.'" "Der alte Bund im Neuen," *Freiburger Rundbrief* 19/20 (January 1953), 25.

51. Edward Flannery, "Hope and Despair at Evanston," *The Bridge: A Yearbook of Judeo-Christian Studies* 2 (1956), 290–291.

52. Oesterreicher to Thieme, Feast of Assumption 1954, John M. Oesterreicher Collection, Seton Hall University Archives & Special Collections Center, South Orange, N.J. [SHU—SCC, JMO Collection], SHU—SCC, JMO Collection, RG 26.4.1, box 10.

53. For Thieme's theses, see "L'espérance du monde: L'action rédemptrice de Dieu en union avec son Oint," *Istina* 1 (1954), 160.

54. Subordinationism is the belief that the Son is inferior to the Father. John E. Thiel, *Senses of Tradition: Continuity and Development in Catholic Faith* (Oxford and New York, 2000), 135.

55. Baum, *Jews and the Gospel*, 252.

56. Oesterreicher to Thieme, Feast of Assumption 1954, SHU—SCC, JMO Collection, RG 26.4.1, box 10.

57. Thieme to Oesterreicher, 7 July 1954 (ibid.).

58. Ibid.

59. See Hildebrand's making the Prodigal son the Jew in "Rückkehr des verlorenen Sohnes," in Dietrich von Hildebrand, *Memoiren und Aufsätze gegen den Nationalsozialismus, 1933–1938*, ed. Ernst Wenisch (Mainz, 1994), 347. But Thieme claimed that from the time of Augustine the prodigal son was understood to be the Gentile. Thus, Christian tradition had neglected the idea that the Elder Son was always with the Father. Karl Thieme, "Der ältere Bruder," *Freiburger Rundbrief* 19/20 (January 1953), 7.

60. For the influence of Augustine on Rosenzweig's thought, see Amos Funkenstein, *Perceptions of Jewish History* (Berkeley and Los Angeles, 1993), 298–299.

61. Cited in Paula Fredriksen, *Augustine and the Jews: A Christian Defense of Jews and Judaism* (New Haven, Conn., 2010), 329.

62. "We shall never understand the maniacal, world-wide seizure of antisemitism unless we transpose the terms," Maurice Samuel had written. "It is of Christ that the Nazi Fascists are afraid; it is his omnipotence that they believe; it is him that they are determined madly to obliterate." *The Great Hatred* (New York, 1940), 36, 56, passim, cited in John M. Oesterreicher, *Auschwitz, the Christian, and the Council* (Montreal, 1965), 23–24.

63. Karl Thieme, "Der religiöse Aspekt der Judenfeindschaft," *Freiburger Rundbrief* 37/40 (October 1957), 14.

64. As evidence of the ultimately religious character of racist antisemitism, he cited the statement of Hitler to Rauschning that conscience was a Jewish invention. Thieme, "Der religiöse Aspekt," 14.

65. New English Bible. Thieme wrote, "for the very reason that he called Israel to His own sonship out of all the nations of the earth, He also punishes it all the harder, according to Amos, for all its sins." *The Church and the Jews: A Memorial Issued by Catholic European Scholars*, Catholic Association for International Peace series no. 26, trans. Gregory Feige (Washington, D.C., 1937), 13.

66. Thieme, "Neue christliche Sicht," 285.

67. These segments are also quoted in a letter of Thieme to Oesterreicher of 1 July 1960. SHU—SCC, JMO Collection, RG 26.4.1, box 10.

68. In 1962, Thieme wrote that the new view did not idealize Jews and make them "blameless nobles"; rather, Jews are a people of "saved sinners like Christians." "Neue christliche Sicht," 286.

69. To hold "that a sin of a few is laid by God on an entire people till the end of time is poor, is bad theology." Oesterreicher, *Auschwitz*, 24–25.

70. Alan Davies, *Antisemitism and the Christian Mind*, 33–34.

71. Like Karl Kraus, a person who "serves God according to the best dictates of will and conscience, or is of good will." John M. Oesterreicher, "Zum Ritualmordbuch von Christian Loge, *Die Erfüllung*," 1, no. 2 (1935), 43–47; "Die Juden und Das Reich Gottes," *Die Erfüllung* 3, no. 1/2 (June 1937), 107.

72. Hildebrand, *Memoiren und Aufsätze*, 89, 109; Albert Raffelt, "'Anonyme Christen' und 'konfessioneller Verein' bei Karl Rahner," *Theologie und Philosophie* 72 (1997), 556.

73. Oesterreicher to Felix Braun, 8 February 1946, SHU—SCC, JMO Collection, RG 26.4.1, box 1.

74. For Augustine, "God is not unjust, so as to deprive the just of the reward of justice, if the sacrament of the divinity and humanity of Christ was not announced to them." From Augustine, "Contra Iulianum," 4. 3. 25. PL 44. 750, cited in William Most, "Is There Salvation outside the Church?" available at http://www.ewtn.com/library/scriptur/outsid.txt (accessed 12 April 2011).

75. John M. Oesterreicher, Review of "The Enigma of Simone Weil," *The Bridge* 1 (1955), 118–158, in *Freiburger Rundbrief* 33/36 (October 1956), 62–63.

76. Oesterreicher to Thieme, 29 May 1957, SHU—SCC, JMO Collection, RG 26.4.1, box 10.

77. Edward H. Flannery, "The Finaly Case," *The Bridge: A Yearbook of Judeo-Christian Studies* 1 (1955), 312.

78. Ibid.

79. Ibid., 313.

80. Thieme to Oesterreicher, 1 July 1960, SHU—SCC, JMO Collection, RG 26.4.1, box 10.

81. Oesterreicher to Thieme, 15 July 1960 (ibid.).

82. Oesterreicher to David Connor, 1 May 1961, SHU—SCC, JMO Collection, RG 26.4.1, box 2.

83. Oesterreicher to Thieme, 30 June 1960, SHU—SCC, JMO Collection, RG 26.4.1, box 10.

84. Thieme to Oesterreicher 7 July 1960 (ibid.).

85. Füllenbach, "Shock, Renewal, Crisis," 213.

86. He cautioned a correspondent in 1968 regarding his 1952 book *The Walls Are Crumbling* that "not everything the book describes [is] my present position." Letter to Louis Huguet, 30 January 1968, SHU—SCC, JMO Collection, RG 26.4.1, box 4.

87. John M. Oesterreicher, *The Rediscovery of Judaism: A Re-examination of the Conciliar Statement on the Jews* (South Orange, N.J., 1971), 56.

88. Interview with Rosemary Lloyd in the *Asbury Park Press*, 17 August 1986.

89. "How much is changed by death," he wrote to Luckner. He also wrote Luckner in 1969 that he was "especially happy" that the *Rundbrief* had featured a section in memorial to Karl Thieme. Letter of 30 April 1969, SHU—SCC, JMO Collection, RG 26.4.1, box 6.

90. Thieme to Démann, 7 June 1962, IfZG, ED 163/12.

91. Heide Fehrenbach, *Race after Hitler: Black Occupation Children in Postwar Germany and America* (Princeton, N.J., 2005), 10.

8. The Second Vatican Council

1. John O'Malley, *What Happened at Vatican II?* (Cambridge, Mass., 2008), 9.

2. Thomas Stransky, "The Genesis of *Nostra Aetate*," public lecture at Georgetown University, 4 October 2006.

3. John M. Oesterreicher, "Declaration on the Relationship of the Church to Non-Christian Religions," in *Commentary on the Documents of Vatican II*, vol. 3, ed. Herbert Vorgrimler (New York, 1969), 128–129.

4. John M. Oesterreicher, *The New Encounter between Christians and Jews* (New York, 1986), 126.

5. O'Malley, *What Happened*, 293.

6. George Tavard, A.A. (France, U.S.), a leading proponent of ecumenism, joined the subcommission in 1961, and in October 1964 the following priests also entered the subcommission's work: Barnabas Ahern, C.P. (U.S.), Pierre Benoit, O.P. (Jerusalem), Bruno Hussar, O.P. (Israel), Nicolaus Persich, C.M. (USA), Thomas Stransky, C.S.P. (U.S.), Msgr. Antonius Ramselaar (Utrecht, the Netherlands). Oesterreicher, "Declaration," 22, 96.

7. The theses were a collaborative effort based on drafts drawn up by the Father Paul Démann in Paris. Oesterreicher, "Declaration," 12.

8. Judaism's presence in the world was a basic part of God's plan of salvation, and therefore Christians should "draw nourishment for themselves" from it. Ibid., 15.

9. Ibid.

10. Ibid., 18.

11. For a lucid discussion see O'Malley, *What Happened*, 42–43.

12. Thomas Stransky, "The Foundation of the SPCU," in *Vatican II by Those Who Were There*, ed. Alberic Stacpoole (London, 1986), 81.

13. Stransky, "Genesis of *Nostra Aetate*."

14. Oesterreicher, *The New Encounter*, 138, 140.

15. Ibid., 137–139.

16. Ibid., 140, 133.

17. The Apeldoorn veteran Father Jean-Roger Hené wrote to congratulate Oesterreicher after his appointment as consulter, but confided that it "took quite some time and persuasion to push your name through, because there seems to be somebody here who doesn't like the ground you're walking on. But you've got a lot of friends here also." Letter of 11 March 1961, SHU—SCC, JMO Collection, RG 26.4.1, box 8.

18. Arthur Gilbert, *The Vatican Council and the Jews* (Cleveland, Ohio, 1968), 34, 120.

19. Oesterreicher wrote that Jews had been "'unreceptive' towards the truth of God's grace" and had stumbled, seeking to "thwart . . . God's plan of salvation." *The New Encounter*, 134–137.

20. Thieme supposedly loved to theorize at the expense of sound exegesis. Oesterreicher to Rudloff, 12 November 1962, SHU—SCC, JMO Collection, RG 26.3.1.11; to Stransky, 7 February 1963, RG 26.3.1.12. Gregory Baum too felt the

Freiburg group (he mentions Gertrud Luckner) "goes to extremes." Baum to Oesterreicher, 4 September 1961, RG 26.3.1.13.

21. Oesterreicher, *The New Encounter*, 139.

22. Oesterreicher, "Declaration," 39.

23. They met from April 16 to 20 at Ariccia; August 26 to 31 in Bühl, Germany; and November 27 to December 2 at Ariccia.

24. Typewritten notes by Leo Rudloff of Secretariat meeting of 28 November 1961, 4, Paulist Office for History and Archives, North American Paulist Center, Washington, D.C. Thomas Stransky papers, box 2, folder 7. [Hereafter: POHA, NAPC, Stransky Papers.]

25. For the disputes between Thieme and Thijssen on the question of the identity of the Jewish people, see *Freiburger Rundbrief* 25/28 (September 1954), 37–38. On Thijssen's work on ecumenism, see Jerome-Michael Vereb, *"Because He Was a German!" Cardinal Bea and the Origins of Roman Catholic Engagement in the Ecumenical Movement* (Grand Rapids, Mich., 2006), 30–31.

26. Typewritten notes by Rudloff of Secretariat meeting of 28 November 1961, 3, POHA, NAPC, Stransky Papers, box 2, folder 7.

27. "Sessio Generalis mensis Augusti," 30 August 1961, 1–2, POHA, NAPC, Stransky Papers, box 2, folder 7.

28. In his history, Oesterreicher recounted the exchange without naming names. *The New Encounter*, 149–150.

29. Bea was refuting the claim of Frans Thijssen that Matthew 27:25 is a prophecy, bringing punishment as well as salvation. He said, "Matthew 27:25 is no prophecy. The crowd simply accepts responsibility for the sentence to be pronounced by Pilate. However the decision of a few often provokes misery even for the many. In Luke we read that Jesus tells the women of Jerusalem to weep for their children." "Discussion on the Jews," SHU—SCC, JMO Collection, RG 26.3.1.13.

30. The second theologian was Diewold. Typewritten notes by Rudloff of Secretariat meeting of 28 November 1961, POHA, NAPC, Stransky papers, box 2, folder 7.

31. Point five stated that the church "believes that at the appointed time, the fullness of the Children of Abraham according to the flesh will embrace Him who is salvation" (Romans 11:12, 26). Oesterreicher, *New Encounter*, 158–159.

32. Ibid., 149–150.

33. Oesterreicher, "Declaration," 41–42; Stransky, "Genesis."

34. He also permitted John Oesterreicher and Leo Rudloff to lobby American and European bishops. Among others, they contacted cardinals Spellman (New York), Liénart (Lille), and König (Vienna) as well as archbishops Alter (Cincinnati) and O'Boyle (Washington). Oesterreicher to Bea, 2 October 1962, SHU—SCC, JMO Collection, RG 26.3.1.8. At the same time Bea was lobbying among German bishops. Rudloff to Oesterreicher, 29 August 1962, ibid., RG 26.3.1.11.

35. Undated (December 1962) memorandum of Bea to John XXIII. Oesterreicher, *The New Encounter*, 152–163.

36. Edward K. Kaplan, *Spiritual Radical: Abraham Joshua Heschel in America, 1940–1972* (New Haven, Conn., and London, 2007), 242.

37. Ibid., 246. Bea wrote Abbot Leo Rudloff that he had met Heschel and spoken with him at great length, and had formed a "superb opinion" of him, and would be happy if Heschel could act as "representative of Jewry at the Council," though such a position did not exist. Letter of 1 October 1962, SHU—SCC, JMO Collection, RG 26.3.1.11.

38. Oesterreicher, "Declaration," 52–53.

39. "Pope Said to Back Council Liberals on Jews," *New York Times*, 14 October 1964.

40. Giovanni Miccoli, "Two Sensitive Issues: Religious Freedom and the Jews," *History of Vatican II*, vol. 4, ed. Giuseppe Alberigo and Joseph A. Komonchak (Leuven, Belgium, 2002), 150.

41. Oesterreicher to König, 30 May 1964, SHU—SCC, JMO Collection, RG 26.4.1, box 6.

42. Jean Dujardin, *L'Église Catholique et le Peuple Juif: Un autre regard* (Paris, 2003), 301.

43. The texts are reprinted in Philip Cunningham, Norbert Hofmann, Joseph Sievers, eds., *The Catholic Church and the Jewish People: Recent Reflections from Rome* (New York, 2007), 191–200.

44. Oesterreicher wrote König that the "second text ('appendix') has got into the hands of a number of non-Catholics through the indiscretion of a monk [*Ordenspriester*] living in Rome." This was probably the Jesuit Malachi Martin. Letter of 6 June 1964, SHU—SCC, JMO Collection, RG 26.4.1, box 5.

45. U.S. bishops mobilized before the meeting. "Cushing May Talk on Draft on Jews," *New York Times*, 19 September 1964.

46. "Council Gets Text on Jews with Hint of Amending It," *New York Times*, 26 September 1964.

47. Floyd Anderson, ed., *Council Daybook*, Vatican II, Session 3 (Washington, D.C., 1965), 61.

48. Anderson, *Council Daybook*, 82.

49. Letter of 21 August 1964, POHA, NAPC, Stransky Papers, box 10, folder 4.

50. Oesterreicher, "Declaration," 67–85.

51. Cited in ibid., 71.

52. Anderson, *Council Daybook*, 69, 71.

53. Miccoli, "Two Sensitive Issues," 160n239.

54. Cunningham, Hofmann, Sievers, eds., *The Catholic Church*, 195.

55. "Ecumenism: What Catholics Think about Jews," *Time*, 11 September 1964.

56. Anderson, *Council Daybook*, 82.

57. Oesterreicher, *The New Encounter*, 230–231.

58. See the *Freiburger Rundbrief*, 25/28 (September 1954), 27, 39. The *Treatise on Kings* of Maimonides makes the point (citing Zephaniah 3:9) that Jesus and Mohammed had helped "pave the way to the King-Messiah and at preparing the

whole world to serve God together." Giuseppe Laras, "Jewish Perspectives on Christianity," in Cunningham, Hofmann, Sievers, eds., *The Catholic Church*, 26.

59. "From Mission to Dialogue," *Conservative Judaism* 21, no. 3 (Spring 1967), 10ff, cited in Eva Fleischner, "Heschel's Significance for Jewish/Christian Relations," 23, manuscript in SHU—SCC, JMO Collection, RG 26.4.1, box 3 (Fleischner correspondence).

60. Ehrlich to Oesterreicher, 10 September 1964, SHU—SCC, JMO Collection, RG 26.4.1, box 2.

61. Ehrlich to Oesterreicher, 15 September 1964 (ibid.).

62. Rolf Vogel, ed., *Ernst Ludwig Ehrlich und der christlich-jüdische Dialog* (Frankfurt, 1984), 23.

63. Ehrlich to Oesterreicher, 15 September 1964, SHU—SCC, JMO Collection, RG 26.4.1, box 2.

64. John T. Pawlikowski, Hayim Goren Perelmutter, *Reinterpreting Revelation and Tradition: Jews and Christians in Conversation* (Franklin, Wisc., 2000), 25. Particularly noticeable is the absence of any reference to Hebrews, the epistle that describes the Old Covenant as obsolete. In Pawlikowski's words, this failure "showed that the Council fathers saw it as a theologically inappropriate source for thinking in keeping with our time on the connection between Church and Jewish people." See Markus Himmelbauer, "Ein neuer Geist in Kirche und Gesellschaft," Jüdisch-christliche Beziehungen, www.jcrelations.net/de/?item=2588 (accessed 26 January 2011).

65. Thieme to Adorno, 4 June 1949, IfZG, ED 163/1.

66. Thieme to Winter, 19 December 1950, IfZG, ED 163/98.

67. Oesterreicher to Fleischner, 28 April 1983, SHU—SCC, JMO Collection, RG 26.4.1, box 3. Thomas Stransky, the American secretary to Cardinal Bea, also disputed claims supposedly made by Rabbi Tanenbaum that the American Jewish Council had decisively influenced the final text. The American Jewish Council memoranda were only "part of a vast amount of preparatory material," wrote Stransky. "At no time during the Secretariat plenary sessions were they referred to." Letter to Harold G. Gardiner, 14 July 1967, POHA, NAPC, Stransky Papers, box 10, folder 7.

68. Oesterreicher's view was that the final draft came about as a result of multiple influences in the context of a "fresh appreciation of scripture," through decisive actions of the Council Fathers themselves (Yzermans, *American Participation*, 599). Of a "Jewish lobby," he wrote, "All rumors to the contrary, it must be said that the influence of that lobby or, or of individual rabbis, on shaping the text was minimal" (Oesterreicher, *The New Encounter*, 213–214).

69. Marc Tanenbaum of the American Jewish Council prepared a statement ("The Jewish Decree") containing an interpretation of New Testament revelation on the Jews (esp. Romans 10–11) at the request of Cardinal Cushing, dated 29 September 1964. (POHA, NAPC, Stransky Papers, box 10, folder 5.) Tanenbaum recognized the directive of Matthew 28:19–20 applying to "the whole of humanity," and urged that reference to it *not* be made in the Jewish statement, but rather at the "close of the declaration on the Jews and other non-Christians . . . This

approach would allow the Church to be true to herself, would be consistent with the spirit of religious liberty, would avoid the inevitable antagonizing of the Jewish people." Stransky's files also contain letters from Zachariah Shuster (AJC), Arthur Gilbert (NCCJ), Philip Hiat (Synagogue Council of America).

70. Oesterreicher, *The New Encounter*, 231.

71. The words were cited by Archbishop Heenan in his address to the bishops of 29 September 1964, POHA, NAPC, Stransky Papers, box 10, folder 6.

72. Letter to Eva Fleischner (23 April 1983) cited in Fleischner, "Heschel's Significance," 21.

73. Miccoli, "Two Sensitive Issues," 150.

74. Reinhard Neudecker, "The Catholic Church and the Jewish People," in *Vatican II Assessment and Perspectives*, vol. 3, ed. René Latourelle (New York, 1989), 284.

75. In its meeting of 9 October 1964, the subcommission on the Jews (Stransky, Oesterreicher, Baum, Hussar, Ramselaar, Benoit, and Holland) altered the final words in "*Sacra haec Synodus meminit vinculi, quo populus Novi Testamenti cum Iudaeis coniunctus*" to "*cum stripe Abrahae coniunctus.*" See "Paragraphus emendata de Iudaeis" 9 October 1964, POHA, NAPC, Stransky Papers, box 10, folder 1. A marginal notation indicates the inspiration as coming from Cardinal Lercaro. For Lercaro's words at the Council, see his "Chiesa cattolica e popolo ebraico: 28.IX.1964," in *Per la forza dello spirito. Discorsi conciliari del card. Giacomo Lercaro* (Bologna, 1984), 108.

76. In fact, the framers chose the word "stock" [*stirpe*] *because* they wanted to indicate the Jews' existence in a religious sense. Communication from Gregory Baum, 19 October 2007.

77. Erich Kahler, *Israel unter den Völkern* (Zurich, 1936), 33.

78. Ellen Smith, George Goodwin, eds., *The Jews of Rhode Island* (Hanover, N.H., 2004), 228.

79. In the study prepared in 1961, Oesterreicher spoke of the Jews as the "stock" from which Christ came. "Quaestiones de Judaeis," undated (February 1961), POHA, NAPC, Stransky Papers, box 2, folder 7, 2. Speaking of the Catholic liturgy during the "Great Debate," Cardinal Lercaro noted that every day Catholics proclaim Abraham "our Patriarch, the father of our race [*stirpis*]." Oesterreicher and Stransky concurred that Lercaro was the origin of this phrase. See the records from October 1964 at RG 26.3.2, box 9, JMO Collection, SHU—SCC.

80. In an interview with radio station WHBI (Newark) of 1959, Oesterreicher said "to be a Jew is to be a descendant of Abraham either by birth or by 'adoption.' When Moses took a Madianite woman to wife, she became a daughter of Abraham" (SHU—SCC, JMO Collection, RG 26.1.9, box 1). Boston's Cardinal Cushing called the Jews "children of Abraham according to the flesh," in his comments on the council floor of 28 September 1964; in 1960, the Pontifical Biblical Institute drafted a petition for the council called "On Shunning Antagonism to Jews," which spoke of the Jews as "children of Abraham by birth." Oesterreicher, *The New Encounter*, 84, 197.

81. They were translated and reprinted in Oesterreicher's *The Bridge*. Flannery, "Hope and Despair in Evanston," 290.

82. Karl Barth, *Die kirchliche Dogmatik*, vol. 2, Part 2, 4th ed. (Zurich, 1959), 224.

83. Romans 9:6–8. The traditional Catholic reading was that "only the Jews accepting the Gospel are the true Israel, while the unbelieving Jews (the majority) remained in some sense Israel." G. M.-M. Cottier, "La religion juive," in *Les relations de l'église avec les religions non chrétiennes: Declaration "Nostra aetate,"* ed. A. M. Henry (Paris, 1966), 240–241.

84. According to Arthur Gilbert, the word "spiritually," added in 1964, assures Jews that the church makes no "pretense of being linked to them in any direct sense as a people." Gilbert, *The Vatican Council*, 188.

85. It combines the view of Galatians 3:7 (which is cited in *Nostra Aetate:* "it is men of faith who are the children of Abraham") with the vision from Paul's sermon in Acts 13:26, in which Jews are called "sons of the family [or stock: *genos*] of Abraham."

86. The point is developed by Cottier: for Paul, there was no firm distinction between Israel and the Jews. Sometimes he signals continuing promises adhering to the Jews, at others he proclaims that Israel had not "attained the righteousness of the law" (Romans 9:31). Cottier, "La religion juive," 241.

87. According to Fr. Stanisław Musiał, Paul's Greek contained no verb [*Israelitai, hon he hiothesia*], and traditionally Israel's sonship was translated into the past tense. To use the present tense in *Nostra Aetate* signaled a "theological turning point." Witold Bereś and Krzysztof Burnetko, *Duchowny niepokorny: Rozmowy z księdzem Stanisławem Musiałem* (Warsaw, 2006), 139.

88. Oesterreicher to Michael McGarry, 15 April 1987, SHU—SCC, JMO Collection, RG 26.4.1, box 6. See also Baum's letter to Bishop Willebrands, 29 July 1964, referring to Romans 9:4, where Paul speaks of the "Israelites," my "natural kinsfolk." "Paul was speaking of the Israel before the coming of Jesus. The prerogatives of Israel are today fulfilled in the Church, the true Israel." At the same time, Baum warned not to "foster a more ardent missionary movement towards the Jews." POHA, NAPC, Stransky Papers, box 10, folder 4.

89. Miccoli, "Two Sensitive Issues," 163n251.

90. Romans 9:2.

91. Oesterreicher, *The New Encounter*, 138.

92. POHA, NAPC, Stransky Papers, box 9, folder 5.

93. Oesterreicher, *The New Encounter*, 250–251; Secretariat Meeting, 12 May 1965, POHA, NAPC, Stransky Papers, box 9, folder 6, 9.

94. These included Bishop Emiel-Jozef De Smedt, Thomas Stransky, Yves Congar, Bruno Hussar, and Oesterreicher himself.

95. Secretariat meeting of 12 May 1965, POHA, NAPC, Stransky Papers, box 9, folders 5–6.

96. Other members of the commission were not "entirely aware of the pertinent discussion" among Jews on these issues. Oesterreicher to Palmieri-Billig, 31 December 1965, SHU—SCC, JMO Collection, RG 26.4.1, box 7.

97. Oesterreicher, "Declaration," 123.

98. The declaration was approved 1,763 to 250 on October 15; then on October 28 before promulgation by 2,221 to 88, 2 with reservations, 1 null. Gilbert, *The Vatican Council*, 193.

99. Members of the Secretariat feared the burning of churches, closing of Catholic schools, and the destruction of Christian life. The altering of the deicide charge was thus considered a compromise, achieved after struggle. Oesterreicher, "Declaration," 109–111.

100. Ibid., 124. Gilbert notes that the 1928 papal statement on the Jews had "condemned" antisemitism (*The Vatican Council*, 255n.13).

101. Romans 11:28; Oesterreicher, "Declaration," 126–127.

102. Rachel Donadio, "Pope Calls Any Denial of Holocaust 'Intolerable,'" *New York Times*, 12 February 2009, A8.

103. POHA, NAPC, Stransky Papers, box 9, folder 6.

104. Gilbert, *The Vatican Council*, 194.

105. Ibid., 175.

106. From the remarks of Gregory Baum in a Secretariat debate about deicide on 4 March 1965, Cardinal Bea concurring, POHA, NAPC, Stransky Papers, box 9, folder 4.

107. Gilbert, *The Vatican Council*, 168–169.

108. Cited in Michael A. Hayes, "From *Nostra Aetate* to 'We Remember': A Reflection on the Shoah," in *Christian-Jewish Relations through the Centuries*, ed. Stanley E. Porter and Brook W. R. Pearson (Sheffield, 2000), 429.

109. Gary Spruch, *Wide Horizons: Abraham Joshua Heschel, AJC, and the Spirit of Nostra Aetate* (New York, 2008), 16.

110. Geoffrey Wigoder, *Jewish-Christian Relations since the Second World War* (Manchester and New York, 1988), 77–79.

111. Ibid., 80.

112. Ibid., 77–79.

113. Karl Plank, "The Eclipse of Difference, Merton's Encounter with Judaism," in *Merton and Judaism: Holiness in Words: Recognition, Repentance, and Renewal*, ed. Beatrice Bruteau (Louisville, Ky., 2003), 70.

114. Gilbert, *The Vatican Council*, 202, 207; Wigoder, *Jewish-Christian Relations*, 80.

115. Oesterreicher, "Declaration," 77.

116. Lercaro had turned his comfortable diocesan villa into an orphanage and lobbied bishops at the Council to have "Church of the Poor" made an organizing principle. Ian Linden, *Global Catholicism: Diversity and Change since Vatican II* (New York, 2009), 65.

117. Oesterreicher, "Declaration," 74–75.

118. Miccoli, "Two Sensitive Issues," 161–163.

119. Jules Isaac, *Has Antisemitism Roots in Christianity?* (New York, 1961), 58.

120. Cited in Oesterreicher, "Declaration," 74–75.

121. Bea to Gertrud Luckner, 26 April 1965. Archiv des Caritas Verbandes, Freiburg, Germany, 093.2 N24/1A.

122. Gilbert, *The Vatican Council*, 170–171.

123. He was willing to contribute the preface for a volume with antisemitic insinuations: Angelo Alberti, *Le message des Evangiles*, Préface de Monseigneur Montini, Archevêque de Milan (Paris, 1961). Zachariah Schuster to Thomas Stransky, 22 January 1963, POHA, NAPC, Stransky Papers, box 10, folder 7.

124. Father Musiał believes that the extraordinary majority of 2,221 for and 88 against can be explained by a sense of guilt: the knowledge among bishops that without centuries of religious antisemitism, Hitler would not have had a chance to carry out his "demented" ideas. Bereś and Burnetko, *Duchowny niepokorny*, 144.

125. Ernst Ludwig Ehrlich, "Die Juden und das Konzil," in *Judenhass: Schuld der Christen?* ed. Willehad Paul Eckert and Ernst Ludwig Ehrlich (Essen, 1964), 403; Miccoli, "Two Sensitive Issues," 152.

126. "Wenn der Papst nun von der Bekehrung der Juden spricht," KATH.net, 7 February 2008, www.kath.net/detail.php?id=18969 (accessed July 15, 2011).

127. For a recent appraisal see John Borelli, "Troubled Waters: Catholic-Jewish Relations in the United States Have Grown Strained," *America*, 22 February 2010, 20–23.

128. This was contrary to the efforts of American Bishop Avery Dulles to re-emphasize the Epistle to the Hebrews. See the exchange between Dulles and his critics: Mary Boys, John Pawlikowski, and Phillip Cunningham, "Theology's Sacred Obligation," *America*, 14 October 2002; Avery Dulles, "The Covenant with Israel," *First Things*, November 2005.

9. A Particular Mission for the Jews

1. Karl Thieme, *Kirche und Synagoge: Die ersten biblischen Zeugnisse ihres Gegensatzes im Offenbarungsverständnis* (Olten, 1945), 211.

2. Thieme to Oesterreicher, 1 January 1948, John M. Oesterreicher Collection, Seton Hall University Archives & Special Collections Center, South Orange, N.J. [SHU—SCC, JMO Collection], RG 26.4.1, box 10.

3. Thieme to Adorno, 9 June 1949, Thieme Papers, Institut für Zeitgeschichte [IfZG], Munich, Germany, ED 163/1; Thieme to Buber, 15 October 1949, ED 163/10.

4. Karl Thieme, "Das neue Bild des Jüdischen in Christlicher Sicht," *Freiburger Rundbrief* 41/44 (1958/59), 37–38. He had argued for ecumenism between Christians and Jews as early as 1952. Michael Phayer, *The Catholic Church and the Holocaust, 1930–1965* (Bloomington, Ind., 2000), 188.

5. Thieme, "Das neue Bild des Jüdischen," 38.

6. Joseph Fitzmyer, "The Letter to the Romans," in *The New Jerome Biblical Commentary* (Englewood Cliffs, N.J., 1990), 862.

7. John M. Oesterreicher, *The New Encounter between Christians and Jews* (New York, 1986), 139.

8. Oesterreicher to Thieme, 10 May 1938, IfZG, ED 163/59.

9. John M. Oesterreicher, *The Rediscovery of Judaism: A Re-examination of the Conciliar Statement on the Jews* (South Orange, N.J., 1971), 56–57.

10. An example was the Halachic sources of Canon law. Oesterreicher to Isaac Jakob, 14 January 1972, SHU—SCC, JMO Collection, RG 26.4.1, box 5.

11. See Baum's revealing preface to Rosemary Ruether, *Faith and Fratricide: The Theological Roots of Antisemitism* (New York, 1974), 4.

12. John M. Oesterreicher, *Wider die Tyrannei des Rassenwahns: Rundfunkansprachen aus dem ersten Jahr von Hitlers Krieg* (Salzburg, 1986), 16.

13. Connor to Oesterreicher, 12 April 1961, SHU—SCC, JMO Collection, RG 26.4.1, box 2.

14. Letter to David Connor, 1 May 1961 (ibid.).

15. Christopher M. Clark, *The Politics of Conversion: Missionary Protestantism and the Jews in Prussia 1728–1941* (Oxford, 1995), 154–155. In seventeenth-century China, Jesuit missionaries went beyond learning the local language to dressing in the silk robes of mandarins and formulating a "Chinese rite" that permitted a form of ancestor veneration. Liam Matthew Brockey, *Journey to the East: The Jesuit Missions to China* (Cambridge, Mass., 2007).

16. Oesterreicher, *Rediscovery of Judaism*, 40–41.

17. Generally he sought the company of those with more favorable attitudes toward the Vatican, such as Pinchas Lapide or Joseph Lichten.

18. He concluded his letter to Oesterreicher (which begins "Dear sir"): "In my future contacts with literature emanating from the Institute of Judaeo-Christian Studies I shall, of course, be guided and warned by the precedent which your circulation department has set." In response, Oesterreicher sent volume 2 of *The Bridge*. Petuchowski to Oesterreicher, 25 February 1957, SHU—SCC, JMO Collection, RG 26.4.1, box 7.

19. See his introduction to Oesterreicher's *Rediscovery of Judaism*, 13.

20. Oesterreicher to Stransky, 7 August 1963, SHU—SCC, JMO Collection, RG 26.3.1.12.

21. He belonged to the left Zionist organization Hashomer Hatzair. Gerhart M. Riegner, *Never Despair: Sixty Years in the Service of the Jewish People and the Cause of Human Rights* (Chicago, 2006), 246.

22. Letter of 26 May 1970 in SHU—SCC, JMO Collection, RG 26.4.1, box 10.

23. Ibid., letter to Moshe Tavor, 12 February 1970.

24. These words were cited by the U.S. Congressman Robert Drinan, S.J., in 1977. Paul Charles Merkley, *Christian Attitudes towards the State of Israel* (Montreal, 2001), 135.

25. The all-day meeting took place at the America Israel Friendship House. Oesterreicher said, "I am not in favor of Zion because I feel it's a national liberation movement. It's my theology that makes me appreciate and love Zion. Judaism and Christianity are missions of the impossible—the hope that the impossible is possible. What draws me to Zionism is that I realize that Zion is divine folly—the idea that people dispersed for 2,000 years should be able to come together this way." Deirdre Carmody, "Professor Scores Arabs and Soviet," *New York Times*, 11 February 1976, 9.

26. Letters of Prof. Paul Jersild to Oesterreicher, 23 February 1976; Oesterreicher to Jersild, 4 March 1976. SHU—SCC, JMO Collection, RG 26.4.1, box 5.

27. *Ketman* is sometimes mistakenly considered an opportunist who merely hides his opinion, but Miłosz makes clear that in the original Persian context *ketman* was a kind of missionary. *The Captive Mind*, trans. Jane Zielonko (New York, 1953), 57–60.

28. On his friendship with Cardinal Innitzer: "Es hat nie so einen schönen März gegeben," in Gerhard Jelinek, ed., *Nachrichten aus dem 4. Reich* (Salzburg, 2008), 150.

29. Czesław Miłosz writes, "After long acquaintance with his role, a man grows into it so closely that he can no longer differentiate his true self from the self he simulates . . ." (*Captive Mind*, 55).

30. A suspicion expressed by the journalist and later American Jewish Committee representative Lisa Palmieri-Billig. Letter to Oesterreicher, 30 November 1965, SHU—SCC, JMO Collection, RG 26.4.1, box 7.

31. In 1969, he came out in support of Iraqi Jews. Dr. Heskel Haddad (Beth Israel Medical Center) wrote Oesterreicher on 20 May 1969: "It was gratifying to see men like you interested and sympathetic with the cause of a small community in such a remote place as Baghdad." SHU—SCC, JMO Collection, RG 26.4.1, box 4.

32. Oesterreicher to Bruno Hussar, 18 February 1969, SHU—SCC, JMO Collection, RG 26.4.1, box 5.

33. Letter of 15 January 1963, SHU—SCC, JMO Collection, RG 26.4.1, box 3.

34. Ibid., letter of 23 January 1963.

35. Letter of 10 September 1964, SHU—SCC, JMO Collection, RG 26.4.1, box 2.

36. John Gilchrist, "A Lot Is Learned through Tough but Respectful Dialogue," *The Catholic Advocate* 52, no. 21 (19 November 2003).

37. Pfliegler has a reputation of being a worker priest, a proponent of progressive causes. Oesterreicher to Hermen von Szalag-Kleeborn, 20 April 1959, SHU—SCC, JMO Collection, RG 26.4.1, box 5.

38. Oesterreicher to Sandra A. Hawrylchak, 22 April 1974. SHU—SCC, JMO Collection, RG 26.4.1, box 4.

39. Interview with Rosemary Lloyd in the *Asbury Park Press*, 17 August 1986.

40. Clyde Haberman, "The Cardinal Visits, and the Chief Rabbi Is Pained," *New York Times*, 28 April 1995, A4.

41. John Tagliabue, "Jean-Marie Lustiger, French Cardinal, Dies at 80," *New York Times*, 6 August 2007, B7.

42. John M. Oesterreicher, "Christians, Jews, and Cardinal Lustiger," *The Catholic Digest*, August 1986, 61.

43. Tagliabue, "Jean-Marie Lustiger."

44. Oesterreicher, "Christians, Jews, and Cardinal Lustiger," 66.

45. Oesterreicher has marked out everything that promotes reconciliation. SHU—SCC, JMO Collection, RG 26.4.1, box 6.

46. Allemand to Oesterreicher, 16 January 1947, SHU—SCC, JMO Collection, RG 26.4.1, box 1.

47. Ibid., 28 May 1947.

48. Ibid., 16 January 1947.

49. Ibid., 28 May 1947.

50. Suzy Allemand, "Simone Weil ou l'identité récusée," in *Simone Weil: Philosophe, historienne et mystique*, ed. Gilbert Kahn (Paris, 1978), 137–140.

51. Oesterreicher to Allemand, 13 September 1977, SHU—SCC, JMO Collection, RG 26.4.1, box 1.

52. Allemand to Oesterreicher, 11 November 1977 (ibid.).

53. Letters of 27 January; 5 March 1984 (ibid.).

54. "I once gave a talk on the church and the Jews to a protestant group. One came over and gave me a pin like this because that was the emblem of an honor society. I've worn it ever since. What more ecumenical sign (can there be than this pin), given to a Catholic priest by a Protestant minister on account of the talk I gave about the Jews?" Interview with Rosemary Lloyd in the *Asbury Park Press*, 17 August 1986.

55. Of the origins of antisemitism Oesterreicher said, "Antisemitism derives from the fact that the various groups cannot stand the fact that other people are the chosen people." Carmody, "Professor Scores," 9.

56. Baum's parents came from Jewish families but had converted to Protestantism. He was included in a *"Kindertransport"* in 1939, then educated in Canada. Hussar was born into a Jewish family in Egypt in 1904 and was baptized in 1935. Like Oesterreicher, he never ceased thinking of himself as Jewish. See Bruno Hussar, *Quand la nuée se levait . . . Juif, prêtre, Israélien: Un itinéraire* (Paris, 1983).

57. Her parents gave Jane up to foster parents, the Luckners from Thuringia. Hans-Josef Wollasch, *Gertrud Luckner: "Botschafterin der Menschlichkeit"* (Freiburg, 2005).

58. On efforts to find a "third way," see George Mosse, *Germans and Jews: The Right, the Left, and the Search for a "Third Force" in Pre-Nazi Germany* (New York, 1970).

59. "Gertrud Luckner, Germany," The Righteous among the Nations (Yad Vashem), www1.yadvashem.org/yv/en/righteous/stories/luckner.asp (accessed 18 February 2011).

60. Angela Borgstedt, "Gertrud Luckner," *Menschen aus dem Land*, no. 12 (2008), www.lpb-bw.de/publikationen/menschenausdemland/luckner.pdf (accessed 7 August 2011).

61. Richard Francis Crane, *Passion of Israel: Jacques Maritain, Catholic Conscience and the Holocaust* (Scranton, Pa. and London, 2010), 44.

62. Barré, *Jacques and Raïssa*, 334–335.

63. Jacques Maritain, "Lettre à un juif Chrétien," *Cahiers Jacques Maritain*, 23 (1991), 41–42.

64. On Parkes portraying himself as of Jewish heritage, see Chaim Chertok, *He Also Spoke as a Jew: The Life of the Reverend James Parkes* (London, 2006), 377. Karl Thieme and Ernst Karl Winter were proud of Jewish ancestors they supposedly had in the deep past. Thieme to Winter, 16 February 1950, Thieme Papers, Institut für Zeitgeschichte [IfZG], Munich, Germany, ED 163/98.

65. On his idea of Israel's vocation, see Crane, *Passion*, 122.

66. Leonard Dinnerstein, "American Jews and the Civil Rights Movement," *Reviews in American History* 30 (2002), 136–140; Stuart Svonkin, *Jews against Prejudice: American Jews and the Fight for Civil Liberties* (New York, 1997).

67. There is a tradition whereby rabbis have signaled to Christians neglected aspects of Christ's teaching (which themselves have Jewish origins). The Prussian-born reform rabbi Joseph Kraus wrote in 1909, "Long have we hoped that the teachings of Jesus will at length convert the Christian. Long have we hoped that if Christians, professing enthusiastic admiration of the Sermon on the Mount, find it difficult to follow its principle teaching, they will at least endeavor not to do ill to those that do no ill. The persistent prejudices prove only too clearly that we have hoped in vain." *Prejudice* (Philadelphia, 1909), 69. Also see Abram Leon Sachar, *Sufferance Is the Badge* (New York and London, 1940), 15.

68. Thieme, "Neue christliche Sicht," 280–281.

69. This is Thieme citing Adorno in his own letter of 9 June 1949. IfZG, ED 163/1.

70. Thieme to Oesterreicher, Assumption 1954, SHU—SCC, JMO Collection, RG 26.4.1, box 10.

71. Maurice Samuel, *The Great Hatred* (New York, 1940), 39, 41. For the influence of Samuel's thought on Jacques Maritain, see Crane, *Passion*, 71, 80.

72. Rolf Vogel, ed., *Ernst Ludwig Ehrlich und der christlich-jüdische Dialog* (Frankfurt, 1984), 22.

73. *Jüdische Wochenschrift Die Wahrheit*, 21 February 1936, 3.

74. Ibid.

75. Johannes M. Oesterreicher, "Die Ansprüche der Judenmission," *Die Erfüllung* 2, no. 1 (April 1936), 35.

76. Oesterreicher, "Christians, Jews, and Cardinal Lustiger," 66.

77. For the critique of parliamentary democracy in Hildebrand's circles, see Rudolf Ebneth, *Die österreichische Wochenschrift "Der Christliche Ständestaat": Emigration in Österreich 1933–1938* (Mainz, 1976), 144.

78. Two prominent Polish Catholics who came out in print for tolerance of Jews as fellow Polish citizens were the Wilno law professor Marian Zdziechowski and the Wilno student activist Henryk Dembiński. The charismatic and courageous Dembiński later became a Communist, and hoped to marry Catholicism and Marxism. He was executed by the Germans in 1941. See Leon Brodowski, *Henryk Dembiński: Człowiek dialogu* (Warsaw/Krakow, 1988). In his exhaustive three-volume study, Adam Michnik locates one other Catholic who came out in print in the 1930s against antisemitism: Maria Winowska. See his *Przeciw antysemityzmowi 1936–2009*, vol. 1 (Krakow, 2010), 348–366.

79. Klaus Schatz, *Zwischen Säkularisation und Zweitem Vatikanum: Der Weg des deutschen Katholizismus im 19. und 20. Jahrhundert* (Frankfurt am Main, 1986), 214.

80. Josef Seifert, "Personalistische Philosophie und Widerstand," in *Dietrich von Hildebrands Kampf gegen den Nationalsozialismus* ed. Josef Seifert (Heidelberg, 1998), 108.

81. On France, see John Hellman, *The Communitarian Third Way: Alexandre Marc and Ordre Nouveau 1930–2000* (Montreal, 2002).

82. See his letter to Thomas Stransky of 21 July 1963: "with the help of Cardinal König and others I gently try to explain to any Council father who is ready to listen to me, the importance of the statement on the Jews for the inner life of the Church." SHU—SCC, JMO Collection, RG 26.3.1.12. In 1939 he wrote, "Racism is hatred of grace and mercy." John M. Oesterreicher, *Racisme, antisémitisme, antichristianisme: Documents et critique* (Paris, 1940; New York, 1943); German translation: *Rassenhass ist Christushass* (Klagenfurt, 1993).

83. "The insistence that Chesterton's antisemitism needs to be understood 'in the context of his time' defines the problem, because his time—from the end of the Great War to the mid-thirties—was the time that led to the extermination of the European Jews. Adam Gopnik, "The Back of the World," *The New Yorker*, 7/14 (July 2008).

84. The quote comes from Uriel Tal, "Religious and Anti-religious Roots of Modern Antisemitism," in *Religion, Politics and Ideology in the Third Reich* (London and New York, 2004), 182.

85. "Israel did tear its heart out of its body, because the Messiah is everything for which Israel was created, everything for which it lived. If it did not die of this horrible deed, then that is a miracle of God . . . like a dying person Israel must suffer unspeakable pains until it declares itself for the One who is life." Review of R. N. Coudenhove-Kalergi, "Judenhass von Heute" and H. Coudenhove-Kalergi, "Das Wesen des Antisemitismus," *Die Erfüllung* 2, no. 4 (November 1936), 212–213.

86. O'Malley, *What Happened at Vatican II?* 221. For reflections upon the interconnectedness of the Vatican II statements, see Stephen Schloesser, "Against Forgetting: Memory, History, and Vatican II," in *Vatican II: Did Anything Happen?* ed. David Schultenover (New York, 2008), 92–152.

Acknowledgments

First I want to thank Prof. Omer Bartov for inviting me (some eleven years ago) to submit a paper for a conference he was organizing at Brown University on "extreme interethnic violence" in the East European borderlands. I decided to focus on East Europeans who *opposed* interethnic violence. To make the project more easily comparative, I placed at the center of my research people who came out against violence for religious reasons. Our meeting, scheduled to begin at Brown University's Watson Center in the second full week of September 2001, had to be rescheduled to the following year. By the time we finally met, my project had mutated: after reading the Polish Catholic press of the interwar years and discovering virtually no advocacy for ethnic others, I became attentive to Catholics farther west like Irene Harand, Johannes Oesterreicher, and Jacques Maritain, and the circles within which they operated.

Thanks to generous support of the University of California President's Research Faculty Fellowship, as well as a sabbatical year spent at the Institute for Advanced Studies in Princeton (2002–2003), I was able to build upon these early ideas and form a foundation for the present study. I want to thank my mentor José Cutileiro as well as the wonderful staff at IAS (in particular Marian Zelazny and Marcia Tucker) for a productive and peaceful year. Thanks also to Seth Koven for inviting me to speak about Irene Harand at Villanova University in the spring of 2003, as well as to Bill O'Donnell for motoring me up to Seton Hall University, where the Oesterreicher papers are stored in the Msgr. William Noé Field Archives and Special Collections Center. I am deeply grateful for the kind assistance of the Seton Hall archivists Alan Delozier and Kate Dodds, as well as for the insights of Monsignor Oesterreicher's successor at the Institute for Judeo-Christian Studies at Seton Hall, Father Lawrence Frizzell. During my leave I also made use of the Ernst Karl Winter papers at Dokumentationszentrum des österreichischen Widerstandes in Vienna.

In subsequent years I was offered opportunities to develop my thoughts in public presentations and would like to thank the following scholars and institutions for making this possible: James Felak (University of Washington at Seattle); John Mc-Greevy, Robert Sullivan, Brad Gregory (University of Notre Dame); Padraic Kenney, Carl Ipsen (Indiana University); Amir Weiner, Norman Naimark (Stanford University); Raphael Jung, Karl Schlögel (Viadrina University, Frankfurt [Oder]); Stefan-Ludwig Hoffmann (Institute for Contemporary History, Potsdam); Mirjam Voerkelius, Martin Schulze Wessel, Benjamin Schenk (University of Munich); Guido Hausmann (University of Freiburg); Eric Weitz (University of Minnesota); James Heft (Institute for Advanced Catholic Studies, University of Southern California); Vladimir Tismaneanu (University of Maryland); and David Tompkins, Vejas Liulevicius (University of Tennessee).

I am grateful to John Boyer and the editors at the *Journal of Modern History* for providing me an opportunity in the December 2007 issue ("Catholic Racism and Its Opponents") to explore some of the ideas developed in this book.

Special thanks to Chair Mary Elizabeth Berry for inviting me to address the Department of History at the University of California, Berkeley in the fall of 2009 and the following colleagues who offered extremely helpful thoughts: Kathleen Frydl, James Vernon, Beshara Doumani, Thomas Gertler, Peter Sahlins, David Hollinger, David Henkin, Maureen Miller, Susanna Elm, Jim Sheehan, Peggy Anderson, Richard Abrams, Irv Scheiner, Emily Mackil, Massimo Mazzotti, Wen-Hsin Yeh, Mark Healey, Nicholas Riasanovsky, Carlos Norena, and Mary Elizabeth Berry. Yuri Slezkine and Ned Walker permitted me access to a lunchtime audience at the Center for Slavic, East European, and Eurasian Studies at UC Berkeley, and spared me some grave errors. Thanks also to Sarah Cramsey and Andrew Kornbluth for inviting me to speak at the Institute's krouzek reading group.

The Institute of International Studies at UC Berkeley awarded me a grant to host a "mini-conference" on my book in the spring of 2010, at which I benefited from the critical remarks of John Pawlikowski (Catholic Theological Union) and Kevin Spicer (Stonehill College), as well as Berkeley colleagues Amos Bitzan, Noah Strote, Andrew Barshay, Thomas Brady, Jonathan Sheehan, Victoria Frede, Maria Mavroudi, Martin Jay, John Efron, and Peggy Anderson (ein zweites Mal). I would not have known about this opportunity but for the friendly advice of Brian DeLay.

At various occasions over the years I have profited from insights provided in conversation or in writing from Norbert Leser, Susannah Heschel, Suzanne Marchand, Dagmar Herzog, Tony Levitas, Paul Baumann, Peter Burg, Brian Porter-Szűcs, Paul Hanebrink, Bruce Berglund, Norman Tobias, John Henry Crosby, Reinhold Knoll, Andreas Laun, Otto Hentz, John Borelli, Fiona Grigg, Bernard Campbell, Carolyn Walker Bynum, Samuel Moyn, Dirk Moses, Timothy Snyder, Markus Lahner, Joseph Komonchak, Christoph Lüthy, Victor Conzemius, John O'Malley, Elisabeth Weidinger, Alwin Renker, Kostek Gebert, Gene Zubovich, and Kate Brown. Charles Maier and Joyce Seltzer helped me figure out what I wanted to say in this book. I want also to thank Terence Renaud, Mark Sawchuk, Peggy O'Donnell, and David DeVore for crucial assistance in finding and understanding sources. Melody Negron did a superb job in preparing the manuscript for print.

I have been fortunate to have questions answered by two of John Oesterreicher's colleagues from the Secretariat for Promoting Christian Unity: Gregory Baum and Thomas Stransky. I am very grateful for the opportunity to look at Father Stransky's papers at the Paulists' archive in Washington, DC, where I enjoyed the assistance of Father John E. Lynch.

Finally I would like to acknowledge scholars I have never met but whose work provided an intellectual structure for the development of my own: Heinrich Lutz, Michael Phayer, Bonaventure Hinwood, Alan Davies, and especially Hermann Greive, whose book *Theologie und Ideologie* remains a towering achievement that deserves to be translated into many languages.

Index